This Book Comes With Lots of
FREE Online Resources

Nolo's award-winning website has a page dedicated just to this book. Here you can:

KEEP UP TO DATE. When there are important changes to the information in this book, we'll post updates.

GET DISCOUNTS ON NOLO PRODUCTS. Get discounts on hundreds of books, forms, and software.

READ BLOGS. Get the latest info from Nolo authors' blogs.

LISTEN TO PODCASTS. Listen to authors discuss timely issues on topics that interest you.

WATCH VIDEOS. Get a quick introduction to a legal topic with our short videos.

And that's not all.
Nolo.com contains thousands of articles on everyday legal and business issues, plus a plain-English law dictionary, all written by Nolo experts and available for free. You'll also find more useful **books, software, online apps, downloadable forms,** plus a **lawyer directory.**

With
**Downloadable
WORKSHEETS**

Get worksheets and more at
www.nolo.com/back-of-book/FIBA.html

7th Edition

The New Bankruptcy

Will It Work for You?

Attorney Cara O'Neill

SEVENTH EDITION	JANUARY 2018
Editor	CARA O'NEILL
Cover Design	SUSAN PUTNEY
Production	SUSAN PUTNEY
Proofreading	SUSAN CARLSON GREENE
Index	UNGER INDEXING
Printing	BANG PRINTING

ISSN 2326-7089 (print)
ISSN 2326-6473 (online)
978-1-4133-2430-3 (pbk)
978-1-4133-2431-0 (epub ebook)

This book covers only United States law, unless it specifically states otherwise.

Please note

We believe accurate, plain-English legal information should help you solve many of your own legal problems. But this text is not a substitute for personalized advice from a knowledgeable lawyer. If you want the help of a trained professional—and we'll always point out situations in which we think that's a good idea—consult an attorney licensed to practice in your state.

About the Author

Cara O'Neill is a legal editor and writer at Nolo, focusing on bankruptcy, consumer credit, and debt. She edits and authors several Nolo book titles. Prior to joining Nolo, Cara practiced for over 20 years in civil litigation and bankruptcy. During that time, she served as an Administrative Law Judge mediating disputes in the automotive industry, taught undergraduate and graduate law courses, and served as house counsel for a large insurance company. She earned her law degree in 1994 from the University of the Pacific, McGeorge School of Law, where she served as a law review editor and graduated a member of the Order of the Barristers—an honor society recognizing excellence in courtroom advocacy. Cara maintains a bankruptcy practice in Roseville, California at the Law Office of Cara O'Neill.

Table of Contents

The Bankruptcy Law: A Work in Progress

On October 18, 2005, a new law took effect that substantially changed the bankruptcy system. Shortly afterwards, *The New Bankruptcy* hit the bookshelves. Now, twelve years later, the fledgling law is no longer new. This seventh edition accounts for the many court interpretations and rules that have put the 2005 law into effect. During that period, we have counseled numerous bankruptcy filers on their rights and duties in Chapter 7 and Chapter 13 bankruptcies. This edition reflects the advice and information we've provided regarding how bankruptcy works and which type of bankruptcy is best for each individual.

More specifically, this book explains how eligibility for Chapter 7 and Chapter 13 bankruptcy is determined, what debts are cancelled (discharged), what happens to your home, car, and other property, what complications might occur, what paperwork is involved, and where you can find help with your bankruptcy. Taken together, this information will help you decide whether it makes sense to handle your debt problems through bankruptcy and, if so, which type of bankruptcy is the best choice for you.

Although it provides valuable guidance for consumers who are considering bankruptcy,

this book isn't intended as an authoritative reference on every detail of bankruptcy law. Nor should it be viewed as a guide on how to handle your own bankruptcy. For more detailed information on bankruptcy, see Nolo's *How to File for Chapter 7 Bankruptcy*, and *Chapter 13 Bankruptcy: Keep Your Property & Repay Debts Over Time*.

Despite the years that have passed since the new law took effect, courts throughout the country are still weighing in on a number of key issues, regularly publishing opinions that are contradictory. Because only the U.S. Supreme Court can ultimately resolve these conflicts—which can take years—those of us in the bankruptcy field must live with some degree of uncertainty. Fortunately, for most readers, these contentious issues will never arise should you decide to file for bankruptcy. Still, when you run across language like, "Some courts say this while other courts say that," you'll want to do your best to learn how the courts in your area have ruled, if at all, in the unlikely event that the issue rears its head in your case. You can find out by using the resources described in Chapter 11, or by finding a public-spirited bankruptcy attorney who is willing to share this information without demanding an arm or a leg in return.

Download Worksheets, Get Updates, and More Online

When there are important changes to the information in this book, we'll post updates online, on a page dedicated to this book:

www.nolo.com/back-of-book/FIBA.html

You will find other useful information there, too, including author blogs, and forms.

What Is Bankruptcy?

If you've picked up this book, you probably have more debt than you can handle.

You may feel overwhelmed by your financial situation and uncertain about what to do next. Maybe a friend, relative, or even a lawyer suggested bankruptcy, describing it as the best thing in the world for you. Someone else may have said the opposite—that bankruptcy is a huge mistake and will ruin your life.

This book will help you sort through your options and choose the best strategy for dealing with your economic plight. It explains:

- how bankruptcy works
- how filing for bankruptcy under Chapter 7 or Chapter 13 (the two bankruptcy options for consumers) will affect your debts, property, home, and credit
- the procedures you'll have to follow (and paperwork you'll have to complete) to file for bankruptcy
- some common mistakes people make before, during, and after bankruptcy, and how to avoid them, and
- some alternative ways to handle your debt problems, outside of the bankruptcy system.

Armed with this information, you'll be ready to decide whether you qualify for Chapter 7 or Chapter 13 bankruptcy and, if so, which chapter makes the most sense.

As you consider the strategies available to you, keep in mind that you're not alone. Despite the recent uptick in the economy, bankruptcy remains a necessary and pervasive part of our economic system.

And bankruptcy may be just the ticket for you. You may be able to stop creditor collection actions (such as wage garnishments and bank account levies) and:

- usually will be able to wipe out all or most of your debts in a Chapter 7 bankruptcy while hanging on to your home, car, and other necessary items, or
- use Chapter 13 bankruptcy to stop foreclosures, reinstate mortgages, remove junior mortgages, and pay back a portion of your debts over three to five years and discharge the rest.

Bankruptcy may, in fact, seem like a magic wand, but it also has its drawbacks. And, because everyone's situation is a little bit different, there is no one-size-fits-all formula that will tell you whether you absolutely should or should not file. For many, the need for and advantage of bankruptcy will be obvious. Others will be able to reach a decision only after closely examining their property, debts, income, and recent financial transactions—and how persistent their creditors are. For some, simple nonbankruptcy options might do the trick—these are explained in Ch. 12 of this book.

This chapter provides some basic background information about the two types of bankruptcies most often filed by individuals: Chapter 7 and Chapter 13. In the chapters that follow, you'll find more detailed information on the issues you are likely to be interested in, including:

- whether you are eligible to file
- which debts will and will not be cancelled
- what will happen to your home, car, and other essential property items
- how your postbankruptcy credit will be affected
- how bankruptcy will affect your personal life, and
- whether you need to be represented by a lawyer or can represent yourself, perhaps with some outside help.

Types of Bankruptcy

Consumers and small business owners can choose from among several types of bankruptcy "chapters," including Chapter 7, Chapter 11, Chapter 12, and Chapter 13. Let's look at each one quickly—more about Chapters 7 and 13 just below.

Chapter 7. Chapter 7 bankruptcy is by far the most popular. In Chapter 7 bankruptcy, you fully disclose your property, debts, and financial activities over the past several years. Approximately three months later you receive a discharge (cancellation) of most types of debts and emerge with all or most of the property you owned going in—luxury items and investment real estate (in which you have equity) commonly excepted.

Chapter 11. Chapter 11 bankruptcy helps a business stay afloat by encouraging negotiation and compromise by all concerned, so that the business can keep going and at least pay the creditors something. While individuals may file under Chapter 11, the process is unaffordable for most primarily because attorneys' fees can easily surpass $20,000. Even a business that starts off in Chapter 11 will often end up in Chapter 7, where the business is liquidated. Because this book is intended primarily for individual consumers, we don't discuss Chapter 11 further (except briefly in Ch. 12).

Chapters 12 and 13. Chapter 12 and Chapter 13 are reorganization programs designed for individuals, except that Chapter 12 is especially designed for owners of family farms, while Chapter 13 is designed for everybody else, including farmers if they wish. Here we discuss only Chapter 13. As used in Chapter 13, the term "individual" includes sole proprietors and independent contractors, but not business entities, such as corporations or limited liability companies (LLCs). However, if you own a corporation or an LLC in order to operate a small business, you are still eligible to file for Chapter 13 as an individual and thereby get rid of your personal liability for the business debts (but your business will still owe the debts).

In a Chapter 13 bankruptcy, you prepare and file the same basic forms as you do in a Chapter 7 bankruptcy. However, you also propose a three- or five-year plan under which you typically must repay certain types of debt in full (such as back child support) and usually some portion of your unsecured debt, although some judges will approve of plans that pay 0% of unsecured debt. Chapter 13 provides some remedies that aren't available in Chapter 7—such as the opportunity to pay off missed mortgage payments over the life of the plan—but usually isn't the bankruptcy of choice because of the extra legal fees it entails, and because people would rather get their fresh start in three months instead of three or five years.

Chapter 7 Bankruptcy

As we mentioned just above, Chapter 7 is a three-month process that usually only requires the filing of some paperwork and one brief appearance before the bankruptcy trustee, the official appointed to handle the case for the court. You may have to make additional brief appearances before a bankruptcy judge if you seek to waive the bankruptcy filing fee or seek approval of a reaffirmation agreement you signed in order to keep a car or other property you are making monthly payments on. (You can learn more about reaffirmation agreements in Ch. 6.)

Prefiling Credit Counseling Requirement

Before you can file your papers, you must have completed a credit counseling session from a nonprofit agency, which typically costs about $50 or less, depending on your income. The agency provides a certificate of completion that you file with your other papers. There are a couple of exceptions to this prefiling counseling requirement, discussed in Ch. 2. The counselor is available online, over the telephone, and through the mail. Take the time to shop around; you may be able to get counseling for as little as $8.

The Automatic Stay

After completing the credit counseling, your next step is to obtain a bankruptcy filing number. You can do this by filing what's known as a skeleton or an emergency petition, or by filing all the required paperwork at the same time. Either way, once you have a filing number, you have a powerful shield—called the automatic stay—against any efforts by your creditors to collect their debts. All you have to do if a creditor calls you after you file is to produce your case number, the date of filing, and the name of the court in which you filed. The creditor will immediately back off. All proceedings to garnish wages, repossess cars, and foreclose homes will also grind to a halt.

There are a few exceptions to the automatic stay, as you might guess. Collection of child support and alimony can proceed, and the stay may expire sooner than you would want if you have had a bankruptcy case dismissed in the previous year. Still, as a general rule, filing for bankruptcy will give you almost total relief from your creditors while the bankruptcy is pending. For more information about the automatic stay, see "How Bankruptcy Stops Collection Efforts" later in this chapter.

Lifting the Stay

In some situations, creditors can successfully request that the court remove (lift) the stay as to their particular situation. For instance, if the automatic stay derailed a foreclosure action, the mortgage owner can request permission from the bankruptcy judge to proceed with the foreclosure. Other common reasons for lifting the stay are car repossessions and evictions of month-to-month tenants.

The Skeleton Petition

Sometimes it's important to obtain a filing number pronto. For instance, if you're faced with an imminent foreclosure or car repossession, you'll need the automatic stay to keep things as they are so you can figure out a way to keep your house or car. But a complete bankruptcy filing involves a lot of forms and disclosure of information, and you may not have the time to prepare them all. Fortunately, you can file a skeleton petition, which requires just a few forms, and file the rest of your paperwork within 14 days. The required forms in a skeleton filing are:

- the petition (three pages plus exhibits)
- a mailing list of your creditors
- a form showing your complete Social Security number, and

- the certificate showing you've completed your credit counseling.

A Brief Description of the Chapter 7 Paperwork

Ch. 9 gives you a more detailed look at these and other official forms, and in Appendix C, you'll find a sample of the paperwork involved in a typical Chapter 7 case. The text that follows is just an overview.

In addition to the paperwork required for a Chapter 7 skeleton petition, you'll need to file forms that:

- describe all your personal property and real estate, including where it is located and its approximate value
- provide information about your debts and creditors
- describe certain economic and financial transactions that occurred within the previous several years, such as property you sold or gave away within the previous two years, or certain payments you may have made to creditors, especially family and other "insiders"
- state how you want to handle debts concerning cars and other property that is collateral for loans (called secured debts)
- disclose your monthly income and monthly expenses
- state whether you want to keep any leases and contracts you have in effect or cancel them, and
- summarize your assets and liabilities.

The Big Choice: Use a Lawyer or Handle Your Own Case?

When you file your bankruptcy, your case will automatically fall within one of two categories:

- You will be represented by a lawyer who will sign your petition as your representative.
- You will be representing yourself (that is, you'll be acting as your own lawyer).

If you are represented by a lawyer, the lawyer's responsibility is to help you select the type of bankruptcy that will best work for you, get the right information in your forms, and make the choices that will be most appropriate for your situation. If, on the other hand, you are acting as your own lawyer, you will be responsible for these same tasks. While print and online resources will give you the information you need to make informed decisions and properly complete the paperwork, you will be solely responsible for the outcome of your case.

The court wants to make sure you understand these duties. It requires you to sign a form that explains:

- the different types of bankruptcies (discussed earlier)
- the services available from credit counseling agencies
- the penalties for knowingly and fraudulently concealing assets or making a false statement under penalty of perjury, and
- the fact that all information you supply is subject to examination by the employees of the U.S. Department of Justice.

In addition, you'll need to complete a form in which you provide your average monthly gross income for the six months prior to the month in which you plan to file. As explained in Ch. 2, that income figure will be your starting point for deciding whether you are eligible to file a Chapter 7 bankruptcy or whether you'll have to use Chapter 13. This form is popularly known as the "means test" and must be filed in every Chapter 7 case.

The Creditors' Meeting

About 30 days after you file your bankruptcy papers, you will be required to attend a hearing known either as the "creditors' meeting" or the "341 hearing." You and your spouse (if your spouse is filing with you) are required to attend. You both must bring photo identification and official proof of a Social Security number. This event is held in a hearing room in the courthouse or federal building, but not in the bankruptcy court itself. A bankruptcy trustee, the official appointed to handle your case for the court, conducts the meeting. Another official known as the U.S. Trustee may also attend your meeting and may ask you questions that bear on your possible ineligibility for Chapter 7 because of your income level (see "The Bankruptcy Trustee" later in this chapter).

The primary purpose of the creditors' meeting is to have you affirm under oath that the papers you filed were honest, complete, and accurate to the best of your ability. The trustee may also question you about property you've described in your paperwork, to see whether you gave it a proper value and whether you have equity that could be used to make some payment toward your unsecured debt (debt that isn't attached to collateral). In addition, the trustee may inquire further about:

- anticipated tax refunds
- recent large payments you made to creditors or relatives, if applicable
- methods you used to arrive at the value of big-ticket property items you are claiming as exempt, such as a house or car
- whether you should be required to proceed under Chapter 13 rather than Chapter 7
- your failure to file any of the required documents, if applicable
- inconsistencies in information you provided that might indicate you are being less than honest, and
- if you didn't have a lawyer prepare your papers, how you got the information necessary to make certain choices, such as which property is exempt (your answer would typically be the Internet, a Nolo book, or a telephone advice lawyer).

If you've done a good job on your paperwork, your income and expenses clearly qualify you for filing under Chapter 7, and you filed all required documents, your particular "moment of truth" in the creditors' meeting will likely be brief. Creditors rarely show up at these meetings,

and the bankruptcy trustee is typically the only one asking the questions. Before ending the meeting, the trustee will ask whether all the information in your papers is 100% correct and whether you expect to receive any further money.

The Role of Lawyers in Creditors' Meetings

Many people hire lawyers to represent them because they don't want to attend creditors' meetings on their own. When the trustee questions you, you—not your lawyer—must answer the questions. That's because you are required to cooperate with the trustee and are expected to be knowledgeable about the information you provided in your papers.

Having an experienced lawyer at your side can be helpful if anything you'll need to explain to the trustee requires legal analysis. In addition, having a lawyer can help you relax and soothe jangled nerves.

Which Debts Are Discharged

In approximately 60 to 90 days after the creditors' meeting, you will receive a discharge order from the court. The discharge order won't refer to your specific debts, but instead will say that all legally dischargeable debts are discharged in your case. In a Chapter 7 bankruptcy, absent a successful objection by a creditor (which is rare), most credit card, medical, and legal debts are discharged, as are court judgments, deficiencies owed because of a foreclosure or repossession, and personal loans. For many filers, this means that all of their debts are discharged.

Some types of debts are not discharged in Chapter 7 bankruptcy. The most common of these are:

- debts incurred to pay nondischarge-able taxes (see Ch. 3)
- court-imposed fines and restitution
- back child support and alimony
- debts owed to an ex-spouse as a result of a divorce or separation
- loans owed to a retirement plan, such as a 401(k) (because you are the creditor as well as the debtor in this situation, bankruptcy doesn't discharge the debt)
- student loans (unless you can show that repaying the loans would be an undue hardship, which is tougher than you might think and requires a separate trial in the bankruptcy court)
- federal and state taxes that first became due less than three years before your bankruptcy filing date (for example, taxes due on April 15, 2017, for tax year 2016 will not qualify for discharge until April 16, 2020), and
- debts for personal injuries or death resulting from your drunk driving.

Some types of debt will survive your bankruptcy, but only when the creditors seek and obtain orders from the bank-

ruptcy court excluding the debts from your bankruptcy. These are: debts arising from your fraudulent actions, recent credit card charges for luxuries, and willful and malicious acts causing personal injury or property damages. (For more on which debts are and are not discharged in a Chapter 7 bankruptcy, see Ch. 3.)

What Happens to Your Property?

With few major exceptions, as of your filing date all the property you own or are entitled to receive becomes part of your bankruptcy estate and is managed by the bankruptcy trustee. In addition, property you transferred within the previous two years (longer if the statute of limitations for fraudulent transfers is more than two years) for significantly less than its value, and certain types of property you have come to own within the six-month period after you file, are also considered part of your bankruptcy estate. Marital property in community property states is also part of the bankruptcy estate, even if only one spouse files. There are other categories of property that may belong in your estate, but these are the main ones. See Ch. 4 for more on what property belongs in your bankruptcy estate.

What does the bankruptcy trustee do with the bankruptcy estate? He or she is looking for any property that, when sold, will generate a profit that can be used to pay your creditors. In fact, that's how these trustees earn a living—from commissions on property from the bankruptcy estate that they sell to benefit creditors. For this reason, the trustee has no interest in property that you legally own but that lacks equity. That's because property without equity won't produce any proceeds for your creditors. For example, if you owe more on your house or car than it's worth, you have no equity and the trustee won't be interested in selling it because proceeds from the sale would, by law, all go to the lender. On the other hand, if you have equity in your house or car (or any other property, for that matter), the trustee will evaluate the property's worth and consider selling it for the benefit of the creditors (and the trustee).

How Exemptions Help You Keep Your Property

Fortunately, all states have laws that allow you to keep a substantial portion of your property when you file for Chapter 7 bankruptcy. This is accomplished through laws—called exemptions—that let you protect the equity you have in various property items from being used by the trustee to benefit your creditors. In some instances, property is exempted regardless of its equity value. For instance, under one of the two California exemption systems, your furniture is exempt regardless of what it's worth. In the other California exemption system, furniture is only exempt up to $650 per item (as are appliances, animals, musical instruments, personal effects, and clothing).

You can keep up to $165,550 worth of equity in your home in New York, and up to $500,000 in Massachusetts.

Most people who file for bankruptcy use the exemptions in the state where they file. But if you haven't been residing in that state for at least two years, you may have to use the exemptions from the state from which you came.

In 15 states, you have a choice of exemptions —you may use your state's exemptions or a list of federal exemptions. To find out whether your state gives you this choice, turn to the exemption chart for your state in Appendix A and look at the entry just below your state's name. It will say either that federal exemptions are allowed or (in most cases) that they are not. If your state allows the federal exemptions, you can find those exemptions after Wyoming in Appendix A. In California, you have a choice of two state exemption systems— System 1 and System 2. If you are using the California exemptions, check out the two California charts in this appendix.

Houses and Cars

People often ask whether they can keep their home and car in a Chapter 7 bank-ruptcy. The answer is yes in the following circumstances:

- You are current on your mortgage or car note.
- You have no significant nonexempt equity in the house or car.

Mortgages

If there is no nonexempt equity, the trustee won't be interested in selling the house, which means you can keep it—unless you are behind on your mortgage payments. If you're behind, although the trustee won't be interested in selling the house, your mortgage lender may initiate foreclosure proceedings and will probably be able to get permission from your bankruptcy judge to proceed.

It works a bit differently if you have equity that you can't protect with an exemption. The trustee will sell the home, give you the exemption amount, and use the remaining proceeds to pay creditors.

Car Loans

Cars and car notes work pretty much the same way as houses. If you have no non-exempt equity in your car, you can keep it as long as you are current on the note, but if you are behind, the lender will attempt to get permission from the judge to proceed with repossession.

Your Car or Home After Bankruptcy

Meeting the requirements for keeping your home or car as described just above doesn't mean that your bankruptcy will end your obligation to the mortgage holder or bank. To understand what happens next, let's back up a little bit.

When you take out a mortgage or car loan, you are actually doing two things:

- signing a promissory note for the amount of the loan, and
- agreeing that if you default on the loan the lender can foreclose or repossess.

What Happens If You Have Nonexempt Equity in Property?

If your equity in property is worth more than an applicable exemption allows, the trustee can:

- seize and sell the property at auction, even if you own the property jointly with others
- pay any lender in the picture the amount that's owed on the property, if any
- give you the amount you are entitled to under the exemption system you are using
- distribute what remains to your unsecured creditors, and
- put in for a commission on the sale.

Frequently, before selling property with nonexempt equity, the trustee will give you an opportunity to buy it back at whatever amount you can agree upon. For instance, if you have a motorcycle that could be sold for $8,000 and you only have $3,000 worth of exemption (meaning $5,000 is nonexempt), the trustee might let you buy it back for the amount the trustee would end up with after a sale. Since sales of personal property cost time and money, the trustee might let you buy the motorcycle back for as little as $4,000.

When the mortgage is recorded at your local land records office, it becomes a lien (a claim) against the house. Similarly, when you take out a car loan, you are signing a promissory note and a "security agreement" that allows the car to be repossessed in case you default. When the seller records the security agreement, it becomes a lien against the car (unless you agree to reaffirm the debt—see Ch. 6).

When you file for bankruptcy, the promissory note part of a secured debt is cancelled. However, the lien securing your payment remains. For example, if you owe $400,000 on your house when you file, the $400,000 promissory note is cancelled. However, that doesn't mean that you can stop paying on your mortgage. If you default, the mortgage lender still has the lien—which hasn't been affected by your bankruptcy—and can foreclose on the lien. Similarly, for secured debts involving a car, your Chapter 7 bankruptcy will cancel the amount you owe on the promissory note but it won't affect the lien—which means the lender can repossess the car if you default. To avoid foreclosure, you must continue paying the amount that you owe.

Especially in the case of car notes, many lenders don't like the idea of your not being legally liable for the balance after bankruptcy. Their right to repossess the car in case of nonpayment isn't enough for them. They want you on the hook for the underlying debt so you don't, at some point in the future, trash the car, give it back, and walk away from the whole thing. Bank-

ruptcy gives them the option of requiring you to sign an agreement reaffirming the underlying promissory note (called a "reaffirmation agreement") so you can't just walk away from the debt after bankruptcy.

EXAMPLE: Marisol owes $25,000 on her GMC Denali when she files for Chapter 7 bankruptcy. If she doesn't reaffirm the debt, the bankruptcy will cancel the $25,000 debt and just leave the lender with the lien—which means she'll still have to make her payments under power of the lien but won't owe the actual debt. If, after her bankruptcy, Marisol decides to turn in the car, she won't owe a cent on it. On the other hand, if Marisol reaffirms the debt, she will continue to be liable under the underlying debt after bankruptcy. Clearly, Marisol is better off not owing the money (that is, not reaffirming), but the lender will be better off having her owe the money to prevent her from escaping scot-free if the car is repossessed or she gives it back.

See Ch. 6 for more on reaffirmation agreements and how secured debts are treated in Chapter 7 bankruptcy.

As for houses, reaffirmation is rare. Instead, lenders have historically relied on foreclosure as their enforcement remedy and haven't worried about your walking away from the house. See Ch. 5 for more about houses in bankruptcy.

RELATED TOPIC

Later chapters include detailed information on exemptions. Ch. 4 covers exemptions in general, Ch. 5 explains exemptions for a home, and Ch. 6 covers cars and other property that secure a loan.

Costs and Fees

As of this writing, the filing fee for a Chapter 7 bankruptcy is $335. If you can't afford the fee, you can apply for a fee waiver or permission to pay in installments. You'll have to file an Application for Waiver (or payment in installments) when you file your bankruptcy papers. The court clerk will set a hearing date for you to appear before the judge—who will decide whether you qualify for the waiver. The form, rules, and eligibility guidelines for getting a fee waiver are available at www.uscourts.gov/bankruptcy-forms/application-have-chapter-7-filing-fee-waived. If you want to be represented by a lawyer, you will likely have to pay an additional $1,200 to $2,000 in attorneys' fees.

If you decide to handle your own case, you will probably want to get some outside help. This will typically consist of some of the following:

- one or more do-it-yourself books on bankruptcy (roughly $30 a pop)
- telephonic legal advice from a lawyer (roughly $100 an hour, although many lawyers provide free consultation as a marketing device), and

- clerical assistance with your forms from a bankruptcy petition preparer (between $100 and $200 depending on your jurisdiction).

See Ch. 11 for more on resources you can use to file for bankruptcy.

Issues That Must Be Decided by a Judge

Chapter 7 bankruptcy is designed to run smoothly with very few bankruptcies requiring a decision by an actual judge. Instead, the bankruptcy trustee oversees the case for the most part. However, you and your attorney (if you have one) will have to appear before a judge in the following cases:

- Your income appears to make you ineligible for Chapter 7 bankruptcy and you want to argue that an exception should be made in your case.
- A creditor contests your right to file for Chapter 7 bankruptcy or discharge a particular debt (which is rare).
- You want the judge to rule that you are entitled to discharge a particular type of debt (such as student loans— see Ch. 3 for more information on debts that can be discharged in Chapter 7 bankruptcy only with the judge's approval).
- You want to eliminate a lien on your property that will survive bankruptcy (see Ch. 10).
- You are handling your own case, are making payments on a car or other

personal property, and want to keep the property and continue the contract after bankruptcy. This is called "reaffirming" the contract. (See Ch. 6 for more on reaffirmation agreements.)

See Ch. 10 for more on these and other types of issues that require action by a judge.

How a Chapter 7 Case Ends

Chapter 7 bankruptcy ends with a discharge of all qualifying debts. (For information on which debts can be discharged in Chapter 7, see Ch. 3.) When a debt is discharged, the creditor is forever barred from trying to collect it from you. However, the debt may still appear on your credit report, but it should be tagged as "discharged in bankruptcy." Government entities may not discriminate against you simply because you've received a bankruptcy discharge, but private companies can and do in some circumstances. (See Ch. 9 for more on the consequences of receiving a bankruptcy discharge.)

Mandatory Budget Counseling

In addition to the requirement that you obtain credit counseling before you file for bankruptcy, you must also participate in a course on budget management before you can get your discharge. Most filers use the same agency for the budget counseling as they used for the prefiling credit counseling. See Ch. 2 for more information about this requirement.

Changing Your Mind

If you file for Chapter 7 bankruptcy and then change your mind, you can ask the court to dismiss your case. As a general rule, the court will not do so if it wouldn't be in the best interests of your creditors. For example, your request to dismiss might be denied if you have significant nonexempt assets that the trustee could sell to raise money to pay your creditors.

> **EXAMPLE:** Jake files for Chapter 7 bankruptcy, thinking all of his property is exempt. Shortly after he files, Jake's mother tells him that he is on the deed for a 20-acre ranchette that he, his sister, and his mother inherited from his father. Under the exemption laws applicable to Jake's bankruptcy, his share of the ranchette is not exempt which means the trustee can sell the property and distribute Jake's share to his unsecured creditors. Jake wants to hold on to the property and so requests that his case be dismissed. His request is denied because it would not be in the best interest of Jake's creditors. The moral? Don't file Chapter 7 unless and until you know what property you own and what will happen to it in bankruptcy.

If you do dismiss your case, you can file again later, although in some circumstances you may have to wait 180 days and pay a new filing fee. Instead of dismissing your Chapter 7 case, you can always convert it to another type of bankruptcy for which you qualify (typically Chapter 13 for individuals). In Jake's case, for example, he could convert to a Chapter 13 bankruptcy in order to save the ranchette. However, in his plan, Jake would have to pay his unsecured creditors at least as much as they would have received had Jake filed under Chapter 7— essentially, the market value of his share of the ranchette, less sale costs and the trustee's commission. (See below, to learn more about the Chapter 13 repayment plan.)

Chapter 13 Bankruptcy

Chapter 13 bankruptcy works quite differently from Chapter 7 bankruptcy. In Chapter 13, the trustee does not sell your assets to repay your creditors. Instead, you use a portion of your income to pay some or all of what you owe to your creditors over time (anywhere from three to five years, depending on your income and how much of your debt you can afford to repay). The trick to successfully using Chapter 13 to get out of debt is to make sure you have enough income to meet all of your payment obligations under the Chapter 13 laws. (See Ch. 2 to learn about the eligibility requirements for filing under Chapter 13.)

How a Chapter 13 Case Begins

To file a Chapter 13 bankruptcy, first you must complete a credit counseling course, then fill out and file a packet of forms— mostly the same forms as you would use in a Chapter 7 bankruptcy, and also provide the court with:

- a feasible plan to repay some or all of your debts over the plan period (either three or five years, depending on your income and Chapter 13 legal requirements)
- proof that you've filed your federal and state income tax returns for the previous four years, and
- a copy (or transcript) of your most recently filed IRS income tax return. (See Ch. 10 for more on Chapter 13 paperwork.)

The Repayment Plan

Under a Chapter 13 repayment plan, you make payments, usually monthly, to the bankruptcy trustee, the official who oversees your case. The trustee uses that money to pay the creditors covered by your plan and to pay his or her own statutory fee (usually 10% of the amount distributed under your plan).

Under Chapter 13, you are required to devote all of your "projected disposable income" to your plan (essentially, the amount left over after paying your allowed expenses). Your repayment period may be as short as three years if your gross average income over the six months before you file is below your state's median income, and five years if it is above. (See Ch. 2 for more on making this calculation.) In some cases, the filer needs a five-year plan to make all required payments regardless of whether his or her income is above or below the median income.

Postconfirmation Increases in Income

If your repayment plan is based on an income level that increases after the court confirms your plan, the trustee can request the court to order a jump in your monthly payments due to your new ability to pay this extra amount. The basic idea in Chapter 13 is that you have to devote all your disposable income to your plan payments.

In Chapter 13, some creditors are entitled to receive 100% of what you owe them, while others may receive a much smaller percentage or even nothing at all. For example, a Chapter 13 plan must propose that any child support you owe to a spouse or child (as opposed to a government agency) will be paid in full over the life of your plan; otherwise, the judge will not approve it.

Why File a Chapter 13 Bankruptcy?

Most people who have a choice between Chapters 13 and 7 choose Chapter 7. After all, it lasts about three months instead of three to five years, is cheaper than Chapter 13 if you hire a lawyer, and you don't have to pay down any of your dischargeable debt. So, why would you choose to file a Chapter 13 bankruptcy? Here is a brief list of some reasons (all of these are discussed in more detail throughout the book):

- In Chapter 13, you can get rid of a second mortgage lien on your real estate—called a lien strip-off—if the market value of the house is less than the amount owed on the first mortgage.
- Chapter 13 sometimes provides a way to reduce your secured debts to the value of the collateral (for instance, reducing a $10,000 car note on a $5,000 car to $5,000, which lowers the payments).
- Chapter 13 lets you make up for missed payments on a house, car, or other collateral over a three- to five-year period.

- Chapter 13 gets rid of certain types of debts that aren't discharged in Chapter 7 (for instance debts owed because of divorce or a separation agreement, but not support).
- Chapter 13 allows you to operate a business while you are in bankruptcy (unlike Chapter 7, which may require that you close the business).
- If you previously received a Chapter 7 discharge, you can't get another Chapter 7 discharge for eight years, but you can get a Chapter 13 discharge after only four years. And you can file for Chapter 13 immediately after a Chapter 7 discharge (but you won't get a discharge). (See Ch. 2 for reasons why this can help.)

See Ch. 7 for a mock conversation between a bankruptcy lawyer and client in which they discuss whether the client should file a Chapter 7 or Chapter 13 bankruptcy.

On the other hand, the judge legally could approve a plan that doesn't repay any portion of your credit card debts if you won't have any projected disposable income left after paying your back child support obligations and other obligations that must be paid in full under the Chapter 13 laws.

Not All Disposable Incomes Are Equal

One of the oddities of the Chapter 13 law is that your qualifying disposable income may be different than your actual disposable income. Your qualifying disposable income is initially based on your average gross income over the six-month period prior to your filing date. For example, if your income was $8,000 a month for the first three months of that period and $4,000 for the second three months, your qualifying monthly disposable income will be $6,000—the six-month average—even though your actual income through the life of your plan will only be $4,000. (Ch. 2 explains qualifying disposable income in more detail, as well as how these figures and requirements might be juggled to come up with a workable repayment plan that a judge will approve.)

To have your debts fully discharged under Chapter 13, you must usually make all payments required by your plan and:

- remain current on your federal and state income taxes

- remain current on any child support or alimony obligations, and
- annually file a copy of your federal income tax return or transcript of the return with the court.

You also have to provide your creditors with copies of the income tax returns or transcripts you file with the court, if they request them.

Which Debts Are Discharged

If your Chapter 13 bankruptcy pays your unsecured debts in full, then you will receive a complete discharge of those debts no matter what type they are. If your plan pays less than 100% of a debt, the balance will be discharged unless it is a type of debt that isn't discharged in Chapter 13 bankruptcy.

As a general rule, most credit card, medical, and legal debts are discharged, as are most court judgments, deficiencies from foreclosures or repossessions, and personal loans. Debts that have to be fully paid in a Chapter 13 bankruptcy are:

- court-imposed fines and restitution
- back child support and alimony owed to an ex-spouse or child
- student loans
- recent back taxes
- unfiled taxes, and
- debts you owe because of a civil judgment arising out of your willful or malicious acts or for personal injuries or death caused by your drunk driving.

Chapter 13 Plan Must Pay Unsecured Creditors as Much as They Would Receive in a Chapter 7 Bankruptcy

People sometimes choose to avoid Chapter 7 bankruptcy because they stand to lose certain property that isn't exempt. Chapter 13 bankruptcy initially looks like a good alternative, because in Chapter 13 you don't have to give up any property. Rather, your obligations under your plan are based on your disposable income.

However, even though Chapter 13 won't take your property, it does require that you pay your unsecured creditors the value of what they would have received in Chapter 7. For example, if you have $50,000 equity in your home that isn't protected by an exemption, you wouldn't lose the home in Chapter 13 bankruptcy, but you would have to propose a plan that pays your creditors at least $50,000 less sale costs and the trustee's commission. This rule often makes it difficult to propose a feasible Chapter 13 plan, due to the size of the required payment.

Debts arising from your fraudulent actions or recent credit card charges for luxuries will not be discharged if the creditor gets a court order to that effect. Ch. 3 explains which debts are discharged in a Chapter 13 bankruptcy.

Which Property Is at Risk in Chapter 13 Bankruptcy

As mentioned, you are not required to give up any property you own when you file your Chapter 13 bankruptcy case. (However, you may choose to give up property. For example, your plan could state your intention to sell or refinance an item of property at a later date.) In Chapter 13, your income is used to pay off some portion of your debt, not your property. However, as mentioned earlier, the value of your non-exempt property can be the determining factor regarding your ability to propose a valid repayment plan.

Houses and Cars

Filing for Chapter 13 bankruptcy lets you keep your house and car as long as you stay current on the payments. You can also pay off arrearages you owe when you file. For instance, if you are $5,000 behind on your mortgage payments, you can pay an extra amount into your plan to pay it off in a reasonable amount of time. That's why Chapter 13 has typically been the remedy of choice for people facing foreclosure. (See Ch. 5 for more on what happens to your home when you file for either type of bankruptcy.)

Costs and Fees

The filing fee for a Chapter 13 bankruptcy is currently $310. If you can't afford the fee, you can apply for a fee waiver. If you want to be represented by a lawyer, you will probably have to pay $2,500 to $4,000 in legal fees, some of which can be paid through your plan.

If you decide to handle your own case (as some do), you will likely want to get some outside help. This will typically consist of one or both of the following:

- one or more self-help law books on Chapter 13 bankruptcy (roughly $40), and
- telephonic legal advice from a lawyer (roughly $100 an hour).

Unlike the situation in Chapter 7, bankruptcy petition preparers are seldom, if ever, willing to handle Chapter 13 cases. See Ch. 11 for more on resources you can use to file for bankruptcy.

The Meeting of Creditors

When you file your Chapter 13 bankruptcy petition, the court schedules a "meeting of creditors" (usually within about a month), and sends an official notice of the bankruptcy filing and the meeting to you and all of your creditors. You (and your spouse if you have filed jointly) are required to attend. You'll need to bring two forms of identification—a picture ID and proof of your Social Security number.

A typical creditors' meeting in a Chapter 13 case lasts less than 15 minutes. The trustee will briefly go over your paperwork with

you. No judge will be present. The trustee is likely to be most interested in whether your repayment plan meets all legal requirements and whether you will be able to make the payments you have proposed. (See Ch. 2 for more on Chapter 13 requirements.) The trustee has a vested interest in helping you successfully navigate the Chapter 13 process because the trustee gets paid a percentage of all payments doled out under your plan.

The trustee will also make sure you have filed your tax returns for all taxable periods during the four prior years. If not, the trustee will continue the creditors' meeting to give you a chance to file these returns or provide proof of filing if you've already done so. You cannot proceed with a Chapter 13 bankruptcy unless and until you bring your tax filings up to date.

When the trustee is finished asking questions, any creditors who show up will have a chance to question you. Secured creditors might come if they have any objections to the plan you have proposed as part of your Chapter 13 filing (but will usually file a motion with the court instead). They may claim, for example, that your plan isn't feasible, that you're giving yourself too much time to pay your arrears on your car note or mortgage, or that your plan proposes to pay less on a secured debt than the replacement value of the collateral property. (See Ch. 6 for more information on collateral and other property that secures a loan.)

An unsecured creditor who is scheduled to receive very little under your plan might object, too, if that creditor thinks you should cut your living expenses and thereby increase your disposable income (the amount from which unsecured creditors are paid).

Challenging the Legality of a Mortgage in Chapter 13 Bankruptcy

When you file Chapter 13 bankruptcy, creditors are supposed to file a proof of claim setting out how much they think you owe. This proof of claim will determine how much they get paid as part of your Chapter 13 plan. If a secured creditor fails to file a proof of claim, you can file one on their behalf.

If the court does not approve the claim, don't expect to get out from under the mortgage entirely. It's much more likely that legal defects in lenders' claims will result in negotiated settlements reducing the amount of your mortgage principal and interest.

Come to the meeting prepared to negotiate with disgruntled creditors. If you agree to make changes to accommodate their objections, you must submit a modified plan and have it served on all of your creditors. While any objections raised by creditors won't be ruled on during the creditors' meeting (because the judge won't be there), the trustee may raise these objections on behalf of the creditors at your confirmation hearing before the judge, which will be scheduled for a couple of weeks later. In most cases, this is when your creditors will object, as well.

The Confirmation Hearing

Unlike Chapter 7, Chapter 13 bankruptcy requires at least one appearance in court. At this appearance, called the confirmation hearing, the judge either confirms (approves of) your proposed plan or sends you back to the drawing board for various reasons—usually because your plan doesn't meet Chapter 13 requirements in one or more particulars. For example, a judge might reject your plan because you don't have enough projected disposable income to at least pay your priority creditors in full and stay current on your secured debts—such as a car note or mortgage. For more information on Chapter 13 confirmation hearings, see Ch. 10.

You are entitled to amend your proposed plan until you get it right, or until the judge decides that it's hopeless. Each amendment requires a new confirmation hearing and appropriate written notice to your creditors.

Other Common Reasons to Go to Court

In addition to attending the confirmation hearing, you may need to go to court to:

- modify your plan after it has been confirmed (if necessary)
- value an asset (if your plan proposes to pay less for a car or other property than the creditor thinks it's worth)

- respond to requests by a creditor or the trustee to dismiss your case
- respond to a creditor who opposes your right to discharge a particular debt (perhaps because you engaged in fraud when incurring the debt)
- discharge a type of debt that can be discharged only if the judge decides that it should be (such as discharging a student loan because of hardship)
- eliminate a lien on your property that will survive your Chapter 13 bankruptcy unless the judge removes it, or
- oppose a secured or unsecured claim filed by a creditor.

These procedures are described in Ch. 10.

How a Chapter 13 Case Ends

If you complete your full three- or five-year repayment plan, are current on your income tax returns and your child support or alimony payments, and complete a budget management course approved by the U.S. Trustee, the remaining unpaid balance on any of your debts that qualify for discharge will be wiped out. If any balance remains on a debt that doesn't qualify for discharge (like a student loan), you will continue to owe the unpaid amount. (The debts that qualify for discharge in a Chapter 13 bankruptcy are explained in Ch. 3.)

Modifying the Plan and Alternatives to Full Discharge

If you can't complete your Chapter 13 plan as written, you can ask the court to modify

it. As long as it's clear that you're acting in good faith, the court is likely to approve your request. If it isn't feasible to modify the plan, you may still be able to get what's called a "hardship" discharge if both of the following apply:

- You failed to complete your plan due to circumstances "for which you should not justly be held accountable" (like a job loss).
- Your unsecured creditors have received at least what they would have gotten if you had filed for Chapter 7 bankruptcy (that is, at least the value of your nonexempt property less sale costs and the trustee's commission).

If the bankruptcy court won't let you modify your plan or give you a hardship discharge, you can:

- convert your Chapter 13 bankruptcy to a Chapter 7 bankruptcy, unless you received a Chapter 7 discharge in a case filed within the previous eight years (this is explained in Ch. 10), or
- dismiss your Chapter 13 case. This means you'll owe your creditors the balances on your debts from before you filed your Chapter 13 case, less the payments you made, plus the interest that accrued while your Chapter 13 case was open.

As you can imagine, Chapter 13 bankruptcy requires discipline. For the entire length of your case, you will have to live strictly within your means—and even more strictly if your income exceeds the state's median income. The Chapter 13 trustee will not allow you to spend money on anything deemed nonessential. In past years, only about half of Chapter 13 plans were successfully completed. Some Chapter 13 filers drop out early in the process, without ever submitting a feasible repayment plan to the court. Keep in mind though, that even if you fail to complete your plan, filing Chapter 13 bankruptcy could provide you with valuable time to get your finances under control or make other adjustments.

How Bankruptcy Stops Collection Efforts

One of the most powerful features of bankruptcy is that it stops most debt collectors dead in their tracks and keeps them at bay for the rest of your case. Once you file, all collection activity (with a few exceptions, explained below) must go through the bankruptcy court—and most creditors cannot take any further action against you directly. It's like hitting a line of ants with bug spray.

TIP
You don't need bankruptcy to stop your creditors from harassing you. Many people begin thinking about bankruptcy when their creditors start phoning their homes and/or places of employment. Federal law prohibits this activity by third-party debt collectors once you tell the collector, in writing, that you don't want to be called. And if you orally tell debt collectors that you refuse to pay, they cannot, by law, contact you except to send one last letter making a final demand for payment before filing a lawsuit. While just telling the collector to stop usually works, you may have to send a written follow-up letter. (See Ch. 12 for a sample letter.) The downside to this strategy is that you leave the creditor with no choice other than to forget about the debt or sue you.

Credit Card Debts, Medical Debts, and Attorneys' Fees

Anyone trying to collect credit card debts, medical debts, attorneys' fees, debts arising from breach of contract, or legal judgments against you (other than child support and alimony) must cease all collection activities after you file your bankruptcy. They cannot:

- file a lawsuit or proceed with a pending lawsuit against you without court permission
- record liens against your property
- report the debt to a credit reporting bureau, or
- seize your property or income, such as money in a bank account or your paycheck.

Public Benefits

Government entities that are seeking to collect overpayments of public benefits, such as unemployment, SSI, Medicaid, or TANF (welfare) benefits, cannot do so by reducing or terminating your benefits while your bankruptcy is pending. If, however, you become ineligible for benefits, including Medicare benefits, bankruptcy doesn't prevent denial or termination of the benefits on that ground.

Domestic Relations Proceedings

Almost all proceedings related to a divorce or paternity action continue as before—they are not affected by the automatic stay. These include:

- the setting and collection of current child support and alimony
- the collection of back child support and alimony from property that is not in the bankruptcy estate (see Ch. 4 for more on what's in the bankruptcy estate)
- the determination of child custody and visitation
- a lawsuit to establish paternity
- an action to modify child support and alimony
- proceedings to protect a spouse or child from domestic violence
- withholding of income to collect child support
- reporting of overdue support to credit bureaus
- the interception of tax refunds to pay back child support, and
- withholding, suspension, or restriction of drivers' and professional licenses as leverage to collect child support.

Criminal Proceedings

If a case against you can be broken down into criminal and debt components, only the criminal component will be allowed to continue—the debt component will be stayed while your bankruptcy is pending. For example, if you were convicted of writing a bad check and have been sentenced to community service and ordered to pay a fine, your obligation to do community service will not be stopped by the automatic stay (but your obligation to pay the fine might be).

Landlord-Tenant Proceedings

With a few exceptions (check your state law), the automatic stay does not stop the eviction of a tenant if:

- the landlord obtained a judgment of possession prior to the bankruptcy filing, or
- the tenant is endangering the property or using controlled substances on it.

Ch. 5 explains when evictions on these grounds may occur. It also covers the new requirements imposed on both the tenant and the landlord if there is a dispute about whether an eviction can proceed.

Tax Proceedings

The IRS can continue certain actions, such as a tax audit, issuing a tax deficiency notice, demanding a tax return, issuing a tax assessment, or demanding payment of a post petition assessment. The automatic stay does, however, stop the IRS from issuing a lien or seizing (levying against) any of your property or income.

Pension Loans

The stay doesn't prevent withholding from a debtor's income to repay a loan from an ERISA-qualified pension (this includes most job-related pensions and individual retirement plans). See Ch. 4 for more on how pensions are treated under bankruptcy.

Foreclosures

Foreclosure is the way a mortgage holder obtains title to the property that secures the mortgage. It is the main (and sometimes only) remedy available to a mortgage holder when the homeowner defaults. Foreclosure procedures differ from state to state. In about half the states, foreclosures are carried out in court just like any other civil proceeding (these are called judicial foreclosures). In the other states, foreclosures occur outside of court (called nonjudicial foreclosures) and typically involve complex state rules regarding notices, reinstatement periods, and redemption periods.

When you file bankruptcy, pending foreclosure proceedings are stopped dead in their tracks and won't resume until your bankruptcy is completed or the bankruptcy judge lifts the stay upon request by the mortgage holder. Importantly, one thing that bankruptcy doesn't stop is the passage of time required by a particular foreclosure notice. For instance, in California, a foreclosing party must provide the homeowner with a 90-day notice of default prior to setting a date for the actual foreclosure sale. While a bankruptcy filing would delay the issuance of the 90-day notice in the first place, it won't prevent the passage of time under the 90-day period once the notice is filed. So, a Chapter 7 filing would substantially delay the foreclosure process if it were filed prior to the 90-day notice, but would have little or no effect on the foreclosure if it were filed during the 90-day notice period. See *The Foreclosure Survival Guide* by Amy Loftsgordon (Nolo) for a more detailed look at how bankruptcy works to delay or prevent foreclosures.

Although foreclosure activities initially are stayed by your bankruptcy filing, the stay won't apply if you filed another bankruptcy within the previous two years and the court, in that proceeding, lifted the stay and allowed the lender to proceed with the foreclosure, or if you filed two bankruptcies within the past year. In other words, the law doesn't allow you to prevent a foreclosure by filing serial bankruptcies.

Utilities

Companies providing you with utilities (such as gas, heating oil, electricity, telephone, and water) may not discontinue service because you file for bankruptcy.

However, they can shut off your service 20 days after you file if you don't provide them with a deposit or another means to assure future payment. They can also cut you off if you don't pay for services you receive after you file for bankruptcy.

Special Rules for Multiple Filers

If you had one bankruptcy case pending during the previous year, then the stay will terminate 30 days after you file unless you, the trustee, the U.S. Trustee, or the creditor asks for the stay to continue as to certain creditors and proves that the current case was filed in good faith.

This rule doesn't apply to any case that was dismissed because you should have filed under Chapter 13 instead of Chapter 7 (see Ch. 2 for more on when a case may be dismissed on that ground).

If a creditor had a motion to lift the stay pending during a previously dismissed case, the court will presume that you acted in bad faith in your current case. You will have to overcome this presumption in order to obtain continuing stay relief. If you had two or more cases pending during the previous year, then there will be no automatic stay. You'll have to seek a court order to obtain any stay relief.

CAUTION

It is particularly important to be aware of these rules if you are dealing with a foreclosure.

The Bankruptcy Trustee

Until your bankruptcy case ends, your financial assets and problems are in the hands of the bankruptcy trustee, who acts under the supervision of another type of trustee called the U.S. Trustee.

The Bankruptcy Trustee's General Duties

With few exceptions, the bankruptcy trustee assumes control of your case.

The bankruptcy trustee's primary duties are:

- in a Chapter 7 bankruptcy, to see that your nonexempt property is seized and sold for the benefit of your unsecured creditors
- to make sure that the paperwork submitted in your bankruptcy is accurate and complete
- to schedule and operate the creditors' meeting (the 341 hearing), and
- to administer the case for the court.

The bankruptcy trustee may be a local bankruptcy attorney or a nonlawyer who is very knowledgeable about Chapter 7 or Chapter 13 bankruptcy generally and the local court's rules and procedures in particular.

Just a few days after you file your bankruptcy papers, you'll get a Notice of Filing from the court, giving the name, business address, and business phone number of the bankruptcy trustee. The trustee may follow up with a list of any financial documents the trustee wants to see, such as bank statements, property appraisals, or insurance documents. In addition, you are supposed to send the trustee paycheck stubs and a copy of your most recently filed federal tax return. You'll provide all documents at least seven days before the creditors' meeting.

As used in this book, the term "trustee" means the bankruptcy trustee who will actually be handling your case on behalf of the bankruptcy court, unless otherwise stated.

The U.S. Trustee's Office

In addition to the bankruptcy trustee assigned to your case, another type of trustee—a U.S. Trustee—will be involved, usually behind the scenes. The Office of the U.S. Trustee is a part of the United States Department of Justice. Its role is to supervise the bankruptcy trustees who actually handle cases in the bankruptcy court, to make sure that the bankruptcy laws are being followed and that cases of fraud and other crimes are appropriately handled. There are 21 regional U.S. Trustee offices throughout the country.

If a U.S. Trustee decides to take an active part in your case, the parties to the case—including you—will be sent a notice about the proposed action, and you will be given an opportunity to oppose whatever action the U.S. Trustee proposes. Later chapters in this book suggest some ways to respond to various actions the U.S. Trustee might propose.

If You Owe Back Child Support

If you owe back support, the trustee is also required to provide notices to the holder of the support claim and the state child support agency to keep them abreast of your bankruptcy and help them find you after your bankruptcy discharge. Specifically, the trustee is required to provide:

- the payee with information about the state child support enforcement agency and his or her rights under the bankruptcy law
- the state child support enforcement agency with information about the back support and the payee, and
- the state child support agency and payee with information about the discharge, your last known address, the last known name and address of your employer, and the name of any creditor who holds a nondischargeable claim or a claim that has been reaffirmed.

Both the payee and the child support enforcement agency can ask these creditors to provide your last known address. The laws specifically authorize these creditors to release such information without any penalty.

Happily, most filers never have to deal with the U.S. Trustee. It is unlikely, unless they file Chapter 7 bankruptcies and their bankruptcy papers—or their testimony at the creditors' meeting—indicate that they:

- have a "current monthly income" that is more than the median income for their state (see Ch. 2)
- earn enough actual income to support a Chapter 13 plan (see Ch. 2), or
- have apparently engaged in illegal actions that warrant investigative follow-up (such as perjury).

Also, some cases are selected for random audits (the number of bankruptcy cases audited varies depending on current budget funding).

Chapter 7 Bankruptcy Trustee

In a Chapter 7 bankruptcy, the trustee is mostly interested in what you own and what property you claim as exempt. This is because the court pays the trustee a commission on property that is sold for the benefit of the unsecured creditors. The trustee may receive up to 25% of the first $5,000, 10% of any amount between $5,000 and $50,000, and 5% of any additional money up to $1,000,000.

If your papers indicate that all of your property is exempt (which means you get to keep it), your case initially is considered a "no-asset" case and your creditors are told not to file claims (because you don't have any property that will be sold to pay them). The trustee also won't show much interest in a no-asset case unless the facts of your case suggest that you may be hiding or mischaracterizing assets. After all, if there is no property for the trustee to seize and sell

to pay your unsecured creditors, then there is no commission for the trustee.

The first time you will personally encounter the trustee in a Chapter 7 case is when you appear at your creditors' meeting, which you must attend if you don't want your bankruptcy dismissed. Typically, if all of your assets are exempt, you will hear nothing further from the trustee. However, if there are (or it appears that there might be) nonexempt assets in your bankruptcy estate, the trustee may continue your creditors' meeting to another date and ask you to submit appropriate documentation in the meantime. More rarely, the trustee may hire an attorney to pursue nonexempt assets you appear to own or to recover money or assets that you transferred prior to bankruptcy. The trustee might even refer your case to the U.S. Trustee's office for further action if it looks like you have engaged in dishonest activity or that you should be in a Chapter 13 case instead of Chapter 7.

If there are nonexempt assets for the trustee to seize and sell, you will be expected to cooperate in getting them to the trustee for disposition. You will also be given the opportunity to "buy the assets back" from the trustee at a negotiated price or substitute exempt assets for the nonexempt assets.

If you have nonexempt property that isn't worth very much or would be cumbersome for the trustee to sell, the trustee can—and often will—abandon the property, which means you get to keep it. For example, no matter how much your used furniture may be worth in theory, many trustees won't bother selling it. Arranging to sell used furniture is expensive and rarely produces much, if any, proceeds for the creditors.

Many people wonder whether a trustee can inventory their homes to determine whether they are hiding property. While unusual, part of your duty to cooperate with the trustee could consist of opening up your home upon the trustee's request. And if you don't voluntarily cooperate, the trustee can obtain an order from the court to force the issue.

The trustee is also required, under the supervision of the U.S. Trustee, to assess your bankruptcy papers for accuracy and for signs of possible fraud or abuse of the bankruptcy system.

Chapter 13 Bankruptcy Trustee

In a Chapter 13 bankruptcy, the trustee's role is to:

- examine your proposed plan and make sure it complies with all legal requirements
- object to the approval of your plan if the trustee feels you have not met all legal requirements
- receive the payments you make under the plan and distribute them to your creditors in the manner required by law

- monitor your duty to file tax returns with the appropriate federal and state taxing authorities for the four years previous to your filing date and annually while your Chapter 13 case is pending, and
- if you owe back child support, provide the payee and your state's child support enforcement agency with information described in "If You Owe Back Child Support," above.

Chapter 13 trustees pay themselves by keeping up to 10% of the payments they disburse to creditors.

Many Chapter 13 trustees play a fairly active role in the cases they administer. This is especially true in small suburban or rural judicial districts, or in districts with a lot of Chapter 13 bankruptcy cases. For example, a trustee may:

- help you create a realistic budget (the trustee cannot, however, give you legal advice)
- explain how to modify your plan, if necessary, or
- give you a temporary reprieve or take other steps to help you get back on track if you miss a payment or two.

Despite the trustee's great interest in your success, your financial relationship with the trustee is not as stifling as it may sound. In most situations, you control your money and the property you acquire after filing—as long as you make the payments called for under your repayment plan and you make all regular payments on your secured debts. However, if your income or property increases during the life of your plan (for instance, you receive a substantial promotion or you win the lottery), the trustee can seek to amend your plan to pay your creditors a greater percentage of what you owe them rather than the lesser percentage originally called for in your plan.

Famous Chapter 13 Bankruptcy Filers

Comedian Jerry Lewis (the telethon guy) filed for Chapter 13 bankruptcy in the 1970s after losing stage bookings. Singer/songwriter Marvin Gaye also filed for Chapter 13 bankruptcy in the 1970s. He dedicated his 1983 megahit album to his Chapter 13 trustee, Elsie Davis.

It's important to remember that the trustee is a very important person in your life for the duration of your case. Your cooperation with the trustee will probably speed the process of gaining court approval for your plan.

Business Bankruptcies

If you own your own business as a sole proprietor or an independent contractor, you and your business are considered the same when it comes to filing for bankruptcy. All debts owed and all assets owned by your business are also considered to be yours. While you may have to provide some additional paperwork for your bankruptcy, such as a profit and loss or income and expense statement, the procedures are the same as if you weren't in business—with one important exception. If your business has assets that frequently change, such as inventory, and you file under Chapter 7, the bankruptcy trustee may require you to shut the business down while your bankruptcy is pending, which is usually about three months. If, however, you have a service business, or a manufacturing business that doesn't carry a large or valuable inventory, you may be allowed to continue business operations during the pendency of the bankruptcy provided your assets are clearly exempt (expect to provide proof of liability insurance, as well).

If you own a corporation or limited liability company, things are different. You and your corporation (or LLC) are different entities and cannot file together. Also, if your business needs to go through bankruptcy, you'll need a lawyer do it. Owners of their own corporations and other business entities cannot represent those entities—unless they themselves are lawyers.

If you do decide to take a corporation or limited liability company into bankruptcy, you cannot use Chapter 13—only Chapter 7 and Chapter 11 are available to business entities. In Chapter 11, the business can continue operations, but you'll have to pay an attorney to represent the business in the bankruptcy, and the fees you will pay will probably be well in excess of $20,000. In Chapter 7, you must liquidate (close) the business.

If you file a personal bankruptcy under Chapter 7 or Chapter 13, corporate-owned assets and liabilities are not automatically

---

Nolo Resources on Bankruptcy, Debt, and Credit

Nolo publishes a number of books on bankruptcy, dealing with debt, and credit repair. Look for the latest editions of these books:

- *How to File for Chapter 7 Bankruptcy,* by Cara O'Neill and Albin Renauer. This do-it-yourself bankruptcy book takes you step-by-step through the filing process for a liquidation bankruptcy.
- *Chapter 13 Bankruptcy: Keep Your Property & Repay Debts Over Time,* by Stephen Elias and Kathleen Michon. This book explains the Chapter 13 bankruptcy process in detail.
- *Solve Your Money Troubles: Debt, Credit & Bankruptcy,* by Amy Loftsgordon and Cara O'Neill. A practical book to help you prioritize debts, negotiate with creditors, stop collector harassment, challenge wage attachments, contend with repossession, respond to creditor lawsuits, and rebuild your credit.

- *Credit Repair,* by Amy Loftsgordon. This book shows how to fix your credit report, rebuild credit, and avoid credit problems in the future.
- *Divorce & Money: How to Make the Best Financial Decisions During Divorce,* by Violet Woodhouse. This book can help you with the overwhelming financial decisions of divorce: selling the house, dividing debts, discovering assets, setting alimony and child support, handling retirement benefits and taxes, and negotiating a fair settlement.

Nolo also provides tons of free bankruptcy information online at www.nolo.com. You'll find hundreds of articles and FAQs on bankruptcy topics, including information particular to each state.

part of the bankruptcy, although you can discharge any personal liability you have for corporate debt. If you own 100% of corporate stock, as part of a personal bankruptcy filed under Chapter 7, the trustee can liquidate the corporation and treat the assets as the debtor's personal assets—which means they can be sold for the benefit of your creditors unless you protect them under the exemptions available to you for this purpose. By contrast, if you own less than 100%, the trustee is limited to selling your shares and distributing the proceeds to the creditors.

CAUTION

If you owe debts jointly with your corporation or LLC, and you file a personal bankruptcy, your bankruptcy discharge may protect you personally but it does not protect your business. Business creditors will still be able to collect against the business assets and income. If you are in this situation, it might make sense to dissolve your corporation or LLC before you file a personal bankruptcy case. However, be aware that if you open a similar business shortly after the bankruptcy, a discharged creditor might accuse you of fraudulently doing so in an attempt to avoid paying your debt. Be sure to talk to a bankruptcy attorney before you file.

Who Can File for Bankruptcy

Bankruptcy might be a good solution to your debt problems —but only if you are eligible to file. For example, you won't be allowed to file for Chapter 7 or Chapter 13 bankruptcy if you don't first seek credit counseling. Before reading the rest of this book to find out what effect bankruptcy will have on your life, you should figure out whether you'll be eligible to file for bankruptcy in the first place.

Unlike Chapter 7 bankruptcy, Chapter 13 eligibility is intended, in large part, to require people to pay back at least a portion of their debts if they are able. And if you do file under Chapter 13, your repayment plan will have to repay certain types of debts in full. This chapter explains these and other eligibility rules for Chapter 7 and Chapter 13. You'll also find a hypothetical discussion between a bankruptcy lawyer and a would-be filer regarding which type of bankruptcy would be more appropriate given that person's circumstances.

Getting Help With Eligibility Issues

As you'll see from this chapter, eligibility rules for Chapter 7 and Chapter 13 bankruptcy are not always simple. Thanks to the bankruptcy means test and Chapter 13 repayment plan requirements, among other things, figuring out if you can file for Chapter 7 or Chapter 13 bankruptcy can be tricky. And even if you qualify to file for bankruptcy, rules about presumed fraudulent transactions and prebankruptcy payments to certain creditors might mean you should think carefully about *when* you file.

If you want to file for Chapter 7 bankruptcy but something in this chapter raises a red flag, be sure to consult with an experienced bankruptcy attorney. A bankruptcy specialist can often help you overcome eligibility problems and other tricky issues.

Credit Counseling

Before you can file for Chapter 7 or Chapter 13 bankruptcy, you must consult a nonprofit credit counseling agency. The purpose of this consultation is to see whether there is a feasible way to handle your debt load outside of bankruptcy, without adding to what you owe.

Counseling Requirements

To qualify for bankruptcy relief, you must show that you received credit counseling from an agency approved by the U.S Trustee's office within the 180-day period before you file your bankruptcy. Once you complete the counseling, the agency will give you a certificate of completion to file with your petition. It will also give you a copy of any repayment plan you may have worked out with the agency. You can find out which agencies have been approved for your judicial district by visiting the Office of the U.S. Trustee's website at www.justice. gov; click "Credit Counseling & Debtor Education" to see the list.

The supposed purpose of credit counseling is to give you an idea of whether you really need to file for bankruptcy or whether an informal repayment plan would get you back on your economic feet. Counseling is required even if it's pretty obvious that a repayment plan isn't feasible (that is, your debts are too high and your income is too low) or you are facing debts that you find unfair and don't want to pay. (Credit card balances inflated by high interest rates and penalties are particularly unpopular with many filers, as are emergency room bills, debts you cosigned, and deficiency judgments based on auctions of repossessed cars.)

Bankruptcy law requires only that you participate in the counseling—not that you go along with whatever the agency proposes. Even if a repayment plan is feasible, you aren't required to agree to it. However, if the agency does come up with a plan, you must file it along with the other bankruptcy documents described in Ch. 10.

CAUTION

The court might agree with the agency's plan. If it's clear from the documents you file that you could complete the repayment plan proposed by the agency, the court may use this as a reason to question your Chapter 7 filing and try to push you into a Chapter 13 repayment plan (see Ch. 10). If that happens, at least you'll have an opportunity to argue about whether you should have to repay all of your debts.

Rules Counseling Agencies Must Follow

In addition to providing services without regard to the debtor's ability to pay, counseling agencies have to meet a number of other requirements. They must:

- disclose to you their funding sources, their counselor qualifications, the possible impact of their proposed plan on your credit report, the costs of the program, if any, and how much of the costs will be borne by you
- provide counseling that includes an analysis of your current financial condition, factors that caused the condition, and how you can develop a plan to respond to the problems without adding to your debt
- use trained counselors who don't receive any commissions or bonuses based on the outcome of the counseling services (that is, kickbacks to individual counselors are not allowed, although kickbacks to the agency may be legal), and
- maintain adequate financial resources to provide continuing support services over the life of any repayment plan (that is, if they propose a three-year payment plan, they must have adequate reserves to service your case for three years).

Counseling Costs

Credit counseling agencies may charge a reasonable fee for their services. However, if a debtor cannot afford the fee, the counseling agency must provide services free or at reduced rates. This means that the service must offer a sliding fee scale and a waiver of fees altogether for people below a certain income level (below 150% of the poverty level for a family of equal size). The Office of the U.S. Trustee, the law enforcement agency that oversees credit counseling agencies, has indicated that a "reasonable" fee might range from free to $50, depending on the circumstances.

Exceptions to the Counseling Requirement

You don't have to get counseling if the U.S. Trustee certifies that there is no appropriate agency available to you in the district where you will be filing. However, counseling can be provided by telephone or (usually) online, so it is unlikely that approved debt counseling will ever be "unavailable."

You can also avoid this requirement if you certify to the court's satisfaction that:

- You had to file for bankruptcy immediately (perhaps to stop a wage garnishment or foreclosure).
- You were unable to obtain counseling within seven days after requesting it.

If you can prove that you didn't receive credit counseling for these reasons, you must certify that to the court and complete the counseling within 30 days after filing (you can ask the court to extend this deadline by 15 days).

Incentive for Creditors to Settle?

If a credit counseling agency proposes a settlement that would repay at least 60% of your debt to a creditor, and that creditor refuses to go along with the plan, the creditor may be penalized when and if your property is distributed in bankruptcy. The creditor will be allowed to collect a maximum of 80% of the total claim if you can show, by clear and convincing evidence, that the creditor was offered the deal at least 60 days before you filed and the creditor unreasonably refused the offer.

Although this 20% penalty is billed as an incentive for creditors to accept settlement prior to bankruptcy, the creditor stands to lose only 20 cents on the dollar for turning down an offer to lose 40 cents on the dollar. It's not clear why a creditor would agree to take a large hit early to avoid the possibility of a smaller hit down the road. Also, it will generally cost you more to prove that the creditor's refusal was unreasonable than the penalty is worth. And finally, this will be a factor only in Chapter 13 cases; creditors of Chapter 7 debtors rarely recoup 60% of their debt, let alone 80%.

In actual practice, most judges won't believe that counseling was not available. It's best to figure out a way to get the counseling before you file. Most counseling agencies can provide immediate service if you request it. Some even provide 24-hour service.

You may also escape the credit counseling requirement if, after notice and hearing, the bankruptcy court determines that you couldn't participate because of:

- a physical disability that prevents you from attending counseling (this exception probably won't apply if the counseling is available on the Internet or over the phone)
- mental incapacity (you are unable to understand and benefit from the counseling), or
- your active duty in a military combat zone.

Calculating Your Income Status

In 2005, Congress decided that higher-income people with primarily consumer debts should file Chapter 13 bankruptcy if possible, given their income and expenses. To learn whether you fit within the Chapter 7 or Chapter 13 group, take the following steps:

1. Calculate your current monthly income (CMI).
2. Compare your CMI to the appropriate median income figure.

Calculate Your Current Monthly Income

The bankruptcy law defines your CMI as your average monthly income received during the six-month period that ends on the last day of the month preceding your filing date—whether or not the income is taxable. When including wages or other sources of income, you must include the gross amount, not the net income you actually receive after deductions from taxes and other withholdings are made.

In Chapter 7, your CMI includes income from all sources except:

- payments you receive under the Social Security Act (including Social Security Retirement, SSI, SSDI, and TANF)
- payments to victims of war crimes or crimes against humanity based on their status as victims of such crimes, or
- payments to victims of international or domestic terrorism.

In Chapter 13, CMI includes income from all sources, with the same exclusions as for Chapter 7.

Use Worksheet A: Current Monthly Income, below, to calculate your CMI:

1. Add up all of the income you received during that six-month period.
2. Divide by six to come up with a monthly average.

Worksheet A: Current Monthly Income

Use this worksheet to calculate your current monthly income; use figures for you and your spouse if you plan to file jointly.

Line 1. Calculate your total income over the last six months before any deductions from wages, salary, tips, bonuses, overtime, and so on.

    A. Month 1 $ _____

    B. Month 2   _____

    C. Month 3   _____

    D. Month 4   _____

    E. Month 5   _____

    F. Month 6   _____

    G. TOTAL WAGES (add Lines 1A–1F) $ _____

Line 2. Add up all other income for the last six months.

    A. Net business, profession, or farm income   _____

    B. Interest, dividends, and royalties   _____

    C. Net income from rents and real property   _____

    D. Pension and retirement income   _____

    E. Alimony or family support   _____

    F. Spousal contributions (if separated and not filing jointly)   _____

    G. Unemployment compensation   _____

    H. Workers' compensation   _____

    I. State disability insurance   _____

    J. Annuity payments   _____

    K. Other   _____

    L. TOTAL OTHER INCOME (add Lines 2A–2K) $ _____

Line 3. Calculate total income over the six months prior to filing.

    A. Enter total wages (Line 1G).   _____

    B. Enter total other income (Line 2L).   _____

    C. TOTAL INCOME OVER THE SIX MONTHS PRIOR TO FILING. Add Lines 3A and 3B together. $ _____

Line 4. Average monthly income over the six months prior to filing. This is called your "current monthly income."

    A. Enter total six-month income (Line 3C).   _____

    B. CURRENT MONTHLY INCOME. Divide Line 4A by 6. $ _____

You can download this form (and all other forms in this book) from Nolo.com; for details, see Appendix B.

EXAMPLE: John and Marcia are married and have two young children. They fell quickly into debt after John was forced out of his job because of a work-related injury on April 1, 20xx. Three months later, on July 1, 20xx, John and Marcia decide to file for bankruptcy.

To calculate their CMI, Marcia reviews the family's income for the period between January 1 and June 30, 20xx (the six-month period ending in the calendar month prior to their bankruptcy filing date). This includes John's *gross* salary for the first three months (he made $8,000 a month as a software engineer), plus $1,800 in workers' compensation benefits for each of the last three months. Marcia made $1,000

How to Determine Your Household Size

Determining your household size is very important—the more members you have in your household, the less likely it is that your income will exceed the median for a similar size household. For example, assume that your CMI is $6,000, the median income for a household of three is $5,800, and the median income for a household of four is $6,500. It will be to your benefit to have four people in your household instead of three.

Unfortunately, neither Congress nor the courts have given clear guidance on how to calculate your household size. Most courts adopt the census test for a household, which includes all of the people, related and unrelated, who occupy a house, an apartment, a group of rooms, or a single room that is intended for occupancy as separate living quarters. Under this test, you can count your children or stepchildren even if they are not dependents for tax purposes, called "heads on beds." However, some courts count only dependents as part of the household and require that you list in your bankruptcy papers any money donated to the household by any other person or entity.

Domestic partners count as one household. But mere roommates are not a single household when they have separate rooms within a house but don't act as one economic unit by commingling their incomes and jointly paying expenses. One vexing issue yet to be decided is whether children can be counted as part of a household in situations where they are only living with the parent part-time under a custody and visitation agreement. For clarification, call your local trustee's office and speak with one of the attorneys.

a month during the first three months and had no income for the last three months. The total family income for the six-month period is $32,400. Divided by six, the family's CMI is $5,400 (the six-month average), even though the monthly amount they actually took in during each of the three months before filing was only $1,800.

The following types of income should be included in the form:

- wages, salary, tips, bonuses, overtime, and commissions
- net income from the operation of a business, profession, or farm (the amount you report as taxable income, after subtracting reasonable and necessary business expenses on IRS Schedule C)
- interest, dividends, and royalties
- net income from rents and other real property income
- pension and retirement income, including any one-time withdrawals
- regular contributions to the household expenses of the debtor or the debtor's dependents, including child or spousal support
- regular contributions by the debtor's spouse if he or she isn't part of the household either because of a separation or a joint debtor in the bankruptcy
- unemployment compensation

- workers' compensation insurance
- state disability insurance, and
- annuity payments.

Compare Your Household Income to Your State's Family Median Income

The census bureau periodically publishes family median income figures for all 50 states. To compare your current monthly income to the family median income for your state, you'll need to multiply your CMI by 12 (remember that for this calculation, your CMI, or "current monthly income," is the average monthly amount received during the full six months immediately preceding your bankruptcy). In John and Marcia's case, the family's CMI ($5,400) multiplied by 12 would be $64,800.

Once you've computed your CMI and located the same size household (for your state), compare the two figures to see whether your CMI is more or less than the median income for the same size household for your state. You can find the state median figures (as of the publication date of this book) in the Median Family Income chart, in Appendix B. You can also find up-to-date figures at www.justice.gov/ust by clicking "Means Testing Information" (the figures change regularly).

You can see from the chart in Appendix B that John and Marcia's current monthly income would be more than the family median income in many states.

If Your Current Monthly Income Is Less Than or Equal to Your State's Family Median Income

If your CMI is less than or equal to your state's family median income, you don't have to take the Chapter 7 bankruptcy means test. If you decide to file for Chapter 13, you can propose a plan that is based on your actual expenses and lasts for only three years.

For Larger Families

Although the U.S. Census Bureau generates median figures for families that have up to seven members, Congress does not want you to use these figures if you have a larger family. The Census figures are to be used for families that have up to four members (these are the numbers you will find in Appendix B). If there are more than four members of your family, you must add $8,400 per additional person to the four-member family median income figure for your state. This figure increases periodically, so check the means testing numbers on the U.S. Trustee's website.

If Your Current Monthly Income Is More Than Your State's Family Median Income

If your current monthly income, as calculated above, exceeds your state's family median income, the consequences depend on whether you are filing for Chapter 7 or Chapter 13 bankruptcy.

Chapter 7: If the majority of your debt is consumer debt (meaning it doesn't come from operating a business, tax debts, or debts for personal injury or property damage you caused to someone else), you'll have to take what's called "the means test." If you can't pass the means test, your Chapter 7 case will be dismissed on the basis of "abusing" the bankruptcy law. The means test starts with your current monthly income (explained earlier in this chapter). You then subtract a combination of real and hypothetical living expenses (these are called "allowable expense deductions" and are explained later in this chapter). The final figure will show whether you have enough projected disposable income to pay some of your debts.

The presumption of abuse is automatic for debtors with above-median income if they have enough projected disposable income to pay general unsecured creditors:

- at least $12,850 or more over a period of 60 months, or
- at least 25% of general unsecured debts if the projected disposable income totals between $7,700 and $12,850 over a period of 60 months.

If your remaining income would be less than $7,700 when projected over the next five years, you will pass the means test and can file for Chapter 7 if you meet the other eligibility requirements explained in this chapter. (The means test is explained in more detail in "Chapter 7 Eligibility Requirements," below.)

EXAMPLE: Jonas makes $4,500 a month as a section manager in a large general-purpose store. His current monthly income is more than the median income for his state, so he has to pass the means test to file for Chapter 7 bankruptcy. He deducts allowable expenses from his income and comes up with $300 a month extra. Because his excess income comes to $18,000 when projected over the next five years ($300 x 60 months), Jonas fails the means test.

If Jonas had only $130 a month extra ($7,800 over a five-year period), he would have to figure out whether this amount would pay at least 25% of his unsecured, nonpriority debt in that five-year period. For instance, if Jonas owed $36,000 in credit card debt, he would be barred from Chapter 7 if he could pay $9,000 (25% of the debt) over a five-year period. Because Jonas only has $7,800 extra, however, he would pass the means test and be eligible for Chapter 7, as long as he meets the other eligibility factors.

No matter how high your income is, you don't have to take the means test if you fit into either of the following situations:

- **You are a disabled veteran.** You don't have to take the means test if you are a disabled veteran with a disability rating of at least 30% and your debts were primarily incurred while on active duty or performing a homeland defense activity.

- **Your debts are not consumer debts.** You can skip the means test if your debt is not primarily consumer debt—that is, if more than 50% of your debt load comes from business debts, taxes, or debts for personal injury or property damage you caused to someone else (called "tort debts"). However, a personal mortgage is considered to be consumer debt (unless it was used for business or an investment) and is often high enough to swing your overall debt into the consumer category.

Chapter 13: If your current monthly income is more than the median for your state and you file for Chapter 13, you must propose a five-year repayment plan to which you commit all of your disposable income. You will also have to use the IRS expense standards—and other allowable deductions—to calculate your projected disposable income (the amount of income you'll have to pay into the plan every month for the benefit of your nonpriority, unsecured creditors). These rules are explained in "Chapter 13 Eligibility Requirements," below.

TIP

Choose your filing date to lower your CMI. If your income has been uneven during the six months prior to your projected filing date, you may want to delay or speed up your filing if either strategy would move your CMI from the high-income to the low-income category. For instance, if you received a large bonus or had a high-paying job during the first three months and a low-paying job during the second three months, each month you wait before filing will reduce your CMI. On the other hand, if you've recently landed a high-paying job after having a low-income job, the sooner you file, the lower your CMI will be. However, in order to remain in Chapter 7, you will still have to show that your ongoing income is completely used up by reasonable and necessary regular living expenses.

If your income and expense forms (Schedules I and J) show that you have extra money each month, the trustee might recommend a conversion to a Chapter 13 bankruptcy, even if you passed the means test.

Chapter 7 Eligibility Requirements

There are several basic eligibility requirements you must meet to file a "consumer" Chapter 7 bankruptcy. In addition, if your current monthly income is more than your state's family median income for a family of your size, and your debts are primarily consumer debts, you will have to pass the means test, explained below. To figure out whether you can meet these requirements, you'll first need to know how various debts are classified.

The Means Test

By now you know that if your CMI exceeds your state's median income for a similar size household, you are required to take what's

known as the means test. The means test measures certain expenses and deductions against your CMI to see whether you have any income you can spare to propose a Chapter 13 bankruptcy plan. In the words of the law, the means test determines whether a "presumption of abuse" arises —that is, whether filing a Chapter 7 bankruptcy would be presumed to be an abuse of the bankruptcy laws in the absence of facts proving the contrary.

SKIP AHEAD
If your CMI is below the median income, no need to take the means test. But see the discussion below regarding "abuse under all the circumstances."

When a presumption of abuse arises, it's up to the filer to rebut the presumption, which means the filer has to convince the court that special circumstances entitle him or her to file under Chapter 7, even though the means test indicates a different result. On the other hand, if no presumption of abuse arises, then the way is clear to file under Chapter 7 (with some exceptions discussed below).

Take the Means Test

The means test itself is contained in Official Forms 122A-1, 122A-1Supp, and 122A-2. You'll find filled-out samples in Appendix C. To complete the test, you must use certain predetermined expenses formulated by the

IRS that vary according to state and region. These expense figures are available only online, at www.justice.gov/ust. The following is a rough guide to help you organize the information you'll need to actually take the test.

Use Worksheet B: Allowable Monthly Expenses, in Appendix B, to help you with the actual figures as you work through the following steps.

Enter Actual Expenses

In addition to your CMI, which is the starting point for the means test, and the predetermined expenses, you'll also have to provide the following information about your actual expenses computed on a monthly basis:

- all federal, state, and local taxes, such as income taxes, self-employment taxes, Social Security taxes, and Medicare taxes (but not excess tax withholding that will result in a tax refund). Do not include property taxes or sales taxes.
- total payroll deductions that are required for your employment, such as retirement contributions, union dues, and uniform costs. Do not include discretionary amounts, such as voluntary 401(k) contributions.
- term life insurance premiums for yourself. Do not include premiums for insurance on your dependents, for whole life, or for any other form of insurance.

You Cannot Use the Car Ownership Deduction If You Don't Have Car Payments

In the past, some courts allowed you to deduct the standard predetermined transportation ownership expense for purposes of the means test, even if you weren't making payments on your car. Other courts ruled that you couldn't take this deduction if you weren't making car loan or lease payments.

However, in 2011, in *Ransom v. FIA Card Services, MBNA, America Bank*, 131 S. Ct. 716 (2011), the United States Supreme Court held that in a Chapter 13 bankruptcy, a debtor cannot use the car ownership deduction if the debtor does not make car loan or lease payments. In a Chapter 13 bankruptcy, the car ownership deduction is one of the deductions used to determine the amount of debtor's disposable income, and thus the amount that the debtor must repay creditors.

Although the *Ransom* case deals with Chapter 13 bankruptcies, some courts have applied the same reasoning to the car ownership deduction in Chapter 7 bankruptcies for means test calculations. Others (but not all), have gone even further by applying the *Ransom* case to house payments. In such courts, a debtor can't factor a mortgage payment into the Chapter 7 means test calculation if the debtor intends to surrender the home.

- payments you are required to pay under a court or administrative agency order, such as spousal or child support payments. Do not include payments on arrearages.
- payments expended for education that is a condition of employment and for education that is required for a physically or mentally challenged dependent child for whom no public education providing similar services is available
- payments for child care, such as baby-sitting, day care, nursery, and preschool (this includes money you pay to a family member to care for your children). Do not include other educational payments.
- payments for health care that is required for the health and welfare of yourself or your dependents, that is not reimbursed by insurance or paid by a health savings account, and that is in excess of the standard health care expense entered on Form 122A-2, Line 7g. Do not include payments for health insurance or health savings accounts listed in Form 122A-2, Line 25.
- payments for telecommunication services other than your basic home telephone and cell phone service—such as pagers, call waiting, caller ID, special long distance, or Internet service—to the extent necessary for your health and welfare or that of your dependents. Do not include any amount previously deducted.

Mortgage Obligation Payments When Surrendering Your Home

It's not uncommon for people filing bankruptcy to be in some stage of foreclosure and months behind on their payments. Some courts refuse to allow a deduction for mortgage payments when it's clear that the filer doesn't intend to keep the house. Other courts let you deduct them as long as you are still liable for them, regardless of what your intent might be for the future. The best approach is to first run the means test without counting the mortgage. If you pass without this deduction, then don't make it. If you need the deduction, however, then you'll need to be prepared to argue in a hearing that your court should follow the courts that allow it. This issue has not yet been decided by the U.S. Supreme Court.

You might want to contact the local U.S. Trustee's office and ask about the approach in your area. Otherwise, speak with a local bankruptcy attorney.

- payments to care for a member of your household or immediate family because of the member's age, illness, or disability
- payments for security systems and any other method of protecting your family
- actual payments for home energy costs that exceed the IRS expense
- payments for your children's education. (The maximum you can deduct is $160.42.)

- payments for food and clothing that exceed the predetermined expense, but no more than 5% of the predetermined expense, and
- charitable contributions (tithing), but only if you have a history of making them.

Understanding How Debts Are Classified

When you take the means test, different types of debts are handled differently in the calculations. This section includes definitions that will help you figure out which numbers to use.

Secured Debts

A debt is "secured" if you stand to lose specific property when you don't make your payments to the creditor. Most secured debts are created when you sign loan papers giving a creditor a security interest in your property—such as a home loan or car loan. But a debt might also be secured if a creditor has filed a lien (a legal claim against your property that must be paid before the property can be sold). Here is a list of common secured debts and liens:

- **Mortgages.** Called deeds of trust in some states, these are loans to buy or refinance a house or other real estate. If you fail to pay, the lender can foreclose on your house.
- **Home equity loans (second mortgages).** If you fail to pay, the lender (typically a bank or finance company) can foreclose on your house.

- **Loans for cars, boats, tractors, motorcycles, or RVs.** If you fail to pay, the lender can repossess the vehicle.
- **Store charges with a security agreement.** Almost all store purchases on credit cards are unsecured. Some stores, notably Best Buy and Home Depot, however, claim to retain a security interest in all hard goods (durable goods) purchased, or they make customers sign security agreements when they use their store charge card.
- **Personal loans from banks, credit unions, or finance companies.** Often, you must pledge valuable personal property, such as a paid-off motor vehicle, as collateral for these loans. The property can be repossessed if you don't make the payments.
- **Judicial liens.** A judicial lien can be imposed on your property only after somebody sues you and wins a money judgment against you. In most states, the judgment creditor then must record (file) the judgment with the county or state. The recorded judgment creates a lien on your real estate and, in some states, on some of your personal property as well.
- **Statutory liens.** Some liens are automatic, by law. For example, in most states, when you hire someone to work on your house, the worker and the supplier of materials can assert a mechanic's lien (sometimes called a materialman's or contractor's lien) on the house if you don't pay.

- **Tax liens.** If you owe money to the IRS or other taxing authority, the debt is secured if the agency has recorded a lien against your property.

Unsecured Debts

An unsecured debt is any debt for which you haven't pledged collateral and for which the creditor has not filed a lien against you. If the debt is unsecured, the creditor is not entitled to repossess or seize any of your property if you don't pay.

Most debts are unsecured. Some of the common ones are:

- credit and charge card purchases and cash advances
- department store credit card purchases for clothing and other apparel
- gasoline company credit card purchases
- back rent
- medical bills
- alimony and child support
- student loans
- utility bills
- loans from friends or relatives, unless you signed a promissory note secured by some property you own
- health club dues
- lawyers' and accountants' bills
- church or synagogue dues, and
- union dues.

Priority Debts

Priority debts are unsecured debts that are considered sufficiently important to jump to the head of the bankruptcy repayment line. This means they are paid first if a Chapter 7 trustee disburses property in the course of the case. This can be very helpful when the priority debt can't be discharged in your bankruptcy (which is usually the case). For example, liability for a recent income tax is both a priority debt and a debt that can't be discharged in bankruptcy. Having your property pay off the tax debt—which you will have to pay anyway—is a lot better than having your property go to pay off debts that would otherwise be discharged in your bankruptcy.

Priority debts that may come up in consumer bankruptcies include:

- wages, salaries, and commissions owed by an employer
- contributions to employee benefit plans
- debts of up to $6,325 (each) owed to certain farmers and fishermen
- up to $2,850 in deposits made for the purchase, lease, or rental of property or services for personal, family, or household use that were not delivered or provided
- alimony, maintenance, or support, and
- income taxes that became due within the three-year period before the bankruptcy filing date and taxes that were collected or withheld from an employee (trust fund taxes); also, customs, duties, and penalties owing to federal, state, and local governmental units.

Enter Monthly Contractual Payments or Secured Debts

You are entitled to deduct the contractual monthly payments you owe on your mortgage, car, and other collateral you are making payments on. The deduction will be based on the total payments due over the next five years, divided by 60. However, if your monthly payments are due to end prior to the end of the five-year period, you still divide the total due by 60 and use the resulting number as your deduction.

> **EXAMPLE:** You are paying $1,500 a month on a mortgage that has ten years left on it. You also pay $300 a month on a home equity loan that has three years left on it. And you have a car note for $200 a month that has two years left. The monthly deduction for the mortgage will be $1,500, since the mortgage is due to last beyond the next five years. To calculate the deduction for the home equity loan, you first multiply $300 by 36 (the number of months left on the loan) and then divide that amount by 60 (the amount left amortized over a five-year period). The resulting deduction will be $180 a month. Finally, multiply $200 by 24 to obtain the amount you have left to pay on the car note ($4,800) and divide by 60, for a monthly deduction of $80. In this example, the total deduction for the mortgage, home equity loan, and car note is $1,760 a month.

Use Worksheet C in Appendix B to help you calculate the actual figures.

Enter One-Sixtieth of Arrearages

You are entitled to deduct a monthly amount equal to one-sixtieth of the arrearage you owe on a secured debt, such as a mortgage or car note. Incidentally, the one-sixtieth fraction represents a monthly payment over a five-year period. For example, if you owe three missed payments on your mortgage totaling $4,500, the deduction would be $75 a month (one-sixtieth of $4,500). Before using this deduction, however, see "Mortgage Obligation Payments When Surrendering Your Home," above.

Enter One-Sixtieth of Your Priority Debts

You are entitled to deduct a monthly amount equal to one-sixtieth of your priority debts. The reason for this is that priority debts must be paid in full over the life of a Chapter 13 plan, and this deduction represents the amount you'll have to pay. For instance, recent taxes (taxes that first became due within the three years immediately preceding your bankruptcy filing date) are priority debts. If you owe $5,000 in recent taxes, you'll deduct one-sixtieth of that amount, or about $83 a month.

The Trustee Fee

You are entitled to deduct the commission the trustee would earn in a Chapter 13 case if you filed one, which is roughly 10% of all payments that would be made under the plan (but it could be less—check with the trustee's office). This is a difficult figure to come up with without more information about which payments you must make under the plan and which payments you can make directly, so you should wrestle with it only if you can't pass the means test by some other way.

A sample completed means test (Forms 122A-1, 122A-1Supp, and 122A-2) is included in Appendix C.

Special Circumstances

If the U.S. Trustee seeks to dismiss or convert your Chapter 7 bankruptcy to a Chapter 13 case on the ground of presumed abuse, you can defend against that motion by showing that special circumstances apply in your case. These special circumstances must increase your expenses or decrease your income to bring your net monthly income down to a level that passes the means test. While the bankruptcy law does not define the term "special circumstances," Congress cited as examples "a serious medical condition" or "a call or order to active duty in the Armed Forces."

And recently the U.S. Trustee's office noted that common special circumstances it may consider include:

- job loss or reduction in income for which there is no reasonable alternative

- a one-time "bump" in prepetition income that is not likely to happen again, such as a one-time pension withdrawal or taking cash out of an IRA
- debtors who have separate households due to pending divorce or job relocation, and have filed a joint bankruptcy petition, and
- a postpetition household size increase due to pregnancy or a reasonable need to support an additional person.

For instance, assume you were activated from the reserves and faced a sharp drop in income as well as the costs of moving your family. If the judge agrees that these are special circumstances, and your changed economic picture gives you a net monthly income that passes the means test, you will be able to file a Chapter 7 bankruptcy.

This is the time to be creative, although keep in mind that your argument will have to be strong enough to persuade the judge. See Ch. 10 for more on using special circumstances to get you past the means test.

When Your Leftover Is Between $128.33 and $214.16

If you have some income left over after all the deductions, and the monthly income is less than $128.33, you are home free. On the other hand, if the monthly income is over $214.16, abuse is presumed (unless you can show special circumstances). What happens if your income is right in the middle? You'll need to determine whether the amount of leftover income will pay at least 25% of your unsecured, nonpriority debt. If it will, a Chapter 7 case will be considered presumptively abusive, and you'll have to file for Chapter 13 bankruptcy. If not, you qualify for Chapter 7 bankruptcy.

Abuse Under All the Circumstances

Even if you pass the means test, you aren't out of the woods. As you know, the means test is based on your CMI, a figure that may have no relationship to your actual income at the time you file bankruptcy. For instance, you may have been unemployed during that six-month look-back period, but when you file your bankruptcy you've just landed a plum job. Even though you pass the means test with flying colors, your actual income, when compared to your actual expenses leaves you a few hundred extra dollars every month. Bankruptcy law allows the trustee to challenge your Chapter 7 bankruptcy on the basis that this extra actual income would fund a Chapter 13 program. The trustee will ask the court to dismiss or convert a case upon a finding of "abuse under all the circumstances." Most courts agree with this approach (using your actual income and expenses to determine abuse rather than your CMI).

Cases are sometimes ordered dismissed or converted with your consent to Chapter 13 under the "abuse under all the circumstances"

test when the filer's mortgage and car payments are unreasonably high for someone filing bankruptcy and the judge decides that lesser obligations would free up some money for a Chapter 13 plan. For example, if Andy's monthly mortgage payments are $5,000 on a $750,000 note in an area where the median home price is $400,000, or Brianna is paying $900 a month on a note secured by a new-model Mercedes, the court may disallow a portion of these expenses and rule that Andy and Brianna could now afford Chapter 13 plans. Of course this means that Andy would have to give up his house and Brianna her car, if they wanted to proceed in the bankruptcy court, rather than having their cases dismissed.

Bad Faith

Another doctrine that may affect your eligibility for a consumer Chapter 7 bankruptcy is what's commonly called "bad faith." Under this doctrine, a judge can dismiss your bankruptcy if he or she believes you filed for reasons other than to get a fresh start, or you engaged in prebankruptcy behavior that is inconsistent with the need for a bankruptcy discharge. For example, in one case, the court dismissed a case because the debtor purchased an expensive motorcycle shortly before filing and could have easily paid off his debts in a Chapter 13 bankruptcy had he not had to make the high monthly payments on his motorcycle.

Individuals and Businesses Can File for Chapter 7 Bankruptcy

Individuals and businesses can file for Chapter 7 bankruptcy. When individuals file, they get rid of their debts and go on with their lives. When business entities file, the business is liquidated, the assets are sold, and the proceeds go to the unsecured creditors. In between these extremes are individuals who are also in business as sole proprietors or independent contractors.

Sole Proprietors

If you run your business as a sole proprietor, you and your business are considered to be one and the same. If there are business assets, they are subject to being sold for the benefit of your creditors—unless they qualify for an exemption (see Ch. 4). If, on the other hand, your business is service or profession oriented—such as contractors, lawyers, accountants, electricians, real estate agents, and the like—there are usually no assets worth selling and your business can continue without interruption. Retail businesses that have inventories or other assets that might generate income for the creditors typically must cease operations upon filing bankruptcy. This gives the trustee time to inventory and value the assets as of the date of the bankruptcy filing and decide whether they are covered by any exemption you claim or whether they can be seized and sold for the benefit of your creditors. Also, in some circumstances, a

trustee may close a business in order to avoid potential liability in the event that a customer is injured.

Owners of Small Business Entities

The owner of a small business that has incorporated or formed as a limited liability company (LLC) often has a choice to make, because there are two potential bankruptcy debtors: the owner personally and the business entity. You can:

- file as an individual and leave the business intact
- file as an individual and also have the business entity file separately
- have the business entity file and not file as an individual, or
- dissolve the business and file as an individual.

These decisions will depend on the following factors:

- the degree to which you have followed the necessary formalities in maintaining the business as a separate entity. For instance, did you maintain corporate minutes, issue stock or memberships, hold corporate meetings and pass resolutions as appropriate? Did you title business assets in the name of the business and keep your individual and business financial transactions separate (by using separate checkbooks, maintaining separate books, and observing basic rules of accounting regarding use of the business assets, income, and expenses)?

- the degree to which the business entity has its own debts and property separate and apart from the owner's, and
- the degree to which the owner has personally signed off on loans and other debt.

One large downside to taking a business entity through Chapter 7 is that you have to use a lawyer. Even if you are the sole owner of the entity, you can't represent it in the bankruptcy court. Lawyers don't come cheap, and this fact alone may drive your decision as to whether to have the entity file or just let it lapse and deal with your personal liability for any corporate debt in a personal bankruptcy.

TIP

If you are filing a business-related bankruptcy, make sure you have good records. Although all bankruptcy debtors may be required to produce records of certain financial transactions as part of their bankruptcy cases, this requirement is especially common when a debtor is in business (or has recently been in business). The records that trustees most commonly request of businesses are profit and loss statements, bank statements, and cancelled checks for the previous 12 months. If the bankruptcy trustee moves to dismiss a case on the ground that the absence of financial records makes the case impossible to administer, the court might not accept the excuse that you're a sloppy bookkeeper, especially if you are a professional or in a type of business that requires some degree of sophistication. Lack of records can also be grounds to deny a discharge.

Partnerships

Similarly, if you are a member of a business partnership with people other than your spouse, you can file for Chapter 7 bankruptcy as a consumer and include all business debts on which you are personally liable. Your partners will remain fully liable for the debts you wipe out, however.

SEE AN EXPERT

If you are a member of a business partnership, consider consulting a small business lawyer before you file for bankruptcy. Your obligation to your partners may be governed by a buy-sell agreement that requires you to terminate your partnership interest before filing for bankruptcy. If you don't follow that agreement or any other understanding you and your partners have, you probably will be putting the partnership's property at risk. And your partners (or ex-partners) may ask the bankruptcy court to lift the automatic stay so they can file a lawsuit against you. A lawyer can help you assess your obligations and options.

You Haven't Had a Previous Bankruptcy Discharge

You can't get a Chapter 7 discharge if you previously had your debts discharged in:

- a Chapter 7 bankruptcy *filed* within the previous *eight* years, or
- a Chapter 13 bankruptcy *filed* within the previous *six* years.

EXAMPLE: On June 14, 2017, you filed for Chapter 7 bankruptcy. You received your discharge on November 2, 2017. You've fallen on hard times again and are considering filing another Chapter 7 case. You cannot file before June 15, 2024.

You Aren't Barred by a Previous Bankruptcy Dismissal

You can't file for Chapter 7 bankruptcy if your previous bankruptcy case was dismissed within the past 180 days for any of the following reasons:

- You violated a court order.
- The court ruled that your filing was fraudulent or an abuse of the bankruptcy system.
- You requested the dismissal after a creditor asked the court to lift the automatic stay.

EXAMPLE: You filed for Chapter 7 bankruptcy on February 12, 2017, after your landlord started eviction proceedings. A week after you filed, your landlord filed a motion with the bankruptcy court to have the automatic stay lifted to continue the eviction proceedings. You dismissed your case. You've found a new place to live, but your debt problems haven't gone away and you want to refile. You must wait at least 180 days before filing again—that is, until August 12, 2017.

You Can Produce a Tax Return, Wage Stubs, and a Credit Counseling Certificate

To file a Chapter 7 case, you must produce your most recently filed tax return. You'll also need a certificate showing that you completed a credit counseling course, as well as wage stubs for the previous 60 days. (See Ch. 10 for more on these requirements.)

You Have Taken an Approved Personal Financial Management Course

You are required to take an approved personal finance course before the court will discharge your debts in a Chapter 7 bankruptcy. The agencies providing this service must be approved by the Office of the U.S. Trustee and must offer approximately two hours of required curriculum. Unlike the credit counseling agencies, personal financial management agencies don't have to be nonprofits, but they must offer in-person services on a sliding fee scale. For more information about the requirements for these agencies and how to find one in your area, visit the U.S. Trustee's website at www. justice.gov/ust; click "Credit Counseling & Debtor Education."

Before you can receive your Chapter 7 discharge, you must file an official form (Form 423) with the bankruptcy court, showing that you have completed this counseling. This must be accompanied by a certificate of completion from the counseling agency. You must file these forms no later than 45 days after the date on which your creditors' meeting was first scheduled. If you miss this deadline, the court may close your case without discharging your debts. This means you'll have to pay another filing fee to reopen your case so you can file the form and request a discharge.

Chapter 13 Eligibility Requirements

Like Chapter 7 bankruptcy, Chapter 13 bankruptcy has several important eligibility requirements.

Prior Bankruptcy Discharges

You can't get a Chapter 13 discharge if you received a discharge in a previous Chapter 13 case in the last two years, or a discharge in a Chapter 7 case filed within the last four years. You aren't barred from filing a Chapter 13 in these circumstances, but you can't get a discharge. For instance, you can file a Chapter 13 bankruptcy the instant you receive a Chapter 7 discharge (to handle liens that survived your Chapter 7 case or pay debts that weren't discharged in that case), and you can operate under a plan confirmed by the court for a three- to five-year period. But you can't get the Chapter 13 discharge, which means you'll still owe any debt that you don't pay off in the course of your Chapter 13 case. (Filing for Chapter 13 after receiving a Chapter 7 discharge is informally known as a "Chapter 20 bankruptcy.")

You may be wondering what good it would do you to file a Chapter 13 case when you don't qualify for the discharge. Doing so may provide a structured way for you to handle your debt load under the protection of the stay. For instance, suppose that you owe a substantial debt, and the creditor is threatening to garnish your wages or take your property. You can stop these actions by paying off the debt in Chapter 13 bankruptcy.

However, keep in mind that you might not be able to take advantage of every Chapter 13 tool. For example, many courts have ruled that a Chapter 13 debtor who is not eligible for discharge cannot "strip off" a junior mortgage. (See Ch. 5 for more about lien stripping.)

Business Entities Can't File for Chapter 13 Bankruptcy

To file a Chapter 13 bankruptcy case, you must be an individual (or a husband and wife filing jointly). If you own your own business as a sole proprietor or partner, you can include all business debts on which you have personal liability. You have to file your case in your name, however, and not in the name of your business, because a business cannot file for Chapter 13 bankruptcy. On your bankruptcy papers, you will need to list all fictitious business names or DBAs ("doing business as" names) that you've used as a sole proprietor or partnership.

EXAMPLE: Shelby Ferra operates a graphic design business under the name "Shelby Designs," and also has a seasonal tax preparation business called "AAA Tax Preparation Services." Shelby's bankruptcy petition would read as follows: Shelby Ferra AKA Shelby Designs AKA AAA Tax Preparation Services. There is no limit to the number of "AKAs" in a bankruptcy petition, provided that they aren't separate business entities requiring their own bankruptcy filings.

As with Chapter 7 bankruptcy, if you operate your business as a sole proprietorship or in a partnership with your spouse or another party, you or you and your partner are personally liable for the debts of the business. For bankruptcy purposes, you and your business (or your share of a partnership) are one and the same. There is one exception: Stockbrokers and commodity brokers cannot file Chapter 13 bankruptcy cases, even for personal (not business) debts.

You cannot file a Chapter 13 bankruptcy on behalf of a corporation, limited liability company (LLC), or partnership as such. If you want to file a reorganization bankruptcy in that situation, you must file a business Chapter 11 bankruptcy, which is beyond the scope of this book.

Your Debts Must Not Be Too High

You do not qualify for Chapter 13 bankruptcy if your secured debts exceed $1,184,200 or your unsecured debts are more than $394,725. If you need help figuring out which of your debts are secured and which are unsecured, see "How Debts Are Classified," above.

Chapter 11 Alternative for Business Entities

Although business entities don't qualify to file Chapter 13 bankruptcy, they certainly can file under Chapter 11. Unfortunately, Chapter 11 bankruptcy is very expensive because of attorneys' fees and the need for both intensive and endless negotiations with secured creditors and creditor committees. Still, if you have a going business and the ability to raise cash in the range of $20,000 to $100,000 or more, Chapter 11 may be workable.

You Must Be Current on Your Income Tax Filings

You will have to offer evidence that you have filed your federal and state income tax returns for the four tax years prior to your bankruptcy filing date. This evidence can be provided by the returns themselves or by transcripts of the returns obtained from the IRS. You have to provide this evidence no later than the date set for your first meeting of creditors (about a month after you file). The trustee can keep the creditors' meeting open for up to 120 days to give you time to file the returns, and the court can give you an additional 120 days. Ultimately, if you don't produce your returns or transcripts of the returns or transcripts for those four preceding years, your Chapter 13 will be dismissed. Keep in mind that filing the returns is different from owing taxes; you can owe taxes and file for bankruptcy, but you must still file the returns.

Your Proposed Repayment Plan Must Satisfy Legal Requirements

Your eligibility for Chapter 13 bankruptcy depends on your ability to propose a plan that the court will approve of (confirm).

To determine whether a judge will confirm your plan, follow these steps:

Step 1: Compute your current monthly income (CMI) and compare it to the median income figure for your state (see Appendix B).

If you are married (not separated), you must count the income of both spouses when computing your disposable income on Forms 122C-1 and 122C-2, even if only one spouse is filing. However, you may exclude certain kinds of income, like Social Security benefits, received by either spouse when making that computation.

Step 2A: If your CMI exceeds the median income figure, use Worksheet C in Appendix B to compute your disposable income (income available to pay your unsecured nonpriority debt after all required payments have been taken care of under your plan). A copy of Worksheet C is in Appendix B.

Step 2B: If your CMI is less than the median income for your state, compute your disposable income by subtracting your actual living expenses from your net income (see sample Forms I and J in Appendix C).

Step 3A: If you have enough disposable income to pay the percentage of your unsecured nonpriority debt that is required by your court (after paying all required debt under the plan), you qualify for Chapter 13.

Step 3B: If you have negative disposable income, forget about Chapter 13, unless you can reduce your living expenses or sell some property to create a positive disposable income.

CAUTION

Your plan might not be confirmed if your actual expenses look too low. If your current monthly income is less than your state's family median income, you can use your actual expenses to calculate how much you could devote to a Chapter 13 plan, provided those expenses are reasonable. Some people are tempted to decrease their stated expenses in order to increase their disposable income so they can qualify for Chapter 13. If it appears that your expenses are unreasonably low, however, the court may reject your plan. And even if the court approves your plan, remember that you still need enough money to live on. So, be realistic.

When Your CMI Is Different From Your Actual Monthly Income

Because your CMI is based on the six-month average prior to your filing date, your actual income may be much less or much more.

Since the bankruptcy laws changed in 2005, courts have differed on what to do when a debtor's "current monthly income" figure is different from the debtor's actual monthly income. Some judges have based Chapter 13 plan payments on projected disposable income that was calculated using the CMI, even if the CMI was different from the debtors' actual monthly incomes. Other judges have been more flexible and permitted plans based on the debtors' actual incomes going forward. Similarly, in some cases, judges considered phantom expenses (such as mortgage payments even though the debtor's intention was to walk away) while others did not.

Fortunately, in 2010, the U.S. Supreme Court provided some guidance on this issue in *Hamilton v. Lanning*, 130 S. Ct. 2464 (2010).

The Court ruled that, when deciding whether to confirm a Chapter 13 plan, bankruptcy courts can take into consideration changes in income or expenses that have occurred, or are known or virtually certain to occur, at the time of confirmation (confirmation usually occurs about two to three months after a petition is filed). In other words, when called on to confirm a Chapter 13 plan, a court can base its decision on the reality of the debtor's income going forward rather than on the formula created by Congress, which looks backward six months. However, the key word here is change. If there has been no significant change from the time the current monthly income and allowable expenses were computed, those figures will determine the amount to be repaid to unsecured creditors under the plan.

In Step 2A, you calculated your mandatory debts and deducted them from the income you had left after deducting IRS-allowed amounts or actual expenses. If you have any remaining income after paying your mandatory debts, you will have to commit that income to paying your unsecured, nonpriority debts.

If your current monthly income is more than your state's median, you have to commit all of your projected disposable income to your plan for a five-year period. If your current monthly income is less than your state's median, you have to commit all of your disposable income to your plan for at least three years. Depending on which category you fit into, your plan will have to show what your projected disposable income can accomplish during the period in question.

For instance, if you are in the five-year category, will your projected disposable income cover all mandatory debts and necessary payments when spread out over 60 monthly payments? If there is anything left, does your plan apply that money to your unsecured, nonpriority debts? If so, then your plan should be confirmed by the court.

Similarly, if your current monthly income is less than the state's median, you need only commit to a three-year plan. So if you can make all required payments within 36 monthly payments, your plan will be confirmed provided that anything left over goes to your unsecured, nonpriority creditors.

If you'll need a longer repayment period to pay all required debts, you can propose a 60-month plan.

In fact, many debtors who qualify for a 36-month plan instead opt for a 60-month plan so that their plan payment is lower. For example, suppose you are trying to save your home from foreclosure and you owe $36,000 in back mortgage payments. If you are eligible for and propose a 36-month plan, you will have to pay at least $1,000 per month to catch up in 36 months ($1,000 x 36 months = $36,000). However, if you propose a 60-month plan, your plan payment might be as low as $600 per month ($600 x 60 months = $36,000). This can be critical to your bankruptcy's success if you have a tight budget.

By now, you should understand that it's possible to propose a confirmable Chapter 13 plan without paying anything to your unsecured, nonpriority creditors—including credit card companies and hospital bills—

assuming you have no nonexempt property (see below).

RESOURCE

Get help calculating expenses in Chapter 13. If your disposable income falls short, it may be because you've deducted too many expenses or misinterpreted the meaning of a particular expense. There are many twists and turns to accurately computing the appropriate expenses in a Chapter 13 case, whether you are using the IRS expenses or actual expenses. A bankruptcy lawyer versed in the new law can be very helpful in this situation. You'll find additional guidance in *Chapter 13 Bankruptcy: Keep Your Property & Repay Debts Over Time*, by Stephen Elias and Kathleen Michon (Nolo).

Child Support and Alimony Owed to the Government

The general rule is that a Chapter 13 plan may be confirmed only if it provides for all priority debts to be paid in full over the life of the plan. However, if all of your disposable income is dedicated to repayment of debts over a five-year period, the plan may be confirmed even if you won't be able to fully repay back child support and alimony you owe to a governmental unit (such as a child support enforcement agency) during the five-year period. But, you will still be liable for the remaining back support after your Chapter 13 discharge.

Your Proposed Payments Must Equal the Value of Your Nonexempt Assets

The total amount of payments to your unsecured creditors under your proposed plan must equal at least what those creditors would have received had you filed for Chapter 7 bankruptcy—that is, the value of your nonexempt property less what it would cost to sell the property and the amount of the trustee's commission. (Exempt property is the property you are allowed to keep if you file a Chapter 7 case. The important topic of exempt property is discussed in Ch. 1 and explained in more detail in Chs. 4 and 5.)

As emphasized throughout this book, many bankruptcy filers have little or no nonexempt property, and thus, probably need not be concerned with this particular eligibility requirement.

However, if you do have nonexempt property, you will have to perform what's called a "liquidation analysis" to determine how much your unsecured creditors would actually receive if you used Chapter 7 (and, therefore, how much they are entitled to receive under your Chapter 13 plan).

Start with the value of your equity in the property. If a portion of the property is exempt, subtract the exempt amount. For example, many states exempt up to a certain amount of equity in a car. If you own a car outright that's worth $10,000, and the exemptions you are using allow you to exempt $4,000 of equity in a car, your total nonexempt amount is $6,000.

Next, subtract the trustee's commission. This amount represents what the trustee would get to keep if your property were taken and sold in a Chapter 7 case. Because this amount would not be distributed to your creditors, you can subtract it from the amount you have to pay them in a Chapter 13 case.

For each item of property sold, the trustee gets 25% of the first $5,000, 10% of the next $50,000, and 5% of the rest up to $1 million. So, if you have a nonexempt bank account containing $25,000, the trustee gets to keep $1,250 (25% of $5,000) plus $2,000 (10% of the remaining $20,000) for a total of $3,250. Put another way, your creditors would receive $21,750 instead of $25,000.

In addition to the trustee's commission, you can also subtract the costs of taking the property and selling it. For certain types of property, there are few (if any) costs of sale. Cash on hand, bank accounts, and investments that can easily be converted to cash fit within this category of property. However, other types of property—such as a home, a car, or furniture—have significant resale costs. Because your unsecured creditors wouldn't get any of this money in a Chapter 7 case, they also aren't entitled to it in your Chapter 13 case. And, because personal property (a piano or furnishings, for example) often sells at auction for significantly less than its replacement value, you might be able to argue for an even lower total.

You Have Taken an Approved Personal Financial Management Course

As in Chapter 7, you (and your spouse, if you're filing jointly) are required to take a course on personal financial management before you can obtain a Chapter 13 discharge. This course is known by several names, including predischarge counseling and budget counseling. It's important to distinguish this mandatory counseling from the credit counseling you were required to take before you filed your bankruptcy. This course takes about two hours and can be taken online or by phone, the same as with credit counseling. As with the credit counseling, you are entitled to pay on a sliding scale if you can't afford the full price. As a general rule, you can save some money if you sign up with the same company for both counseling sessions—the one before you file and the one after you file.

You must provide evidence that you've completed the counseling on or before the date of your last plan payment. Otherwise, the court will not issue your Chapter 13 discharge. For more information about these counseling agencies, visit the U.S. Trustee website at www.justice.gov/ust. Click "Credit Counseling & Debtor Education."

Avoidable Transfers Don't Require a Guilty Mind

The concept of avoidable transfers is actually a simple one. When you file bankruptcy, all your property is part of your bankruptcy estate. This property consists of the property you own on the date you file (if there is sufficient equity) and, in some circumstances, the property you had before you filed. Whether you sold the property for less than its market value—for instance, a $3,000 car to a friend for $1,000—or just gave it away, it doesn't matter. It also doesn't matter whether your method of sale was direct—cash in exchange for the property—or a retitling that resulted in your interest being transferred to the other party. The property belongs to your bankruptcy estate and it's the trustee's job to avoid the transfer (collect it for the benefit of your creditors).

If your mindset was innocent—you had no idea you were going to file for bankruptcy when you transferred the property—the trustee will simply collect it from the transferee and distribute it to your creditors according to bankruptcy priority rules. Your bankruptcy won't be affected. However, if it appears that you deliberately got rid of it because you were planning your bankruptcy, the trustee can take your case to the bankruptcy judge and ask that your bankruptcy discharge be denied. Whether the judge denies your discharge will depend on the individual facts of your case.

Other Issues That Might Affect Your Decision to File

Sometimes you find yourself in a situation that does not prohibit you from filing for bankruptcy, but might produce consequences you don't want—such as the dismissal of your case, your inability to discharge a debt, or the trustee's taking back money that you recently paid to a relative or business associate. Understanding the rules for prefiling transfers of property and presumptions of fraud will help you decide if you should wait before filing for bankruptcy.

Prefiling Transfers of Real and Personal Property

Certain types of prefiling activities have such serious consequences that, as a practical matter, they render you ineligible to file bankruptcy for a period of time. Transactions involving the gift or sale of any type of personal property or real estate during the two-year period immediately preceding your filing date are heavily scrutinized in bankruptcy.

The basic problem here is that some filers are tempted to unload various assets so that the bankruptcy trustee won't find and seize the property and sell it for the benefit of the creditors. These transactions often take the form of selling the property to a friend or relative for a nominal amount, such

as $1.00 with the understanding that the friend will cough up the property after the bankruptcy is completed. Other common examples are taking one's name off of a joint account, deed, or vehicle title (which is really a gift of half of the property to the other owner).

> **EXAMPLE:** You want to file for Chapter 7 bankruptcy but you realize that you are listed on a deed as the co-owner of property where a friend is living—which was necessary to buy the property because your friend had bad credit. After learning that the trustee could take that property and sell it for the benefit of your unsecured creditors, you have yourself taken off the deed before filing. In your bankruptcy papers, you would have to list that transaction, and then the bankruptcy trustee might sell the property and recover your share of the proceeds.

Whatever form it takes, a prebankruptcy gift or sale for substantially less than the property is worth is frequently judged to be a fraudulent transfer, which can result in the transferred property being seized and sold for the benefit of the creditors, and the bankruptcy being dismissed. And even if you convince the bankruptcy trustee that you had an honest intent, the trustee can still demand that the person to whom you transferred the property give it back to be sold for the benefit of the creditors. And in these situations, it usually is not possible to claim the transferred property as exempt, which means you won't get any of the sale proceeds.

Lawyers are often asked, how will the trustee find out about a particular transfer? If title is involved (as with cars, boats, and real estate), the transfer will show up in the trustee's routine search of the various state and local databases (such as the DMV) that would document the transfer. Also, when you go to your creditors' meeting, you must affirm under oath that you've truthfully answered the questions in the Statement of Intention for Individuals Filing Under Chapter 7, the form where you are asked about prebankruptcy transfers. Trustees are skilled in picking up any discrepancy on this point. If they suspect something is wrong, they can follow up the meeting by questioning you under oath in a deposition-like proceeding. The bottom line: Don't ever assume that the trustee won't find out about your transfers. And, more importantly, it's a bad idea to commit perjury. The punishment could involve going to jail.

When all is said and done, some property that is transferred prior to bankruptcy could easily have been retained and claimed as exempt. As for any remaining property, it's better to let it go, or, if you don't want to lose (or pay for) it, not to file at all.

Preference Payments

A basic principle of bankruptcy law is that all creditors deserve to be treated fairly in comparison to each other. In many cases, fair treatment means that no one gets anything. In some cases, it means that your unsecured creditors share in the proceeds if the trustee takes your nonexempt property and sells it.

This principle is undermined if you make a payment to some creditors and not others before you file for bankruptcy. Payments like these may be considered "preferences" because you are favoring some creditors over others. When payments qualify as preferences, the trustee can demand that the creditor return the money to your bankruptcy estate, where it will be divided equally among all of your creditors (subject to any exemptions you can claim).

For consumer debtors (those whose debts are primarily for personal debt rather than business debt), any payment of more than $600 might be considered a preference if it was made within a year to insider creditors (business associates or close relatives), or within three months to others (see below). If, however, you are a business debtor—that is, a majority of your debt arises from your business activities—the court will look only at transactions that exceed $6,225. (How to determine whether you are a business debtor for purposes of this rule is explained above.)

Payments to Insiders

The time period during which payments will be considered a preference depends on whether the creditor is an insider (a business associate, friend, or relative). If you pay more than $600 (or $6,425 if you are primarily a business debtor) to any creditor who's an insider during the year before you file for bankruptcy, that payment is a preference. For example, if you use your tax refund to pay back an emergency loan from your sister, brother, or mother, you have preferred that creditor over your other unsecured creditors. Bluntly put, when in bankruptcy, you are required to treat your mother and Visa equally.

> **EXAMPLE:** In October, Robin borrows $2,000 from her mother to pay off a supplier. In March of the following year, Robin receives a tax refund of $3,000. She pays her mother back and uses the remaining $1,000 to catch up on other bills. Even though no one could blame Robin for paying back her mom, this would likely be considered a preference payment if she files for bankruptcy within the year. She'll have to disclose it in her bankruptcy paperwork, and her mom may have to cough up the money.

There is one important exception to this rule: A payment to an insider won't be considered a preference if you made the payment more than 90 days prior to filing for bankruptcy and you weren't insolvent at the time. For example, if you repaid a $3,000 loan from your mother more than three months before you file, and you can show that the value of your assets was greater than your liabilities at the time you repaid her, the payment won't be considered a preference. This insolvency rule also applies to preferences to noninsiders.

Insolvency is presumed during the 90-day period before you file for bankruptcy, so if you made a preference payment within the past 90 days, you should expect it to be undone if you file for bankruptcy.

Payments to Others

If the creditor is not an insider, but instead is a regular "arms-length" creditor like most of your business creditors, such as a vendor or credit card company, the rules are different. The court will look at your transactions with that creditor for only three months before you file for bankruptcy. During this time period, any payment of more than $600, or $6,425 if you are primarily a business debtor, will be considered a preference.

Payment of criminal restitution, like other debts, can be considered a preference if it is made within the three-month period prior to your bankruptcy filing and is over the $600 threshold.

Antecedent Debt Rule

To qualify as a preference, the payments must be made on an "antecedent" debt. In other words, the debt must already be past due and owing. Even if you are current on an account, it might still qualify as an antecedent debt. For example, you may be current on a large credit card debt because you have been making the minimum monthly payments. As long as interest is being charged on the underlying debt, however, it will be considered an antecedent debt, and paying off the debt would be considered a preference.

Payments Made in the Ordinary Course of Business or Financial Affairs

A payment is not a preference if it is made in the ordinary course of business or the debtor's financial affairs.

> **EXAMPLE:** Tim, a masonry contractor, owes Tom's Tile $3,500 from a past job. Although it's always been Tim's practice to immediately pay for his supplies as soon as he's paid for the job, he hasn't paid Tom's Tile because of a dispute over the quality of materials provided. Tim lands another job, for which he secures $10,000 worth of tile on credit from ABC Masonry Supplies. Two months later, when he is paid for the job, he pays ABC $10,000, which brings his ABC account current. This transaction would most likely qualify as one made in the ordinary course of Tim's business, because it meets his normal practice of immediately paying his suppliers.

Regular payments for personal expenses—such as utilities or services—

typically also qualify as payments made in the ordinary course of business or financial affairs, rather than preferences. And regular monthly payments on long-term debt (for example, making a usual monthly payment on a mortgage, credit card bill, or student loan) also fall within this exception.

Even if a payment to a creditor was not made in the ordinary course of business or financial affairs, it still may escape the trustee's clutches if the debtor receives "new value" as a result of making the payment. This means the debtor is receiving some current benefit for making the payment, not just paying off an old debt. For instance, let's say Tim, from the example above, paid off Tom's Tile so he could order more materials on credit from that company. This extension of credit might be considered new value received for paying off the old debt, which means the payment wouldn't be a preference.

 TIP

Transferring balances may be a preference. At least one court has found that transferring a balance from one credit card to another might be considered a preference. In this case, the debtor used her credit on one credit card to pay off her debt on another credit card. Because she made the transfer within three months of filing for bankruptcy, and she could have used the money for any purpose (in other words, she didn't have to use it to pay off her other card), the court ruled that the transfer was a preference. (*In re Dilworth*, 560 F.3d 562 (8th Cir. 2009).)

If You've Made Preference Payments

The consequences of violating the preference rules can be harsh for the person who received the payment. The bankruptcy trustee is authorized to take back the money and distribute it among your creditors. If you paid back a family member, this may cause some tension. Even if you paid back a creditor that isn't an insider, it could cause problems. For example, if you paid back a credit card issuer so you could keep your card, the issuer will probably revoke your credit card if it has to cough up the money to the trustee. The same problem could come up if you paid a debt to a core vendor or a commercial landlord or an equipment leasing company.

The trustee doesn't have to go after every preference payment. For example, the trustee might decide not to go after a preference if the cost of suing to collect it would outweigh the amount to be gained.

If you can claim an exemption that covers an involuntary preference, the trustee has even less incentive to pursue it. (An example of an involuntary preference is when a creditor takes your money through wage garnishment or a bank levy.) However, you cannot claim an exemption to cover voluntary preference payments.

Even though you can't pay a favorite creditor before you file, nothing prevents you from doing so after you file, as long as you do it with income earned after you file for bankruptcy or with property that isn't in your bankruptcy estate.

Presumptions of Fraud

If you charge a credit card for an amount exceeding $675 for luxuries within three months of filing, or take out a cash advance from any one creditor exceeding $950 within 70 days before filing, the charge or advance will be presumed to be fraudulent if the creditor challenges it in court. As a general rule, few if any creditors will actually challenge such small amounts, because it will cost more in attorneys' fees. But to be safe it's advisable to wait out the three-month, or 70-day period, before filing.

You can also get into trouble if you:

- run up large debts for luxury items when you clearly are broke and have no way to pay the debts, or
- conceal property or money from your spouse during a divorce proceeding.

These activities cast a suspicion of fraud over your entire bankruptcy case. (These debts are discussed further in Ch. 3.) ●

How Bankruptcy Affects Your Debts

Most people consider bankruptcy because they want to get rid of debts—either immediately (in a Chapter 7 bankruptcy) or over time (in a Chapter 13 repayment plan bankruptcy). Many of your debts will, in fact, be wiped out in a bankruptcy of either type. Some, however, will not—which means you will still be responsible for paying them.

If you successfully complete your bankruptcy, whether Chapter 7 or Chapter 13, you will receive a notice from the court discharging all debts that are legally dischargeable. Although the notice lists the types of debts that are dischargeable, it doesn't tell you which of your particular debts are discharged and which are not. This chapter explains what types of debts are discharged in Chapter 7 and Chapter 13 bankruptcies, and which debts you might still owe after your bankruptcy case is over.

Debts That Will Be Discharged in Bankruptcy

Whether you file for Chapter 7 or Chapter 13 bankruptcy, certain types of debts will be discharged—that is, you will no longer be responsible for repaying them— at the end. In a Chapter 7 bankruptcy, you won't have to repay any portion of these debts directly: The bankruptcy trustee will divide your nonexempt assets (if you have any) among your creditors, then the court will discharge any amount that remains

unpaid. In a Chapter 13 bankruptcy, your repayment plan will most likely provide for some portion of these debts to be paid back but not necessarily in full. If you complete your plan successfully, the remaining unpaid amount will be discharged.

Credit Card Debts

Without a doubt, the vast majority of those who file for bankruptcy are trying to get rid of credit card debts. Happily for these filers, the vast majority of bankruptcies succeed in this mission. With a few rare exceptions for cases involving fraud or luxury purchases immediately prior to your bankruptcy (outlined in "Debts That Survive Chapter 7 Bankruptcy," below), you can expect to get rid of your credit card debt in a Chapter 7 or Chapter 13 bankruptcy.

Medical Bills

Many people who file for bankruptcy are in financial trouble because of medical bills. Although the rates of the uninsured have dropped due to the Affordable Care Act, millions of Americans still don't have health insurance, are inadequately insured, or have high-deductible plans which require them to pay thousands of dollars out of pocket. Changes to the healthcare system under the Trump administration could reverse this downward trend, and lead to an uptick in bankruptcy filings brought on due to insufficient medical coverage.

Luckily, bankruptcy provides an out: Your medical bills will be discharged at the end of your bankruptcy case.

Lawsuit Judgments

Most civil court cases are about money. If someone wins one of these lawsuits against you, the court issues a judgment ordering you to pay. If you don't come up with the money voluntarily, the judgment holder is entitled to collect on it by, for example, withdrawing the funds in your bank account, levying your wages, or placing a lien on your home.

Money judgments and the debts that underlie them are almost always dischargeable in bankruptcy, regardless of the facts that led to the lawsuits in the first place. There are a couple of exceptions (discussed in "Debts That Survive Chapter 7 Bankruptcy," below), but in the vast majority of cases, money judgments are discharged. Even liens on your home arising from a court judgment can be cancelled if they interfere with your homestead exemption. (See "Voluntary Secured Debts Are Dischargeable, But the Lien Remains the Same," below.)

Obligations Under Leases and Contracts

Increasingly in our society, things are leased rather than owned, be it a lease of real property (such as an apartment) or personal property (such as a car). If you enter into a lease contract and then become unable to make the monthly payment or otherwise perform your obligations under the lease, there will be consequences. The other party may want to hold you to the deal, and failing that, expect you to pay damages as a result of your breach (the damages are typically a reasonable, predetermined amount, or the actual financial hit the other party takes when you don't come through). If you don't pay what you owe, the other party can go after you in a lawsuit.

Some debtors also have ongoing contractual obligations, such as a contract to sell or buy real estate, buy a business, deliver merchandise, or perform in a play. The other party may want to force you to hold up your end of the deal and may sue you for breach of contract damages if you fail to perform.

Obligations and liabilities under these types of agreements can also be cancelled in bankruptcy. Almost always, filing for bankruptcy will wipe out your lease or contractual obligation if you want to get out of it.

If you wish, you can choose to keep the contract or lease in effect by "assuming" it. For example, you may have a time-share contract that you have been paying on for years and are close to paying off. Rather than canceling the contract, you may wish to keep it in effect. Or, you may be leasing your car and want to "assume" the lease. You indicate your choice—whether to assume or reject a lease or contract—in a document called a Statement of Intention.

Personal Loans and Promissory Notes

Money you borrow in exchange for a promissory note (or even a handshake and an oral promise to pay the money back) is almost always dischargeable in bankruptcy. As with any debt, however, the court may refuse to discharge a loan debt if the creditor can prove that you obtained the loan fraudulently. But that rarely happens, and it's unlikely to take you by surprise. Most people know when someone might accuse them of engaging in fraud.

Debts Owed to Coborrowers Who Paid the Original Debt

If you have jointly incurred a debt with another person, and that person pays off the debt in full, the debt you owe to the cosigner for your share of the debt (that was paid off) is dischargeable in Chapter 7 bankruptcy. However, this rule doesn't necessarily apply if the coborrower is your spouse and you have taken responsibility for payment of the debt in a divorce or separation agreement. You should always list coborrowers as creditors in your bankruptcy.

Voluntary Secured Debts Are Dischargeable, But the Lien Remains the Same

Secured debts are typically contractually linked to specific items of property, called collateral. If you don't pay the debt, the creditor can take the collateral. The most common voluntary secured debts include loans for cars and homes.

If you have a voluntary debt secured by collateral, bankruptcy eliminates your personal liability for the underlying debt—that is, the creditor can't sue you to collect the debt itself. But bankruptcy doesn't eliminate the creditor's hold, or "lien," on the property that served as collateral under the contract.

Other types of secured debts arise involuntarily, often as a result of a lawsuit judgment or an enforcement action by the IRS on taxes that are old enough to be discharged. In these cases too, bankruptcy gets rid of the underlying debt, but may not eliminate a lien placed on your property by the IRS or a judgment creditor. However, you may be able to get rid of involuntary judgment liens that are attached to property you can exempt. (See Ch. 6 "Avoiding Judicial Liens" for more on this.)

Chapter 7 bankruptcy offers several options for dealing with secured debts, ranging from buying certain types of property from the creditor for its replacement value, reaffirming the debt, surrendering the property, or (in some cases) getting rid of the debt while keeping the property and continuing to make payments as before. Secured debts and options for dealing with them in Chapter 7 bankruptcy are discussed in Ch. 6.

Other Obligations

The sections above outline the most common debts that are discharged in bankruptcy, but this isn't an exhaustive list. Actually, you can pretty much count on discharging any obligation or debt unless it fits within one of the exceptions discussed below.

Debts That Survive Chapter 7 Bankruptcy

Under bankruptcy law, there are several categories of debt that are "not dischargeable" in Chapter 7 (that is, you will still owe them after your bankruptcy is final):

- Some of these debts can't be discharged under any circumstances.
- Some will not be discharged unless you convince the court that the debt fits within a narrow exception to the rule.
- Some may survive your bankruptcy, but only if the creditor files a formal objection and convinces the court that they should.

Debts Not Dischargeable Under Any Circumstances

There are certain debts that bankruptcy doesn't affect at all: You will continue to owe them just as if you had never filed.

Domestic Support Obligations

Obligations defined as "domestic support obligations" are not dischargeable. Domestic support obligations are child support, alimony, and any other debt that is *in the nature of* alimony, maintenance, or support.

To be nondischargeable under this section, a domestic support obligation must have been established—or must be capable of becoming established—in:

- a separation agreement, divorce decree, or property settlement agreement
- an order of a court that the law authorizes to impose support obligations, or
- a determination by a child support enforcement agency (or another government unit) that is legally authorized to impose support obligations.

Other Debts Owed to a Spouse, Former Spouse, or Child

You can't discharge any debt you owe to a spouse, former spouse, or child that was incurred:

- in the course of a divorce or separation, or
- in connection with a separation agreement, divorce decree, or other court order.

Simply put, debts you owe to a child or former spouse because of a divorce are not dischargeable in Chapter 7. (However, they can be discharged in Chapter 13—see "Debts Discharged in Chapter 13 (But Not in Chapter 7)," below.)

Importantly, while your bankruptcy will get rid of your obligation to pay the creditor, you are still liable to your ex-spouse for your share if the creditor goes after him or her for payment. Assume, for example, that Linda and Paul agree in their marital settlement agreement that Paul will be responsible for the couple's credit card debt (roughly $50,000), while Linda will assume responsibility for the family car, a 2009 BMW on which they owe $50,000. If Paul files for bankruptcy, he will no longer owe anything to the credit card creditors, but if the creditors try to collect from Linda as a joint debtor, Linda can hold Paul responsible. Similarly, if Linda defaults on the BMW and files bankruptcy after a deficiency judgment of $20,000 is obtained, Paul can sue Linda for the $20,000 if he is forced to pay it. Of course if both Linda and Paul file bankruptcy, then they are both freed of obligations to the creditors and each other.

Fines, Penalties, and Restitution

You can't discharge fines, penalties, or restitution that a federal, state, or local government has imposed to punish you for violating a law. Examples include:

- fines or penalties imposed under federal election law (these might be dischargeable in Chapter 13)
- fines for infractions, misdemeanors, or felonies
- fines imposed by a judge for contempt of court

- fines imposed by a government agency for violating agency regulations
- surcharges imposed by a court or an agency for enforcement of a law, and
- restitution you are ordered to pay to victims in federal criminal cases.

Certain Tax Debts

Regular income tax debts are dischargeable if they are old enough and meet the other requirements (discussed below). Other types of taxes may not be dischargeable at all. The specific rules depend on the type of tax.

Fraudulent income taxes. You cannot discharge debts for income taxes if you didn't file a return or you were intentionally avoiding your tax obligations.

Property taxes. Property taxes aren't dischargeable unless they became due more than a year before you file for bankruptcy. Even if your personal liability to pay the property tax is discharged, however, the tax lien on your property will remain. From a practical standpoint, this discharge is not meaningful, because you'll have to pay off the lien before you can transfer the property with clear title. In fact, you may even face a foreclosure action by the property tax creditor if you take too long to come up with the money.

Other taxes. Other types of taxes that aren't dischargeable are business related: payroll taxes, excise taxes, and customs duties. Sales, use, and poll taxes are also probably not dischargeable.

Debt Incurred to Pay Nondischargeable Taxes

In a Chapter 7 bankruptcy, you can't discharge debts that you incurred to pay taxes owed to a government entity. For example, if Jose uses his Visa card to pay his income taxes of $2,000, Visa can bill Jose for the $2,000 after the bankruptcy is over. Similarly, if Valerie borrows $5,000 from her credit union to pay her property tax, the debt will survive her bankruptcy.

This type of debt is dischargeable in a Chapter 13 bankruptcy, however. For instance, if Jona owes $25,000 in back taxes after an audit, and uses a credit card to pay it off, she would be on the hook for $25,000 after a Chapter 7 bankruptcy. However, if she files for Chapter 13, she can get rid of the balance of the debt when her plan ends after three or five years (the length of her plan will depend on her income), even though her plan had been paying pennies on the dollar toward the debt.

SEE AN EXPERT

Get help for business tax debts. If you owe any of these nondischargeable tax debts, see a bankruptcy attorney before you file.

Court Fees

If you are a prisoner, you can't discharge a fee imposed by a court for filing a case, motion, complaint, or appeal, or for other costs and expenses assessed for that court filing, even if you claimed that you were unable to afford the fees. (You can discharge these types of fees in Chapter 13—see "Debts Discharged in Chapter 13 (But Not in Chapter 7)," below.)

Intoxicated Driving Debts

If you kill or injure someone while you are driving and are illegally intoxicated by alcohol or drugs, any debts resulting from the incident aren't dischargeable. Even if a judge or jury finds you liable but doesn't specifically find that you were intoxicated, the debt may still be nondischargeable if you were impaired during the accident. The judgment against you won't be discharged if the bankruptcy court (or a state court in a judgment collection action) makes an independent determination that you were, in fact, intoxicated.

Note that this rule applies only to personal injuries: Debts for property damage resulting from your intoxicated driving are dischargeable. And these types of debts might be dischargeable in Chapter 13 bankruptcy if a judgment has not yet been entered.

Condominium, Cooperative, and Homeowners' Association Fees

You cannot discharge fees assessed after your bankruptcy filing date by a membership association for a condominium, housing cooperative, or lot in a homeownership association if you or the trustee have an ownership interest in the condominium, cooperative, or lot. As a practical matter, this means that any fees that become due after you file for Chapter 7 bankruptcy will survive the bankruptcy, but fees you owed prior to filing will be discharged (assuming you give up the home; if you want to keep your condo or house, you'll have to get current on fees). (You can discharge postfiling fees in Chapter 13—see "Debts Discharged in Chapter 13 (But Not in Chapter 7)," below.)

Debts for Loans From a Retirement Plan

If you've borrowed from your 401(k) or other retirement plan that is qualified under IRS rules for tax-deferred status, you'll be stuck with that debt. You can, however, discharge a loan from a retirement plan in Chapter 13— see "Debts Discharged in Chapter 13 (But Not in Chapter 7)," below. But you might owe income taxes on the discharged amount.

Debts You Couldn't Discharge in a Previous Bankruptcy

If a bankruptcy court dismissed a previous bankruptcy case because of your fraud or other bad acts (misfeasance), you cannot discharge any debts that you tried to discharge in that earlier bankruptcy. (This rule doesn't affect debts incurred since the date you filed the earlier bankruptcy case.)

Debts Not Dischargeable Unless You Can Prove That an Exception Applies

Some debts cannot be discharged in Chapter 7 unless you show the bankruptcy court that the debt falls within an exception. The two most common examples of this type of debt are student loans and certain taxes.

Student Loans

Student loans are very difficult to discharge. The law excludes student loans from the discharge, whether they are issued or insured by the government or a nonprofit institution, or by a private commercial lender (provided that the loan is a qualified education loan incurred by an individual). To qualify as an education loan, the loan must contain certain payback provisions that give the borrower a tax deduction and some slack in times of economic difficulty or when attending an educational institution. The only way out of an educational loan in bankruptcy is to establish undue hardship, which is harder to do than you might think.

To discharge your student loan on the basis of "undue hardship," you must file a separate action in the bankruptcy court and obtain a court ruling in your favor on this issue. To succeed, an action to discharge a student loan debt typically requires the services of an attorney, although it's possible to do it yourself if you're willing to put in the time. (See Ch. 10 for general information about going to bankruptcy court.)

In determining undue hardship, most bankruptcy courts look at three factors (listed below). If you can show that all three factors are present, the court is likely to grant you an undue hardship discharge of your student loan. These factors are:

- **Poverty.** Based on your current income and expenses, you cannot maintain a minimal living standard and repay the loan.
- **Persistence of hardship.** Your current financial condition is likely to continue indefinitely—that is, your situation is hopeless or virtually hopeless. This factor is most likely to be present if you are elderly or you or a spouse has a disability that restricts your opportunities to earn a decent living.
- **Good faith.** You've made a good-faith effort to repay your debt. (You're not likely to be granted a hardship discharge if you file for bankruptcy immediately after getting out of school or if you haven't looked extensively for employment and made efforts to maximize your income.)

Rules for PLUS Loans

Parents can get Parental Loans for Students (PLUS Loans) to finance a child's education. Even though the parent does not receive the education, the loan is treated like any other student loan if the parent files for bankruptcy. The parents must meet the undue hardship test to discharge the loan.

Although it's changed somewhat in recent years, many courts are reluctant to discharge student loans. They take the position that Congress wants student loans to be repaid, absent exceptional circumstances. They also recognize that federal student loan regulations require a lot of flexibility on the creditor's part, including moratoriums on payments, temporary reductions in payments, and extensions of the repayment period that lower the monthly payments to an affordable amount. These options give debtors other ways (short of filing for bankruptcy) to seek relief from student loan debt.

In some cases, however, courts have found that it would be an undue hardship to repay the entire loan and relieved the debtor of a portion of the debt. Other courts take the position that it's an all-or-nothing proposition—either the entire loan is discharged or none of it is discharged. Ask a local bankruptcy attorney how courts in your area handle student loans.

Regular Income Taxes

People who are considering bankruptcy because of tax problems are almost always concerned about income taxes they owe to the IRS or the state equivalent. There is a myth afoot that income tax debts are not discharged in bankruptcy. This is not true if you are able to meet certain conditions. Here are the specifics.

You can discharge federal or state income tax debt in Chapter 7 bankruptcy if all of the following are true:

- You filed a tax return for the tax year or years in question.
- The return was filed at least two years before your bankruptcy filing date.
- The tax return was due at least three years before you file for bankruptcy (usually that is either April 15th of the following year or October 15th if you requested an extension).
- The taxing authority has not assessed your liability for the taxes within the 240 days before your bankruptcy filing date (this time period can be extended if the IRS has suspended collection activities because of an offer in compromise or a previous bankruptcy filing).
- You did not willfully attempt to evade the tax.

EXAMPLE: Fred filed a tax return in August 2012 for the 2011 tax year. In March 2014, the IRS audited Fred's 2011 return and assessed a tax due of $8,000. In May 2015, Fred files for bankruptcy. The taxes that Fred wishes to discharge were for tax year 2011. The return for those taxes was due on April 15, 2012, more than three years prior to Fred's filing date in May 2015. The tax return filed in August 2012 was at least two years prior to Fred's bankruptcy filing date. Finally, the assessment date of March 2014 was well prior to 240 days of the filing date. There is no evidence that Fred schemed to not pay his tax (in other words, that he illegally tried to avoid paying). Because Fred met all five conditions for discharging an income tax liability, Fred can discharge those taxes.

Even if you meet each of the five requirements for discharging tax liability, any lien placed on your property by the taxing authority will remain after your bankruptcy. The result is that the taxing authority can't go after your bank account or wages, but you'll have to pay off the lien before you can sell your real estate with a clear title.

However, if your property is essentially worthless or has no equity after your bankruptcy discharge, ask for an "abatement" of the lien; the taxing authority might release the lien.

Taxes Due Under Late-Filed Returns

According to most bankruptcy courts, a late-filed return does not constitute a "return" for purposes of the second prong in the above criteria for discharging tax debt. Your return is "late" if all of your filing extensions have expired and the IRS has filed a substitute return without your assistance. (These courts make an exception if the IRS files a substitute return with your assistance under Internal Revenue Code Section 6020(a)—something the IRS may, but is not obligated, to do.) However, some courts (notably the Eighth Circuit Court of Appeals as well as various lower courts in other jurisdictions) don't follow this reasoning. Instead, they may allow you to discharge income taxes even if you file a late return, as long as you meet the other criteria. If you have filed a late tax return, talk to a bankruptcy lawyer.

CAUTION

Debts incurred to pay nondischargeable taxes will also be nondischargeable in Chapter 7 bankruptcy. If you borrowed money or used your credit card to pay taxes that would otherwise not be discharged, you can't eliminate that loan or credit card debt in Chapter 7 bankruptcy. In other words, you can't turn a nondischargeable tax debt into a dischargeable tax debt by paying it on your credit card. (Note: These debts can be discharged in Chapter 13 bankruptcy, however, as explained below.)

Debts Not Dischargeable in Bankruptcy If the Creditor Successfully Objects

Four types of debts may survive Chapter 7 bankruptcy, but only if both:

- the creditor files a formal objection—called a complaint to determine dischargeability—during the bankruptcy proceedings, and
- the creditor proves that the debt fits into one of the categories discussed below.

If Your Debts Will Be Discharged Unless a Creditor Objects

Even though creditors have the right to object to the discharge of certain debts, many creditors—and their attorneys—don't fully understand this right. And a creditor might decide to write off the debt rather than contesting it. It can cost a lot to bring a "dischargeability action" (as this type of case is called). If your debt isn't huge, a creditor might find it cheaper to forgo collecting the debt rather than to fight about it in court.

Finally, if a creditor or the trustee does object in either of these situations, you may be able to settle the debt for much less than it would have taken to pay it off.

For these reasons, you'll want to consider your total debt burden, as well as the cost and stress involved in defending a dischargeability action (a type of lawsuit). If you are filing primarily to get rid of a debt that won't be discharged if a creditor objects, you might end up with a bankruptcy on your record for nothing. If, on the other hand, you have other debts that will certainly be discharged (such as credit card debts), those debts will be gone after you file for bankruptcy, even if a creditor successfully objects to the discharge of one debt.

If you suspect that a creditor might challenge the dischargeability of a particular debt on fraud grounds, you should discuss your concern with an attorney before moving forward. Such matters can come with penalties, including criminal fines and incarceration.

Debts From Fraud

In order for a creditor to prove that one of your debts should survive bankruptcy because you incurred it through fraud, the debt must fit one of the categories below.

Debts from intentionally fraudulent behavior. If a creditor can show that a debt arose because of your dishonesty, the court probably will not let you discharge the debt. Here are some common examples:

- You wrote a check for something and stopped payment on it, even though you kept the item.
- You wrote a check against insufficient funds but assured the merchant that the check was good.
- You rented or borrowed an expensive item and claimed it was yours in order to use it as collateral to get a loan.
- You got a loan by telling the lender you'd pay it back, when you had no intention of doing so.
- You received payments from unemployment insurance or another benefit program because of your fraud or misrepresentation.

For this type of debt to be nondischargeable, your deceit must be intentional, and the creditor must have relied on your deceit in extending credit or awarding benefits. Again, these are facts that the creditor has to prove before the debt will be ruled nondischargeable by the court. Keep in mind, however, that a creditor will likely have a seemingly valid case—and you'll have to defend against it. Given the seriousness (and potential criminal ramifications) of fraud charges and the complexity of defending yourself in a lawsuit, it's likely that you'll want to bring in an attorney. Therefore, it's not advisable to file a bankruptcy case without first consulting with a bankruptcy professional if you suspect that a creditor might accuse you of fraud.

Debts from a false written statement about your financial condition. If a creditor proves that you incurred a debt by making a false written statement, the debt isn't dischargeable. Here are the rules:

- The false statement must be written— for instance, made in a credit application, rental application, or resume.
- The false statement must have been "material"—that is, it was a potentially significant factor in the creditor's decision to extend you credit. The two most common materially false statements are omitting debts and overstating income.
- The false statement must relate to your financial condition or the financial condition of an "insider"—a person close to you or a business entity with which you're associated.
- The creditor must have relied on the false statement, and the reliance must have been reasonable.
- You must have intended to deceive the creditor. This is extremely hard for the creditor to prove based simply on your behavior. The creditor would have to

show outrageous behavior on your part, such as adding a "0" to your income (claiming you make $180,000 rather than $18,000) on a credit application.

Again, if you suspect that a creditor might accuse you of providing a false written statement, consult with an attorney about the potential risks you'll face if you choose to move forward with bankruptcy.

Recent debts for luxuries presumed fraudulent. If you run up more than $675 in debt to any one creditor for luxury goods or services within the 90 days before you file for bankruptcy, the law presumes that your intent was fraudulent regarding those charges. The charges will survive your bankruptcy unless you prove that your intent wasn't fraudulent. The term "luxury goods and services" does not include things that are reasonably necessary for the support and maintenance of you and your dependents (what that means will be decided on a case-by-case basis).

Recent cash advances presumed fraudulent. If you get cash advances from any one creditor totaling more than $950 under an open-ended consumer credit plan within the 70 days before you file for bankruptcy, the debt is presumed to be nondischargeable. "Open-ended" means there's no date when the debt must be repaid, but rather, as with most credit cards, you may take forever to repay the debt as long as you pay a minimum amount each month. Again, the presumption means that if someone objects, you have to prove your intention was not fraudulent.

 RELATED TOPIC

Additional information on credit card issuers' attempts to have credit card debt declared nondischargeable because of fraud is provided in Ch. 9.

Debts Arising From Debtor's Willful and Malicious Acts

If the act that caused the debt was both willful *and* malicious (that is, you intended to inflict an injury to person or property), the debt isn't dischargeable if the creditor successfully mounts an objection in the bankruptcy court.

Generally, crimes involving the intentional injury to people or damage to property are considered willful and malicious acts. Examples are assaults, battery, rape, arson, or vandalism.

Other acts that would typically be considered to be willful and malicious include:

- kidnapping
- deliberately causing extreme anxiety, fear, or shock
- libel or slander
- illegal acts by a landlord to evict a tenant, such as removing a door or changing the locks, and
- trademark and copyright infringement.

If you were simply careless (you should have taken more care, as is true in most automobile accidents), or even reckless (for example, you caused an injury by driving far too fast), the debt will still be discharged. Because creditors have a hard time proving that a debt arises from both a willful and malicious act, these debts are often ordered discharged by the court when contested on this ground.

Willful and Malicious Acts Are Different in Chapter 13

In Chapter 7 bankruptcy, these debts are nondischargeable only if the underlying act is found by the court to be both willful *and* malicious. Under Chapter 13 bankruptcy, however, the underlying act need only be willful *or* malicious. On the other hand, debts for property damage, which can survive Chapter 7 under the willful and malicious rule, can be discharged in a Chapter 13 bankruptcy.

Debts From Embezzlement, Larceny, or Breach of Fiduciary Duty

A debt incurred as a result of embezzlement, larceny, or breach of fiduciary duty is not dischargeable if the creditor successfully objects to its discharge.

"Embezzlement" means taking property entrusted to you for another and using it for yourself. "Larceny" is another word for theft. "Breach of fiduciary duty" is the failure to live up to a duty of trust you owe someone, based on a relationship where you're required to manage property or money for another, or where your relationship is a close and confidential one. Common fiduciary relationships include those between:

- business partners
- attorney and client
- estate executor and beneficiary
- guardian and ward, and
- husband and wife.

And even a debt resulting from mere negligence committed by a fiduciary may be nondischargeable.

Debts or Creditors You Don't List

Bankruptcy requires you to list all of your known creditors on your bankruptcy papers and provide their most current addresses. This gives the court some assurance that everyone who needs to know about your bankruptcy will receive notice. As long as you do your part, the debt will be discharged (as long as it's otherwise dischargeable under the rules), even if the official notice fails to reach the creditor for some reason beyond your control—for example, because the post office errs or the creditor moves without leaving a forwarding address.

Suppose, however, that you forgot to list a creditor on your bankruptcy papers or carelessly misstated a creditor's identity or address. In that situation, the court's notice may not reach the creditor and the debt may survive your bankruptcy. Here are the rules:

- If the creditor knew or should have known of your bankruptcy through other means, such as a letter or phone call from you, the debt will be discharged even though the creditor wasn't listed. In this situation, the creditor should have taken steps to protect its interests, even though it didn't receive formal notice from the court.

- If all of your assets are exempt—that is, you have a "no-asset" case—the debt will likely be discharged (unless the debt is otherwise nondischargeable). In this situation, the creditor wouldn't have benefited from receiving notice anyway, because there is no property to distribute. However, if the lack of notice deprives a creditor of the opportunity to successfully object to the discharge by filing a complaint in the bankruptcy court (such as for a fraudulent debt), the debt may survive your bankruptcy.

If an Unknown Creditor Pops Up After Bankruptcy

If a creditor comes out of the woodwork after your bankruptcy case is closed, you can always reopen your case, name the creditor, and then seek an amended discharge. If it's the kind of debt that will be discharged anyway, many courts won't let you reopen because there is no need to. The debt is discharged by law and most creditors know this. However, if the creditor continues to try to collect the debt, you can haul the creditor into the bankruptcy court on a contempt charge (for violating the court's discharge order).

Debts That Survive Chapter 13 Bankruptcy

The typical Chapter 13 plan pays 100% of back child support, back taxes, and other debts classified as priority debts, and some percentage of other nonpriority unsecured debts, depending on the debtor's disposable income and the value of the debtor's nonexempt property. (See Ch. 2 for more on Chapter 13 plans.) This section explains what happens to any remaining nonpriority, unsecured debt when your Chapter 13 plan is complete.

As in Chapter 7, several categories of debt may not be discharged in Chapter 13 bankruptcy:

- Some debts can't be discharged under any circumstance and you'll be stuck with them after your case is over.
- Student loans won't be discharged unless you convince the court that it would be an undue hardship to pay off the loan.
- Fraudulent debts won't be discharged, but only if the creditor convinces the court that they shouldn't be.

Debts Not Dischargeable Under Any Circumstances

Certain types of debts survive Chapter 13 bankruptcy, regardless of your income or circumstances.

Domestic Support Obligations

In both Chapter 7 and Chapter 13 bank-ruptcies, child support and alimony debts you owe directly to an ex-spouse or child are nondischargeable. (See "Debts That Survive Chapter 7 Bankruptcy," above, for more on these obligations.) Usually, your Chapter 13 repayment plan must provide for 100% repayment of these debts. In some instances, you might be able to pay less than 100% of these debts through your plan if you commit all of your disposable income to a plan that lasts five years. However, the unpaid portion will not be discharged in your bankruptcy. The same goes for support you owe to a governmental child support collection agency—you might not have to pay 100% through your plan, but you will remain on the hook for the remaining unpaid portion after your bankruptcy.

> **EXAMPLE:** In the final decree issued in his divorce, Fred was ordered to pay his ex-wife $500 a month for child support. Shortly after the divorce, Fred's ex-wife applied for welfare and assigned her child support rights to the county providing the welfare. Over time, Fred fell behind on his child support to the tune of $25,000 principal and interest. When Fred files for bankruptcy under Chapter 13, his plan—later confirmed by the court—requires him to pay $15,000 of the $25,000 arrearage. When Fred receives his Chapter 13 discharge, he will still owe the $10,000 that won't be paid through his plan.

Criminal Penalties

Debts you owe on fines or restitution orders contained in the sentence for conviction of any crime (yes, even traffic tickets) won't be discharged in Chapter 13.

Fines or Penalties Owed to a Government Agency

If you have been fined by a government agency for some reason, or subjected to a penalty or a forfeiture of property, this debt will not be discharged. However, if the government agency assesses the fine because you were overpaid benefits due to your failure to report income or for some other faulty behavior, only the fine itself is not dischargeable. The amount you were overpaid is dischargeable like any other unsecured debt. However, if the agency files an action in court alleging that you obtained the overpayment through fraud, the court can rule that the overpayment is not dischargeable.

> **EXAMPLE:** Mary was receiving unem-ployment insurance benefits, and then found a job. While she originally intended to report the job to the unem-ployment insurance agency—which would result in a termination of the benefits—she found that her wages were insufficient for her needs and decided to continue receiving the unemployment benefits. When she was caught about six months later, she had received over $10,000 in overpayments. She signed an agreement to repay the

$10,000 overpayment as well as a $5,000 fine because of her intentionally fraudulent behavior. In bankruptcy, the $5000 fine is not dischargeable as matter of law. However, the $10,000 would be discharged unless the government agency filed an affirmative action in bankruptcy court, asking the judge to except the overpayment from discharge because of fraud.

Certain Taxes

Recent income tax debts—those that first became due within the three-year period prior to your filing date—are priority debts and have to be paid in full in any Chapter 13 plan. If your Chapter 13 ends prematurely for any reason, the tax debts you have not yet repaid will remain; you will either have to pay them outside of bankruptcy or convert your Chapter 13 to a Chapter 7 bankruptcy. (See "Debts That Survive Chapter 7 Bankruptcy," above, for information on which taxes are dischargeable.) If there is evidence in the tax records that you tried to avoid your duty to file an honest return or pay your taxes, the taxes will survive bankruptcy without exception. If you operated a business, you can't discharge taxes related to the business. A trust tax is an amount that you hold on behalf of the taxing agency, such as employee withholdings and sales tax.

Intoxicated Driving Debts

If you operate a vehicle while illegally intoxicated by alcohol or drugs, and you kill or injure someone, any debt arising out of the injury is not dischargeable if the claimant obtained a court judgment prior to your bankruptcy filing. But what if you are sued and the judge or jury finds you liable but doesn't specifically find that you were intoxicated? This may not help you: The judgment against you won't be discharged if the bankruptcy court (or a state court in a judgment collection action) determines that you were, in fact, intoxicated.

Note that this rule applies only to personal injuries: Debts for property damage resulting from your intoxicated driving will be dischargeable.

Debts Arising From Your Willful or Malicious Actions

To prevent a debt resulting from a willful or malicious action from getting wiped out, a creditor will likely need to bring an action in bankruptcy court and ask the court to determine whether the act involved in the underlying judgment meets the willful or malicious injury standard. It isn't always clear. If the court finds that a creditor's civil court judgment against you was due to your willful or malicious act, the judgment will be nondischargeable.

You can expect the bankruptcy court to give the underlying state court judgment great deference, so unless you can prove that your actions weren't willful or malicious, don't count on prevailing.

For example, O.J. Simpson was acquitted of criminal charges but found liable, in a civil suit, for wrongful death—which fits the definition of a "willful or malicious act." Under this rule, O.J. would likely not be able to discharge the debt in Chapter 13 bankruptcy.

Note that the act which gives rise to the debt need only be willful *or* malicious to be nondischargeable in Chapter 13, which greatly expands the types of debt that will survive discharge. For instance, a judgment for injury caused by your reckless driving would most likely survive Chapter 13 bankruptcy on the ground of "maliciousness," whereas it might be discharged in Chapter 7 because reckless driving, though malicious, is seldom considered willful.

Finally, unlike Chapter 7, which includes damage to property, this exception to a Chapter 13 discharge applies only to debts arising from personal injury or death.

Debts or Creditors You Don't List

Bankruptcy requires you to list all your creditors on your bankruptcy papers and provide their most current addresses. That way, the court can mail out notice of your bankruptcy with the best chance of reaching them. If you do your part and the official notice fails to reach a creditor for some reason beyond your control—for example, because the post office errs, or the creditor moves without leaving a forwarding address—the debt will still be discharged (as long as it is otherwise dischargeable). Also, if the creditor knew or should have known of your bankruptcy through other means, such as a letter or phone call from you, the debt will be discharged.

Student Loan Interest May Be Discharged in a Chapter 13 Plan

In *United Student Aid Funds, Inc. v. Espinosa*, No. 08–1134 (U.S., March 23, 2010), the Chapter 13 debtor submitted a plan, which the bankruptcy court confirmed, that provided for payment of the student loan principal but discharge of the accrued interest. The lender did not object and the interest was discharged upon completion of the plan. The lender then attempted to collect the interest it considered due, arguing that discharge of a student loan, and accompanying interest, may only be accomplished if the debtor sues the lender in an adversary action to determine the loan's dischargeability, and the court finds repayment of the loan would constitute an undue hardship. The U.S Supreme Court refused to set aside the discharge order, ruling that the lender had actual notice of the bankruptcy (and the plan that provided for the discharge of the interest), and could have appeared in the bankruptcy to protect its rights. However, the Supreme Court made clear that discharging student loans (rather than interest) through plan confirmation violates the bankruptcy code and it's uncertain how courts will treat this situation in the future.

Suppose, however, that you forget to list a creditor on your bankruptcy papers or carelessly misstate a creditor's identity or address. In that situation, the court won't notify the creditor and the debt almost always will survive your bankruptcy (unless the creditor wouldn't have received any payments under your plan, a very rare occurrence). The general rule is that debts not listed in a Chapter 13 case survive the bankruptcy. This means, of course, that you should be extra careful to list all of your creditors in a Chapter 13 case. Also, if a creditor fails to file a proof of claim, you would be well advised to file one for it, especially if the claim is for a secured debt.

Student Loans

As in Chapter 7, a student loan cannot be discharged in Chapter 13 unless you show the bankruptcy court that paying the loan back would be a substantial hardship. See "Debts That Survive Chapter 7 Bankruptcy," above, for more on the rules for discharging student loans.

Fraudulent Debts

Debts based on fraud, theft, or breach of fiduciary duty are not dischargeable in Chapter 13. (See "Debts That Survive Chapter 7 Bankruptcy," above, for a description of these types of debts.) However, the discharge is not automatic. Bankruptcy courts in Chapter 13 cases use the same procedure for determining the dischargeability of these debts as they use in Chapter 7 cases— that is, the debt will be discharged if the creditor fails to come forward and establish fraud in the bankruptcy court.

If You Convert From One Chapter to Another

In most cases, bankruptcy filers may convert their cases from one chapter to another. If, for example, a court finds that a Chapter 7 filing is an abuse of the bankruptcy system under the means test, the filer can convert to Chapter 13 rather than dismissing the case altogether. Or, you may decide to convert because a particular debt will only be discharged in Chapter 13, for example, or because you won't be able to complete a Chapter 13 repayment plan. In order to convert your case, however, the court must be convinced that your conversion was made in good faith. Once you make the switch, you are subject to the dischargeability rules of the chapter to which you converted, not the chapter you started out using.

EXAMPLE: Connie files for Chapter 13 bankruptcy because she owes a lot of debt from a divorce and has been told that those debts can be discharged in Chapter 13 but not in Chapter 7. Connie proposes a feasible Chapter 13 plan that pays only 25% of her divorce-related debt. Halfway through the plan, Connie loses her job and can't continue her payments. She converts to Chapter 7. Her Chapter 7 discharge won't include the divorce-related debts. However, Connie will receive a credit for the amounts she paid on those debts during her Chapter 13 case.

Debts Discharged in Chapter 13 (But Not in Chapter 7)

Certain debts that cannot be discharged in Chapter 7 (see "Debts That Survive Chapter 7 Bankruptcy," above) can be discharged in Chapter 13. They are:

- marital debts created in a divorce or settlement agreement
- debts incurred to pay a nondischargeable tax debt
- court fees
- condominium, cooperative, and homeowners' association fees incurred after the bankruptcy filing date on property you have given up (in most courts)
- debts for loans from a retirement plan
- debts that couldn't be discharged in a previous bankruptcy, and
- fines or penalties imposed under federal election law.

How Joint Debts Are Handled

Debts for which you have a joint debtor—another person who owes the debt along with you—raise some tricky issues. Let's look at the different kinds of joint debtors and how your bankruptcy filing might affect them.

Cosigners and Guarantors

A cosigner or guarantor is someone who signs onto your debt in order to back up or guarantee your payment. If you don't pay, the cosigner or guarantor is legally responsible for payment. If you discharge a debt for which you have a cosigner or guarantor, your joint debtor will still owe the entire thing, even though you are no longer on the hook to repay it.

If you want to file for Chapter 7 bankruptcy but don't want to stick your cosigner or guarantor with the debt, you can try to make an agreement with the creditor to reaffirm the debt—that is, to continue to owe it after your bankruptcy ends.

> **TIP**
> **It's usually better to reimburse the cosigner than to reaffirm the debt.** For a variety of reasons, it's almost always a good idea to discharge the debt and agree to owe your cosigner for any potential liability, rather than to reaffirm it and continue to owe your original creditor. This approach gives you more flexibility regarding repayment than you'd have if you defaulted on your payments to the regular creditor under a reaffirmation agreement. Also, the creditor may decide not to try to collect from the cosigner, which means neither one of you would have to repay the debt. And finally, it's possible that the cosigner will also decide to file bankruptcy.

If you file for Chapter 13 bankruptcy, assuming the cosigned or guaranteed debt is a consumer and not a business debt, you can include it as part of your repayment plan,

Bankruptcy, Joint Debtors, and Preferences

If you file for Chapter 7 bankruptcy and have a joint debtor who is a relative, close friend, or business associate, the joint debtor may have to pay the bankruptcy trustee any amount that you owe the creditor on the loan. Here's how this works.

As mentioned in Ch. 2, when you file for bankruptcy, the bankruptcy trustee will look to see whether you made any payments to creditors within the 90 days before you filed—or within one year of filing, if those payments were made to, or for the benefit of, a relative or close business associate. These payments are called "preferences" and they're not permitted if they exceed certain limits. The idea is that you shouldn't be allowed to single out certain creditors for special treatment just before you file for bankruptcy.

If you make a preferential payment to a creditor, the bankruptcy trustee can demand that the creditor turn over the amount of payment to the trustee, so that it can be divided equally among your unsecured creditors. If the creditor pays up and the debt is then discharged in bankruptcy, you won't owe anything, but your joint debtor will be on the hook for whatever remains of the original debt.

If the creditor can't or won't cough up the preference money you paid, the trustee could sue the creditor. But an easier route for the trustee may be to go after your joint debtor—who benefited from the preference because your payment wiped out or reduced his or her liability for the debt. In this scenario, believe it or not, the joint debtor would have to pay the trustee the amount of the preference. The joint debtor then continues to be liable for the debt, less the amount of the preference kept by the creditor.

Fraudulent transfers are closely related to preferences. If, in the applicable statute of limitations period before filing for bankruptcy, you transfer property to a friend, a relative, or another insider without an exchange of equal value, the transfer may be considered fraudulent. (The applicable statute of limitations period is always two years or more, depending on state laws applied by the trustee.) Fraudulent transfers give the trustee the right to seize the transferred property for the benefit of your creditors. They may also result in the denial of your bankruptcy discharge.

and your joint debtor will not be pursued during your bankruptcy case—typically, at least three years. If you can, you should pay the debt in full during your case. If you don't, you will be entitled to discharge whatever balance remains when your case is over (assuming the debt is otherwise dischargeable in a Chapter 13 bankruptcy). But in that situation, the creditor can still go after the joint debtor for the balance.

Spousal Responsibility for Debts

Married people can file for bankruptcy jointly or separately. If they file jointly, all of their debt is subject to the rules explained above. If only one spouse files, state marital property rules determine which debts qualify for discharge.

Community Property Rules

Some states use what's called a "community property" system to determine who owns marital property, including debts. These states are Arizona, California, Idaho, Louisiana, Nevada, New Mexico, Texas, Washington, and Wisconsin. (Spouses in Alaska can elect to have their property treated as community property, if they make a written agreement to that effect.)

In community property states, both spouses owe debts incurred by either spouse during the marriage even if one spouse incurs a debt without the other spouse's knowledge. These are termed "community" debts. Debts incurred by a spouse prior to the marriage are considered separate debts, as are debts incurred after separation and divorce.

For example, when Justine and Paul marry in California, each has about $10,000 in credit card debt. In addition, Paul owes taxes to the IRS and Justine owes her uncle $3,000 on a loan she used to buy a car. After they marry, Justine and Paul buy a home and take out a second mortgage a few years later. They also obtain an unsecured loan of $15,000 from a bank to buy a car.

When hard times hit in 2008, they separate. Shortly after the separation, Justine starts using the credit cards that are in her name only and adds an additional $20,000 to her personal debt. Under these facts, all the credit card debt is separate debt because Paul and Justine incurred it either before marriage or after separation. So, too, is Justine's debt to her uncle and Paul's debt to the IRS. However, the home mortgages and the bank loan are community debts.

In bankruptcies filed in community property states, community debts are discharged as to community property, even if only one spouse files—which means the nonfiling spouse will benefit from the filing spouse's discharge. This is often called a "phantom discharge" and it protects all community property, even property that the couple acquires in the future. This discharge of community debts, however, does not protect the nonfiling spouse's separate property. The discharge also does nothing to get rid of the nonfiling spouse's separate debts; these will survive the bankruptcy.

Using the facts in the previous example, if Justine files for bankruptcy in a community property state, she will discharge her credit card debt and her debt to her uncle. The debt owed on the house, although a community debt, will be handled differently because it is secured debt. (See Ch. 7 for more on how secured debts are treated in bankruptcy.) The bank loan is also community debt and will likely be discharged as to Justine's separate property and as to the couple's community property, even though Paul doesn't file. Justine's bankruptcy will not affect Paul's separate credit card debt or his separate debt to the IRS.

Creditors Seldom Sue Nonfiling Spouses for Marital Debts

When a debt is jointly owed because of state marital property rules, and is not discharged as to the nonfiling spouse in a bankruptcy filed by just one spouse, creditors seldom if ever sue the nonfiling spouse for the debt unless his or her name is on the contract underlying the debt. This is primarily because there is a huge aftermarket for buying judgments and then trying to collect on them; to have any value in this market a judgment must be simple to collect. Also, it takes time and money to impose liability on a nonsigning spouse, since state marital property laws are seldom absolute and can require a showing that the debt was not a necessity or in some other category that would allow the nonfiling spouse to escape liability. In short, most creditors determine that it just isn't practical to try to collect the debt from a nonfiling spouse who never signed onto the debt (but it can happen). Similarly, a spouse who is added to an existing credit card owned by the other spouse is not liable for the debt unless he or she signs the request.

However, if Justine had used joint credit cards after separating from Paul, those creditors could still collect from Paul, just as they would be able to collect from any other cosigner. The lesson learned: If you separate from your spouse, consider removing your spouse's name from all your accounts.

Common Law Property Rules

All states that don't use the community property system for dealing with marital debts are termed common law states. The rules for those states are a bit simpler. All debts either spouse incurs before the marriage are that spouse's separate debts. Debts incurred during the marriage might be either separate or joint: If the debt is jointly undertaken (for example, it was incurred from a joint account or the creditor considered the credit information of both spouses in deciding to extend the loan) or the debt benefits the marriage (for example, the debt was for necessary items, such as food, clothing, or child care), it is jointly owed by both spouses. Otherwise, a debt that one spouse incurs separately remains that spouse's separate debt.

When one spouse files for bankruptcy in a common law state, the only debts that come into play are that spouse's separate debts and any debts that can be classified as joint. The other spouse's separate debts continue unaffected by the bankruptcy filing.

Business Partners

As a general rule, all partners are responsible for partnership debts unless the partnership has special provisions limiting the liability of certain classes of partners (as in a limited partnership). If you are in a partnership and file for bankruptcy, you can get rid of your personal liability for partnership debts. However, the remaining partnership and individual partners (if there are any—often partnerships are dissolved if one partner leaves or declares bankruptcy) will still be on the hook. ●

Your Property and Bankruptcy

This chapter explains what happens to the property you own when you file for bankruptcy. It also covers exemptions—the rules that determine which property you can keep, which property you'll have to give up in Chapter 7 bankruptcy, and, in some cases, how much you have to pay out in Chapter 13 bankruptcy.

In Chapter 7, if property is "exempt," you will probably be able to keep it; you may have to forfeit nonexempt property or property that is worth more than the applicable exemption, to the bankruptcy trustee to pay off your creditors.

In Chapter 13, if property is not exempt, your plan will have to provide that your unsecured creditors will be paid at least as much as they would receive from nonexempt assets in a Chapter 7 bankruptcy. In essence, this would amount to the value of the property, less any exemption you would be entitled to, less costs of sale, and less the trustee's commission.

In this chapter, we focus only on what happens to personal property (any type of property other than real estate) you own outright. Ch. 5 discusses what happens to real estate, including how bankruptcy can be used to deal with foreclosures. Ch. 6 explains what happens to personal property that is collateral for a debt you are making payments on.

CAUTION

Exempt property can be taken to pay child support, alimony, and taxes. This chapter explains the rules that protect certain types of property from being seized by creditors or the bankruptcy trustee to pay your debts. However, your exempt property is not protected if you owe money to a former spouse for child support or alimony: These obligations must be met, even if it means that you lose property that would otherwise be exempt. The same goes for overdue taxes: The taxing authority or the bankruptcy trustee may be able to take otherwise exempt property.

Most Chapter 7 filers emerge from bankruptcy with their property intact because most of what they own is exempt and the benefit to the creditors of seizing and selling what is not exempt is often not worth the cost. But that is not always the case. Also, in Chapter 13, you are entitled to keep your property regardless of its value, but your plan must pay your unsecured creditors at least as much as they would have received had you filed a Chapter 7 bankruptcy. (See Ch. 2 for more on this.)

Your Bankruptcy Estate

The assets you own on the day you file for bankruptcy is called your "bankruptcy estate." With a few important exceptions (discussed below), property and income you acquire after you file for Chapter 7 bankruptcy aren't included in your bankruptcy estate. When you file for bankruptcy, the forms you have to fill out require you to list all of your assets.

What's in Your Bankruptcy Estate

The broad categories of property that make up your bankruptcy estate are described below.

Property you own and possess when you file. Everything in your possession that you own, whether or not you owe money on it—for example, a car, real estate, clothing, books, television, stereo system, furniture, tools, boat, artworks, or stock certificates—is included in your bankruptcy estate. Property that you have in your possession but belongs to someone else (such as the car your friend stores in your garage or the television you borrowed from your sister) is not part of your bankruptcy estate, because you don't have the right to sell it or give it away.

Property you own but don't possess when you file. You can own something even if you don't have physical possession of it. For instance, you may own a car that someone else is using. Other examples include a deposit held by a stockbroker, a security deposit held by your landlord or a utility company, or a business in which you've invested money.

Property you are entitled to receive. Property that you have a legal right to receive but haven't gotten yet when you file for bankruptcy is included in your bankruptcy estate. Common examples include:

- wages, royalties, or commissions you have earned but have not yet been paid
- a tax refund legally due you
- vacation or termination pay you've earned
- property you've inherited but not yet received from someone who has died
- proceeds of an insurance policy, if the death, injury, or other event that gives rise to payment has already occurred, and
- money owed you for goods or services you've provided (often called "accounts receivable").

Community property. If you live in a community property state, all property either spouse acquires during the marriage (but not during separation) is ordinarily considered "community property," owned jointly by both spouses. (The community property states are Arizona, California, Idaho, Louisiana, Nevada, New Mexico, Texas, Washington, and Wisconsin, and—if you have a written community property agreement or trust—Alaska.) Gifts and inheritances to only one spouse are the most common exceptions—these are the separate property of the spouse who receives them. If you're married and file jointly for bankruptcy, all the community property you and your spouse own, as well as all of both of your separate property, is considered part of your bankruptcy estate. If your spouse doesn't file, then your bankruptcy estate consists of all of the community property and all of your separate property—your spouse's separate property isn't included.

Marital property in common law property states (all states that aren't community property states). If you are married and filing jointly in a common law state, your bankruptcy estate includes all the property you and your spouse own, together and separately. If you are filing alone for bankruptcy in a common law property state (all states other than the community property states listed above), your bankruptcy estate includes:

- your separate property (property that has only your name on a title certificate or that was purchased, received as a gift, or inherited by you alone), and
- half of the property that is jointly owned by you and your spouse, unless you own the property as tenants by the entirety.

CAUTION

"Tenancy by the entirety" property often is handled differently in bankruptcy. Property you and your spouse jointly own as "tenants by the entirety" usually receives special protection in bankruptcy if (1) it is

located in Delaware, the District of Columbia, Florida, Hawaii, Illinois, Indiana, Maryland, Massachusetts, Michigan, Missouri, North Carolina, Pennsylvania, Tennessee, Vermont, Virginia, or Wyoming and (2) only one spouse files for bankruptcy. In that event, the filing spouse's creditors (and therefore the bankruptcy court) typically cannot take property that both spouses own as tenants by the entirety. If both spouses file, however, this protection doesn't apply. If you and your spouse own "tenancy by the entirety" property, consult a local bankruptcy lawyer before you file.

Certain property you acquire within 180 days after filing for bankruptcy. Most property you acquire or become entitled to after you file for bankruptcy isn't included in your bankruptcy estate. But there are a few exceptions. If you acquire or become entitled to the following items within 180 days after you file, you must notify the trustee:

- an inheritance through a will or by operation of law or through a living trust, a beneficiary designation, or through any other transfer device that occurs upon a person's death where the death occurs within the 180-day period
- property you receive or have a right to receive from a marital settlement agreement or divorce decree, and
- death benefits or life insurance policy proceeds.

Unless an exemption applies, the trustee can take this property and distribute it to your creditors.

Property (revenue) generated by estate property. This type of property typically consists of the proceeds of contracts—such as those providing for rent, royalties, and commissions—that were in effect at the time of the bankruptcy filing, but which produced earnings after that date. For example, if you are a composer or an author and receive royalties each year for work that was written before you filed for bankruptcy, the trustee may collect those royalties as property of your estate. Proceeds from work you do after your filing date belong to you.

Property that appreciates in value after you file. If you own property that has appreciated in value after you file for bankruptcy, the amount of the appreciation is also part of your bankruptcy estate and, absent an available exemption, can be taken by the trustee right up until the time your bankruptcy case is closed. For example, assume your home has equity worth $100,000 when you file and you live in a market where the real estate prices are appreciating. The trustee decides to keep your case open. A few years later, while your case is still open, the equity in your home appreciates to $150,000 and your exemption protects only $100,000. At this point the trustee can decide to sell your home, give you the $100,000 exemption, and use the $50,000 to pay your unsecured creditors.

Property you transferred prior to your bankruptcy. The rules discussed in Ch. 2 regarding preferences and fraudulent transfers create a type of property—

property illegally transferred or paid out in a preference—that is considered part of your bankruptcy estate. However, since by definition you no longer own or have possession of the property, the bankruptcy trustee is authorized to "avoid" the transfer or preference—this means the trustee can sue the party who has received the property to have it returned to the bankruptcy estate, and then sell the property for the benefit of your creditors.

Consignment goods. Under the bankruptcy code, property your business stocks on a consignment basis (for example folk art in a crafts shop or jewelry in a consignment store) is generally considered to be an asset of your business and can be liquidated without payment to the people who have placed the property with you on consignment.

Property That's Not Part of Your Bankruptcy Estate

Property that is not in your bankruptcy estate is not subject to the bankruptcy court's jurisdiction, which means that the bankruptcy trustee can't take it to pay your creditors under any circumstances.

The most common examples of property that doesn't fall within your bankruptcy estate are:

- Social Security payments, whether they be past, present, or future (Section 407 of the Social Security Act)
- property you buy or receive after your filing date (with the few exceptions described above)

- property in your possession that belongs to someone else (for instance, property you are storing for someone), and
- wages that are withheld, and employer contributions that are made, for employee benefit and health insurance plans.

> **CAUTION**
>
> **Even if they are technically part of your bankruptcy estate, most retirement plans are exempt, which means you'll get to keep them anyway.** For example, IRAs and 401(k) plans are exempt in all states (although the exemption for IRAs is limited to $1,283,025 per person). For more information, see Appendix A.

You may be able to exclude funds placed in a qualified state tuition program or Coverdell education savings account from your bankruptcy estate, as long as both of the following apply:

- You deposit the funds into the account at least one year before filing for bankruptcy.
- The beneficiary of the account is your child, stepchild, grandchild, step-grandchild, or in some cases, foster child.

This exclusion applies to all funds placed in the account at least two years previous to your filing date. It is limited to funds of $6,425 or less placed in the account within a one-year period beginning two years before you file for bankruptcy. These rules can be tricky. Consider getting advice from a bankruptcy expert if you have made contributions to these types of accounts.

Inventory Your Property

If you decide to file for bankruptcy, you'll be required to list all property that belongs in your bankruptcy estate. Whether you can hold on to that property, or at least some of the property's value in dollar terms, depends on what the property is worth, which exemptions are available to you, and what type of bankruptcy you file. The best way to start finding out what you'll be able to keep in Chapter 7 or pay out in Chapter 13 is to create an inventory (list) of your property and match it with the available exemptions.

The simplest strategy is to start with the property items that you are most interested in keeping—and worry about the rest of your property only if and when you actually file for bankruptcy. Or, you can be more systematic and make a list of every single thing in your bankruptcy estate. If you're married and would be filing jointly, enter all property owned by you and your spouse (or the property that you both care about). Use Worksheet E: Personal Property Checklist in Appendix B to identify the property in your bankruptcy estate.

Worksheet F: Property Value Schedule

List the total replacement value of each item in your Personal Property Checklist.

Item	Replacement Value
1. Cash	$ _____
2. Bank accounts	_____
3. Security deposits	_____
4. Household goods and furniture	_____
5. Books, pictures, etc.	_____
6. Clothing	_____
7. Furs and jewelry	_____
8. Sports and hobby equipment	_____
9. Interest in insurance	_____
10. Annuities	_____
11. Pensions and profit-sharing plans	_____
12. Stock and interest in business	_____
13. Interest in partnership and ventures	_____
14. Bonds	_____
15. Accounts receivable	_____
16. Alimony and family support	_____
17. Other liquidated debts, tax refund	_____
18. Future interests and life estates	_____
19. Interests due to another's death	_____
20. Other contingent claims	_____
21. Intellectual property rights	_____
22. Licenses and franchises	_____
23. Vehicles	_____
24. Boats, motors, and accessories	_____
25. Aircraft and accessories	_____
26. Office equipment, furniture, and supplies	_____
27. Machinery, fixtures, etc.	_____
28. Inventory	_____
29. Animals	_____
30. Crops—growing or harvested	_____
31. Farm equipment	_____
32. Farm supplies, chemicals, and feed	_____
33. Anything not listed above	_____
TOTAL	$ _____

Value Your Property

Use Worksheet F: Property Value Schedule, above, to figure out what each item is worth.

You can download this form (and all other forms in this book) from Nolo.com; for details, see Appendix B.

It's easy to enter a dollar amount for cash and most investments. If you own a car, start with the middle *Kelley Blue Book* price or, alternatively, the middle price calculated by the National Automobile Dealers Association (at www.nada.org). If the car needs repair, reduce the value by what it would cost you to fix the car. You can find the *Kelley Blue Book* at a public library or online at www.kbb.com. Alternatively, you can use the valuations provided at www.nada.org.

For bankruptcy purposes, you are supposed to compute the property's replacement value: what it would cost to buy identical property—considering its age and condition—from a retail merchant. If you use the Internet, visit eBay (www.eBay.com) to get a fix on the going price for just about anything. Or briefly describe the item in Google (or your search engine of choice) and see what turns up. As long as your valuations are based on the going retail price for the item in question, you should use the lowest value you can find, which means you are more likely to be able to keep the property under your state's exemption laws.

If you are filing separately and own something jointly with someone (other than a spouse with whom you would file for bankruptcy), reduce the value of the item to reflect only the portion you own. For example, you and your brother jointly bought a music synthesizer worth $10,000. Your ownership share is 40% and your brother's is 60%. You should list the value of the property you own as $4,000, not $10,000.

Even if you are married and filing separately in a community property state, include the total value of all the community property as well as the value of your separate property.

If you are married, you own the property with your spouse as tenants by the entirety, and you are filing separately, your ownership interest may not be 50% for purposes of computing your exemption. (Talk to a lawyer to find out what percentage of your tenancy by the entirety property you can claim as exempt.)

Understanding Exemptions

Bankruptcy is intended to give debtors a fresh start—not to leave them utterly destitute. You are entitled to keep certain property that the laws applicable to your bankruptcy categorize as exempt. Creditors cannot take exempt property as part of their collection efforts, and the bankruptcy trustee can't take it, either. Exempt property can literally range from "the shirt on your back" to a million-dollar estate, depending on which exemptions you are entitled to use.

Be Careful of Joint Ownership Accounts

Joint accounts are often created for purposes other than ownership of the funds in the account. For example, a parent commonly puts a child on his or her account to provide an easy means of inheritance. When the parent dies, the account automatically goes to the child. Or, the child may be added to the account to handle economic transactions for the parent. In these situations, it's clear to the parent and child that the funds belong to the parent, but absent a formal statement of this fact when setting up the account, a Chapter 7 bankruptcy trustee (in a bankruptcy filed by the child) might reasonably view the account as also belonging to the child. If so, the account (or at least half the account) might be considered property of the child's bankruptcy estate to be seized and sold unless the child claims it as exempt.

Fortunately, a legal doctrine known as "bare legal title" is sometimes used to exclude this type of property from the bankruptcy estate. In essence, the bankruptcy court rules that the parent has an equitable claim to the funds, which leaves the child with bare legal title to the account but with no right to the funds themselves. However, it's not enough to merely assert that the funds fall into the bare legal title doctrine; the court must believe that this was actually the intention of a chid and a parent when the account was set up.

State Exemption Systems

Every state has its own fairly lengthy list of exempt property. (You can find these lists in Appendix A.) In addition, some states offer bankruptcy filers an alternative choice of exemptions—a list of exempt property found in the federal Bankruptcy Code. States that offer this choice are: Arkansas, Connecticut, Hawaii, Massachusetts, Michigan, Minnesota, New Hampshire, New Jersey, New Mexico, Oregon, Pennsylvania, Rhode Island, Texas, Vermont, Washington, and Wisconsin. In these states, you must choose between the state exemption system and the federal exemption system (no mixing or matching allowed).

Although California doesn't make the federal Bankruptcy Code exemptions available, it has two separate exemption systems—both created by state law. Debtors who use the California exemptions must choose between System 1 (the regular state exemptions available to debtors in and out of bankruptcy) and System 2 (state exemptions available only in bankruptcy and very similar to the federal exemptions). Here, too, no mixing and matching.

How Exemptions Work

Under both the federal and state exemption systems, some types of property are exempt regardless of value. For example, in some states, home furnishings, wedding rings, or clothing are exempt without regard to value. In Washington, DC, homes are exempt regardless of their value or the value of the bankruptcy filer's ownership (equity) in the home.

Other kinds of property are exempt up to a limited value. For instance, cars are often exempt up to a certain amount—typically $2,500 to $5,000. The home equity exemption ranges from nothing in New Jersey to $15,000 in Missouri to $500,000 in Massachusetts, to no limit other than acreage in Florida, Texas, and a few Midwestern states.

When there is a dollar limit on an exemption, any equity above the limit is considered nonexempt. (Your equity is the amount you would get to keep if you sold the property.) Even though a portion of your ownership in these items is exempt, the trustee can seize and sell property in which your equity exceeds the exemption limit, give you your exemption amount, and distribute the remainder to your unsecured creditors.

Many states offer a "wildcard" exemption —a dollar amount that you can apply to any property, in order to make it (or more of it) exempt. This type of exemption typically runs from a few hundred to several thousand dollars (more than $28,000 in California's System 2 exemptions). If you use the federal exemptions, the wildcard is up to $13,100 for individuals and $26,200 for couples.

Where You Make Your Home

When we refer to the state "where you make your home," we mean the place where you are living and intend to remain living for the indefinite future, the place where you work, vote, receive your mail, pay taxes, bank, own property, participate in public affairs, register your car, apply for your driver's license, and send your children to school. Congress refers to this state as your "domicile." Your domicile might be different from where you are actually living if you spend time in one state but consider another state to be your true home. For example, members of Congress or the military, professional athletes, and corporate officials all might spend significant amounts of time working in another state or country; their domicile is the state where they make their permanent home.

Domicile has been defined as "the place where a man has his true fixed and permanent home and principal establishment and to which whenever he is absent he has the intention of returning." This means something more than your residence, which generally means wherever you are living at any given time. Even if you reside in one state, your domicile may be elsewhere—and your domicile determines which exemptions you can use.

EXAMPLE: Lucinda and Freddie file a joint bankruptcy petition in Vermont, which allows a choice between the Vermont state exemptions and the federal exemptions. Lucinda and Freddie rent their home but own a travel trailer with a value of roughly $20,000, which they want to keep. The Vermont state exemptions provide a wildcard allowance up to a maximum of $7,400, not nearly enough to protect the travel trailer. However, the federal exemptions provide a wildcard exemption for couples of $26,200 on any type of property. Lucinda and Freddie choose the federal exemptions, which also protect their other property, such as their furniture, animals, and tools of the trade.

When the Trustee Takes Property

As mentioned earlier, the trustee may seize and sell nonexempt property only in a Chapter 7 bankruptcy. As a practical matter, the trustee won't seize and sell property unless the value of the nonexempt portion, after the costs of storage and sale are deducted, is high enough to make it worth the trustee's while. For example, even if your used furniture exceeds the exemption limit in your state (assuming there is one), the trustee is unlikely to seize and sell the furniture unless it is quite valuable and could obviously be resold for an amount that will cover your exemption (whatever it

is) and still leave enough for your unsecured creditors to generate a decent commission for the trustee. (See "The Bankruptcy Trustee" in Ch. 1 for more on how trustees get paid.)

The kinds of property listed below are typically not exempt unless by application of a wildcard. If you are concerned about keeping any of these items, you should pay close attention to the exemptions that are available to you:

- interests in real estate other than your home (see Ch. 5 for more on residential property exemptions)
- substantial equity in a newer-model motor vehicle
- expensive musical instruments unrelated to your job or business
- stamp, coin, and other valuable collections
- cash, deposit accounts, stocks, bonds, and other investments
- business assets (other than tools of the trade, which are typically exempt)
- valuable artwork
- expensive clothing and jewelry
- antiques, or
- IRAs that have been inherited and that no longer have any restrictions on withdrawal.

Residency Requirements for Exemption Claims

Prior to 2005, filers used the exemptions available in the state where they filed for bankruptcy. Now, however, some filers may have to use the exemptions available in the state where they used to live. Congress became concerned about people gaming the system by moving to states with liberal exemptions just to file for bankruptcy. As a result, it passed residency requirements filers have to meet before claiming a state's exemptions. Here are the new rules:

- If you have made your current state your home for at least two years, you will file in that state and use that state's exemptions (subject to the homestead cap explained in Ch. 5).
- If you have made your current state your home for more than 91 days but less than two years, you will file in that state and use the exemptions of the state where you lived for the better part of the 180-day period immediately prior to the two-year period preceding your filing.
- If you have lived in your current state for fewer than 91 days, you must wait until you have lived there for 91 days to file in that state (then use whatever exemptions are available to you according to the rules above).
- If the state you are filing in offers the federal homestead exemption, you can use that exemption list regardless of how long you've been living in the state.
- If this system deprives you of the right to use any state's exemptions, you can use the federal exemptions, even if the state where you file doesn't offer this choice. For example, some states allow their exemptions to be used only by current state residents, which might leave former residents who haven't lived in their new home for at least two years without any available state exemptions.

A longer residency requirement applies to homestead exemptions: If you acquired a home in your current state less than 40 months before your filing date, your homestead exemption may be subject to a $160,375 cap regardless of which state's exemption system you use. (Ch. 5 covers homestead exemptions in detail.)

RESOURCE

Find state exemptions online. You can search the exemptions for your state at www.nolo.com.

EXAMPLE 1: Sammie Jo lives in South Carolina from July 2015 until January 2016, when she gets lucky at a casino, moves to Texas, and buys a car for $15,000. In March 2017, Sammie Jo files for bankruptcy in Texas. Because Sammie Jo has been living in Texas for only 14 months—not two years—before she files for bankruptcy, she can't use the Texas exemption for cars, which can be up to $50,000 depending on the value of other personal property claimed as exempt. Because Sammie Jo filed in March 2017, the two-year period begins in March 2015. And because Sammie Jo lived in South Carolina for the better part of the two-year period preceding the bankruptcy filing date, the South Carolina state exemptions are the only state exemptions available to her. As it turns out, the South Carolina exemption for cars is only $5,900, which means Sammie Jo will probably lose her car if she uses the South Carolina state exemptions.

However, Texas offers the federal exemptions as an alternative to its state exemptions. The state where a person files determines whether the federal exemptions are available, regardless of how long the person has lived in that state. This means that Sammie Jo can use the federal exemptions instead of the South Carolina state exemptions. Under the federal exemptions, Sammie Jo is entitled to exempt a motor vehicle up to $3,775—still not enough to cover her car, which is now worth $14,000. But wait. The federal exemptions also provide a wildcard of $1,250 plus $11,850 of unused homestead exemption. Sammie Jo rents rather than owns her home (and doesn't need a homestead exemption), so she can add the entire wildcard of $13,100 to her $3,775 vehicle exemption, for a total exemption applicable to her car of $16,875.

EXAMPLE 2: Julia lives in North Dakota for many years until she moves to Florida on January 15, 2016. She files for bankruptcy in Florida on November 30, 2017. Because she hasn't lived in Florida for two years (her two-year anniversary is January 14, 2018), Julia must use the exemptions from the state where she lived for the better part of the 180-day period preceding the two-year period—which is North Dakota. Julia's largest property item is a prepaid medical savings account deposit of $20,000. While this would be exempt under Florida law, North Dakota has no exemption for this item. Nor are the federal exemptions available in Florida. So the trustee will most likely seize the medical savings account and use it to pay Julia's creditors. Had Julia waited another month and a half to file, she would have been able to use Florida's exemptions and keep her medical savings account.

Using the Exemptions Appendix

You can find the exemptions for all 50 states in Appendix A. If you are considering filing for bankruptcy in one of the states listed below, you'll also want to look at the federal exemptions, which are listed right after Wyoming.

Use Appendix A to find the applicable exemptions for your property, using the rules set out above to determine which exemptions to use. Do this by comparing the type and value of your property, and the amount of equity you have in the property, with the exemptions. (You can find definitions of many of the terms in Appendix A in the Glossary at the back of this book.)

States That Offer the Federal Exemptions	
Alaska	New Jersey
Arkansas	New Mexico
Connecticut	New York
District of Columbia	Oregon
Hawaii	Pennsylvania
Kentucky	Rhode Island
Massachusetts	Texas
Michigan	Vermont
Minnesota	Washington
New Hampshire	Wisconsin

Remember, if you are filing in a state that offers the federal bankruptcy exemptions, you should also check the federal exemption chart. Items that aren't exempt under the state exemptions available to you may be exempt under the federal system, and vice versa. However, you must pick one system or the other to use in your bankruptcy—you can't mix and match.

If you are married and filing jointly, you can double the federal exemptions and any state exemptions unless the chart says that you can't. This will be indicated either at the top of the chart for the particular state or next to a particular exemption.

Assuming you live in California and meet the residency requirements for claiming that state's exemptions, you may choose System 1 (the regular state exemptions) or System 2, a state list that is derived from the federal exemptions but differs in important particulars. If you file in California but don't meet the residency requirements, you can't use either California system—you'll have to use the rules set out above to figure out which exemptions you can use.

Federal Nonbankruptcy Exemptions
If you are using the exemptions of a particular state rather than the federal exemptions, you may also exempt property listed in Appendix A under Federal Nonbankruptcy Exemptions. Don't confuse those with the federal bankruptcy exemptions, which may be used only if a state allows, and only as an alternative to the state exemptions.

Your Home

One of the biggest worries you may face in deciding whether to file for bankruptcy is the possibility of losing your home, whether you own or rent. If so, you'll be relieved to know that the bankruptcy system is not designed to put you out on the street.

If you can get and stay current on your mortgage payments, and your equity in your home is fully protected by an available exemption, your chances of keeping your home look good. If, however, your equity in the home is significantly more than the amount you are entitled to keep (called the "homestead exemption"), you might lose your home if you file under Chapter 7. In this situation, Chapter 13 bankruptcy will likely be a better option, assuming you qualify. (You'll have to pay an amount equal to your nonexempt equity—minus liquidation costs—over the course of three to five years.)

If you are behind on your mortgage payments when you file bankruptcy, the story is different. In a Chapter 7 case, your lender will probably be able to get permission from the bankruptcy court to initiate foreclosure proceedings.

If you are a renter facing eviction based on a court order, filing for bankruptcy is unlikely to improve your situation in most cases. If, however, you owe back rent but your landlord has not yet obtained a judgment of eviction, you can use bankruptcy to temporarily postpone the eviction in addition to discharging any liabilities arising from your tenancy.

This chapter covers:

- issues facing homeowners who file under Chapter 7
- issues facing homeowners who file under Chapter 13, and
- issues facing renters who file for bankruptcy under either chapter.

Homeowners Filing for Bankruptcy Under Chapter 7

If you are current on your house payments, you can figure out how bankruptcy will affect your home ownership by doing some simple math:

1. Compute your equity in your home.
2. Choose the appropriate homestead exemption.
3. Compare your equity to the homestead exemption.

If your equity is less than the homestead exemption, your home is protected. If your equity is more than the homestead exemption, your home is at risk. (See "If You Are Behind on Your Mortgage Payments," below, if you aren't current on your payments.)

Compute Your Equity

Your equity in your home is the amount you would end up with if you sold it. This is typically what it would cost you to sell the same property *less* what you will have to pay to others out of the sales price because of legal claims (liens) they have against the property (such as claims by your mortgage lender or the county tax collector). Don't include the costs of selling the house—such as closing costs or broker's fees—in your calculations. These costs will, however, be important in deciding later whether your home is safe from being sold by the trustee for the benefit of your creditors.

> **EXAMPLE:** Your house will sell for $300,000. You have a mortgage for $200,000. There are no other debts that have to be paid out of the sales proceeds. Your equity is $100,000. If there is a lien on your home, you must subtract that as well. For example, if you didn't pay the contractor who remodeled your kitchen and the contractor put a $20,000 lien on your home, your equity would be reduced by that lien amount, to $80,000.

If there's a money judgment lien on your home that would deprive you of your full homestead exemption if the property were sold, you can ask the bankruptcy judge to remove the lien. But even if you plan to petition to have the lien removed, don't include the amount of the lien when calculating your equity in the home. You can find out more about lien avoidance procedures in Ch. 10.

Assess the Fair Market Value of Your Property

When computing your equity, you must first assess your home's fair market value. When home values deteriorate, it's often difficult to know what a home is worth without actually selling it. Home values have traditionally been determined by comparables—what similar homes in the neighborhood have sold for. However, comparables are hard to come by when homes aren't being sold. And even when they are being sold, they aren't necessarily sold under normal market conditions. For example, homes that have sat empty for months as a result of a foreclosure sale may ultimately be sold to investors who are looking for rock bottom prices. If you use sales under those conditions to judge your home's value, you may not get what you think your home is worth. Still, in the final analysis, its value can only be determined by what it would sell for, and it may not sell for much more than was paid for the distressed home down the street. Probably the best way to pin a value on your home is to find a real estate agent who can give you an estimate. The amount will be the agent's best guess at what they could get for it if you put it up for sale. Alternatively, you can use the information databases available on the Internet (see below).

Fortunately, most areas in the country have rebounded after the great recession of 2008. Now you may run into the problem of having too much equity. If your home likely would sell for significantly more than what you owe, you have to determine whether that equity is protected by your state's exemption laws. If the real estate market in your area is appreciating quickly, you must make sure that you know the house value just before your bankruptcy filing date, so you can be sure your homestead exemption covers your equity.

Realtors in your area will know what similar homes have sold for and can give you a pretty accurate estimate of what they could get for your home. Most realtors will provide you with a written broker's price opinion free of charge.

Liens Exist Only If They're Recorded

A lien on real estate exists only if it has been recorded in the local land records office. For this reason, you can tell whether you have any liens against your property by paying that office a visit and searching its database. It's not uncommon for people to assert liens based merely on language in written agreements. For example, an agreement stating that Johnny owes Florence $2,000 and that Florence will have a lien on Johnny's home to secure repayment of the loan, does not by itself create the lien. The contract must be properly recorded.

RESOURCE

Using the Internet to find sales prices for comparable homes in your area. Information (purchase price, sales date, and address) is available free from sites including www.homevalues. com, www.zillow.com, and www.realtor.com. Simply enter your home's address or zip code.

Identify Liens on Your Property

When computing your equity, you must subtract any liens on the property. A lien is a legal claim on property that can only be removed voluntarily by the lienholder or by a court order. A mortgage, for example, is a debt that is secured by the property in the form of a lien.

Because a lien claims a right to some portion of the property's value, it "clouds" the owner's title to the property. Buyers don't want to buy property that is encumbered by liens—and insurance companies don't want to issue title insurance in this situation, either. As a practical matter, this means you will have to pay off liens in order to sell your house (unless you can get rid of the liens in your bankruptcy—which may be the case with liens arising from money judgments).

In addition to a mortgage, other typical liens arise from:
- second deeds of trust
- home equity loans and lines of credit
- money judgments issued by a court
- child support arrearages

- delinquent income or property taxes, and
- debts owed to people who improved the property but who weren't paid for some reason (these are called mechanic's and materialman's liens).

To compute your equity, deduct all liens on your home from its fair market value (what you could sell it for). If a debt is not secured by a lien on your home, you don't have to count it when computing your equity.

As explained above, you shouldn't count liens that can be removed in bankruptcy when calculating your equity. See "Eliminating Liens in Chapter 7 Bankruptcy" in Ch. 6 and "Lien Avoidance Motions" in Ch. 10 for more information on lien avoidance.

Choose Your Homestead Exemption

Your homestead exemption is the amount of equity in your home you are entitled to keep if you file for Chapter 7 bankruptcy. Every state has its own homestead exemption rules—and the exemption available to you will help determine whether you keep or lose your home. Because bankruptcy law imposes strict residency requirements for the use of a state's exemptions, however, you may not qualify for the exemption you want to use. This section explains the various types of homestead exemptions available, and how to figure out which one to use.

Types of Homestead Exemptions

Homestead exemptions vary tremendously from state to state. In fact, in a few states, the homestead exemption isn't a monetary amount at all—it's based on your lot size. On the other hand, in a handful of states there is no homestead exemption at all. Some states are at the other extreme and allow you to protect a very large amount of equity (for example, $500,000 in Massachusetts). In a few states, the homestead exemption is based on a combination of lot size and a monetary amount.

Homestead Exemptions Protect Only Residences

With very few exceptions, you must reside in the home as your primary residence when you file for bankruptcy in order to claim a homestead exemption. Homestead exemption laws do not protect second homes, vacation homes, or other real estate in which you aren't living when you file. They do, however, typically apply to a mobile home, an R.V., or a boat that you use as your primary residence.

Declared Homesteads

In California and many other states, the homestead exemption automatically kicks in when you file for bankruptcy. However, some states (listed below) require you to file a "Declaration of Homestead" with the county recorder in order to use the state's homestead exemption in bankruptcy. In rare cases, some states will allow you to claim an exemption for a declared homestead even if you aren't living in the home when you file.

States That Require a Declaration of Homestead	
Alabama	Nevada
Idaho	Utah
Massachusetts	Virginia
Montana	Washington

States With Two Exemption Systems

In 19 states and the District of Columbia, you must choose between two different homestead amounts—one offered by the state and one offered under the federal Bankruptcy Code. California also offers a choice between two different amounts, but both amounts are offered under California state law. (See Ch. 4 for more on these dual systems.)

Wildcard Exemptions

In some states, you can increase the amount of your homestead exemption with a state "wildcard" exemption—that is, a dollar amount that your state allows you to apply to any property, in order to make it (or more of it) exempt. The chart below lists the state wildcard exemptions that you can apply to real estate; although other states have wildcard exemptions, they can be applied only to personal property.

EXAMPLE: In Connecticut, the base homestead exemption is $75,000. In addition, Connecticut has a wildcard exemption of $1,000 applicable to any property. This means that if you don't use the wildcard exemption for other types of property, you can use it for your homestead, which would increase the exemption from $75,000 to $76,000.

State Wildcard Exemptions Applicable to Real Estate	
Connecticut	$1,000
Georgia	$1,200
Indiana	$10,250
Kentucky	$1,000
Maine	$400
Maryland	$6,000
Mississippi (available if you are 70 years or older)	$50,000
Missouri (more, if head of household)	$600
New Hampshire	$8,000
Ohio	$1,225
Pennsylvania	$300
Rhode Island	$6,500
Vermont	$7,400
West Virginia	$800

Tenancy by the Entirety

In 18 states, spouses are allowed to own property together in a form known as "tenancy by the entirety." If only one spouse files for bankruptcy, property the couple owns as tenants by the entirety is, generally, not part of the bankruptcy estate. In other words, the property is exempt in its entirety, regardless of its value. If, however, both spouses file, the property will be part of their bankruptcy estate and will be subject to the appropriate homestead exemption available to the couple under the rules discussed below.

States That Allow Spouses to Own Property in Tenancy by the Entirety	
Delaware	Missouri
District of Columbia	North Carolina
Florida	Ohio
Hawaii	Pennsylvania
Illinois	Rhode Island
Indiana	Tennessee
Maryland	Vermont
Massachusetts	Virginia
Michigan	Wyoming

Choose the Appropriate Homestead Exemption

As explained in Ch. 4, residency requirements determine which exemptions filers can use. In addition to these general rules, Congress passed even stricter residency requirements for claiming a state's homestead exemption, to discourage people from moving to states with more generous homestead exemptions just to file for bankruptcy.

If You Have Been Domiciled in Your State for at Least Two Years and You Acquired Your Current Home at Least 40 Months Before Filing
You can use your current state's homestead exemption without restriction.

> **EXAMPLE:** Mary and Peter are domiciled in Washington. They have owned their home for five years. They file for bankruptcy in Washington and can use Washington's homestead exemption without limitation (because they lived in Washington for at least two years and acquired their home at least 40 months prior to filing their bankruptcy). Because Washington offers the federal exemption option, Mary and Peter can choose either the Washington state homestead exemption or the federal homestead exemption. As it turns out, the Washington state homestead exemption is $125,000 compared to a maximum federal homestead exemption of $47,350 (for a couple filing together).

If You Have Been Domiciled in Your State for at Least Two Years and You Bought Your Home Within 40 Months of Filing, Using the Proceeds From the Sale of Another Home in the Same State
If you acquired your current home within 40 months of filing, but purchased it with the proceeds from the sale of another home in the same state that occurred at least 40 months earlier, you can use your current state's homestead exemption without restriction.

Choosing Between Exemption Systems Can Be Painful

As mentioned, California has two exemption systems and 17 states plus the District of Columbia give you a choice between the state exemptions and the federal exemptions. Sometimes it is an agonizing choice as to which system to use. For instance California System 1 allows up to $175,000 in home equity protection (depending on age, disability, and other factors) whereas System 2 only allows $26,800. On the other hand, not only does System 2 have a $1,425 wildcard exemption, but you can use any unused portion of the $26,800 homestead exemption to protect any property of your choice—essentially giving you a wildcard exemption worth $28,225. System 1 only lets you use the homestead exemption for home equity and doesn't provide a general-purpose exemption for personal property.

To see how this plays out, assume you have $50,000 worth of equity in your home and a car worth $15,000. If you use System 1, you can keep your home but you may have to give up your car, since that system only allows you to keep $3,050 worth of vehicle equity (more if your vehicle qualifies as a "tool of the trade"). In System 2, you could keep the car (by applying the $28,225 wildcard exemption to the $15,000 equity in your car), but would likely lose your home. Since you can't mix or match, you'll ultimately have to choose one system or the other. However, most people elect to keep their home. In this situation, meeting with a bankruptcy attorney to find out how to minimize your loss will likely be well worth the cost.

EXAMPLE: Violet and Robin have lived in Nevada for six years. When they first moved there, they bought a home for $175,000. Three years later, they sold that home and bought another home for $250,000. Although they have owned their current home for less than 40 months, they bought it with the proceeds of another Nevada home that they purchased more than 40 months before filing. Violet and Robin can claim Nevada's homestead exemption without restriction.

If You Acquired Your Home Within 40 Months of Filing and Have Been Domiciled in Your State Two Years or More

If you acquired your current home within the previous 40 months and have made your home in your state for at least two years, you can use that state's homestead exemption, subject to a $160,375 cap.

EXAMPLE 1: Three years ago, John and Susie moved from Massachusetts to Texas, where they bought a home. If they file for bankruptcy in Texas, they can claim the Texas homestead exemption because they have lived there longer than two years. However, because they bought the Texas home within the 40-month period prior to their bankruptcy filing, they will be limited to a homestead cap of $160,375. The Texas homestead exemption, which protects a home on up to ten city acres regardless of value, would typically protect John and

Susie's equity. However, because they're subject to the cap, their protection will be limited to $160,375.

EXAMPLE 2: Massachusetts provides a homestead exemption of $500,000. After moving from Vermont to Boston in 2015, Julius and his family buy a fine old Boston home in 2016 for $700,000. After borrowing heavily against the home because of financial reversals, Julius files for bankruptcy in early 2017. At the time Julius owns $250,000 equity in the house. Although the Massachusetts homestead exemption of $500,000 would easily cover Julius's equity, Julius may claim an exemption of only $160,375 because he acquired the Massachusetts house after moving from another state within the previous 40 months.

If You Have Lived in Your State for Less Than Two Years

If you moved to your current state within two years before filing bankruptcy, you must use the homestead exemption available in the state where you made your home for the better part of the 180-day period prior to the two-year period, subject to the $160,375 cap. However if the state where you are filing offers the federal homestead exemption, you can use that exemption regardless of how long you've been living in that state or when you bought your home.

EXAMPLE: Eighteen months ago, Fred moved from Florida to Nevada, where he purchased his current home with $400,000 he received from a recent inheritance. Fred files for bankruptcy in Nevada, his current state. Because Fred has not lived in Nevada for two years, and because he lived in Florida for the 180-day period prior to the two-year period preceding his bankruptcy filing, he must use Florida's homestead exemption, subject to the $160,375 cap. The cap imposes an extreme penalty on Fred. Florida's homestead exemption is unlimited while Nevada's is $550,000. However, because Fred can protect only $160,375, most of his equity in his home is nonexempt, which means that the trustee will undoubtedly sell the home, give Fred his $160,375, and distribute the balance to Fred's unsecured creditors.

If You Have Committed Certain Crimes, Torts, or Deception Against Creditors

Even if you qualify for an "uncapped" homestead exemption under the rules explained above, your exemption might be limited if you have engaged in particular types of misconduct. If you have committed a felony, a securities act violation, or certain crimes or intentional torts that have led to death or serious bodily injury, your homestead exemption may be capped at $160,375, depending on how the court sees your circumstances. For instance, the court might decide to lift the cap if it finds that the homestead in question is reasonably necessary for you to support yourself and your dependents.

Even if you haven't committed a crime or tort, your homestead exemption might be limited if you have tried to cheat your creditors. If you have disposed of non-exempt property with the intent to hinder, delay, or defraud a creditor at any time within the ten years before you file for bankruptcy, the value of your interest in your current home could reduced by the value of the property you unloaded, which means you may be left with little or no homestead protection.

Find Your Homestead Exemption

Once you have decided which state's homestead exemption you can use, turn to Appendix A at the back of this book and look in the top box for that state.

If you are married and filing jointly with your spouse, check to see whether you can double your state's homestead amount.

If the chart for your state indicates that the federal exemptions are available, compare your state's exemption with the federal homestead exemption, which currently is $23,675 for a single filer and double that for a married couple filing jointly, plus a general-purpose (wildcard) exemption of $1,250 for a single filer and double that for joint filers. So, under the federal exemptions, a married couple may exempt up to $47,350 plus $2,500, for a combined total homestead exemption of $49,850.

> **CAUTION**
>
> **Special considerations for states with bankruptcy-specific exemptions.** Some states have two sets of exemption schemes, one of which can only be used in bankruptcy. In the past, a few courts have ruled that the bankruptcy-specific exemptions are unconstitutional. (See Appendix A, "Special Considerations in States With "Bankruptcy-Specific" Exemptions.") As of this writing, all bankruptcy courts allow you to use bankruptcy-specific exemptions. However, if you live in one of these states, consider consulting with a local bankruptcy attorney to determine the applicable homestead exemption amount.

Compare Your Equity to the Homestead Exemption

Now that you've computed your equity and located the appropriate homestead exemption, it's time to put the two together. This comparison will tell you whether you can safely file for Chapter 7 bankruptcy and keep your home, or whether you should consider other options—such as filing under Chapter 13.

If You Have No Equity in Your Home or You Are Under Water (Upside Down)

If the total amount of debt against your home is equal to or more than its market value, you have no equity and aren't at risk of losing the home in bankruptcy as long as you keep current on your payments. This is true no matter how large or small the homestead exemption that's available to you and no matter how upside down you are. The trustee wouldn't get any money out of selling your home—all of the proceeds would go to the mortgage company and other creditors who have liens on the property.

> **EXAMPLE:** Your home is worth $325,000. You still owe $425,000. The trustee cannot sell the home because there isn't enough equity to fully repay the mortgage (the mortgage liens assure the mortgage holder of being paid in full). In other words, even if you live in a state that offers little or no homestead protection, you will still keep your home. The trustee can't profit from selling it because the value is less than what you owe on the mortgage.

If You Have Some Equity in Your Home

If the total amount of debt against your home is less than its market value, you will want to compare the difference—your equity—with the homestead exemption available to you. As long as the homestead exemption covers your equity, the trustee won't have any interest in selling your home; there wouldn't be any equity left over to pay your unsecured creditors, and the trustee wouldn't get any commission for the sale. Even if your equity exceeds the homestead limit, the trustee will likely figure in the costs of sale (about 6% of its selling price) before deciding whether it makes sense to sell the home.

> **EXAMPLE:** The real estate broker you used when you bought your home told you that it is currently worth $300,000. You owe your mortgage lender $250,000. The equity in your home is $50,000 ($300,000 minus $250,000). Suppose that if the trustee sells your $300,000 home, he or she will net approximately $275,000 because of the costs of sale and the trustee's commission. After paying the mortgage, the trustee would clear $25,000. If your homestead exemption is equal to or greater than $25,000, the trustee would gain nothing by selling the home. If a significant chunk of the $25,000 is unprotected by a homestead exemption, however, your home is in danger of being sold for the benefit of your unsecured creditors.

CAUTION

Tax liens get priority over homestead exemptions. Tax liens get priority over any exemptions that you can claim. In some cases, the bankruptcy trustee can sell your home for the benefit of the tax lien creditor and cut you out of receiving any homestead exemption. If you have a tax lien and your home is worth more than you owe on your mortgage, then Chapter 13 bankruptcy might be a better choice for you.

If Your Equity Is Significantly More Than Your Homestead Exemption

The homestead exemptions in some states are adequate to cover all or most of a person's equity, but not every state has an exemption.

As the economy has recovered, many homes have increased in value and equity that greatly exceeds the states' homestead exemption. These homes are at risk in Chapter 7 bankruptcy filings.

If you have nonexempt equity in your home (equity that isn't protected by your homestead exemption) and would lose it if you filed for Chapter 7 bankruptcy, you'll want to explore other options. For instance, if your home would sell for $300,000, the total liens are $100,000, and your state's homestead exemption is $100,000, you would have $100,000 of unprotected equity. The trustee would sell your home, pay off the $100,000 mortgage, pay you your $100,000 homestead exemption, and use the extra $100,000 (less costs of sale) to pay your remaining creditors. If some of this money were left after all creditors were paid in full (and the trustee took his or her cut), you would get that balance in addition to your homestead exemption.

If you have too much equity in your home, the better option might be to use some of it to pay off your debts and avoid bankruptcy altogether.

If You Are on a Fixed Income

If you have excess equity in your home, you may be tempted to take out a loan and use it to pay your debts. However, if you are on fixed income because of retirement or disability, you may not be able to make the payments on a loan. In other words, by borrowing to pay your debts, you may end up defaulting on the loan and losing your home to the lender.

> **EXAMPLE:** Trudy bought her home in 1956 for $56,000. Over the years, the value of the house has increased to $400,000. Trudy owes $175,000 in credit card debt and is considering filing for bankruptcy. Trudy wants to borrow against her home and pay off the debt, but her sole income is $800 a month from Social Security. She won't be able to make the payments on the loan.

Although this is a difficult situation, Chapter 7 bankruptcy is not the answer—you would lose your home to the trustee. You might be able to buy a new home with the proceeds from your homestead exemption (the trustee would pay you that in cash), but for many, the loss of a home would be traumatic.

In Trudy's case, depending on her age, the best option may be a reverse mortgage she can use to pay off the debt and augment her fixed income while remaining in her home for the rest of her life. The downside to this is that she won't be able to pass the home down to her kids or other heirs when she dies.

If You Are Behind on Your Mortgage Payments

If you are behind on your mortgage payments when you file for Chapter 7 bankruptcy, you will almost certainly lose your home to foreclosure unless you can get current in a hurry. As a general rule, your mortgage lender will ask the bankruptcy court to lift the automatic stay (the court order that bars creditors from trying to collect their debts, discussed in Ch. 1), and the court will probably grant the request, allowing the mortgage lender to begin or resume foreclosure proceedings.

The only way Chapter 7 bankruptcy can help you is if you can stave off foreclosure for the length of your bankruptcy case. When the case is over, and your other debts are wiped out or reduced, you may have an easier time getting and remaining current on your mortgage payments, assuming the lender hasn't yet accelerated (demanded full payment of the principal plus interest) the loan. Or, if you have funds in a retirement plan, you might be able to borrow enough money from the plan so that you can reinstate your mortgage. To reinstate a mortgage, you pay all back and current mortgage payments, plus various costs incurred by the lender due to your default.

Get Some Help Negotiating Your Modification

If you are trying to make your mortgage more affordable, either temporarily or in the long term, consider using a free HUD-certified housing counselor. These nonprofit counselors typically are employed by local community action agencies, but also can be located through a couple of national networks. To become certified, these counselors must attend an intensive week-long training sponsored by HUD, which schools them in every aspect of the mortgage business and the various modification procedures used for mortgages insured or owned by the various federal housing entities (Freddie Mac, Fannie Mae, and FHA). These counselors may have contacts within the various banks and companies involved in servicing mortgages and can assist you in working out a deal to make your mortgage more affordable. You can find a HUD-certified counselor at:

- HUD. Go to www.hud.gov and choose "Resources" and then "Foreclosure Avoidance Counseling."
- The Homeownership Preservation Foundation. Go to www.995hope.org or call 888-995-HOPE.
- The National Foundation for Credit Counseling. Go to www.nfc.org and choose "Housing Counseling" or call 866-557-2227.
- Making Home Affordable. Go to www.makinghomeaffordable.gov, choose "Get Started" and then "Speak With a Housing Expert."

Another option is to seek a loan workout modification from your lender that reduces your payments. You might qualify for a loan modification under one of the federal programs, or you might be able to negotiate a workout directly with your lender. Get Nolo's *The Foreclosure Survival Guide*, by Amy Loftsgordon, for more information on these options.

Negotiating With the Lender

If you've missed only a few mortgage payments, your lender may be willing to negotiate. What the lender agrees to will depend on your credit history, the reason for your missed payments, and your financial prospects.

Here are the possible options your lender might agree to:

- spread out the missed payments over a few months
- reduce or suspend your regular payments for a specified time and then add a portion of your overdue amount to your regular payments later on
- extend the length of your loan and add the missed payments at the end
- suspend the principal portion of your monthly payment for a while and have you pay only interest, taxes, and insurance, or
- modify your loan to reduce the interest rate and monthly payments.

States Where Judicial Foreclosure Is Customary	
Connecticut	Maine
Delaware	New Jersey
Florida	New York
Hawaii	North Dakota
Illinois	Ohio
Indiana	Oregon
Iowa	Pennsylvania
Kansas	South Carolina
Kentucky	Wisconsin
Louisiana	

If the Lender Starts to Foreclose

If your debt problems look severe or long-lasting, the lender may take steps toward foreclosure. In most cases, the lender will accelerate the loan before foreclosure actually occurs. Usually this means you must pay the entire balance immediately, or else the lender will foreclose. However, many states give you additional time to bring your loan current and thereby avoid foreclosure.

There are two different kinds of foreclosure. One is called a "judicial" foreclosure, so named because the lender must file papers in court and obtain the court's approval before foreclosing. In many judicial foreclosure states, this kind of foreclosure can take up to a year before you would lose your house. If you file Chapter 7 bankruptcy, you will add two or three extra months to that period (depending on whether your lender gets permission from the judge to proceed with the foreclosure before your bankruptcy runs its course). And, if you are salting away at least a portion of your mortgage payment each month, even a three-month delay can result in a substantial increase in your savings.

Your Lender Must Wait 120 Days Before Starting to Foreclose—But That Might Change

In 2014, the Consumer Financial Protection Bureau passed regulations that added 120 days to the state foreclosure process. The waiting period gives homeowners time to apply for a program with the mortgage lender that will allow the owner to stay in the home. If a homeowner submits a complete application, the lender must finish the review process before starting the foreclosure process—a protection that is especially important in states with a short foreclosure period. However, the law appears to be in limbo. The Trump administration has made clear that it seeks to dismantle the Dodd-Frank Act (the law that created the Consumer Financial Protection Bureau), and therefore, this protection might come to an end. We'll post updates on the companion page—www.nolo.com/back-of-book/FIBA.html—as changes occur.

States Where Nonjudicial Foreclosure Is Customary

Alabama	Montana
Alaska	Nevada
Arkansas	New Hampshire
California	North Carolina
Colorado	Oklahoma (unless homeowner requests judicial)
District of Columbia	
Georgia	Rhode Island
Idaho	Tennessee
Maryland	Texas
Massachusetts	Utah
Michigan	Virginia
Minnesota	Washington
Mississippi	Wyoming
Missouri	

The other kind of foreclosure is called a "nonjudicial" foreclosure, so named because the lender does not have to go to court in order to foreclose. Instead, a third-party trustee (not the bankruptcy trustee) sells your property after sending you a series of notices. This trustee is the person or business named in the deed of trust that you signed (or their successors in interest) instead of, or in addition to, the traditional mortgage when you purchased or refinanced your property. In some states (especially in the South), nonjudicial foreclosures can happen within a month or two, while in other states nonjudicial foreclosures take as long as or longer than judicial foreclosures—a year or more in some cases.

Using Foreclosure Document Deficiencies to Negotiate New Mortgage Terms

In order to foreclose on real estate, the party bringing the action has to be able to prove that it owns the mortgage. To do this, it must be able to produce the original promissory note or other proof showing that it is the current legal owner of the note. Because of the way mortgages were merchandised in the last few decades, many foreclosing parties have difficulty showing they own the mortgage. During the mortgage crisis, it came to light that many foreclosures were initiated on the basis of affidavits (statements under oath) falsely stating that the affiant had personal knowledge of the facts contained within the documents being sworn to. In fact, common practice was for individuals to swear to thousands of affidavits a month without any knowledge whatsoever of what was in the paperwork.

While such practices are not as prevalant as they once were, problems still exist. Homeowners can use possible defects in the mortgage ownership paper trail and the faulty ways in which foreclosure documents have been prepared to negotiate a way to stay in the home.

When the Automatic Stay Will Be Lifted to Permit Foreclosure

If you file for Chapter 7 bankruptcy and are behind on your payments, expect the mortgage lender to come to court and ask the judge to lift the automatic stay. (See Ch. 1 for more on the automatic stay.) If you have nonexempt equity in your home, the bankruptcy trustee is likely to successfully oppose the motion and sell the property for the benefit of your unsecured creditors (after the lender is paid off and you are paid the amount protected by the applicable exemption). If you have no equity, however, the trustee will probably not oppose the motion to lift the stay and will let the foreclosure go through.

During a foreclosure, you have several options (although if the creditor begins a nonjudicial foreclosure, some of them may not be available to you simply because of time constraints):

- Sell your house. If you don't get any offers that will cover what you owe your lender, the lender may agree to take less. This is called a "short sale."
- Get a new loan that pays off all or part of the first loan and puts you on a new schedule of monthly payments. If the original lender has accelerated the loan, you'll need to refinance the entire balance of the loan to prevent foreclosure.
- Reinstate the loan. If the lender hasn't accelerated the loan in some states, you can prevent foreclosure simply by

paying the missed payments, taxes, and insurance, plus interest.

- File for Chapter 13 bankruptcy. The section below explains how Chapter 13 bankruptcy can save your home if you are behind on your mortgage.
- Plan to lose your home. Take advantage of the foreclosure procedures—and delays inherent in bankruptcy—to stay in your home for as long as possible. (See "If Foreclosure Is Unavoidable," above.)
- Use faulty mortgage documents as a negotiating tool to get the lender to agree to new mortgage terms. If you suspect that a lender is wrongfully foreclosing on your home, it's a good idea to have a knowledgeable attorney review your case as soon as possible. (See "Using Foreclosure Document Deficiencies to Negotiate New Mortgage Terms," just above.)

Homeowners Filing for Bankruptcy Under Chapter 13

If you own your home and file for bank-ruptcy under Chapter 13, you won't face the same issues as you would under Chapter 7. Chapter 13 repayment plans are funded out of your projected disposable income, not your nonexempt property. As long as you can propose a legal plan out of your projected disposable income, you can keep your home no matter how much equity you have—or how large the homestead exemption available to you. As always, however, the devil is in the details.

Under the law governing Chapter 13, you must propose a repayment plan that pays your unsecured creditors at least as much as they would have received if you had filed for Chapter 7 bankruptcy. For example, if your creditors would have received $100,000 worth of unprotected (nonexempt) home equity in Chapter 7, you will have to pay your unsecured creditors at least $100,000 over the life of your plan (less what it would cost to sell the property and pay the trustee's commission). If you don't have adequate projected disposable income to pay that amount, the court will not confirm your plan and you'll find yourself in Chapter 7, or outside of bankruptcy if you choose to dismiss your Chapter 13 case. (See "Chapter 13 Eligibility Requirements," in Ch. 2, for more on how projected disposable income is computed.)

In this situation, an experienced bankruptcy attorney might be able to come up with a creative solution so that you afford your plan payments (although it's the exception, not the rule). For example, the court might approve a plan whereby you have an affordable monthly plan payment, and then later make up the difference with one, large balloon payment. To come up with the cash for the balloon payment, you could sell or refinance property that you own.

Determining Which State's Exemptions Apply

The starting point is to figure out which exemptions are available to you. "Choose Your Homestead Exemption," above, helps you make that determination for homestead exemptions in a Chapter 7 case. The same rules apply in a Chapter 13 case for the purpose of deciding the minimum amount your unsecured creditors must be paid. These rules are:

- If you acquired your home at least 40 months before filing, and have been domiciled in your state for at least two years, you can use your state's homestead exemption without restriction.

- If you acquired your home less than 40 months ago but you have made your home in your current state for at least 40 months and you purchased your current home with the proceeds from the sale of a former home in your current state, you can use your current state's homestead exemption without restriction.

- If you have made your home in your current state for at least two years but you acquired your home less than 40 months previous, you must use your current state's homestead exemption subject to a $160,375 cap.

- If you have made your home in your current state for less than two years, you must use the homestead exemption of the state where you were living for the better part of the 180-day period prior to the two-year period, subject to the $160,375 cap.

- If the state you are filing in offers the federal homestead exemption, you can use that exemption regardless of how long you've been living in the state or when you bought your home.

- If you don't qualify for any state's homestead exemption, you can use the federal homestead exemption.

For a discussion and examples of these rules, review "Choose Your Homestead Exemption," above.

CAUTION

You must count all your nonexempt property. In most cases, the equity you own in your home will be the big-ticket item that determines how much you must pay your unsecured creditors in a Chapter 13 bankruptcy. However, if you own other valuable property that is nonexempt, you must add in the value of that property to determine how much your unsecured creditors must get paid under your repayment plan. Chs. 4 and 6 discuss exemptions for other kinds of property; residency requirements apply to those exemptions as well.

Selling or Refinancing Your Home to Increase Your Disposable Income

As discussed in Ch. 2, you qualify for Chapter 13 only if you have enough projected disposable income to remain current on certain obligations and pay 100% of any arrearages owed on them. For instance, your repayment plan must propose to pay:

- usually 100% of all support arrearages owed to a child or an ex-spouse, as well as your current required payments on those obligations
- 100% of all arrearages on a mortgage as well as the current monthly payments (assuming you plan to keep your home)
- 100% of recent tax debt, and
- an amount to your unsecured creditors equal to the value of your nonexempt property.

These and other requirements often make it difficult, if not impossible, for some people to propose a viable Chapter 13 plan. In this situation, you may wish to use some or all of the equity in your home to help fund your Chapter 13 plan—particularly if your equity, when added to your projected disposable income, is sufficient to make your plan confirmable, but isn't enough to make a serious dent in your debt load.

> **EXAMPLE:** Ethan owes $125,000 in credit card debt and is contemplating bankruptcy. However, his income is insufficient to propose a confirmable Chapter 13 plan (because he owes back child support and taxes that he must pay in full). Chapter 7 also isn't an attractive option for Ethan because he would lose nonexempt property that he really wants to keep:

stock options and shares in a family corporation. Fortunately, Ethan owns a home that would produce $50,000 after costs of sale. If Ethan sells his home and devotes the proceeds to his plan, the plan will then become confirmable.

In order to use property to fund a Chapter 13 plan, you either must have:

- the sale proceeds in hand when you file your bankruptcy petition or shortly afterwards, or
- a feasible plan of sale that will convince the judge that you really will be able to sell the property and devote the proceeds to the plan.

Of course, if refinancing or borrowing against your home would pay off your debts outside of bankruptcy and still leave you with a manageable loan payment, this might be your best option. In fact, if you have (or can get) a sizeable sum of money to pay toward debt, some courts might find your Chapter 13 filing an abuse of the bankruptcy process. If you find yourself in this situation, you'll want to speak with a local bankruptcy attorney before filing your case. If your debts are already delinquent, your creditors may be willing to settle them for less than what you owe. In this situation, you might be able to use the refinance funds or sale proceeds to negotiate lump-sum payments on your debts at a large discount, and avoid filing for bankruptcy.

If Your Mortgage Is in Arrears but Foreclosure Hasn't Started

If you are behind on your mortgage and want to keep your home, immediately apply for a loan modification if time permits. If that is not feasible, then Chapter 13 will likely be your bankruptcy chapter of choice. As discussed above, filing for Chapter 7 bankruptcy usually won't prevent a lender from ultimately foreclosing on a mortgage default. But Chapter 13 is different. If you have enough disposable income to propose a plan that (a) makes your regular payments on your mortgage and (b) pays off your arrearage in a reasonable period of time, you will be allowed to keep your home as part of your Chapter 13 case.

> **EXAMPLE:** Kenny and Zoe, a married couple, pay $2,000 a month on their mortgage. They have fallen five payments behind and owe an arrearage of $10,000. If they file for Chapter 7 bankruptcy, the lender will get the bankruptcy stay lifted and proceed to foreclose on the loan. Because they want to keep their home, Kenny and Zoe file a Chapter 13 bankruptcy and propose a repayment plan that will, among other things:
> - pay their monthly mortgage of $2,000, and
> - pay another $300 (roughly) a month toward the arrearage.
>
> If the judge confirms their plan, and they remain current on their repayment plan payments, they'll be able to stay in the home.

Mortgage Modifications Under Chapter 13

In Chapter 13, the court can reduce the amount of your secured mortgage debt to the value of the property. The remaining mortgage debt becomes unsecured property. This is often referred to as a "cramdown." Unfortunately, you cannot cram down the mortgage on your principal residence. Therefore, this is helpful only for investment and vacation properties (and is used infrequently). Additionally, you must pay the entire crammed down amount of your mortgage over the life of your Chapter 13 plan, which cannot exceed 60 months. This makes many real estate cramdowns unworkable; most people cannot afford to pay off such a large sum in just five years.

> **EXAMPLE:** John and Carrie, a married couple, own their residence and a rental unit. The home is currently worth $200,000, and their mortgage is $250,000. Their rental unit is currently worth $100,000, and the mortgage is $125,000. If John and Carrie file for Chapter 13 bankruptcy, they cannot cram down the mortgage on their residence. However, they can cram down the mortgage on the rental unit to $100,000. But they would need to pay the entire $100,000 through their Chapter 13 plan.

Stripping Off Liens in Chapter 13

Chapter 13 provides another useful tool to homeowners with junior mortgages on their property, called lien stripping. With lien stripping, you are allowed to get rid of junior liens on your home if they are wholly unsecured.

What exactly does this mean? Junior liens are anything other than your first mortgage. So they would include second or third mortgages, HELOCs, and home equity loans. A lien or security interest is wholly unsecured if the equity in your property does not cover any of the lien amount. For example, say your home is worth $500,000, your first mortgage is $550,000, and your second mortgage is $50,000. Since your first mortgage is greater than the equity in your home, there is no equity left to cover your second mortgage. If a lender were to foreclose on your home, the first mortgage holder would get $500,000 and the second mortgage holder would get nothing. If a junior mortgage or home equity line is eligible for lien stripping, the formerly secured debt becomes unsecured debt. As we discussed earlier in this book, most Chapter 13 filers pay pennies on the dollar when it comes to unsecured debt.

You should be aware that you cannot strip junior liens in Chapter 7 bankruptcy. If you keep real estate in a Chapter 7 case, you'll remain responsible for all the associated debt.

Beware of Foreclosure "Rescue" Scams

Beware of foreclosure "consultants," lawyers, and other services claiming they can help you avoid foreclosure. Many of these services claim you have a legitimate defense to the foreclosure, when in fact you don't. Examples of what scammers tell frustrated homeowners include:

- If their lenders won't work with them, they have a legitimate defense to foreclosure (as discussed above, this is not true).
- If the homeowners cannot afford to pay the loans, it must be the lenders' fault.

Other foreclosure consultants claim they will help you avoid foreclosure—and then do nothing.

How do scammers get away with this? They are savvy enough to promise things the homeowner would desperately like to be true. And there just aren't enough resources available to prevent these scams or catch all of the scammers. The end result: You pay the consultant lots of money, and still lose your home.

You can find more information about foreclosure scams in *The Foreclosure Survival Guide*, by Amy Loftsgordon (Nolo).

If Your Mortgage Is in Arrears and the Lender Has Started to Foreclose

If your lender has started to foreclose, you can file for Chapter 13 bankruptcy and take up to five years to make up your missed payments, reinstate the loan, and keep making the payments under the original contract. This is called "curing the default." Your right to cure the default depends on how far along the foreclosure proceeding is. If the lender has accelerated the loan or obtained a foreclosure judgment, you usually can still cure the default. If the foreclosure sale has already occurred, however, Chapter 13 usually won't help. Cases have held that the bankruptcy court has no jurisdiction to undo a sale, even if state law might otherwise allow.

Raising Defenses to Foreclosure in Bankruptcy

If you have a legitimate defense to the fore-closure of your home, in most cases you can raise and litigate the issue in bankruptcy court. For example, if you are not in arrears on your mortgage as the servicer claims, you can raise this defense within your bankruptcy case. However, you will almost always need a lawyer to do this because the process is so complicated.

Some people erroneously believe that if their lender won't "work with" them (for example, by agreeing to a loan modification or some other way to avoid foreclosure), they have a legitimate defense to foreclosure. This is not true. Your mortgage loan is a contract and each party to the contract (that means you and your lender) must live up to the original bargain. If the agreement no longer works for you, the lender is under no obligation to modify your loan to help you out. If it refuses to do so, you can't raise this as a defense to the foreclosure.

If Foreclosure Is Unavoidable

If you owe significantly more on your mortgage than your home is worth, or you can't afford your mortgage (perhaps because of a reset in interest rates or a loss of income), consider using your state's foreclosure procedures to your best advantage. Depending on your state and your mortgage lender's policies, you can easily remain in your home for many months without paying a dime to anyone. By paying yourself all or a part of your mortgage instead of sending it to your lender, you can easily amass a savings of many thousands of dollars that will be available to you when you seek out new shelter. For example, assume that Kenny's mortgage payment increases from $1,200 to $1,500 because of a mortgage interest reset. Kenny has been able to afford the $1,200, but he can't meet the $300 monthly increase. Kenny decides to walk away from the mortgage. He stops making his mortgage payments and instead puts $1,200 a month into his own bank account. Kenny will probably have months of payment-free shelter before he has to move, meaning he will be able to save just by living in his house payment free.

Don't Walk Away From Home Equity—Let the Bankruptcy Trustee Help

Unfortunately, a homeowner who can't meet a mortgage payment or sell a home before a foreclosure can face losing a home with equity. If you find yourself in this situation, you might have another avenue to explore—filing for Chapter 7 bankruptcy. Although this approach won't help you keep the house, it might allow you to retain a portion of your equity—which is better than nothing when you're out of options. Here's how it works: The automatic stay will stop the foreclosure and give the bankruptcy trustee time to sell the home. Once sold, the trustee must pay off the mortgage. Then, in most cases, the trustee must give you the amount of equity that you're entitled to protect (exempt) in your state. After taking a percentage as a fee, the trustee will distribute the remaining proceeds to your creditors. Of course, this plan won't work unless there will be something left over for creditors. If the math doesn't work, it might make sense to give the trustee incentive to sell the house by claiming less than the full exemption amount. Finally, as with any unusual plan, you'll want to speak with a local bankruptcy attorney before proceeding forward. Not only will you want to make sure that you aren't doing anything inappropriate, but the attorney will likely have a working relationship with the trustee and will know the best way to approach the trustee on your behalf.

Importantly, if you react to foreclosure by selling your home (typically in a short sale) or offering the lender the deed back "in lieu of foreclosure," you will have to move out of the house much earlier than if you just wait out the foreclosure procedures in your home, and you will thus forgo this unique opportunity to amass a considerable savings. For more information on your state's foreclosure laws and strategies for remaining in your home payment free for the maximum period of time, see *The Foreclosure Survival Guide*, by Amy Loftsgordon (Nolo).

SEE AN EXPERT

If your lender has sent you a foreclosure notice, it may be time to consult with a bankruptcy or real estate attorney—quickly. You may have special legal options—and risks—in your state that are not discussed above. (See "The Risk of Deficiency Judgments," below.) If you think you can't afford an attorney, remember that you won't be paying your mortgage. For most people, just one month's mortgage payment is enough to buy an attorney's advice, if not outright representation. And if the attorney can help you stay in your home, payment free, for longer than you could stay there without the attorney's help, which is frequently the case, the attorneys' fees would be well worth it.

The Risk of Deficiency Judgments

In most states and with certain property and types of loans, the lender can get a deficiency judgment following a foreclosure. A "deficiency judgment" is a judgment for the difference between what you owe and what the lender gets for the property at auction. The creditor can use this deficiency judgment to collect the rest of the debt by seizing your other available property.

The possibility of a deficiency judgment could affect your strategy when facing a foreclosure. For instance, if you are at risk of a deficiency judgment, you might try to deed the property back to the lender, in exchange for a release from liability (commonly called a "deed in lieu of foreclosure"). But if your state doesn't permit deficiency judgments (called nonrecourse states), or your property is not subject to a deficiency judgment, you might benefit from fighting the foreclosure as long as possible without making any payments in the meantime.

These laws vary from state to state, which is one reason you may need to consult a real estate or bankruptcy attorney if you get a notice of foreclosure.

Renters Filing for Bankruptcy

If you're current on your rent payments and you file for either Chapter 7 or Chapter 13 bankruptcy, your bankruptcy should have no effect on your tenancy. Although your landlord might not like the idea that you filed for bankruptcy, chances are good that he or she won't even find out about it. Because you are current on your rent, you don't have to list your landlord as a creditor entitled to notice of the proceeding. Although you have to list on your bankruptcy papers any security deposits held by your landlord, you will probably be able to claim those deposits as exempt. And even if you can't, it's a rare trustee who actually will go after that money because it serves as collateral for the rental agreement (but be prepared just in case you have a hungry trustee).

If You Are Behind on Your Rent When You File

Back rent is dischargeable in both Chapter 7 and Chapter 13 bankruptcies. However, if you get very far behind on your rent, your landlord will likely file an action in court to evict you. If you file for bankruptcy before the court issues a judgment for possession (an eviction order), the automatic stay will prohibit your landlord from trying to evict you on the basis of your prefiling rent default during your bankruptcy—unless the landlord files a motion to lift the stay. However, if you don't stay current on your rent after you file, the landlord is free to seek your eviction on the basis of the postfiling rent default.

EXAMPLE: Aldo owes two months' back rent when he files for bankruptcy. At the time Aldo files, his landlord hasn't yet obtained a judgment of possession. The landlord can't evict him for this debt while the bankruptcy is pending unless he files a motion to lift the stay. However, if Aldo fails to pay rent on time after he files for bankruptcy, the landlord can give him a delinquency or "pay or quit" notice and file an eviction action in court if he doesn't move and the rent isn't paid as required. Also, many states and localities give landlords the right to evict tenants for no reason at all, as long as the tenant receives adequate notice and the landlord strictly complies with the state's eviction procedures. So, even if Aldo faithfully pays his rent on time after his bankruptcy, he might still lose his apartment.

If the Landlord Already Has a Judgment

If your landlord has already obtained a judgment of possession (or "eviction") against you when you file for bankruptcy, the automatic stay won't help you (with the possible exception described below). The landlord is entitled to proceed with the eviction just as if you never filed for bankruptcy.

If the eviction order is based on your failure to pay rent, you may be able to have the automatic stay reinstated. However, this exception applies only if your state's law allows you to stay in your rental unit and "cure" (pay back) the rent delinquency after the landlord has a judgment for possession. Here's what you'll have to do to take advantage of this exception:

Step 1: As part of your bankruptcy petition, you must file a certification (a statement under oath) stating that your state's laws allow you to cure the rent delinquency after the judgment is obtained and to continue living in your rental unit. Very few states allow this. To find out whether yours is one of them, ask the sheriff or someone at legal aid (if you have legal aid in your area). In addition, when you file your bankruptcy petition, you must deposit with the court clerk the amount of rent that will become due during the 30-day period after you file.

Once you have filed your petition containing the certification and deposited the rent, you are protected from eviction for 30 days unless the landlord successfully objects to your initial certification before the 30-day period ends. If the landlord objects to your certification, the court must hold a hearing on the objection within ten days, so theoretically you could have less than 30 days of protection if the landlord files and serves the objection immediately.

Step 2: To keep the stay in effect longer, you must, before the 30-day period runs out, file and serve a second certification showing that you have fully cured the default in the manner provided by your state's law. However, if the landlord successfully objects to this second certification, the stay will no longer be in effect and the landlord may proceed with the eviction. As in Step 1, the court must hold a hearing within ten days if the landlord objects.

SEE AN EXPERT

If you really want to keep your apartment, talk to a lawyer. As you can see, these new rules are somewhat complicated. If you don't interpret your state's law properly, file the necessary paperwork on time, and successfully argue your side if the landlord objects, you could find yourself put out of your home. A good lawyer can tell you whether it's worth fighting an eviction—and, if so, how to go about it.

Endangering the Property or Illegal Use of Controlled Substances

Under the new bankruptcy law, an eviction action will not be stayed by your bankruptcy filing if your landlord wants you out because you endangered the property or engaged in the "illegal use of controlled substances" on the property. And your landlord doesn't have to have a judgment in hand when you file for bankruptcy: The landlord may start an eviction action against you or continue with a pending eviction action even after your filing date if the eviction is based on property endangerment or drug use.

To evict you on these grounds after you have filed for bankruptcy, your landlord must file and serve on you a certification showing either of the following:

- The landlord has filed an eviction action against you based on property endangerment or illegal drug use on the property.
- You have endangered the property or engaged in illegal drug use on the property during the 30-day period prior to the landlord's certification.

If your landlord files this certification, he or she can proceed with the eviction 15 days later unless, within that time, you file and serve on the landlord an objection to the truth of the statements in the landlord's certification. If you do that, the court must hold a hearing on your objection within ten days. If you prove that the statements in the certification aren't true or have been remedied, you will be protected from the eviction while your bankruptcy is pending. If the court denies your objection, the eviction may proceed immediately.

As a practical matter, you will have a very difficult time proving a negative—that is, that you weren't endangering the property or using drugs. Similarly, once allegations of property endangerment or drug use are made, it's hard to see how they would be "remedied."

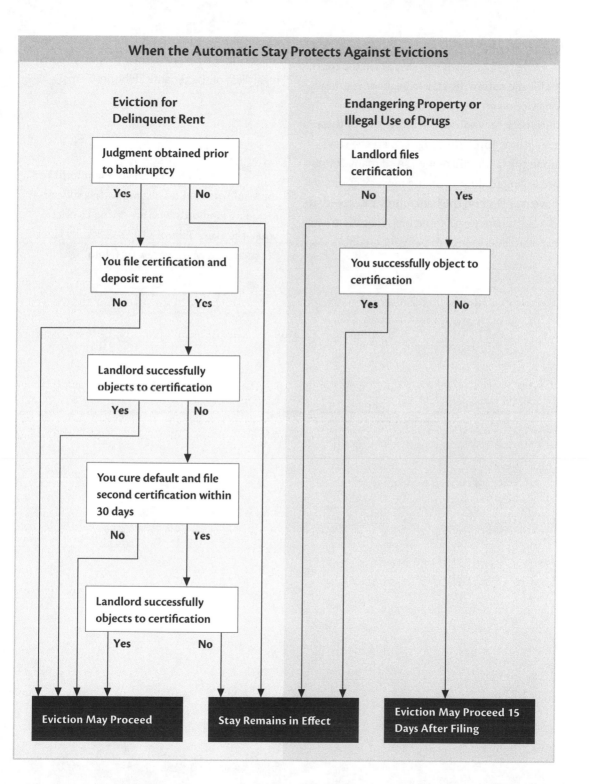

When the Automatic Stay Protects Against Evictions

Eviction for Delinquent Rent

Judgment obtained prior to bankruptcy
- Yes
- No

You file certification and deposit rent
- No
- Yes

Landlord successfully objects to certification
- Yes
- No

You cure default and file second certification within 30 days
- No
- Yes

Landlord successfully objects to certification
- Yes
- No

Endangering Property or Illegal Use of Drugs

Landlord files certification
- No
- Yes

You successfully object to certification
- Yes
- No

Eviction May Proceed

Stay Remains in Effect

Eviction May Proceed 15 Days After Filing

CAUTION

Landlords can always ask the court to lift the automatic stay to begin or continue an eviction on any grounds. Although the automatic stay will kick in unless one of these exceptions apply, the judge can lift the stay upon the landlord's request. And many courts are willing to do so, because most evictions will have no effect on the bankruptcy estate—that is, your tenancy isn't something that the trustee can turn into money to pay your creditors. As a general rule, bankruptcy courts are inclined to let landlords exercise their property rights regardless of the tenants' debt problems.

RESOURCE

Need help with your landlord? For more information on dealing with landlords— including landlords who are trying to evict you—see *Every Tenant's Legal Guide,* by Janet Portman and Marcia Stewart (Nolo). ●

What Happens to Personal Property That Secures a Loan

This chapter explains what happens to personal property you are making payments on when you file for bankruptcy—typically, a car or major household furnishings, such as living room or bedroom sets. It also covers other collateral: property you already owned that you pledged as security for a personal or business loan.

What Are Secured Debts?

Almost without exception, if you are making payments on property, you have agreed that the property will serve as collateral for repayment of the debt. This means that if you default on your payments, the creditor (or lender) can repossess the property, sell it, and obtain a court judgment against you (a deficiency judgment) for the difference between what you owe and what the property sold for. In bankruptcy, debts secured by collateral are called "secured debts."

How Secured Debts Are Handled in Chapter 7 Bankruptcy

Secured debts are treated differently in bankruptcy than other kinds of debts. Unlike a credit card debt or medical bills, a secured debt has a piece of property attached to it. Although the debt itself may be discharged in bankruptcy (and usually is), the creditor may still have a right to take the property back if you default on the payments.

A secured debt has two parts:

- **Personal liability.** You have personal liability for a secured debt just as you would for any other debt. This is what obligates you to pay the debt to the creditor. Chapter 7 bankruptcy wipes out this personal liability if the debt is otherwise dischargeable. Once your personal liability is eliminated, the creditor cannot sue you to collect the debt.

- **Security interest.** The second part of a secured debt is the creditor's legal claim (lien or security interest) on the property that serves as collateral for the debt. The lien gives the creditor the right to repossess the property or force its sale if you do not pay the debt. And liens are not affected by the bankruptcy discharge. In other words, by failing to remain current on payments, you can lose the property, even if the debt itself is discharged. (In some cases, however, you can ask the bankruptcy court to remove the lien as part of your bankruptcy case.)

If You Are Current on Your Payments

If you are current on your payments for a secured debt when you file Chapter 7 bankruptcy, you can surrender the property and discharge the underlying debt (that is, you can walk away from the contract free and clear). Or, you can keep the property if both of the following apply:

- Your equity in the property, if any, is protected by an applicable exemption (see below).
- You are willing to take one of the two available options for secured debts—reaffirmation or redemption (see below).

Does an Exemption Protect Any Equity You Have in the Property?

You have equity in property serving as collateral if it could be sold for more than you owe. For instance, if you owe $3,000 on a car loan and the car could be sold for $6,000, you have $3,000 worth of equity. This equity is part of your bankruptcy estate (see Ch. 4), which means the trustee can take it unless it's protected by an exemption. In this example, if you have $3,000 equity in your car and the exemptions available to you allow only $1,000 for motor vehicles, the trustee could sell the car, pay your secured creditor the $3,000 you still owe, give you your $1,000 exemption in cash, and distribute the remaining $2,000 (less costs of sale and the trustee's commission) to your unsecured creditors.

 RELATED TOPIC

Information for homeowners. See Ch. 5 for information on computing your equity in a home.

Debtors frequently owe more on a secured loan than the property securing the debt is worth—which by definition means they have no equity in the property. Typically, the interest that is charged on a secured loan often makes your total payment much higher than it would be if you had paid cash for the property. Also, even though the value of the property decreases (depreciates) over time, your loan and accompanying interest is based on the value of the property when you bought it.

If you have no equity in the property, or if your equity is fully protected by an available exemption, the trustee will have no interest in the property. You can either surrender it to the secured creditor or take one of the actions explained in "Redemption and Reaffirmation," just below, if you want to hold on to the property.

Redemption and Reaffirmation

Even if the trustee isn't interested in taking your property (because there is insufficient equity to produce payments to your unsecured creditors), that doesn't necessarily mean you get to keep it. The creditor still has that lien on the property, which means you might lose it to repossession unless you are current on your payments and use one of the remedies explained in this section.

Of course, you always have the option of simply giving the secured property to the creditor. Surrendering the property completely frees you from the debt, quickly and easily: The lien is satisfied by your surrender of the property, and your personal liability is discharged by the bankruptcy. The downside, obviously, is that you lose the property.

If you want to hang on to secured property, you have two options: redemption or reaffirmation.

Redeem the Property

In Chapter 7 bankruptcy, you have the right to "redeem" property—that is, to buy it back from the creditor with a lump sum, rather than have the creditor take it and sell it to someone else. Under the new bankruptcy law, if the property is used for personal, family, or household purposes, you can redeem it by paying the replacement value—the price a retail merchant would charge for property of that kind, considering the age and condition of the property at the time you redeem it. This means, for example, that you can redeem a car for the middle price listed in the *Kelley Blue Book* (www.kbb.com) or similar car valuation systems, such as www.nada.com.

At first glance, redemption doesn't seem like much of a remedy. After all, if you are filing for bankruptcy, how can you afford to buy the property outright? The answer is that all cash and other property you acquire after your bankruptcy filing date is yours to do with as you please (with the few exceptions explained in Ch. 4) and can be used to redeem property. For instance, you can sell some of your exempt property (with the trustee's permission during the time you are in bankruptcy), get a loan from family or friends, or work overtime to raise the money.

Redemption is a great option if your debt substantially exceeds the property's value. The creditor must accept the replacement value of the item as payment in full, even if you owe much more. However, you do have to come up with the replacement value of the property in a lump sum. If you can't afford to do that, you may be able to file a Chapter 13 case and pay off the property's replacement value over the life of your plan rather than through a lump sum payment.

You have the right to redeem property in a Chapter 7 bankruptcy only if all of the following are true:

- The debt is a consumer debt on goods used for personal or household purposes. This means you cannot redeem property that secures business debts or a car that you use for business purposes.
- The property is tangible personal property. "Personal property" includes everything but real estate. "Tangible property" is property you can touch, such as a car or stereo system. (Examples of intangible personal property, for comparison purposes, include investments, like stocks and bonds, or intellectual property rights, like patents, trademarks, and copyrights.)
- You have either claimed the property as exempt or the trustee has abandoned it because it has little or no equity.

Reaffirm the Debt

When you "reaffirm" a debt, you and the creditor use an official form to set out the amount you owe and the terms of the repayment. In essence, this restores the old

Negotiate for Better Terms

There is no requirement that your reaffirmation agreement contain the same terms as your current agreement, although you have a right to reaffirm under the same terms if you can't get better terms through negotiation. While your lender ultimately has the right to hold you to the same terms, bankruptcy law gives you the right to surrender the property and walk away from the note without paying a penny. Because the lender will lose a ton of money if it has to auction off the property after you surrender it, you do have some leverage to negotiate a better deal.

Assume you are paying $350 a month on a 2015 Ford F-250 truck. When you file bankruptcy in 2017, the truck is worth $14,000 but you still owe $22,000. The lender sends you a reaffirmation agreement containing the same terms as the old note. You call the lender back and explain that you won't be able to afford $350 a month but that you are willing to reaffirm if the lender reduces the principal to the current value of the truck, and the payment from $350 to $250 a month. The lender rejects your offer but counteroffers with a plan that will require payments of $300 a month and a longer time to pay off the note. Because you really do want to keep the truck, you accept the offer and the lender sends you a new reaffirmation agreement to be signed and filed with the court.

debt with the same terms set out in the original contract. You might even be able to negotiate better terms. Although getting better terms is rare for car loans, many debtors can negotiate much better terms for loans on appliances, jewelry, furniture, and electronics. In return, you get to keep the property as long as you keep current on your payments under the new agreement. If the debt is reaffirmed, both the creditor's lien on the collateral and your personal liability under the new contract survive bankruptcy.

Reaffirmation can be used when redemption is unavailable or impractical. It provides a sure way to keep property, as long as you abide by the terms of the reaffirmation agreement. But because reaffirmation leaves you personally liable, there is no way to walk away from the debt after your bankruptcy, even if the property becomes worthless or you simply decide you no longer want it. (Remember, you will have to wait eight years to file another Chapter 7 bankruptcy case.)

As a general rule, you should sign a reaffirmation agreement only if it is the sole way to keep property you can't be without, and you have good reason to believe you'll be able to pay off the balance. For example, many people use reaffirmation to keep a car, one of the few essential items of property in today's world.

The reaffirmation agreement form contains a number of disclosures about what you are getting into by reaffirming the debt. If you are represented by an attorney, the agreement becomes effective upon its signing unless the attorney refuses to approve the reaffirmation (perhaps because the attorney believes the payments would be a substantial hardship). If you are not represented by an attorney, or the attorney refuses to sign off on it, the agreement will become effective only after it has been filed with the court and approved by the bankruptcy judge in a court hearing near the end of your bankruptcy that you must attend.

At the hearing, the judge will only approve the agreement if he or she determines that it is in your best interest. To that end, the judge will look at the income and expense schedules you filed with your other bankruptcy paperwork and consider whether continuing to make payments on the debt will be a substantial hardship or interfere with your ability to get a fresh start through bankruptcy. While the judge will probably be sympathetic to your desire to keep your ride, he or she may nevertheless disapprove the reaffirmation agreement. Some courts have ruled that if you do everything you are supposed to do to reaffirm—that is, agree to reaffirm in your Statement of Intention, sign and file the reaffirmation agreement in court, and appear at the reaffirmation hearing—bankruptcy law authorizes you to retain possession of the car as long as you remain current, regardless of whether the judge approves or disapproves the agreement. Oddly, you will be better off if the judge disapproves

the agreement because then you won't owe a deficiency if you have to return the car after bankruptcy. But you'll be able to keep the car as long as you remain current on your payments. However, this approach won't help your credit. To do that, you'll need to sign a reaffirmation agreement. That's because the creditor won't report your on-time payments to the credit reporting agencies unless you have a reaffirmation agreement.

TIP

Most bankruptcy judges won't approve the reaffirmation of an unsecured debt. Some debtors want to keep a credit card that has a balance and are told by the credit card company that they can do that if they agree to reaffirm the debt. While this may technically be true, very few judges would approve such a reaffirmation agreement. Why not? From the judge's viewpoint, a reaffirmation agreement on an unsecured debt provides no benefit to the bankruptcy debtor (other than the right to keep the card) and is therefore not a legal contract.

The Statement of Intention for Individuals Filing Under Chapter 7

As part of your bankruptcy case, you are required to file an official form called a "Statement of Intention," which tells your secured creditors what you plan to do with the collateral. That is, you must tell them whether you plan to surrender the collateral, redeem it, or reaffirm the debt.

Keeping Property Without Reaffirming or Redeeming

Prior to the 2005 changes in the bankruptcy law, many bankruptcy courts allowed a debtor to keep secured property without going through the reaffirmation process, provided he or she remained current on payments under the contract with the creditor. If the debtor fell behind, the creditor could take the property, but the debtor's personal liability for the debt was wiped out by the bankruptcy. This method was often referred to as the "retain and pay" or "ridethrough" option.

According to recent court decisions, this remedy is no longer available under bankruptcy law. However, if the law of your state forbids creditors from enforcing a lien on your property as long as you are current under the contract, your creditors may have to let you keep the property as long as you remain current, no matter what the new bankruptcy law says. Many creditors are perfectly happy with this arrangement to this day; they would rather have a steady payment stream on the original contract than repossess used property that has to be sold at auction. However others—especially credit unions—have increased repossessions even when the debtor's payment is current.

If you don't file the Statement of Intention within 30 days after you file your bankruptcy petition, your creditor can repossess the property in the manner permitted by state law. Repossession may also occur if you fail to carry out your stated intention within 45 days of filing the statement.

If You Are Not Current on Your Payments

If you're behind on your payments to a secured creditor and don't have the ability to get current, Chapter 7 bankruptcy probably won't prevent the creditor from repossessing the property. While your bankruptcy filing will initially stop any repossession activity, the creditor can ask the court to lift the automatic stay or repossess the property after your bankruptcy case is closed. If you are behind on your payments, most courts will lift the stay in order to let the creditor proceed with repossession. (For more on the automatic stay, see Ch. 1.) If you want to keep the property, you'll need to reinstate the loan outside of bankruptcy, by making up the missed payments (and fees associated with the default) and by resuming your regular payments.

If your lender has already accelerated the loan (declared the entire balance due) and won't let you reinstate it, you can file for Chapter 13 bankruptcy. You can make up the missed payments in your plan as long as you also make the regular payments called for under your original agreement. (See Ch. 2.) Also, in Chapter 13, you may be able to reduce the total amount of your payments to the property's actual value.

Eliminating Liens in Chapter 7 Bankruptcy

During your Chapter 7 bankruptcy case, you may be able to eliminate a lien on an item of secured property. If you can eliminate, or "avoid," a lien, you get to keep the property free and clear, without paying anything more to the creditor. To avoid a lien, you must be able to claim an exemption in the property that is impaired by the lien—that is, that the lien deprives you of your right to benefit from the exemption because you can't sell the property without paying off the lien. (See Ch. 4 for more on exemptions.)

For the purpose of lien avoidance, there are two types of liens: (1) judicial liens, and (2) liens you agree to have placed on property you already own in exchange for a personal loan. A judicial lien is one that was placed on your property to collect a court judgment for money. The second type of lien is called a nonpossessory, nonpurchase money lien because the lienholder doesn't possess the collateral (as would be the case if the lien were owned by a pawnbroker), and you didn't use the loan to buy the collateral.

A judicial lien may be "avoided" (wiped out) on any type of property, including real estate, to the extent the lien "impairs an exemption." A nonpossessory, non-purchase money lien, on the other hand, may be avoided only on certain types of personal property (see below).

In most courts, lien avoidance actions are relatively simple. Most of the time, the lien owner doesn't contest the motion, so you'll just have to make sure you get the paperwork right. On occasion, however, a lien owner may object, which means you will have to participate in one or more court hearings, depending on the type of objection. (The procedural steps necessary for lien avoidance are described in more detail in Ch. 10.)

Avoiding Judicial Liens

Most judicial liens occur when:

- You've been sued for money and lost.
- The judgment creditor (the winner of the lawsuit) obtains a judgment against you for a sum of money.
- The judgment is recorded against your property in the form of a lien.

Most often, judicial liens are imposed on real estate. Judicial liens can also be imposed on business assets; almost all states provide a way to do this under the Uniform Commercial Code. However, liens are seldom, if ever, attached to consumer goods because ownership of consumer personal property is rarely recorded in public documents.

If paying a judicial lien would deprive you of any part of the exemption you are entitled to claim on the property, you can get rid of the lien by following the lien avoidance process outlined in Ch. 10. A few courts have ruled that you can avoid a judicial lien even if you have no equity in the property. Be sure to speak to an attorney about the possibility of avoiding the lien even if you are underwater on the mortgage.

Avoiding Nonpossessory, Nonpurchase Money Liens

A nonpossessory, nonpurchase money security lien is almost always created when a consumer obtains a personal loan from a finance company. These liens can be avoided only on the following types of property (and only if the property is exempt without regard to your equity in the property):

- household furnishings, household goods (see the list below), clothing, appliances, books, musical instruments, or jewelry
- health aids professionally prescribed for you or a dependent
- the first $6,425 of a lien attaching to animals or crops held primarily for your personal, family, or household use, and
- the first $6,425 of a lien attaching to tools used in your trade.

Under bankruptcy law, the term "household goods" is limited to:

- clothing
- furniture
- appliances
- one radio
- one television

- one VCR (the statutory language hasn't been updated to take DVDs into account)
- linens
- china
- crockery
- kitchenware
- educational equipment and materials primarily for the use of your minor dependent children
- medical equipment and supplies
- furniture exclusively for the use of your minor children or elderly or disabled dependents
- your personal effects (including the toys and hobby equipment of your minor dependent children and your wedding rings) and those of your dependents, and
- one personal computer and related equipment.

The following are not considered to be household goods, and you cannot avoid liens on them:

- works of art (unless they are by you or a relative)
- electronic entertainment equipment with a fair market value of more than $675 in the aggregate (excluding the one television, one radio, and one VCR listed above)
- items acquired as antiques with a fair market value of more than $675 in the aggregate
- jewelry with a fair market value of more than $675 in the aggregate (excluding wedding rings), and

- a computer (excluding the computer equipment listed above), a motor vehicle (including a tractor or lawn tractor), a boat, or a motorized recreational device, conveyance vehicle, watercraft, or aircraft.

To avoid a nonpossessory, nonpurchase money lien, you must have owned the property before the lien was "fixed" on it. This will almost always be the case with this type of lien. See Ch. 10 for more on lien avoidance.

How Secured Debts Are Handled in Chapter 13 Bankruptcy

Secured debts are handled completely differently in Chapter 13 than in Chapter 7. By filing for Chapter 13 bankruptcy, you can keep property subject to a secured debt even though you are behind on your payments when you file. Under your Chapter 13 plan, you can pay off the arrearage (the defaulted payments) over the course of the plan, as long as you meet your current payment obligations during that time.

Surrendering Property

If you don't want to keep property that is subject to a secured debt, you can surrender it to the creditor and schedule what you still owe on the contract as an unsecured debt. This means that you may have to pay a portion of the debt over the life of your plan, depending on the factors described in Ch. 2, "Chapter 13 Eligibility Requirements."

Reducing Secured Debt to the Property's Value (Cramdowns)

If you want to keep property that is worth less than what you still owe on it, you can propose a plan that pays off the replacement value of the property over the life of the plan (rather than what you owe on the contract). For example, if you owe $20,000 on the property and its replacement value is $10,000, you can propose a plan that pays only $10,000. If you complete your plan, then you'll own the property free and clear. This remedy of reducing a secured debt to the replacement value of the collateral is known as a "cramdown," a most descriptive term.

> EXAMPLE: Dave owes $13,000 on his car, and its replacement value is $8,000. Dave can propose to pay $8,000 in equal payments over the life of his plan, and then own the car outright once he obtains a discharge.

If you fail to complete your Chapter 13 plan, the cramdown is cancelled and you must pay the full balance of the debt before obtaining title.

There are three important exceptions to the cramdown rule:

- You can't cram down a debt owed on a motor vehicle purchased within 30 months of your filing date if you bought the car for your personal use. However, if you use the car as part of your business, you can cram down the debt without regard to the 30-month restriction.

- You can't cram down a debt owed on other personal property purchased within a year of your filing date.
- You can't cram down a mortgage that is used exclusively for your primary residence.

The purpose of these restrictions is to prevent people from purchasing cars or other property with the intent to file for bankruptcy and use the cramdown remedy. The good news is that, because you can't cram down the debt, you might be able to surrender the vehicle and perhaps get off the hook for the entire debt. However, the majority of the courts that have decided this issue require you to include the deficiency as an unsecured debt when you formulate your plan.

Continuing the Contract

If you want to continue the secured debt as before, all you have to do is provide in your proposed plan that you will remain current on the contract during the life of the plan. If you don't complete your Chapter 13 plan, but are still making payments on the secured debt, you can either convert to Chapter 7 and use one of the remedies described in "How Secured Debts Are Handled in Chapter 7 Bankruptcy," above, or continue making the payments outside of bankruptcy. Keep in mind, however, that if you have crammed down a debt in Chapter 13 and then convert to Chapter 7, you'll lose the benefit of the cramdown. This means you'll owe the original amount of the debt (minus any amount paid through the plan) to the creditor. If you want to keep the property, you'll have to cure the default or make some other arrangement with the creditor. If you are still in Chapter 13 and something happens to the collateral (for example, it is destroyed in an accident), it is usually possible to amend your plan and reschedule what you still owe as unsecured debt.

Making the Decision

The previous chapters explain how bankruptcy works in general to stop collection efforts and give you a fresh start, how the two main types of consumer bankruptcy—Chapter 7 and Chapter 13—will affect your debts and property, and how to determine your eligibility for each. It's a lot of information to absorb, especially when making the choice between chapters.

To help you sort through this information, weigh the pros and cons, and reach a decision, this chapter gives you a transcript of a consultation between a debtor and a lawyer. As you'll see, the debtor, Georgia Cox, is trying to figure out whether to file for bankruptcy under Chapter 7 or Chapter 13. She has decided to consult with a bankruptcy lawyer to help her with her decision. The questions the lawyer asks will help remind you of factors you should consider as you evaluate your own situation.

Lawyer: Hi, Georgia. How can I help you today?

Debtor: Well, I've run up quite a bit of debt, and I might want to file for bankruptcy. I know there are different types of bankruptcy, but I need some help figuring out what my options are.

Lawyer: Okay, I can help you with that. The two basic types of bankruptcy for individuals are Chapter 7 bankruptcy and Chapter 13 bankruptcy. There are a couple of major differences between them. In a Chapter 13 bankruptcy, you pay down some or all of your debts over a three- to five-year period and discharge (cancel) whatever is left over at the completion of your plan. In a Chapter 7 bankruptcy, you don't pay down any of your debt, and the entire process takes between three and four months. But you may have to give up property you own so it can be sold and the proceeds distributed to your creditors.

In either type of bankruptcy, some types of debts aren't discharged, but will survive your bankruptcy. For instance, overdue child support must be paid in full as part of a Chapter 13 bankruptcy. Also, some debts that can be discharged in Chapter 13 will survive a Chapter 7 bankruptcy. But we'll get to that later. Do you have any questions so far?

Debtor: I kind of already knew most of what you just told me and I'm leaning toward Chapter 7 since it's over a lot sooner and seems like it's a lot simpler. But would Chapter 13 would be the better choice for me?

Lawyer: Okay. Well, let's think this through. Some people aren't eligible to file for Chapter 7 bankruptcy. Let's start there. Then, if both options are available to you, we can talk about which one makes more sense.

Debtor: Sounds good.

Lawyer: I'm going to start by asking you a few questions: What state do you live in?

Debtor: New Hampshire.

Lawyer: Who lives with you as part of your household? Tell me about relatives, dependents, and anyone else whose income and expenses are regularly combined with yours to maintain your home.

Debtor: Just me and my two children. One is eight and the other just turned 12.

Lawyer: Okay. And do you operate a business?

Debtor: Actually, I do. Does it matter?

Lawyer: Well, business debts are sometimes treated differently than consumer debts when it comes to deciding your eligibility for filing Chapter 7. Also, Chapter 13 is often the better type of bankruptcy for an ongoing business if you're the sole owner, because you can keep your business assets and use your business earnings to make your required payments, but we'll get to that later.

Debtor: Okay. I run my own business, repairing used electronic equipment.

Lawyer: Have you incorporated your business or is it a partnership?

Debtor: No, just me, a sole proprietor.

Lawyer: And do you have other work? Do you have a regular job and operate your business on the side?

Debtor: No, just the business.

Lawyer: Is your income pretty steady?

Debtor: It was until recently. Near the end of the year, my business dropped off and I'll be lucky to bring in half of what I was earning not too long ago. Also, I receive alimony and child support, which helps stabilize my income, but my ex told me just last week that his company is starting to lay people off and he may be next.

Lawyer: Looking at your debts as a whole, were more of them due to your business or more due to your personal needs? When making this assessment, your mortgage counts as a consumer debt and back taxes count as a business debt.

Debtor: Why are you asking?

Lawyer: If your debts were primarily incurred for your business, you wouldn't have to worry about something we call the means test—essentially a questionnaire that determines whether you can afford to pay back some of your debts in a Chapter 13 bankruptcy.

Debtor: I would say about 40% were from my business and 60% were personal.

Lawyer: Okay, too bad. That makes you a consumer debtor rather than a business debtor and we'll have to evaluate your income to see whether you need to take the means test. For starters, how much did you earn in the last six months? That's gross earnings less your reasonable business expenses.

Debtor: About $3,000 a month after expenses for the last six months.

Lawyer: You mentioned that you receive child support and alimony. How much, and do you have any other income?

Debtor: About $1,000 a month in alimony and $800 a month for child support. That's it.

Lawyer: Have those amounts been steady over the last six months?

Debtor: Yes, there haven't been any changes.

Lawyer: So, it looks like your average monthly earnings over the past six months are $3,000 from your business, $1,000 in alimony, and $800 for child support, for a total of $4,800. Does that sound right?

Debtor: Yes.

Lawyer: Under the bankruptcy law, if your income is less than the median annual income for a family of your size in your state, you are presumed to be eligible to file for Chapter 7 bankruptcy. You don't have to go fill out a lengthy form comparing your income to your expenses and your deductions for contractual obligations, such as a car note and mortgage. Does any of this sound familiar to you?

Debtor: Yes, I remember reading a few years ago that higher-income people aren't able to file for Chapter 7. Is that what you are talking about?

Lawyer: Yes, that's it. Also, if your income is less than the median for your state and you decide to file a Chapter 13 bankruptcy anyway, your repayment plan can last for three years instead of five. If, on the other hand, your income is more than the median, your plan would have to last for five years.

Debtor: I didn't know that.

Lawyer: So, let's see how these numbers work out. Your annual income based on your gross income for the last six months is $57,600. The New Hampshire median income for a household of three people is $89,188. So, you're under the median income and don't have to take the means test to prove your eligibility for Chapter 7 bankruptcy. And if you decide to use Chapter 13, you can repay your debts over three years, instead of five.

Debtor: I guess that's good news, but when it comes right down to it, I wish I earned more, even if that meant I had to take the means test and have a Chapter 13 case last longer. Of course, if I had more money, I guess I wouldn't be talking to you about filing for bankruptcy in the first place.

Lawyer: Even though you qualify for Chapter 7 bankruptcy on the basis of your average income over the past six months, you can still be disqualified if, going forward, your actual monthly net income is substantially more than your actual monthly expenses, leaving you with some extra income every month to pay down your debt under a three-year Chapter 13 repayment plan.

Debtor: I wish I did have some extra income. When I recently compared my net income to my expenses, I definitely didn't have any money left over. Of course there are probably ways I could reduce my expenses if I had to.

Lawyer: Well, (because your income is below the state median income) as long as your basic living expenses are more or less equal to your net income, you have the option of filing for Chapter 7 bankruptcy.

Let's turn now to your residence. How long have you lived in New Hampshire?

Debtor: About three years.

Lawyer: Have you lived there continuously for the last three years, or did you live or maintain a residence somewhere else?

Debtor: I've lived here the whole time. I moved here from Vermont because of a job, but I didn't keep a home in Vermont. I vote and get my mail here.

Lawyer: Great. Because you've been living in New Hampshire for more than two years, we'll use our state's property exemptions. These will determine what property you can keep if you file a Chapter 7, and the minimum amount you'll have to pay your unsecured creditors if you file a Chapter 13 bankruptcy.

Debtor: Why do the exemptions matter in a Chapter 13 bankruptcy? I thought I could keep all of my property if I use Chapter 13.

Lawyer: Yes, you're right about that. But the law doesn't want your creditors to be worse off because you use Chapter 13. So a Chapter 13 repayment plan has to give your unsecured, nonpriority creditors at least as much they would have received had you filed a Chapter 7 bankruptcy. Roughly speaking, you have to pay for any nonexempt property that you keep.

Debtor: Okay, I guess that's fair.

Lawyer: Also, priority creditors have to be paid 100% in Chapter 13 cases. This would include back taxes, child support and alimony, and a portion of wages owed to employees. Nonpriority creditors are the rest of your creditors, typically credit card issuers, banks, doctors and lawyers, and holders of money judgments for repossessed and foreclosed property. For example, in your case, if you owed your employees wages or you owed contributions to a retirement plan, these would be priority debts and those creditors would be paid first in a Chapter 7 case if you have nonexempt assets. In a Chapter 13 case, priority debts must be paid in full over the life of your plan.

Debtor: Thanks for explaining that.

Lawyer: You're welcome. Now, let's figure out what you can protect. Do you own your home?

Debtor: Yes.

Lawyer: Are you making payments on a mortgage?

Debtor: Yes.

Lawyer: What's your monthly payment?

Debtor: $1,200.

Lawyer: Are you current on your payments?

Debtor: Yes.

Lawyer: What's your home worth?

Debtor: $150,000.

Lawyer: And how much do you owe on it?

Debtor: About $100,000.

Lawyer: That's a total?

Debtor: Yes.

Lawyer: Okay. Under the New Hampshire homestead exemption, you are entitled to protect $120,000 of equity in your home. You have $50,000 of equity, so all of your equity is protected.

Debtor: What's a homestead exemption?

Lawyer: That's an exemption that protects equity in your home. You are entitled to keep that much equity, even if you file for Chapter 7 bankruptcy. If your equity exceeded the exemption, you might lose the extra equity if you filed for Chapter 7. The trustee could sell your home, pay off the mortgage, pay you your exemption, and distribute the balance among your creditors. But because your equity is protected by the exemption, there wouldn't be anything left for your creditors after you got your exemption amount and the mortgage was paid. That's how exemptions work.

In Chapter 13, if you have property that isn't exempt, your repayment plan has to pay at least the portion of that property's value to your unsecured creditors.

Debtor: I remember reading back in 2005 that the new bankruptcy law makes it harder for people to keep their homes. Will that affect me?

Lawyer: No. The new law puts a cap of $160,375 on the exemption amount for people who bought their home within the 40 months before they filed for bankruptcy. So it affects only people who bought homes more recently, and then only if their states would otherwise allow them to take higher exemptions. For example, even if you bought your home in New Hampshire within the previous 40 months, the New Hampshire homestead is only $120,000, so the $160,375 cap wouldn't make any difference.

Debtor: So, I don't have to worry about that.

Lawyer: Right. Your exemption might be affected if you used nonexempt property in the last ten years to buy your home in order to cheat your creditors but that probably didn't happen. I guess I should ask how you got the money to pay for your home, just in case.

Debtor: I borrowed money from my parents.

Lawyer: Great. Your home equity is covered by your state's homestead exemption and you can keep it if you file for Chapter 7 bankruptcy.

Debtor: What happens to my home if I file for Chapter 13 bankruptcy?

Lawyer: As long as you keep making your mortgage payments and the other payments required by your Chapter 13 plan, there won't be a problem. However, if you fall behind on your payments, your lender could foreclose, just as if you hadn't filed bankruptcy. On the other hand, if you have reason to believe that the mortgage or foreclosure papers are defective, you can challenge the mortgage or foreclosure as part of your Chapter 13 case.

Debtor: So unless I have some basis to challenge the mortgage, I have to keep my mortgage payments current, no matter which type of bankruptcy I file?

Lawyer: That's right. What other debts do you owe?

Debtor: Mainly credit card debts. And one SBA bank loan for my business.

Lawyer: Is the SBA loan secured by any of your property?

Debtor: No, it's just a bank loan.

Lawyer: How much are you paying on that loan?

Debtor: About $300 a month.

Lawyer: And how much credit card debt do you owe?

Debtor: About $23,000.

Lawyer: What were the credit card debts for?

Debtor: About $14,000 for personal expenses and $6,000 for paying off back taxes. Also, $3,000 for a credit card charge by my husband that I assumed in our divorce.

Lawyer: Oh yeah? What period did you owe the taxes for?

Debtor: The last couple of years.

Lawyer: That's interesting. I'll come back to this later, but bankruptcy law allows you to discharge credit card charges used to pay off taxes in a Chapter 13 bankruptcy but not in a Chapter 7 bankruptcy. So, if there is no other reason to choose one type of

bankruptcy over the other, you would be wise to choose Chapter 13.

So, having paid those taxes, are you now current on your taxes for the past four years?

Debtor: Yes.

Lawyer: That's good. You can't file for Chapter 13 unless you have filed your state and federal taxes for the previous four years. How much was the bank loan for?

Debtor: $40,000

Lawyer: Did anybody cosign on that loan?

Debtor: As matter of fact, my mother cosigned that loan.

Lawyer: Did any of the money from the loan go to your mother? Or did you get all of it?

Debtor: All of the loan money was received by me and used by me.

Lawyer: Hmm. Even if you could get rid of that debt in bankruptcy, your mother would still be on the hook to repay it if you filed under Chapter 7. Even though you wouldn't be responsible for the debt any more, she would be.

But if you file for Chapter 13 bankruptcy, your mother won't have to repay it while your plan is in place, as long as your plan provides for payment of some or all of that debt. So, assuming your plan lasts for three years, your mother won't be on the hook during that period. However, she will still be responsible for any amount you haven't paid when your plan ends. So, again, if there is no other reason to choose one type of bankruptcy instead of the other, it looks like Chapter 13 might be a good choice.

Do you have any other debts?

Debtor: Nothing significant, maybe a total of $2,000 in miscellaneous bills. And, oh, does child support count?

Lawyer: I thought you were receiving child support.

Debtor: I am, but I also owe child support, for a child from a previous marriage. I never paid because my ex never asked, but now he's seeking current support as well as $5,000 in back support.

Lawyer: How much will you owe?

Debtor: Under the court order, $300 a month.

Lawyer: Have you started paying the support?

Debtor: No. I have to start paying it next month.

Lawyer: If you decide to file for Chapter 13, you will have to remain current on your child support payments throughout the life of your plan. If you don't, your case will be dismissed or converted to a Chapter 7 bankruptcy.

Debtor: I understand.

Lawyer: Let's talk later about the back support you owe. When were you divorced?

Debtor: A couple of years ago.

Lawyer: Did you assume any of the debts in the course of your divorce?

Debtor: Yes, I assumed the credit card charges for personal expenses in exchange for my ex-husband's share of our home.

Lawyer: Okay. How much were these charges?

Debtor: About $3,000

Lawyer: Hmmm, in a Chapter 7 bankruptcy you can discharge this debt with regard to the creditor, but your ex can come after you for this debt if he is sued by the creditor. In Chapter 13 bankruptcy, the debt would be fully discharged, both in respect to the creditor and your ex.

Debtor: It sounds like I should probably file for Chapter 13.

Lawyer: Maybe, but we're not through yet. Let's talk about your other property. And this is where exemptions will become important. Other than your home, do you have any other property you would want to keep in your bankruptcy?

Debtor: Oh, yes. I have a concert piano and some copyright interests in several songs I wrote. Also, I have a car I want to hold on to and the tools I use in my business.

Lawyer: How much are the tools worth?

Debtor: About $3,000.

Lawyer: Great. New Hampshire allows you to keep up to $5,000 worth of tools for your occupation, so those are covered. How much is the car worth?

Debtor: About $4,000 according to *Kelley Blue Book*.

Lawyer: Are you making payments on it?

Debtor: Yes.

Lawyer: How much is left on your note?

Debtor: About $8,000.

Lawyer: When did you buy it?

Debtor: Three years ago.

Lawyer: If you file for Chapter 13, you can pay off the value of the car rather than what you still owe on the note. This is called a cramdown, and it's another great reason to file for Chapter 13. And it's a good thing you didn't buy your car more recently: You couldn't use this cramdown procedure if you bought the car within 2½ years of your bankruptcy filing date.

Now let's take a look at the New Hampshire exemptions to see whether your other property is covered. Remember, exemptions like the homestead exemption and the tools of your occupation exemption are laws that determine what property you can keep in your bankruptcy. As I read them, the car is covered because you owe more than it's worth, so your creditors wouldn't get anything if it were sold. Because you don't have any equity in the car, you don't need to protect it with an exemption. As for the piano and your copyright interests, there are no state exemptions that specifically cover those items.

Debtor: Does that mean I'll lose my piano?

Lawyer: Not necessarily. Remember, if you file for Chapter 13, you don't lose any property—you just have to make sure you pay your creditors at least what they would have received from a sale of the piano in a Chapter 7 bankruptcy. And even though New Hampshire doesn't specifically exempt pianos, it has a $3,500 exemption for all your furniture. So depending on your piano's value, it might be covered by the furniture exemption.

Debtor: I think my piano would sell for about $8,500 and I guess my copyrights are pretty much worthless.

Lawyer: Why do you say your copyright interests are worthless?

Debtor: Well, they belong to three songs I wrote, but I've never had the songs published, so there is no one to sell them to.

Lawyer: Okay, let's forget about the songs. We're only talking about the piano. Looking at the New Hampshire exemptions, in addition to the portion of the piano's value arguably covered by the furniture exemption—$3,500—there are also some wildcard exemptions. This type of exemption can be used to protect any property you choose. New Hampshire's wildcard exemptions will provide an additional $8,000 that you can put toward the piano: That takes into account a $1,000 straight wildcard, plus a $7,000 wildcard that you can use if you don't fully take advantage of certain other exemptions. If you use these wildcards for your piano, only about $500 of its value is not exempt. Since the costs of sale and the trustee's commission, on top of the exemptions, would more than eat up that $500, there is a chance that you won't have to pay any of the piano's value to your creditors in a Chapter 13 case. Of course, if you need part of the furniture exemption for other pieces of furniture, that would take away from the exemption available for your piano. And, the trustee might object to a piano being classified as furniture.

Debtor: Okay.

Lawyer: Here is a copy of the New Hampshire exemptions. (Lawyer hands Georgia a page showing the New Hampshire bankruptcy exemptions.) Other than the piano, do you have any property that exceeds the exemption limit or that isn't listed in the exemption list?

Debtor: No, the piano is the only problem. But if I use the furniture exemption for my piano, my furniture won't be exempt. It's old furniture I bought at the Goodwill. I have nothing that would be of any value.

Lawyer: Well, that's up to the trustee. If you choose to use the entire furniture exemption for your piano, you might have to place some value on your furniture equal to what it would cost you to replace it.

Debtor: That would probably be about $1,000.

Lawyer: Okay, so you may have a couple of thousand dollars in nonexempt property depending on how you use the wildcard. That's under the New Hampshire state exemptions. If your state allows it, you may choose to use a different set of exemptions set out in the bankruptcy code termed the "federal exemptions." As it turns out, New Hampshire does allow use of the federal exemptions. You can choose from the federal exemption list or from the New Hampshire state list, but you can't mix or match.

Let's take a look and see if the federal exemptions would do you any good. The federal exemptions protect only $23,675 in your home equity. You have $50,000 equity to protect, so you wouldn't want to choose the federal exemptions.

So, we know you can file for Chapter 7 bankruptcy if you wish. You could keep your home and perhaps your piano, even though it isn't completely exempt. If you can't use the furniture exemption for the piano, the trustee would probably take it and sell it, and use the proceeds to pay your unsecured creditors. Or, you could keep the piano if the trustee were willing to sell it to you for a negotiated price. But that's all in a Chapter 7 bankruptcy.

Debtor: It's still sounding to me like Chapter 13 is a good idea. But you said I have to make sure I'm eligible. What are the requirements?

Lawyer: Before we get to that, I have a couple of more questions.

Debtor: Okay.

Lawyer: During the previous year, have you made payments on any loans you owe to relatives?

Debtor: Nope.

Lawyer: Good. If you had, the trustee might require the relative to return the money so it could be added to the amount your creditors would get.

Debtor: I wouldn't want that to happen.

Lawyer: Have you given away or sold any property to anyone within the past two years?

Debtor: No.

Lawyer: That also simplifies things. If you had given away some property, or you had sold some property for less than what it was worth, the difference in value would be considered nonexempt property. You'd have to add that to the amount you have to pay under your Chapter 13 plan. But you didn't sell any property, so this rule doesn't affect you.

Debtor: Wow, there's a lot to consider here. Are we done—isn't it clear that Chapter 13 is the right route for me?

Lawyer: Bear with me; just a few more issues to consider. Chapter 13 has some limitations on how much debt you can owe. Let's see, you owe a total of $69,000 of unsecured debt: a $40,000 bank loan, $23,000 in credit card debts, $5,000 in child support arrearage, and $2,000 in other debts. You owe a total of $108,000 secured debt (your home and car). This means you fall within the eligibility guidelines, which are $1,184,200 for secured debts and $394,725 for unsecured debts.

Debtor: That's good.

Lawyer: Now let's see what debts you would have to pay in your Chapter 13 bankruptcy. Some debts have to be paid in full while others could be paid in part, depending on your income. The debts that would have to be paid in full over the life of your plan would be at least the $5,000 arrearage for your child support and the $500 for the nonexempt portion of your piano and your furniture, or $5,500 total debt payable in full over the course of your Chapter 13 plan.

Debtor: So how much would that be a month?

Lawyer: People whose average gross income for the preceding six months is less than the state median income—which is your situation—can propose a three-year repayment plan. If your income were higher than the median, you'd have to propose a five-year program.

So, when spreading out $5,000 over three years, you would have to pay at least $139 a month, plus the monthly payment on your car as modified downwards to reflect its value ($111), your current mortgage payment, and other expenses related to Chapter 13 bankruptcy, such as the trustee's fee and your attorney's fee if you use an attorney. If you don't have enough income to pay that after you subtract your living expenses (including your mortgage payment and your car payment) you won't qualify for a three-year Chapter 13 plan.

Debtor: How can I tell whether I have enough income to meet the Chapter 13 requirements?

Lawyer: If you decide to file a Chapter 13 bankruptcy, you have to fill out some forms to determine your income and your expenses. These forms will basically show whether you can afford a Chapter 13 bankruptcy. If you don't have enough income to pay all necessary debts in three years, you can ask the judge to let you propose a five-year plan, so you can pay less each month. If you still won't have enough left, after paying your expenses, to make your payments, you probably won't be able to use Chapter 13.

Debtor: So, do you suggest that I file for Chapter 7? Or should I use Chapter 13?

Lawyer: Well, before I answer that, I've saved the best for last. Let's talk about attorneys' fees. I charge $3,500 for a Chapter 13 and $1,500 for a Chapter 7. So, by filing a Chapter 7, you'll save at least $2,000 in legal fees. But in Chapter 13 cases, I charge only $2,000 up front; the additional $1,500 can be paid through your plan. Overall, it will cost less up front for you to file a Chapter 7 bankruptcy. Also, in your case, I see no reason why you couldn't handle your own Chapter 7 bankruptcy with the help of the ABC Bankruptcy Petition Preparation Service down the street. They have the same computer program as I use, but all they do is help you complete your paperwork. They can't give you legal advice. If you are up to handling your own case, which I think you are from this conversation, you should explore the self-help option.

If you do decide to do it yourself, I would be happy to consult with you for a flat rate of $150. Under my consultation agreement you could ask me as many questions as you want, over the telephone. Even with a good self-help book, you might miss important information that you need to have a good result in your bankruptcy.

Debtor: I want you to handle my case. I don't think I'm up for self-representation.

Lawyer: Okay, now I'm ready to answer your basic question. As long as you have enough income left over in your budget to use Chapter 13, that would be an excellent choice for you because:

- It will protect your codebtor—your mother—for the life of the plan.
- It will allow you to keep your car and pay it off at market value rather than reaffirming the current note, which is twice what it's worth.
- Unlike Chapter 7, it fully discharges the credit card debts you assumed in your divorce.
- Unlike Chapter 7, it will allow you to discharge the credit card debts you incurred to pay off your taxes.
- It will allow you to pay off your child support arrearage—that is, the back child support you owe—over the life of your plan, without worrying about wage garnishments and bank levies.

So, assuming you have enough income to propose a confirmable Chapter 13 plan, and pay my fees, I recommend Chapter 13. If you can't propose a confirmable Chapter 13 plan, even over a five-year period, or you can't afford my fees, I suggest you go with Chapter 7. ●

Your Credit Cards

What will happen to your credit cards when you file for bankruptcy depends largely on the current status of your accounts, and to a lesser degree on the creditors. For this discussion, most credit cards fall into three possible categories:

- cards on which you have a zero balance—that is, you're all paid up
- cards on which you have a balance but are current—that is, you make at least the minimum payment each month, and
- cards on which you are in default—that is, you haven't made any payments in a while.

The Uncertain Future of Credit Cards

The information in this chapter is based on the history of credit card practices in the United States. This history may no longer be a guide to future policies. Because millions of people with previously solid credit scores may lose some or all of their income in the coming months and years, credit card issuers may radically change their policies, as to existing credit card accounts and the issuance of new cards to people who may be considered "subprime" because of a bankruptcy, a foreclosure, or other causes of bad credit.

If Your Balance Is Zero

On your bankruptcy papers, you'll have to list your creditors—all of the people and businesses to whom you currently owe money. If you have a balance of zero on a credit card, you don't currently owe the card issuer any money, and you don't have to list it on your bankruptcy papers there is a good chance you *might* come through bankruptcy—Chapter 7 or Chapter 13—still owning that credit card. But there are exceptions.

The Trustee May Take Your Card

It's possible that the bankruptcy trustee will confiscate your credit cards, ask you about the creditors with whom you have a zero balance, or demand that you write to them and tell them about your bankruptcy. This is much more likely to happen in a Chapter 13 case, where the trustee must supervise your finances for three to five years, than in a Chapter 7 case, where the trustee won't care about debts you incur after filing.

The Credit Card Issuer May Find Out About Your Bankruptcy

Most credit card companies constantly review your credit reports for any sign of economic weakness. For example, credit card companies often raise interest rates on cards if the cardholder makes a late payment on another card or to another creditor (although the Credit Card Accountability and Disclosure Act of 2009 placed some restrictions on interest rate hikes and requires companies to provide a certain amount of notice before increasing your interest rate). Therefore, a credit card company with which you have a zero balance may find out about your bankruptcy even though you haven't listed it as a creditor.

> **EXAMPLE:** You file for bankruptcy and include the following debts, among others: BigBank Visa, MediumBank MasterCard, and LittleBank Visa. Your balance on your TinyBank MasterCard is $0, so you don't include that creditor on your bankruptcy papers. TinyBank learns of your bankruptcy anyway from the credit bureaus it checks to monitor the creditworthiness of its customers.

Your Credit Card Issuer May Cancel Your Zero-Balance Card

On learning of your bankruptcy, the company that issued your credit card may decide to terminate your account, even though you don't owe that business a penny, on the ground that you are no longer a good credit risk. On the other hand, some credit card companies will be happy to continue doing business with you believing that you are now an excellent credit risk because you won't be able to file a Chapter 7 bankruptcy again for eight years. Often enough, you will be able to keep your zero-balance credit card account.

Even if you lose all your credit cards in your bankruptcy, don't get too worked up over it. Especially if you file for Chapter 7 bankruptcy, there are other ways to get a credit card, if you really think you need one. Although you may have trouble getting a card with a large credit balance, you will be able to obtain a debit card that gives you all the advantages of a credit card, with one important exception—the amount you can charge will be limited to the amount in your bank account (unless you opt into the bank's overdraft protection program—which many consumer advocates advise against).

The Trustee Might Recover Recent Payments on Your Credit Card

It may not be wise to pay off a credit card just before you file bankruptcy. When you file for bankruptcy, you must indicate on your papers all of your recent financial transactions. For filers whose debts are primarily consumer debts, payments of more than $600 to any one creditor in the 90 days prior to filing may be retroactively cancelled. For filers whose debts are primarily business debts, payments of more than $6,425 to any one creditor in the 90 days prior to filing may be retroactively cancelled.

These "eve of bankruptcy" payments are called "preferences." The trustee can recover preferences from the creditor you paid and use the money for the benefit of all your creditors, not just the creditor who received the payment. There are exceptions to this rule for business debtors who make the payment in the normal course of their business, and for payments made for regular ongoing expenses like your mortgage or utilities (as opposed to one-time expenses, like paying off a delinquent bill).

If You Owe Money But Are Current

If you owe money on a credit card but have managed to eke out at least a minimum payment each month, you will have to list this creditor on your bankruptcy papers even though you aren't behind. Your bankruptcy—Chapter 7 or Chapter 13—may come as a great surprise to the creditor.

If you file for Chapter 7 bankruptcy and want to keep your credit card, you might be able to do so by offering to sign a reaffirmation agreement with the credit card issuer. In a reaffirmation agreement, you agree to repay the balance in full, as if you never filed for bankruptcy. However, you will have to convince the court that reaffirming the debt is in your best interest. (See Ch. 6 for more on reaffirming debts.)

Reaffirming a Credit Card Debt May Not Be a Good Idea

Before you reaffirm a credit card debt, ask yourself whether it really makes sense. For most people, it doesn't. The purpose of filing for bankruptcy is to get rid of debts, not to still owe money. Admittedly, some people choose to file, even though they know that they won't be able to eliminate certain debts. But even in that situation, it almost never makes sense to come out of bankruptcy owing a credit card balance you had before you filed. And it's unlikely that a bankruptcy judge would approve the agreement. More likely, you will come out of bankruptcy still owing taxes or a student loan. If you want to have a credit card after bankruptcy, chances are very good that you'll be able to get one (but one that starts with a zero balance, not with the amount you owed before you filed). A debit card will probably serve all of your needs—and won't get you back into debt.

The credit card issuer may ask you to sign a reaffirmation agreement when you file for Chapter 7 bankruptcy, even if you intend to wipe out the debt (although this is unusual). The creditor may offer tempting terms—a reduction in the interest rate, a reduction of the balance you owe, or an increase in your line of credit. But you should resist. To sign a reaffirmation agreement would probably defeat a major, if not the sole, reason you filed—to get rid of your credit card debt. (If the creditor gets insistent or starts claiming that you incurred the credit card debt fraudulently, you still have options—see Ch. 10.)

If you file for Chapter 13 bankruptcy, your plan will propose to repay your unsecured creditors, including your credit card issuers, some percentage of what you owe. Chapter 13 plans are sometimes referred to by this percentage—for example, "this couple filed a 55% plan." (Remember that unlike credit card debts, some types of debts, including priority debts and secured debts, must be repaid in full, even in Chapter 13. For more on secured debts, see Ch. 6.) In most cases, even if you propose to pay 100% of what you owe on a card, the creditor will cancel your account. And the Chapter 13 trustee may confiscate your card anyway.

Your Job, Freedom, and Self-Respect

For most people, the thought of filing for bankruptcy raises a number of troubling questions. Many of these have to do with eliminating debts. (Those are answered in Ch. 3.) Other questions concern the potential loss of property. (Those are addressed in Chs. 4, 5, and 6.)

But many of the questions go beyond debts and assets and hit at the core of what it means to be a member of our society— earning a living, bringing up your children, and keeping your freedom and self-respect.

Will You Lose Your Self-Respect?

Americans learn almost from birth that it's a good thing to buy all sorts of goods and services. A highly paid army of persuaders surrounds us with thousands of seductive messages each day that say "Buy, buy, buy." Easily available credit makes living beyond our means easy—and resisting the siren sounds of the advertisers difficult. But we're also told that if we fail to pay for it all right on time, we're failures. In short, much of American economic life is built on a contradiction.

Adding to this contradiction is the system of high interest and penalties employed by most credit card companies that cause our debt to soar beyond any reasonable expectation. In many cases, the interest rates are so high that the companies involved would have been prosecuted for loan sharking in the not-too-distant past—before the credit card industry systematically lobbied to do away with usury laws or to create exceptions to those laws for credit card interest rates.

Credit card companies keep this system working by encouraging us to make the minimum payment, which stimulates us to make more credit purchases and eases us into debt loads far beyond our ability to ever pay them off. We now all owe our soul to the company store. To feel guilty about being caught in this deliberately contrived economic trap is nonsense. There's much more to life than an A+ credit rating and bigger things to feel guilty about than the failure to pay bills on time.

What About Friendly Creditors?

While you may not care about discharging your credit card debts in bankruptcy, you may feel bad about doing the same to the debts you owe to friends, family, or business creditors in your community— such as a doctor, dentist, chiropractor, pharmacist, accountant, lawyer, contractor, or hardware store. You have to list all debts in your bankruptcy papers, including those obligations that you'd rather pay. While qualifying debts you owe to creditors close to you will get discharged, there's nothing to prevent you from voluntarily paying the debts after you file. Communicating your intent to repay to these friendly creditors will make everybody involved feel a whole lot better about your bankruptcy.

Fortunately, it's been recognized that debts can get the better of even the most conscientious among us. Bankruptcy provides a sensible way for debt-oppressed people to start new economic lives. It's a truly worthy part of our legal system, based as it is on forgiveness rather than retribution. Certainly, it gives people a fresh start in our increasingly volatile economy, helps keep families together, reduces suicide rates, and keeps the ranks of the homeless from growing even larger. So, don't let the word "bankruptcy" cause you stress.

Will You Lose Your Job?

No employer—government or private—may fire you because you filed for bankruptcy. Nor may an employer discriminate against you in other terms and conditions of employment—for example, by reducing your salary, demoting you, or taking away responsibilities—because of your bankruptcy.

Termination for Other Reasons

If there are other valid reasons for taking these actions, the fact that you filed for bankruptcy won't protect you. In other words, an employer who wants to take negative action against you can do so provided there are other valid reasons to explain the action—such as tardiness, dishonesty, or incompetence. But if you are fired shortly after your bankruptcy is brought to your employer's attention, you might have a case against the employer for illegal discrimination because of your bankruptcy.

How Employers Find Out About Bankruptcy Filings

In practice, employers rarely find out about Chapter 7 bankruptcy filings. However, if a creditor has sued you, obtained a judgment, and started garnishing your wages, you (or your attorney) must notify your employer about the bankruptcy to stop the garnishment. In that case, your employer will get the news. In that situation, your employer (or at least the payroll department) already knew you were having financial problems and will probably welcome the bankruptcy as a way for you to take affirmative steps to put your problems behind you.

If you fall behind on your Chapter 13 bankruptcy payments, your employer might learn of your bankruptcy case. If you have a regular job with regular income, the bankruptcy judge may order your Chapter 13 payments to be automatically deducted from your wages and sent to the bankruptcy court. (This is called an "income deduction order." It's used in some jurisdictions, but not all.) In effect, if you default on your payments, your employer will act as a sort of collection agency, to make sure you honor your Chapter 13 plan.

Income Deduction Orders Work

You may not like the idea of the income deduction order, but the bankruptcy court might deny your Chapter 13 plan if you refuse to comply with it. And the order will probably make it easier for you to complete your plan. The success rate of Chapter 13 cases is higher for debtors with income deduction orders than for debtors who pay the trustee themselves, for the very obvious reason that it's hard to spend money you never receive.

Security Clearances

Many jobs require a security clearance. If you are a member of the armed forces or an employee of the CIA, FBI, another government agency, or a private company that contracts with the government, you may have a security clearance. Do you risk losing your security clearance if you file for bankruptcy? Probably not—in fact, the opposite may be true. According to credit counselors for the military and the CIA, a person with financial problems—particularly someone with a lot of debt—is at high risk for being black-mailed. By filing for bankruptcy and getting rid of the debts, you substantially lower that risk. Bankruptcy usually works more in your favor than to your detriment.

Effect of Bankruptcy on Job Applicants

Federal, state, and local government agencies cannot consider your bankruptcy when deciding whether to hire you. There is no corresponding rule for private employers, however, and some people find that having a bankruptcy in their past comes back to haunt them, particularly when applying for jobs that require them to deal with money (bookkeeping, accounting, payroll, and so on).

Many private employers conduct a credit check on job applicants as a matter of course and will find out about your bankruptcy from the credit report. While employers need your permission to run credit checks, employers can also refuse to hire you if you don't consent. If you're asked to give this authorization, consider speaking candidly about what the employer will find in your file. Being honest up front about problems that are truly behind you may outweigh any negative effects of the bankruptcy filing itself.

Other Forms of Discrimination Because of Bankruptcy

Federal, state, and local governmental units can't legally discriminate against you because you filed for bankruptcy.

Discrimination by Government Agencies

Governmental units may not deny, revoke, suspend, or refuse to renew a license, permit, charter, franchise, or other similar grant on the basis of your bankruptcy. Judges interpreting this law have ruled that the government cannot:
- deny or terminate public benefits
- deny or evict you from public housing

- deny or refuse to renew your state liquor license
- exclude you from participating in a state home mortgage finance program
- withhold your college transcript
- deny you a driver's license
- deny you a contract, such as a contract for a construction project, or
- exclude you from participating in a government-guaranteed student loan program.

In general, once any government-related debt has been discharged, all acts against you that arise out of that debt must also end. If, for example, you lost your driver's license because you didn't pay a civil court judgment that resulted from a car accident, you must be granted a license once the debt is discharged. If the debt isn't discharged, however, you can still be denied your license until you pay up.

Discrimination by Private Entities

Prohibitions against private discrimination aren't nearly as broad as prohibitions against government discrimination. As mentioned above, private employers may not fire you or punish you because you filed for bankruptcy. Other forms of discrimination in the private sector, however, such as denying you rental housing or a surety bond or withholding a college transcript, are legal.

The best way to confront this type of discrimination is to build a solid credit history after bankruptcy. You can find

sound strategies for getting back on your financial feet in *Credit Repair*, by Amy Loftsgordon (Nolo).

If a potential landlord does a credit check, sees your bankruptcy, and refuses to rent to you, there's not much you can do except try to show that you'll pay your rent and be a responsible tenant. You probably will need to go apartment hunting with a "renter's résumé" that shows you in the best possible light. Be ready to offer a cosigner, find roommates, offer to pay more rent, or even pay several months' rent up front in cash.

Effect of Bankruptcy on Child Custody

Bankruptcy and divorce (or separation) are so often related these days that one frequently follows the other. Bankruptcy judges are becoming experts on family law matters, and family law judges are becoming experts in bankruptcy. Don't worry about your bankruptcy affecting your custody status. Keep in mind, however, that bankruptcy does not relieve you of your child support and alimony obligations, past or present.

Effect of Bankruptcy on Your Freedoms

We Americans are used to some basic freedoms, and many people fear the loss of those freedoms if they file for bankruptcy. Relax. Except in some unusual cases, this is just not going to happen.

Consequences of Dishonesty

When you file for bankruptcy, you swear, under "penalty of perjury," that everything in your papers is true to the best of your knowledge. If you deliberately commit a dishonest act, such as failing to disclose property, omitting material information about your financial affairs, unloading nonexempt assets just before filing (especially if you don't disclose the transfer), or using a false Social Security number (to hide your identity as a prior filer), you can be criminally prosecuted for fraud.

Bankruptcy law streamlines the process by which fraud-related cases can be referred to the U.S. Attorney's office for prosecution. Also, the law requires the government to audit one out of every 250 bankruptcy cases. It is important to disclose all of your property and debts in your bankruptcy papers, provide accurate answers to the questions in your Statement of Financial Affairs for Individuals Filing for Bankruptcy (see Ch. 10), and not try to hide property from the trustee or your creditors prior to filing.

Examples of criminal prosecutions abound. A debtor in Massachusetts went to jail for failing to list on his bankruptcy papers his interest in a condominium and $26,000 worth of jewelry. Another Massachusetts debtor served time for listing her home on her bankruptcy papers as worth $70,000 when it had been appraised for $116,000. An Alaska debtor was jailed for failing to disclose buried cash and diamonds. A Pennsylvania debtor omitted from her papers $50,000 from a divorce settlement and was sentenced to some time in prison.

The message is simple: Bankruptcy is geared toward the honest debtor who inadvertently gets in too deep and needs the help of the bankruptcy court to get a fresh start. A bankruptcy judge will not help someone who has played fast and loose with creditors or tries to do so with the bankruptcy court. If you lie, hide, or cheat, it may come back to haunt you in ways much worse than your current debt crisis ever could.

Moving

You are free to change your residence after you file. Just be sure to send the trustee and court a written notification of change of address if your case is still open. If your move involves selling your house and you've filed for Chapter 13 bankruptcy, the trustee may want to use proceeds of the sale to pay off your creditors (if your plan doesn't already propose full payment).

Changing Jobs

You can certainly change jobs while your bankruptcy case is pending, and after it ends. If you've filed a Chapter 13 case, be sure to tell the trustee so he or she can transfer the income deduction order.

Divorce

No one can force you to stay married, not even a bankruptcy judge. Here's how a divorce will fit (or not) into your bankruptcy.

Chapter 7. If you've filed for Chapter 7 bankruptcy and want to end your marriage, go ahead. Your bankruptcy case will probably end long before your divorce case does. However, it often makes sense to wait until a divorce is completed before filing for bankruptcy (unless you and your spouse can streamline debt distribution by filing together). Your property ownership and personal debt situation will be much clearer after your divorce becomes final—and your marital debts and property have been divided between you and your former spouse.

If you assume responsibility for debts in a divorce, you will still owe those debts after your bankruptcy to the extent that the creditor goes after your ex. For instance, if you agree in your divorce agreement to pay off a particular credit card and then you file bankruptcy, your liability to the creditor is discharged, but you are still responsible to your ex if the credit card company sues him or her for the amount owed. For this reason, it sometimes makes sense to file bankruptcy before you assume responsibility for any debt in the course of your divorce. Note that unlike the situation in Chapter 7, in Chapter 13 you are permitted to fully discharge debt you've assumed responsibility for in your divorce as long as it's not for support.

Chapter 13. If you've filed a Chapter 13 case with your spouse, you may face some complications if you want to continue your case and get divorced. Bankruptcy law states that you must be a married couple to be eligible to file a joint case. If you have a "final decree" of divorce, you are no longer eligible to file a joint bankruptcy.

> **TIP**
>
> **Who's going to know?** It's highly unusual for anyone to find out about your bankruptcy other than your creditors, businesses that obtain a copy of your credit report, and the people you tell. Although your bankruptcy filing might be listed in a local newspaper, these notices often appear in low-circulation papers, and few people sit around reading such notices anyway. Bankruptcy filings aren't broadcast on local television or radio unless you are very famous. ●

Bankruptcy Forms and Procedures

Chapter 7 bankruptcy is a relatively straightforward process for most filers. You can look forward to smooth sailing—whether you represent yourself or are represented by a lawyer—if all of the following are true in your situation:

- Your average gross monthly income over the six-month period prior to the month you file is less than the median income for a household of your size in the state where you are filing (which fits many would-be filers).
- If you are in business for yourself and your business has few or no assets or inventory.
- Your only real estate is your home and you have little or no equity in it.
- You have lived in the state where you are filing for at least two years.
- Your net monthly income doesn't exceed your reasonable living expenses by more than a few hundred dollars.
- You haven't given any property away (or sold it for less than it's worth) during the previous two years.
- Property you care about keeping is clearly exempt (that is, the trustee can't take it under your state's exemption laws or, if available in your state, under the federal exemption law).
- You haven't repaid a debt owed to a relative or business associate within the previous year.

If you meet all of these criteria, it is unlikely that your case will produce any disputes that will have to be resolved by a bankruptcy judge, rather than by agreement between you and the trustee or your creditors. Your only personal appearance is likely to be at the creditors' meeting (see Ch. 1). However, if you are reaffirming a car note or another debt connected to collateral, you may have to appear at a brief hearing where the bankruptcy judge will decide whether reaffirmation is in your best interest (see Ch. 6 for more on the reaffirmation hearing). But, to the extent that your case is more complex—perhaps because of multiple real estate holdings, an ongoing retail business, or inappropriate prebankruptcy transfers of property—it makes good sense to hire a lawyer in order to achieve the best possible result.

Some brief descriptions of the Chapter 7 proceedings that might require some legal help are explained in this chapter. (Ch. 11 explains what type of help is available and how to find it.)

While many Chapter 7 filers successfully represent themselves, most people who file for Chapter 13 bankruptcy hire an attorney to represent them. Chapter 13 bankruptcy is almost always too difficult for people to successfully complete without representation. Some of the trouble points are outlined later in this chapter.

If, after you file your bankruptcy, you want to change course and convert to another type of bankruptcy or get out of bankruptcy altogether, you'll find the rules that apply in this chapter. And, no matter what type of bankruptcy you file, you can look forward to completing plenty of paperwork. The basic forms required in both types of bankruptcy are explained in this chapter as well.

The Means Test

A single dollar's difference in your income can have a large impact on your bankruptcy plans. If your "current monthly income" (CMI, defined and described in Ch. 2) is one dollar less than your state's median income, you can:

- file for Chapter 7 bankruptcy without completing the means test (Form 122A-2)

- use your actual expenses (rather than the IRS's expense standards, which are often lower) to compute your disposable income (and thus your Chapter 13 plan payments), and
- propose a three-year plan if you file for Chapter 13 bankruptcy.

On the other hand, if your CMI is even one dollar more than the state's median income, you must:

- complete the means test and produce results showing that you have insufficient funds in your budget to support a Chapter 13 repayment plan

---

The Means Test Forms

The means test consists of three bankruptcy forms, but you won't have to fill out all of them. Here's how it works:

- Form 122A-1 *Chapter 7 Statement of Your Current Monthly Income*. Everyone filing for Chapter 7 bankruptcy must complete this form. It calculates your CMI and compares it to the median income in your state for the same family size. If your income is above the state median, you must also complete Form 122A-2. If your income is below the state median, then you don't have to complete Form 122A-2.
- Form 122A-1-Supp. *Statement of Exemption from Presumption of Abuse Under § 707(b)2)*. There are several instances when you do not have to

pass the Chapter 7 means test in order to be eligible for Chapter 7 bankruptcy. If any of these apply to you, you must complete Form 122A-1-Supp.
- Form 122A-2. *Chapter 7 Means Test Calculation*. If your income is above the median income in your state, you must complete Form 122A-2. This is what is traditionally referred to as the "means test." If you pass this part of the test, you can file for Chapter 7 (assuming you meet other eligibility criteria). If you don't pass, you cannot file for Chapter 7.

Although all filers used to use the same forms, this has changed. You'll want to be sure that you're using the individual version for your filing (businesses use the "non-individual" forms).

- use the IRS standards to compute your disposable income if you decide to file a Chapter 13 bankruptcy, and
- propose a five-year plan if you file for Chapter 13 bankruptcy.

For many filers, this won't be a close call: It will be fairly easy to figure out where you stand. But how should you proceed if a modest change in your income or expenses would put you below the median income or change the outcome of the means test?

Sometimes waiting a month or two before filing will take care of the problem. For example, if you have recently become unemployed but your income for the months prior to your unemployment put you over the top, just waiting another month might sufficiently lower your average income for the six-month period to squeeze you under the bar. Let's see how this works. Assume Denis makes an average monthly gross income of $5,000 for the five-month period of March through July 2015. He gets laid off in August and receives $1,800 in unemployment insurance payments. His average gross income for the entire six-month period (March to August) is $4,466. If Denis files bankruptcy in September, his average monthly gross income for the preceding six-month period will exceed the median income or a family of his size ($4,000). However, if Denis waits another month to file, his average income for the six-month period preceding

his filing date will decrease to $3,933, putting him under the median income level applicable to his case.

If waiting to file bankruptcy won't solve the problem, the stakes may well be worth the cost of a consultation with a bankruptcy attorney who will be familiar with the categories and definitions of income and expenses. In addition to appreciating the nuances contained within the means test, attorneys in close cases can raise novel arguments on behalf of their clients. These arguments result in court decisions that a bankruptcy attorney can use to suggest legal ways to decrease your income or increase your expenses to achieve a more desirable outcome. Also, in some courts you can file a Chapter 13 bankruptcy and then later convert the case to Chapter 7 without having to take the means test. This might not be the most direct route to your objective—a Chapter 7 discharge—but it would still get the job done.

Challenges for Abuse

Bankruptcy law describes two kinds of abuse that can sink your Chapter 7 filing:

- failure to pass the means test (known as presumptive abuse because the trustee will presume that you aren't entitled to file under Chapter 7 if you flunk the means test), and
- abuse under the totality of the circumstances (general abuse).

If abuse is presumed because you fail the means test, you may not be allowed to proceed with your Chapter 7 bankruptcy unless you can rebut the presumption by showing special circumstances (see "Defending a Motion to Dismiss or Convert," below). If you are accused of abuse under the totality of the circumstances, however, the party bringing the charge (usually the U.S. Trustee) has the burden of proving abuse. Needless to say, you are much more likely to be barred from Chapter 7 when abuse is presumed than when it must be proved.

TIP

Abuse laws apply only to consumer cases. The law on abuse, both general and presumed, applies only to filers with primarily consumer debts. Filers who have primarily business debts are not subject to abuse motions on either general or presumptive grounds. Your debts are primarily business debts if more than half of the total value of your debt arises from the operation of a business.

If you file under Chapter 7, you won't know for sure whether your bankruptcy filing will be challenged on abuse grounds until the trustee (or in some cases, a creditor) asks for a court hearing to dismiss or convert your case.

Presumed Abuse

If your bankruptcy paperwork demonstrates that you don't pass the means test, you can expect the U.S. Trustee to file a motion to dismiss your case or (with your consent) convert the case to Chapter 13. The bankruptcy trustee or any creditor can also file a motion to dismiss or convert your case on the grounds of abuse, but the U.S. Trustee will probably be the one bringing the motion: The U.S. Trustee is legally responsible for assessing your eligibility for Chapter 7 bankruptcy and otherwise seeing that the bankruptcy laws are complied with.

General Abuse

As mentioned, even if you pass—or don't have to take—the means test, your Chapter 7 filing can still be challenged for general abuse.

If you were subject to the means test but passed it on the face of your paperwork, the court, U.S. Trustee, bankruptcy trustee, or a creditor can still file a motion to dismiss your bankruptcy or convert it to Chapter 13 if the totality of the circumstances demonstrates abuse. For example, you could be subject to an abuse motion if you seek to reject a personal services contract—a contract in which you've agreed to provide services to another person or business—without adequate financial justification. For instance, if you sign a three-year recording contract and then file for Chapter 7 bankruptcy just to get out of it, your case could be challenged on general abuse grounds.

Motions to Dismiss for Abuse Under All the Circumstances

As we've explained, it's possible to have your case dismissed if it appears that your Chapter 7 filing is an abuse of the bankruptcy code under all the circumstances. Motions to dismiss for this reason tend to focus primarily on whether the debtor's expenses are unnecessarily extravagant. For example, one very strict Ohio bankruptcy court ruled that a mortgage expense on a $400,000 home and an expense for repayment of a 401(k) loan should not be allowed. Without those expenses, the debtors had adequate income to fund a Chapter 13 plan, which made their case an abuse under all the circumstances. (*In Re Felske*, 385 B.R. 649 (N.D. Ohio 2008).)

The grounds for dismissal don't necessarily have to exist when you file for bankruptcy. A motion to dismiss for abuse may be brought on the basis of events occurring anytime before the discharge. So if you get a new job or win the lottery, or some other event happens while your case is pending that would enable you to proceed under Chapter 13, you may face a challenge to your Chapter 7 case. (See also *In re Henebury*, 361 B.R. 595 (S.D. Fla. 2007).)

If you face dismissal on this ground, you will need to explain why it's unlikely you could complete a Chapter 13 bankruptcy, or why expenses that are challenged by the trustee are really necessary for you to get a fresh start. There is no clear test of what constitutes abuse under all the circumstances. As with obscenity, the judges will know it when they see it. Fortunately, the U.S. Trustee (usually the party bringing these motions) has the burden of proving the abuse. If you pass the means test, your eligibility for Chapter 7 bankruptcy is presumed and the trustee has to overcome that presumption.

If your average monthly income (calculated according to the formula explained in Ch. 2, "Calculating Your Income Status") is less than the state's median income, you aren't subject to the means test and your filing won't be presumed to be abusive. Your Chapter 7 filing can still be challenged on the ground of general abuse, but only if the judge or U.S. Trustee files the motion; no creditors allowed at this party. Again, absent the presumption, the court or U.S. Trustee must prove abuse.

The U.S. Trustee is likely to challenge your Chapter 7 bankruptcy filing on general abuse grounds if you could easily propose a feasible Chapter 13 plan, even though you weren't subject to the means test or you passed the means test. For instance, if you otherwise qualify for Chapter 13 and can pay $12,850 or more over a five-year period toward a Chapter 13 plan—or you could pay at least 25% of your unsecured, nonpriority debt—you might face an abuse motion.

Charitable Contributions

Assuming you have a record of making set charitable contributions to a qualified religious or charitable entity or organization, a court may not consider these contributions as part of your disposable income. In other words, the trustee cannot argue that you should pay your money into a Chapter 13 repayment plan rather than to the charity of your choice.

> **EXAMPLE:** You pass the means test but the U.S. Trustee files a motion to dismiss your case for abuse because you give 25% of your income to your church (and have over a substantial period of time). The U.S. Trustee argues that if you only tithed (gave 15% of your income), you could propose a feasible Chapter 13 repayment plan. Following this law, the court dismisses the U.S. Trustee's motion and allows your Chapter 7 bankruptcy to proceed.

For example, during the previous six months, suppose Julian and Edna's combined average monthly gross income is $7,000, which is $1,500 a month over the median income for a similar size family. They pass the means test because they have a number of large deductions, including $1,000 a month for two car notes and $3,500 for their mortgage. As it turns out, shortly before filing, Julian gets a large raise, and his and Edna's actual monthly net income exceeds their actual living expenses by $700 (well over the $12,850 for a five-year period). The U.S. Trustee files a motion to dismiss or convert the bankruptcy on the ground that a Chapter 7 filing would constitute an abuse under all the circumstances. His reasoning is that there is enough excess actual income to fund a Chapter 13 plan, and because Julian and Edna are spending more for their car notes and mortgage than is reasonable in their particular situation. Following other cases decided by courts in his district, the bankruptcy judge grants the motion, giving Julian and Edna 15 days to either convert their case to Chapter 13 or have it dismissed.

Court Procedures

If you fail the means test, the U.S. Trustee must file a statement indicating whether your filing should be considered an abuse within ten days after your meeting of creditors. (See Ch. 1 for more on this meeting.) Five days after the U.S. Trustee's statement is filed, the court must send the notice to all of your creditors, to let them know about the U.S. Trustee's assessment and to give them an opportunity to file their own motions to dismiss or convert on abuse grounds, if they desire.

Within 30 days after filing this statement, the U.S. Trustee must either:

- file a motion to dismiss or convert your case on grounds of abuse, or
- explain why a motion to convert or dismiss isn't appropriate (for example, because you passed the means test).

If your income is below the state median income, the U.S. Trustee doesn't have to file either statement, because abuse will not be presumed. However, your filing can still be challenged for general abuse, as explained earlier.

Note that these duties and time limits apply only to the U.S. Trustee. If your income is more than the state median, your creditors can file a motion to dismiss or convert anytime after you file, but no later than 60 days after the first date set for your creditors' meeting.

Defending a Motion to Dismiss or Convert

If the U.S. Trustee (or the trustee or a creditor in appropriate circumstances) files a motion to dismiss or convert your case, you are entitled to notice of the hearing at least 20 days in advance. You will receive papers in the mail explaining the grounds for the motion and what you need to do to respond. If the motion to dismiss or convert is based on presumed abuse, the burden is on you to prove that your filing is not abusive. If the motion is based on general abuse, the burden of proof is on the party bringing the motion.

Presumed Abuse

If the motion to dismiss or convert is based on your actual failure to pass the means test, your only defense is to show "special circumstances." However, it's not enough to show that these circumstances exist: You must also show that they justify additional expenses or adjustments of current monthly income "for which there is no reasonable alternative."

In order to establish special circumstances, you must itemize each additional expense or adjustment of income and provide:

- documentation for the expense or adjustment, and
- a detailed explanation of the special circumstances that make the expense or adjustment necessary and reasonable.

You will win only if the additional expenses or adjustments to income enable you to pass the means test.

EXAMPLE: Maureen and Ralph have a child (Sarah) with severe autism. Sarah is making remarkable progress in her private school, for which Maureen and Ralph pay $1,000 a month. No equivalent school is available at a lower tuition. Under the means test guidelines, Maureen and Ralph are entitled to deduct only $1,875 a year from their income for private school expenses. If Maureen and Ralph were allowed to deduct the full $1,000 monthly tuition, they would easily pass the means test. By documenting Sarah's condition, the necessity for the extra educational expense, and the fact that moving her to a less expensive school would greatly undermine her progress, Maureen and Ralph would have a good chance of convincing the court to allow the $1,000 expense, which would in turn rebut the presumption of abuse.

Bankruptcy courts have issued written decisions on a variety of special circumstance claims. If you need to prove special circumstances to pass the mean test, you will definitely want to check with a local attorney or do your own research to find out how bankruptcy court or the courts in your state have treated the special circumstances you're claiming.

A frequently addressed issue is whether payments on nondischargeable student loans can be considered a special circumstance. While a few courts have held that they can be, more courts have gone the other way and ruled that student loan payments do not constitute special circumstances. (See, for example, *In re Champagne*, 389 B.R. 191 (Bkrtcy Kan. 2008) and *In re Pageau*, 383 B.R. 221 (S.D. Ind. 2008).)

Here are some cases in which the court has allowed a particular special circumstances claim, but remember that courts in your area may see the issue differently:

- unusually high transportation expenses (*In re Batzkiel*, 349 B.R. 581 (Bkrtcy N.D. Iowa 2006); *In re Turner*, 376 B.R. 370 (Bkrtcy D. N.H. 2007))
- mandatory repayment of 401(k) loan (*In re Lenton*, 358 B.R. 651 (Bkrtcy E.D. Pa. 2006))
- birth of child and student loan debt (*In re Martin*, 371 B.R. 347 (Bkrtcy C.D. Ill. 2007))
- reduction in income due to voluntary job changes (*In re Tamez*, No. 07-60047 (Bkrtcy W.D. Tex. 2007))
- joint debtors who have two separate households (*In re Graham*, 363 B.R. 844 (Bkrtcy S.D. Ohio 2007); *In re Armstrong*, No. 06-31414 (Bkrtcy N.D. Ohio 2007))
- unusually high rent expenses (*In re Scarafiotti*, 375 B.R. 618 (Bkrtcy D. Colorado 2007)), and
- court-ordered child support payments (*In re Littman*, 370 B.R. 820 (Bkrtcy D. Idaho 2007)).

In addition, the U.S. Trustee's office recently provided some guidance on this issue, noting that it may consider as special circumstances the following:

- job loss or reduction in income for which there is no reasonable alternative
- a one-time "bump" in prepetition income that is not likely to happen again

debtors who have separate households due to pending divorce or job relocation, and have filed a joint bankruptcy petition, and

- a postpetition household size increase due to pregnancy or a reasonable need to support an additional person.

General Abuse

If your filing is challenged for general abuse, the party bringing the motion to dismiss or convert has the burden of proof. If the motion is based on your ability to fund a Chapter 13 plan (even though you passed the means test), you can raise any special expense you have—for example, necessary private tuition, extraordinary child care expenses, or legal fees associated with a continuing legal action—to demonstrate your inability to fund a Chapter 13 plan.

Valuation Hearings

There are two situations when you may need to ask the court to assign a value to a car or other personal property. In a Chapter 7 bankruptcy, you may need a valuation if you propose to redeem property that you are making payments on. (See Ch. 6 for more on redemption.) If the property's replacement value (what the property could be purchased for in a retail market, considering its age and condition) is less than the debt, you can pay

the replacement value in a lump sum and own the property outright.

In a Chapter 13 bankruptcy, you may want the court to determine the replacement value of property that is collateral for a secured debt. If the replacement value is less than the debt, your repayment plan can pay the replacement value. This is called a "cramdown." (See Ch. 6 for more on cramdowns.)

RESOURCE

Getting evidence of value. For cars, *Kelley Blue Book* appraisals are a good start (www.kbb.com). Another good place to look is the website of the National Automobile Dealers Association, www.nada.com, which is recommended by the courts. However, you and the creditor may disagree about the car's value because of its condition, something these websites can't shed much light on. In that case, a private appraisal would be persuasive.

To get a valuation hearing, you or a creditor must file a motion. These motions are handled in the same way as the other motions discussed in "Common Chapter 7 Motions and Proceedings," just below. If you or a creditor requests a valuation hearing in Chapter 13, the court will either postpone your confirmation hearing or hold the valuation hearing immediately before the confirmation hearing.

Common Chapter 7 Motions and Proceedings

In very simple Chapter 7 cases, you will probably have to attend only one official proceeding: the creditors' meeting, supervised by the trustee. But if your Chapter 7 case involves issues that must be decided by a bankruptcy judge—for example, if you are facing a motion to dismiss or convert for abuse—you, or someone helping you, must know the required court procedures. You will have to either take the time to learn how to represent yourself or consult an attorney who already knows what needs to be done. You can also get help from

---

Common Motion Procedures

There are many types of motions. The two main varieties are called "ex parte" motions and "noticed" motions. Ex parte motions are easier to bring because you don't have to send formal notice to all of the parties or schedule a court hearing. These are used primarily for administrative issues that are not controversial, such as a request to reopen a case or to get permission to shorten the required time for giving notice.

Noticed motions are more complex. One party files the motion and sends notice of what is requested to the appropriate parties (this is called "serving" the parties). The notice is accompanied by a legal argument (points and authorities) and a declaration—a sworn statement that sets out the facts of the case under penalty of perjury.

The notice typically includes the date and time at which the court will hear the motion. Sometimes, the notice states that a hearing will be set only if the party served with the motion wants to oppose it. If a hearing is set, all parties must receive notice at least 20 days in advance.

The party against whom the motion is brought typically can file a written opposition to the motion at any time up to five days before the hearing. Other parties in all bankruptcy motion proceedings are the U.S. Trustee and the regular trustee.

The bankruptcy judge will hear argument on the motion and either rule right then and there (from the bench) or take the matter under submission (take it back to his or her chambers and think about it for a while). When the judge makes a decision, he or she typically issues a written decision and orders the prevailing party to prepare a formal order.

Either party may appeal the motion to a U.S. District Court or a Bankruptcy Appellate Panel (if one has been established in the district where the case is heard). Notice of appeal must usually be filed with the bankruptcy court *within ten days* of the date the court's decision or order is "entered." If you don't file this notice on time, you will almost surely lose your right to appeal.

bankruptcy petition preparers, but they are allowed only to fill in the bankruptcy forms in accordance with your instructions—they can't give you legal advice or appear for you in court. (See Ch. 11 for more information on bankruptcy petition preparers.)

This section briefly describes some of the more common court proceedings that might be required in a Chapter 7 bankruptcy (in addition to the abuse motion to dismiss or convert discussed above). This will give you an idea of what you'll be facing if one of these issues pops up in your case.

RESOURCE

Use Nolo resources to help you through the litigation maze. Nolo's *How to File for Chapter 7 Bankruptcy*, by Cara O'Neill and Albin Renauer, provides guidance for some of these procedures. *Represent Yourself in Court*, by Paul Bergman and Sara J. Berman (Nolo), also has an excellent chapter on litigating in bankruptcy court. For a plain-English guide to making your way through law books and other resources, see *Legal Research: How to Find & Understand the Law*, by Stephen R. Elias (Nolo).

Hearing on Relief From Stay

A creditor who wants to collect from you or your property directly may request relief from the automatic stay in order to do so. This is called a "relief from stay" hearing. (For more on the automatic stay, see Ch. 1.) This could come up, for example, if you are behind on your mortgage or car payments.

The creditor asks for this type of hearing by filing a motion in the bankruptcy case. The creditor doesn't need to file a separate lawsuit, as it would with some other types of disputes within a bankruptcy case. The work you have to do to oppose the request and get your side of the case heard in court is not all that difficult. However, you may need to do a little legal research.

Dischargeability Hearing

Ch. 3 explains that some types of debts survive your bankruptcy only if the creditor comes into court and challenges the proposed discharge of the debt. In addition, student loans and certain other types of debts will be discharged only if you (the debtor) file a separate action in the bankruptcy court against the creditor and convince the judge that the debt should be discharged. These court procedures that determine whether debts survive a bankruptcy are called "dischargeability" actions.

Debtors are most likely to bring dischargeability actions to discharge a student loan on the basis of hardship, or to cancel a tax debt on the basis that it meets the requirements for discharge under the bankruptcy code. Creditors are most likely to bring a dischargeability action alleging that a debtor incurred a debt through fraudulent means or caused personal injury through drunk driving or a willful and malicious act.

To start a dischargeability action, a creditor (or you) must file a separate complaint in the bankruptcy court, formally serve the complaint on the other party, and move the case forward to trial before the bankruptcy judge. This requires considerable research and knowledge of court rules. You are likely to have one or two false starts, in which the clerk returns your paperwork or the court tells you to try again. Dealing with formal court procedures can be quite frustrating for self-represented people. On the other hand, if there is enough money at stake, it may be worth your while to spend the time and deal with the frustration that comes with formal court litigation.

Of course, you can hire a bankruptcy attorney just for this part of your case, if there is enough at stake to justify paying the attorney's fees and you are able to find an attorney willing to provide limited services. (See Ch. 11.)

Reaffirmation Hearing

If you aren't represented by an attorney and have agreed with a creditor to "reaffirm" a debt (to recommit yourself to personal liability for a car note or another secured debt, despite your bankruptcy discharge), you will have to attend a hearing at which the judge will warn you of the consequences of reaffirmation: You'll continue to owe the full debt, you may lose the collateral if you default on your payments, and in many states, the creditor can sue you for any balance due after the property is sold at auction.

In some cases, the court will decide (on the basis of the debtor's income and expenses) that making the payments would be too much of a hardship to the debtor after bankruptcy, and will disallow the reaffirmation agreement.

The bankruptcy laws state that you have to enter into an agreement with the lender (assuming the lender requires it), but say nothing about what happens if the judge disallows the agreement. Courts have ruled that you are entitled to keep your vehicle if the only reason the car note is not reaffirmed is that the judge wouldn't allow it. Along this line, when disapproving reaffirmation agreements, some judges order lenders to refrain from repossessing cars as long as debtors are current on their payments. As a general rule, you are better off having the judge disapprove the reaffirmation agreement, since you'll then be able to keep the vehicle as long as you remain current, but you won't owe the car note if you have to give the car back sometime after your bankruptcy is over.

Lien Avoidance Motions

Ch. 6 explains that certain types of liens can be removed from your property in a Chapter 7 bankruptcy case. To do this, you need to file a motion to "avoid" the lien. As with other motions, you must mail the lienholder a written explanation of what you want (to avoid the lien) and why you are entitled to it. You must also provide the lien owner with a notice explaining what the lien owner must do to respond (in order to keep the lien). If there is no response, you can obtain an order to avoid the lien by default. If the creditor responds, you can set the matter for hearing. Sometimes, you set the matter for hearing in your initial notice—it all depends on the rules for your bankruptcy court's district.

Converting From One Chapter to Another

The bankruptcy law allows you to change your bankruptcy from one chapter to another in most circumstances. This process is called conversion. If you want to remain in bankruptcy and you convert, you won't have to pay another filing fee and your creditors are still prevented from taking action against you.

Conversions From Chapter 7

You may voluntarily convert a Chapter 7 case into a Chapter 11 (usually only businesses do this), Chapter 12 (for farmers), or Chapter 13 bankruptcy *at any time* unless you already converted to your Chapter 7 case from one of the other chapters. Some cases have held that a court may deny permission to convert if the conversion is made in bad faith, while other courts have upheld the plain language of the statute, which doesn't mention such a condition.

Upon a creditor's request, after notice and hearing, the court can convert a Chapter 7 case to a Chapter 11 case at any time. The court can convert your Chapter 7 case to a Chapter 13 case only if you

consent. For example, as explained earlier, if you file for Chapter 7 and your filing is found to be abusive, the court can convert the case to Chapter 13 if you consent. If you don't consent, the court will dismiss your case outright.

Your case cannot be converted unless you qualify for relief under the new chapter. For example, you can't convert to Chapter 13 unless you fall within the debt guidelines for that chapter (secured debts not exceeding $1,184,200 and unsecured debts not exceeding $394,725).

Conversions From Chapter 13

Just like a Chapter 7 bankruptcy, you can convert your Chapter 13 case to another chapter, but only if you qualify for relief under that chapter. And your Chapter 13 case can also be converted against your wishes, in some situations.

Voluntary Conversion

You may convert your Chapter 13 case into a Chapter 7 case at any time, as long as you qualify to file for Chapter 7 under the rules discussed in Ch. 2. As mentioned earlier, some courts don't require you to take the Chapter 7 means test upon such a conversion.

Involuntary Conversion

The U.S. Trustee, the trustee, or a creditor may request that the court, after notice and hearing, dismiss your Chapter 13 case or convert it to Chapter 7, whichever is in the best interest of your creditors. Your case might be converted to Chapter 7 rather than dismissed if your Chapter 13 filing was in bad faith and you have valuable nonexempt property that the trustee could seize for the benefit of your creditors. If, on the other hand, you have no nonexempt property, the creditors would benefit more from an outright dismissal.

The court may order the dismissal of your Chapter 13 case, or convert it to Chapter 7, only for cause, such as your:

- unreasonable delay that is prejudicial to your creditors
- nonpayment of any court fees or charges
- failure to file a repayment plan in a timely manner
- failure to start making your plan payments on time
- failure to comply with your plan
- failure to file your bankruptcy papers on time
- failure to stay current on your alimony or child support payments after your filing date, or
- failure to file your state and federal tax returns with the court.

Any time prior to confirming the Chapter 13 plan, the court, after notice and hearing, may order your case converted to Chapter 11 or 12 upon request by the U.S. Trustee, the trustee, or a creditor. If you are a farmer, the court may not order a conversion to Chapter 7, 11, or 12

unless you request it. As with Chapter 7, no conversion may be ordered to another chapter unless you qualify for relief under that chapter.

Effect of Conversion From Chapter 13 to Chapter 7

One issue that often arises in the course of a conversion from Chapter 13 to Chapter 7 is how you treated your property between your filing date and your conversion date. As explained in Ch. 4, the trustee technically owns all of the property in your bankruptcy estate—which is essentially everything you own when you file, except pensions. If you start out in Chapter 13 and sell some of your nonexempt property, then convert to Chapter 7, what happens to the property you got rid of? Not a problem. When you convert from Chapter 13 to Chapter 7, the property of the estate is the property that remains in your possession or under your control on the date of conversion.

What about property you got after you filed for Chapter 13 bankruptcy but before you converted to Chapter 7? In most cases, this property will not be part of your Chapter 7 bankruptcy estate. However, if you acted in bad faith when converting from Chapter 13 to 7, then the court may find that it is part of your bankruptcy estate.

If you are able to cram down a debt in Chapter 13, the lien remains on the property until you complete the plan or the claim is paid in full without regard to the cramdown. If you don't complete the plan, the cramdown becomes ineffective and you will still owe the entire debt with lien attached, less money you have paid to the creditor during your Chapter 13 plan. In Chapter 7, you'll have the opportunity to surrender or redeem the property.

Potential Problems in Chapter 13

As with Chapter 7 cases, there are some potential bumps in the road in Chapter 13 cases. These typically come up in the context of the confirmation hearing, where the judge approves or rejects your proposed repayment plan.

Confirmation Hearing

Unlike Chapter 7, a Chapter 13 bankruptcy requires at least one appearance before a bankruptcy judge—the confirmation hearing. At the confirmation hearing, the court approves or rejects your proposed repayment plan. (Rejecting a plan is also called "denial of confirmation.")

The confirmation hearing must be held between 20 days and 45 days after your meeting of creditors. However, the hearing can be held earlier if no one objects.

Although a judge technically presides over the confirmation hearing, the trustee usually runs the show. If the trustee tells the judge that he or she has no objection to your plan, and no creditor shows up to convince the judge that your plan is unfair, the judge will most likely approve the plan without a further hearing. But if the trustee has some problems with your plan, or a creditor raises issues of fairness, the judge will most likely send you back to the drawing board and reschedule ("continue," in legalese) the confirmation hearing to another date, when you will have to submit a modified plan. Each time you submit a modified plan, you must notify all of your creditors (typically, by using the mailing matrix prepared by the court).

If it becomes obvious that Chapter 13 bankruptcy isn't realistic for you—for example, you earn very little money to pay into a plan—the judge will typically order that your case be dismissed unless you want to convert it to Chapter 7 bankruptcy before the date set for the dismissal.

Objections to Your Plan

The trustee (or a creditor) may raise objections to your proposed plan. (See Ch. 2, "Chapter 13 Eligibility Requirements.")

Listed below are some objections you might face in Chapter 13.

The plan was not submitted in good faith. The bankruptcy law explicitly requires you to file for Chapter 13 in good faith. In determining whether you filed in good faith, courts will look to see whether your proposed plan has any purpose other than sincerely trying for a fresh start. For example, one bankruptcy court ruled that a Chapter 13 filing was not in good faith because the debtor filed for the sole purpose of getting around a judge's decision in an ongoing state court case. If you are filing your papers with the honest intention of getting back on your feet, and you really can make the payments required by the plan, you probably will be able to overcome a good-faith objection.

Most bankruptcy courts will look at the following factors:

- How often you have filed for bankruptcy. Filing and then dismissing multiple bankruptcies does not, in itself, show bad faith. However, if you've filed and dismissed two or more other bankruptcy cases within one year, the court may find lack of good faith if there are inconsistencies in your papers or you can't show that your circumstances have changed since the previous dismissal.

- The accuracy of your bankruptcy papers and oral statements. The court is likely to find a lack of good faith if you misrepresent your income, debts, expenses, or assets, or if you lie at the creditors' meeting.

- Your efforts to repay your debts. If your plan will pay your unsecured creditors a small percentage of what you owe, or nothing at all, you may have to show the court that you are stretching as much as you can. The court will want to see that you are not living luxuriously and that you are making substantial efforts to pay your unsecured creditors, even if it means trading in your fancy new car for a used model.

The plan is not feasible. Probably the most common objection is that your plan is not feasible—that is, you won't be able to make the required payments or comply with the other terms of the plan. To overcome this type of objection, your monthly income must exceed your monthly expenses by at least enough to allow you to make the payments required under Chapter 13 bankruptcy. For instance, a debtor who owes a $50,000 tax arrearage as well as $25,000 in credit card debts must propose a plan that, at a minimum, pays the $50,000 in full over the life of the plan (because taxes are usually a priority debt and must be paid in full).

The trustee or a creditor might also question your job stability, the likelihood that you'll incur extraordinary expenses, and whether you have any outside sources of money. If your plan seems to reflect too much wishful thinking, and your sources of money are uncertain, the court will probably reject the plan on the ground that it isn't feasible. Possible scenarios leading the court to find that your plan isn't feasible include:

- You have a business that has been failing, but you've predicted a rebound and intend to use business income to make your plan payments.

- You propose making plan payments from the proceeds of the sale of certain property, but nothing points to the likelihood of a sale.

- Your plan includes a balloon payment (a large payment at the end), but you have not identified a source of money from which the payment will be made.

The plan fails to promote the "best interest" of the creditors. Under your Chapter 13 repayment plan, you must pay your unsecured creditors at least as much as they would have received had you filed for Chapter 7 bankruptcy—that is, the value of your nonexempt property less the costs of sale and the trustee's commission. (Exemptions are discussed in Ch. 4 and the method for determining what the creditors would have received in a Chapter 7 bankruptcy is explained in Ch. 2.) This is called the "best interest of the creditors" test.

If the trustee or a creditor raises this objection, you will have to provide documents showing the values of the potentially nonexempt portions of your property, such as a recent appraisal of a home in which your equity is equal to or exceeds your state's homestead exemption, or a publication stating the value of an automobile of the same make, model, and year as yours. In determining property value, keep in mind that costs of sale also take into consideration the fact that at an auction (the means used by trustees to liquidate property in a Chapter 7 bankruptcy), property sells for about 60% of wholesale.

The plan unfairly discriminates. Chapter 13 bankruptcy is intended to treat all unsecured creditors fairly, relative to each other. You might be inclined to pay some unsecured creditors more than others—for example, you might propose to pay 100% of a student loan (which isn't dischargeable anyway) but only 35% of your credit card debts (which are dischargeable). In this situation, the trustee or the credit card issuers are likely to object to your plan on the ground that they are unfairly being discriminated against.

The plan doesn't provide adequate protection for collateral. Plans must provide that payments to secured creditors on property serving as collateral will be distributed in equal monthly amounts and will be sufficient to provide the creditor with adequate protection of its interest in the collateral.

You have not provided documents that the trustee requested.

Filling Out the Bankruptcy Forms

When you file bankruptcy, you'll need to complete a large number of official forms. Although all filers used to use the same forms, this has changed. You'll want to be sure that you're using the individual version for your filing (businesses use the "non-individual" forms).

You have several options for completing the forms. You can:

- download the forms from the Internet and fill them in yourself
- hire a bankruptcy petition preparer to complete the forms under your direction (see Ch. 11)

- get limited telephonic advice from a lawyer (this is unusual), or
- hire an attorney to handle everything.

If you use an attorney, the papers will be filed electronically in most courts. If you represent yourself, you will mail the forms to the court or file them in person.

Chapter 7 Documents

There are a number of documents you will have to file in a Chapter 7 case.

The Voluntary Petition

You start a Chapter 7 case by filing a "Voluntary Petition for Individuals Filing for Bankruptcy," the official court form that asks for some basic information, including:

- your name(s), address, and the last four digits of your Social Security number
- whether you have lived, maintained a residence, maintained a business, or had assets in the district for the better part of 180 days prior to filing (this establishes your right to file in a particular district)
- the type of bankruptcy you are filing (Chapter 7, 11, 12, or 13)
- whether your debts are primarily consumer or business
- whether you own a business
- how you will be paying your filing fee (at filing, in installments, or not at all because of a fee waiver)

- the estimated number of creditors
- the estimated amount of your debts
- the estimated value of your property
- whether you have nonexempt assets
- whether a judgment for eviction has been entered against you
- whether you are aware of some bankruptcy basics
- your history of bankruptcy filings within the past eight years, if any, and
- whether you have completed your debt counseling or obtained a waiver.

Additional Documents

A number of additional documents must be filed within 14 days after filing the petition. The best practice is to file all the documents when you file your petition, to keep your case under control (and make sure you don't miss the 14-day deadline).

Here are the documents you must provide:

- a list of all of your creditors, including each one's name, mailing address, and account number (this is called the "creditor matrix")
- lists of your assets (Schedule A/B: Property)
- a schedule of liabilities (Schedule D: Creditors Who Hold Claims Secured By Property and Schedule E/F: Creditors Who Have Unsecured Claims)

> **CAUTION**
>
> **You must list all of your debts.** Some people think they don't have to list debts that they intend to pay in full (for example, car loans). Not so. You must list each and every debt you have. And remember, just because you list a secured debt doesn't mean you'll lose the property that guarantees payment of the debt. (See Ch. 6 for more on secured debts.)

- a statement of your financial affairs for up to ten years prior to your filing date
- a schedule of your current income (Schedule I) and current expenditures (Schedule J)
- wage stubs for the 60 days prior to filing
- a statement of your average monthly gross income over the previous six months, and a means test calculation if your income exceeds the median income for a similar size family in your state
- a certificate showing that you received credit counseling from an authorized provider within the six months prior to filing
- a copy of any debt repayment plan you developed during your mandatory credit counseling
- a form showing that you received counseling in personal financial management from an authorized provider during the course of your bankruptcy case; this is due after filing and before you receive your discharge

- a copy of your most recent tax return or a transcript of the return obtained from the IRS (due to the bankruptcy trustee seven days prior to the creditors' meeting)
- a schedule indicating which assets you are claiming as exempt (Schedule C)
- a schedule of any executory contracts (contracts that are still in force and require action by one or both parties) and leases you have signed (Schedule G)
- a schedule of your codebtors, if any (Schedule H)
- a form called Statement of Intention for Individuals Filing Under Chapter 7, in which you tell your secured creditors how you plan to deal with your secured debt (see Ch. 6)
- if you are being evicted and want your bankruptcy filing to hold the eviction off, the certification and rent described in Ch. 5, and
- a form setting out your full Social Security number.

Chapter 13 Documents

Almost all of the documents required for a Chapter 7 bankruptcy are also required in a Chapter 13 bankruptcy, with the exception of the Statement of Intention for Individuals Filing Under Chapter 7.

In addition to these documents, you must file a proposed Chapter 13 repayment plan (most local courts have a mandatory form that you must use for your plan) and a form that you use to calculate your disposable income available to repay your unsecured creditors. You must also provide evidence that you have filed tax returns (or transcripts from the IRS) for the previous four tax years, prior to the creditors' meeting. The trustee can keep the creditors' meeting open for 120 days after the first date for which it is scheduled to allow you extra time to obtain and file your returns. And the court can give you 30 additional days, if necessary.

While your Chapter 13 case is pending, you must also file with the court:

- any new tax returns and amendments that you file with the IRS
- a statement under oath of your income and expenditures for each tax year, and
- a statement of your monthly income that shows how income, expenditures, and monthly income are calculated.

These statements must show:

- the amount and sources of your income
- the identity of any person who is responsible (along with you) for the support of any of your dependents, and
- the identity of any person who contributed, and the amount contributed, to your household.

Upon request, you must provide the tax returns to your creditors, the U.S. Trustee, and the bankruptcy trustee.

Basic Requirements for Completing Bankruptcy Documents

Whether you file on your own or with the help of a professional, you have a duty to make sure that your papers meet these requirements:

- **You must be thorough.** Always err on the side of giving too much information rather than too little.
- **You must respond to every question.** If a question doesn't apply to you, check the "none" box. If there isn't one, you will have to type "N/A" for "not applicable." Make sure to list and value all of your property, even if you think it has no value. List the property, and either put zero for its value, or check the "unknown" box. Then be prepared to explain your answer at the creditors' meeting.
- **You must be willing to repeat yourself.** Sometimes different forms—or different questions on the same form—ask for the same or overlapping information. You will have to provide the same information multiple times.
- **You must be scrupulously honest.** You must swear, under penalty of perjury, that you've been truthful on your bankruptcy forms. The most likely consequence for failing to be scrupulously honest is a dismissal of your bankruptcy case, but you could be prosecuted for perjury if it's evident that you deliberately lied.

RESOURCE

Finding the forms. You can find samples of the basic forms described in this section in Appendix C. You can also view the current official forms online at www.uscourts. gov/forms/bankruptcy-forms. These forms can be filled in online, but you can't save them (which means you should download the forms, make drafts, and then fill in and print each form based on your draft, one form at a time).

At first glance, you might think that there's no way you can deal with all of this paperwork. However, in Chapter 7 cases, it really isn't as difficult as it looks—especially if you have a simple case. Nolo publishes excellent, up-to-date, line-by-line guides for the forms, and you'll only need to complete the parts of the forms that apply to your personal situation. To paraphrase the old saying, just take it one document at a time.

Getting Help With Your Bankruptcy

You will have three sources of outside help if you wish to file for bankruptcy:

- a debt relief agency (as both lawyers and nonlawyer bankruptcy petition preparers are now called)
- a book that gives you step-by-step instructions on how to file for bankruptcy (such as those published by Nolo), or
- a combination of bankruptcy books, Internet sites, and lawyers.

Debt Relief Agencies

Any person or entity that you pay or otherwise compensate for help with your bankruptcy is considered a debt relief agency. The two main types of debt relief agencies are lawyers and bankruptcy petition preparers (BPPs). Credit counseling agencies and budget counseling agencies are not debt relief agencies. Nor are any of the following:

- employers or employees of debt relief agencies
- nonprofit organizations that have federal 501(c)(3) tax-exempt status
- any creditor who works with you to restructure your debt
- banks, credit unions, and other deposit institutions, or
- an author, publisher, distributor, or seller of works subject to copyright protection when acting in that capacity (in other words, Nolo and the stores that sell its books aren't debt relief agencies).

Lawyers and BPPs are covered separately below. This section explains what the bankruptcy law requires of debt relief agencies generally.

Lawyers Are Debt Relief Agencies

In *Milavetz v. United States*, 130 S. Ct. 1324 (2010), the Supreme Court ruled that lawyers may be considered debt relief agencies under the bankruptcy code and, therefore, are subject to the various notice and contract requirements imposed on all debt relief agencies. As to the rule which prohibits debt relief agencies from advising clients to undertake new debts, the Supreme Court said this section only prohibits lawyers from advising their clients to load up on debt that could later be discharged—and, therefore, did not infringe on lawyers' free speech rights.

Mandatory Contract

Within five days after a debt relief agency assists you, it (or he or she) must enter into a contract with you that explains, clearly and conspicuously:

- what services the agency will provide you
- what the agency will charge for the services, and
- the terms of payment.

The agency must give you a copy of the completed, signed contract.

Mandatory Disclosures and Notices

The debt relief agency must inform you, in writing, that:

- All information you are required to provide in your bankruptcy papers must be complete, accurate, and truthful.
- You must completely and accurately disclose your assets and liabilities in the documents you file to begin your case.
- You must undertake a reasonable inquiry to establish the replacement value of any item you plan to keep, before you provide that value on your forms.
- Your current monthly income, the amounts you provide in the means test, and your computation of projected disposable income (in a Chapter 13 case), as stated in your bankruptcy papers, must be based on a reasonable inquiry into their accuracy.
- Your case may be audited, and your failure to cooperate in the audit may result in dismissal of your case or some other sanction, including a possible criminal penalty.

In addition to these stark warnings, a debt relief agency must also give you a general notice regarding some basic bankruptcy requirements and your options for help in filing and pursuing your case. The agency must give you this within three business days after the agency first offers to provide you with services. Failure to give you this notice can land the agency in big trouble.

Restrictions on Debt Relief Agencies

A debt relief agency may not:

- fail to perform any service that the agency informed you it would perform in connection with your bankruptcy case
- counsel you to make any statement in a document that is untrue or misleading or that the agency should have known was untrue or misleading, or
- advise you to incur more debt in order to pay for the agency's services.

Any contract that doesn't comply with the requirements on debt relief agencies may not be enforced against you. A debt relief agency is liable to you for costs and fees, including legal fees, if the agency negligently or intentionally:

- fails to comply with the law's restrictions on debt relief agencies, or
- fails to file a document that results in dismissal of your case or conversion to another chapter.

In sum, debt relief agencies are on the hook if they are negligent in performing the services required by the bankruptcy law or other services they have agreed to provide.

Bankruptcy Petition Preparers

Bankruptcy petition preparers (BPPs) are basically typing services. Under the law, they are permitted to enter data onto the official bankruptcy forms, print them out, and file them with the court. BPPs cannot provide any legal advice, nor can they tell you what information to include on the forms.

What a Bankruptcy Petition Preparer Cannot Do

BPPs are very different from lawyers. BPPs are legally prohibited from giving you legal advice, which includes information such as:

- whether to file a bankruptcy petition or which chapter (7, 11, 12, or 13) is appropriate
- whether your debts will be discharged under a particular chapter
- whether you will be able to hang on to your home or other property if you file under a particular chapter (that is, which exemptions you should choose)
- information about the tax consequences of a case brought under a particular chapter or whether tax claims in your case can be discharged
- whether you should offer to repay or agree to reaffirm a debt
- how to characterize the nature of your interest in property or debts, and
- information about bankruptcy procedures and rights.

This ban on providing legal advice is important, because BPPs are not trained or licensed to provide legal advice. Many an individual has relied on a BPP's advice or recommendation, only to suffer serious consequences to his or her bankruptcy

case, such as losing assets or being denied a discharge of debts.

Fees

Each bankruptcy district imposes a strict cap on the fees that BPPs can charge, usually between $100 and $200. The U.S. Trustee reasons (and courts have upheld this reasoning) that BPP fees should be set according to what general typists in the community charge per page. This is because BPPs are not supposed to do anything other than type the forms.

Regulation of Bankruptcy Petition Preparers

Anyone can be a BPP. Yes, anyone. There is nothing in the bankruptcy code that requires BPPs to have any particular level of education, training, or experience. Unlike most other jobs, a prison record is no handicap to becoming a BPP. How, then, are BPPs regulated? Regulation is provided by the U.S. Trustee's office, which reviews all bankruptcy petitions prepared by BPPs. BPPs must provide their name, address, telephone number, and Social Security number on bankruptcy petitions, as well as on every other bankruptcy document they prepare. The U.S. Trustee uses this information to keep tabs on BPPs.

At the creditors' meeting, the bankruptcy trustee may ask you questions designed to determine if the BPP gave you legal advice.

For example, the trustee might ask how you chose your exemptions or how you decided which chapter to file under.

BPPs can be fined for certain actions and inactions spelled out in the bankruptcy code (11 U.S.C. § 110). These are:

- failing to put his or her name, address, and Social Security number on your bankruptcy petition
- failing to give you a copy of your bankruptcy documents when you sign them
- using the word "legal" or any similar term in advertisements, or advertising under a category that includes such terms, and
- accepting court filing fees from you. You must pay the filing fee to the court yourself or, in some districts, give the BPP a cashier's check made out to the court.

Finally, a BPP must submit a statement under oath with each petition he or she prepares stating how much you paid in the previous 12 months and any fees that you owe him or her but haven't yet paid. If BPPs charge more than they are permitted, they will be ordered to return the excess fees to their clients.

If a BPP provides legal advice, engages in any fraudulent act in regard to your case, or fails to comply with the rules governing his or her behavior listed above, the court can require the BPP to return your fee and pay a fine for each violation. If the BPP engaged in serious fraud, the court can require the BPP to pay a fine and an amount equal to three times your fee. The court can also order the BPP to stop providing services.

Does Regulation Work?

Unfortunately, many BPPs fail to provide their names, addresses, and telephone numbers on bankruptcy petitions and other documents. And many do not submit fee statements with the petitions they type. This makes it difficult for the U.S. Trustee to keep tabs on some BPPs—often the ones trying to skirt the law. This means that if something goes awry in your case because the BPP violated the law or gave you bad legal advice, the BPP is likely to slink away, leaving you to deal with negative impact on your case. The bottom line: Don't count on the U.S. Trustee or any other agency to protect you from BPP malfeasance.

Having said that, it is true that some districts are trying to crack down on bankruptcy petition preparers who fail to comply with the law or engage in outright fraud. For example, in the Central District of California (Los Angeles and surrounding counties), the court has banned 200 BPPs from providing services because they engaged in serious wrongdoing. But there are many others that the U.S. Trustee has not caught up with yet.

Can a BPP Give You Written Information?

Under the Bankruptcy Code, BPPs may prepare your bankruptcy forms only under your direction. This means you must tell the BPP what exemptions to choose, whether to file under Chapter 7 or Chapter 13, what approach to take in respect to your secured debts (car note, mortgage), and what values to place on your property. That's fine in theory, but unless you have the benefit of this book or another source of legal information, there is no way you would have adequate bankruptcy expertise to tell the BPP how to proceed. In an attempt to bridge this gap, many BPPs hand their customers written materials that contain information their customers need (although some skirt the law altogether by providing legal advice directly to you—which they are not authorized or trained to do). However, providing a customer with written legal information about bankruptcy has itself been held to be the unauthorized practice of law in many states (California is an important exception).

A Bankruptcy Petition Preparer Cannot Represent You

If you decide to use a BPP, remember that you are representing yourself and are responsible for the outcome of your case. This means not only learning about your rights under the bankruptcy law and understanding the proper procedures to be followed, but also accepting responsibility for correctly and accurately filling in the bankruptcy petition and schedules. If, for example, you lose your home because it turned out to be worth much more than you thought, and the homestead exemption available to you didn't cover your equity, you can't blame the BPP. Nor can you blame the BPP if other property is taken from you because you didn't get the necessary information—from a lawyer or from this book—to properly claim your exemptions. The point is, unless you hire a lawyer to represent you, you are solely responsible for acquiring the information necessary to competently pursue your case.

Bankruptcy Lawyers

Bankruptcy lawyers are regular lawyers who specialize in handling bankruptcy cases.

When You May Need a Lawyer

Most Chapter 7 bankruptcies sail through without a hitch if prepared correctly. However, there are some situations in which you may need some help from a bankruptcy lawyer:

- Your average income during the six months before you file is more than your state's median income, and it looks like you won't be able to pass the means test. (See Ch. 2 for more information on these calculations.)

- You want to hold onto a house or motor vehicle and the information we provide on these subjects doesn't adequately address your situation or answer all of your questions.

- You want to get rid of a student loan or income tax debt that won't be wiped out in bankruptcy unless you convince a court that it should be discharged.

- A creditor files a lawsuit in the bankruptcy court claiming that one of your debts should survive your bankruptcy because you incurred it through fraud or other misconduct.

- The bankruptcy trustee (the court official in charge of your case) seeks to have your whole bankruptcy dismissed because you didn't give honest and complete answers to questions about your assets, liabilities, and economic transactions.

- The U.S. Trustee asks the court to dismiss your case—or force you into Chapter 13—because your income is high enough to fund a Chapter 13 repayment plan, or because the trustee believes that your filing is an abuse of the Chapter 7 bankruptcy process for other reasons.

- You have recently given away or sold valuable property for less than it is worth.

- You went on a recent buying spree with your credit card (especially if you charged more than $675 on luxury goods within the past 90 days).

- You want help negotiating with a creditor or the bankruptcy court, and the amount involved justifies hiring a bankruptcy lawyer to assist you.

- You have a large lien on your property because of a court judgment against you, and you want to remove the lien in your bankruptcy case.

- A creditor is asking the court to allow it to proceed with its collection action despite your bankruptcy filing (for instance, a creditor wants to foreclose on your house because you are behind on your mortgage payments).

- You are being evicted by your landlord because you have fallen behind on your rent.

Even if you aren't facing one of these complications, you may still simply want the convenience and comfort of having a lawyer to guide you through your case. If you find the thought of going through the process overwhelming, a lawyer can take charge of your case and relieve you of the responsibility to get everything done. The lawyer can accompany you to the creditor's meeting, work with you to make sure that your documents are complete and accurate, get all your paperwork filed on time, and generally handle all of the little details that go into a successful bankruptcy case. Although representation comes at a price—which can be considerable—you will have the peace of mind of knowing that someone is watching your back. While we obviously believe that many people can handle their own Chapter 7 bankruptcies, it isn't right for everyone, especially if you have other significant sources of stress in your life or simply don't feel up to handling it all by yourself.

Full-Service Lawyer Representation

In a general sense, you are represented by a lawyer if you contract with the lawyer to handle some or all of your bankruptcy case for you. More specifically, there are two types of representation—the type where you hire a lawyer to assume complete responsibility for your bankruptcy and the type where you represent yourself but hire a lawyer to handle one particular aspect of your bankruptcy case. We refer to the first type of representation as "full-service representation" and the second type of representation as unbundled services (discussed below).

When providing full-service representation, a bankruptcy lawyer is responsible for making sure that all of your paperwork is filed on time and that the information in your paperwork is accurate. These duties require the lawyer to review various documents—for instance, your credit report, tax returns, and home value appraisal—both to ensure the accuracy of your paperwork and to make sure that you are filing for bankruptcy under the appropriate chapter. If your paperwork is inaccurate or you filed under Chapter 7 when you should have filed under Chapter 13, the lawyer can be fined a hefty amount and be required to return your fees.

In exchange for their basic fee, full-service bankruptcy lawyers typically are also responsible for appearing on your behalf at the creditors' meeting, representing you if a creditor opposes the discharge of a debt, and eliminating any liens that the bankruptcy laws allow to be stripped from your property.

Sometimes, a case appears to be simple at the beginning but turns out to be complicated later on. In that event, you might start out representing yourself but later decide to hire an attorney to handle a tricky issue that arises.

Before you decide that it's too expensive to get legal representation, go see some lawyers and find out. Many offer free consultations. And fees are almost always negotiable, especially since lawyers want your business.

Unbundled Services

Since the 1990s, some lawyers have been willing to offer their services on a piecemeal basis and provide legal advice over the telephone and Internet to help people who are representing themselves. In bankruptcy cases, lawyers are increasingly willing to step in and handle a particular matter, such as stripping liens from your property or handling a dischargeability action brought by you or a creditor.

When a lawyer does specific jobs at a client's request but doesn't contract for full-service representation in the underlying case, he or she is said to be providing an unbundled service. For example, you may be able to hire an attorney to handle a specific procedure—such as to defend against a motion for relief from stay—while you handle the main part of the bankruptcy yourself.

Few court cases discuss the boundaries of unbundled services. Some courts have held that attorneys can't "ghostwrite" legal documents for nonlawyers—because that would be a type of fraud on the court—but the issue has not been decided by most courts. Also, nothing prevents a lawyer from appearing for you in a limited capacity and putting his or her own name on associated documents.

Lawyers providing unbundled services usually charge an hourly fee. As a general rule, you should bring an attorney into the case for an unbundled service only if a dispute involves something valuable enough to justify the attorney's fees. If a creditor objects to the discharge of a $500 debt, and it will cost you $400 to hire an attorney, you may be better off trying to handle the matter yourself, even though this increases the risk that the creditor will win. If, however, the dispute is worth $1,000 and the attorney will cost you $200, hiring the attorney makes better sense.

Unfortunately, many bankruptcy attorneys do not like to appear or do paperwork on a piecemeal basis. Justified or not, these attorneys believe that by doing a little work for you, they might be on the hook if something goes wrong in another part of your case—that is, if they are in for a penny, they are in for a pound. Also, the bar associations of some states frown on unbundled services on ethical grounds. On the other hand, a number of other state bar associations are starting to encourage their attorneys to offer unbundled services simply because so many people—even middle-income people—are unable to afford full representation.

Bankruptcy Consultations

Some lawyers provide bankruptcy consultations (a category of unbundled service) for a transaction fee (for example, a $100 flat rate) or a fee based on the amount of time your call takes (for example, $3 a minute). There are also free consultations offered by private attorneys and bar associations. Similar services—free and paid—are available on the Internet. To find a telephonic or online consultation service, in addition to those mentioned here, go to Google or another search engine and look for "bankruptcy legal advice telephone or Internet."

You might want an attorney consultation to get advice about whether bankruptcy would be a good option for you. And even if you are planning to file for bankruptcy on your own, you may wish to consult with an attorney about a particular issue or question you have, such as which exemptions you should use or whether you should reaffirm a debt.

As with other debt relief agencies, lawyers offering telephonic services are considered debt relief agencies and must use a contract detailing their services as well as provide the other notices described above.

How to Find a Bankruptcy Lawyer

Where there's a bankruptcy court, there are bankruptcy lawyers. They're listed in the yellow pages under "Attorneys," and often advertise in newspapers. You should use an experienced bankruptcy lawyer, not a general practitioner, to handle or advise you on matters associated with bankruptcy.

There are several ways to find the best bankruptcy lawyer for your job:

- **Personal referrals.** This is your best approach. If you know someone who was pleased with the services of a bankruptcy lawyer, call that lawyer first.
- **Legal Aid.** Legal Aid offices are partially funded by the federal Legal Services Corporation and offer legal assistance in many areas. A few offices may do bankruptcies, although most do not. To qualify for Legal Aid, you must have a very low income.
- **Pro bono panels.** Some organizations help link clients to private attorneys who agree to take some cases for free, called pro bono services. Most likely, you'll have to qualify for pro bono services, which usually means having a low income. The American Bar Institute has a list of pro bono resources on its website. Go to www.bankruptcyresources.org, choose "Find Help," click on your state, then choose "Pro Bono Resources."
- **Legal clinic.** Many law schools sponsor legal clinics and provide free legal advice to consumers. Some legal clinics have the same income requirements as Legal Aid; others offer free services to low- and moderate-income people.
- **Group legal plans.** If you're a member of a plan that provides free or low-cost legal assistance and the plan covers bankruptcies, make that your first stop in looking for a lawyer.
- **Lawyer-referral panels.** Most county bar associations will give you the names of bankruptcy attorneys who practice in your area. But bar associations may not provide much screening. Take the time to check out the credentials and experience of the person to whom you're referred.
- **Internet directories.** Both bar associations and private companies provide lists of bankruptcy lawyers on the Internet, with a lot more information about the lawyer than you're likely to get in a yellow pages ad. A good place to start is Nolo's Lawyer Directory, at www.nolo.com (scroll down to the "Find a Lawyer" box).

Fees

For a routine Chapter 7 bankruptcy, a full-service lawyer will likely charge you somewhere between $1,000 and $2,000 (plus the $335 filing fee). In most situations, you will have to pay the attorney in full before he or she will file your case. This is because once you file your Chapter 7 bankruptcy, any money you owe the attorney is discharged along with your other dischargeable unsecured debts.

On your bankruptcy papers, you must state the amount you are paying your bankruptcy lawyer. Because every penny you pay to a bankruptcy lawyer is a penny not available to your creditors (at least in theory), the court has the legal authority to make the attorney justify his or her fee. This rarely happens, however, because attorneys know the range of fees generally allowed by local bankruptcy judges, and set their fees accordingly. This means that you probably won't find much variation in the amounts charged by lawyers in your area (although it never hurts to shop around).

The scope and range of services that the attorney promises you in return for your initial fee will be listed in the "Disclosure of Compensation of Attorney For Debtor" form. This form is filed as part of your bankruptcy papers. In the typical Chapter 7 case, the attorney's fee will include the routine tasks associated with a bankruptcy filing: counseling, preparing bankruptcy and reaffirmation forms, and attendance at the creditors' meeting. Any task not included in the disclosure form is subject to a separate fee.

If your case will likely require more attorney time, you may—and probably will—be charged extra, according to the attorney's hourly fee or other criteria he or she uses. A typical bankruptcy attorney charges between $200 and $300 an hour (rural and urban) and would charge a minimum of roughly $400 to $600 for a court appearance. Some attorneys will add these fees to their standard fee and require you to pay it all in advance. For instance, if the attorney's standard fee is $1,500, but the attorney sees extra work down the line, you may be charged $2,000 in anticipation of the extra work.

Other attorneys will happily charge you their standard fee up front and wait until after you file to charge you for the extra work. Because these fees are earned after your bankruptcy filing, they won't be discharged in your bankruptcy and the attorney need not collect them up front. Whatever the attorney charges you, you are protected against fee gouging. An attorney must file a supplemental form to obtain the court's permission for any postfiling fees.

Attorneys charge a lot more for Chapter 13 bankruptcies because those cases involve substantially more work. Rates vary significantly depending on where you live. Nationwide, most bankruptcy attorneys charge somewhere between $2,500 and

$5,500 to represent you in a Chapter 13 bankruptcy. If your case is complicated, the fee may be higher.

What to Look for in a Lawyer

No matter how you find a lawyer, these three suggestions will help you make sure you have the best possible working relationship.

First, fight any urge you may have to surrender to, or be intimidated by, the lawyer. You should be the one who decides what you feel comfortable doing about your legal and financial affairs. Keep in mind that you're hiring the lawyer to perform a service for you, so shop around if the price or personality isn't right.

Second, make sure you have good "chemistry" with any lawyer you hire. Ask specific questions. Do you get clear, concise answers? If not, try someone else. Also, pay attention to how the lawyer responds to your knowledge. If you've read this book, you're already better informed than most clients (and some lawyers are threatened by clients who have done their homework).

TIP

Talk directly to the lawyer. When making an appointment, ask to talk directly to the lawyer. If you can't, this may give you a hint as to how accessible he or she is. If you're told that a paralegal will be handling the routine aspects of your case under the supervision of a lawyer, you should not be satisfied with that arrangement.

Finally, once you find a lawyer you like, make an hour-long appointment to discuss your situation fully. The lawyer or a paralegal in the lawyer's office will tell you what, if anything, to bring to the meeting (if not, be sure to ask ahead of time). Some lawyers will want to see a recent credit report and tax return, while others will send you a questionnaire to complete prior to your visit. Depending on the circumstances, you may also be asked to bring your bills and documents pertaining to your home and other real estate you own. Some lawyers prefer not to deal with details during the first visit, and will simply ask you to come as you are.

Your main goal at the initial conference is to find out what the lawyer recommends in your particular case and how much it will cost. Go home and think about the lawyer's suggestions. If they don't make sense or you have other reservations, call someone else.

TIP

Look for a state-bar-certified bankruptcy specialist or member of the NACBA. Membership in the National Association of Consumer Bankruptcy Attorneys (NACBA) is a good sign that your lawyer will be tuned in to the nuances of the law and the court interpretations of the law that are sure to come. And a certified bankruptcy specialist is also a good bet since he or she will have experience plus other credentials (not all states certify bankruptcy specialists). Those credentials vary by state, but might include passing a special bankruptcy exam, handling a certain number of cases, completing a large number of continuing education classes in bankruptcy, and receiving a recommendation from a bankruptcy judge, bankruptcy trustee, and/or other bankruptcy attorneys.

Legal Research

Legal research can vary from the very simple to the hopelessly complex. In this section, we are staying on the simple side. If you would like to learn more about legal research or if you find that our suggestions come up a bit short in your particular case, we recommend that you obtain a copy of *Legal Research: How to Find & Understand the Law*, by Stephen Elias (Nolo), which provides a plain-English tutorial on legal research in the law library and on the Internet.

Sources of Bankruptcy Law

Bankruptcy law comes from a variety of sources:

- federal bankruptcy statutes passed by Congress
- federal rules about bankruptcy procedure issued by a federal judicial agency
- local rules issued by individual bankruptcy courts
- federal and bankruptcy court cases applying bankruptcy laws to specific disputes
- laws (statutes) passed by state legislatures that define the property you can keep in bankruptcy, and

- state court cases interpreting state exemption statutes.

Not so long ago, you would have had to visit a law library to find these resources. Now you can find most of them on the Internet. However, if you are able to visit a decent-sized law library, your research will be the better for it. Using actual books allows you to more easily find and read relevant court interpretations of the underlying statutes and rules—which are crucial to getting a clear picture of what the laws and rules really mean.

There is another important reason to visit the law library, if possible. While you can find superficial discussions and overviews of various aspects of bankruptcy on the Internet, you'll find in-depth encyclopedias and treatises in the law library that delve into every aspect of bankruptcy. In other words, you can find not only the law itself, but also what the experts have to say about all the picky little issues that have arisen over the years. Also, books in a law library are almost always subjected to a rigorous quality control process—as is this book—whereas you never know what you're getting on the Internet. To avoid getting lost in cyberspace, follow our suggestions below for researching bankruptcy law online and avoid the temptation to settle for the first hit in a Google search.

Below, we show you how to get to the resources you'll most likely be using, whether you are doing your research on the Internet or in the law library.

Bankruptcy Background Materials: Overviews, Encyclopedias, and Treatises

Before digging into the primary law sources (statutes, rules, cases, and so on that we discuss below), you may want to do some background reading to get a firm grasp of your issue or question.

The Internet

A number of Internet sites contain large collections of articles written by experts about various aspects of bankruptcy. A good starting place is Nolo's website, www. nolo.com, which offers lots of information and resources.

The Law Library

Providing you with a good treatise or encyclopedia discussion of bankruptcy is where the law library shines. This type of resource is not typically available online unless you find a way to access the expensive legal databases—Westlaw and Lexis—marketed almost exclusively to lawyers. Call your local law library—you might be able to access them at no cost.

Collier on Bankruptcy

It's a good idea to get an overview of your subject before trying to find a precise answer to a precise question. The best way to do this is to find a general commentary on your subject by a bankruptcy expert. For example, if you want to find out whether a particular debt is nondischargeable, you should start by reading a general discussion about the type of debt you're dealing with. Or, if you don't know whether you're entitled to claim certain property as exempt, a good overview of your state's exemptions would get you started on the right track.

The most complete source of this type of background information is a set of books known as *Collier on Bankruptcy*, by Lawrence P. King, et al (Matthew Bender). It's available in virtually all law libraries. *Collier* is both incredibly thorough and meticulously up to date; semiannual supplements, with all the latest developments, are in the front of each volume. In addition to comments on every aspect of bankruptcy law, *Collier* contains the bankruptcy statutes, rules, and exemption lists for every state.

Collier is organized according to the bankruptcy statutes. This means that the quickest way to find information in it is to know what statute you're looking for. (See the Bankruptcy Code sections set out below.) If you still can't figure out the governing statute, start with the *Collier* subject matter index. Be warned, however, that the index can be difficult to use because it contains a lot of bankruptcy jargon you may be unfamiliar with. A legal dictionary will be available in the library.

Foreclosure Resources

If you are facing foreclosure, you'll definitely want to look at *The Foreclosure Survival Guide,* by Amy Loftsgordon (Nolo). This book explains the options available to you, and then walks you through the necessary steps for handling your particular situation.

Other Background Resources

For general discussions of bankruptcy issues, there are several other good places to start. An excellent all-around resource is called *Consumer Bankruptcy Law and Practice.* This volume, published by the National Consumer Law Center, is updated every year. It contains a complete discussion of Chapter 7 bankruptcy procedures, the official bankruptcy forms, and a marvelous bibliography.

Another good treatise is a legal encyclopedia called *American Jurisprudence*, 2nd Series. Almost all law libraries carry it. The article on bankruptcy has an extensive table of contents, and the entire encyclopedia has an index. Between these two tools, you should be able to zero in on helpful material. Finally, some large and well-stocked law libraries carry a looseleaf publication known as the Commerce Clearing House (CCH) *Bankruptcy Law Reporter* (BLR). In this publication, you can find all three primary source materials relating to bankruptcy: statutes, rules, and cases.

If you are looking for information on adversary proceedings (such as how to defend against a creditor's challenge to the dischargeability of a debt), turn to *Represent Yourself in Court,* by Paul Bergman and Sara J. Berman (Nolo). It has an entire chapter on representing yourself in adversary proceedings in bankruptcy court. If you

---

How to Use Law Libraries

Law libraries that are open to the public are most often found in and around courthouses. Law schools also frequently admit the public at least some of the time (not, typically during exam time, over the summer, or during other breaks in the academic year).

If you're using a library as a member of the public, find a way to feel at home, even if it seems that the library is run mostly to serve members of the legal community. Almost without exception, law libraries come with law librarians. The law librarians will be helpful as long as you ask them the right questions. For example, the law librarians will help you find specific library resources, such as where you can find the federal bankruptcy statutes or rules, but they normally won't teach you the ins and outs of legal research. Nor will they give an opinion about what a law means, how you should deal with the court, or how your particular question should be answered. For instance, if you want to find a state case interpreting a particular exemption, the law librarian will show you where your state code is located on the shelves and may even point out the volumes that contain the exemptions. The librarian won't, however, help you interpret an exemption, apply the exemption to your specific facts, or tell you how to raise the exemption in your bankruptcy case. Nor is the librarian likely to tell you what additional research steps you can or should take. When it comes to legal research in the law library, self-help is the order of the day.

need information on court procedures or the local rules of a specific court, consult the *Collier Bankruptcy Practice Manual*.

Finding Federal Bankruptcy Statutes

Title 11 of the United States Code contains all the statutes that govern your bankruptcy.

The Internet

If you are using the Internet, go to the Legal Information Institute of Cornell University Law School, www.law.cornell.edu. Cornell lets you browse laws by subject matter and also offers a keyword search. To help you in your browsing, below is a table setting out the various subject matter sections of the U.S. Code that apply to bankruptcy.

The Law Library

Virtually every law library has at least one complete set of the annotated United States Code ("annotated" means that each statute is followed by citations and summaries of cases interpreting that provision). If you already have a citation to the statute you are seeking, you can use the citation to find the statute. However, if you have no citation—which is frequently the case—you can use either the index to Title 11 (the part of the Code that applies to bankruptcy) or the table we set out below, which matches various issues that are likely to interest you with specific sections of Title 11.

Once you have found and read the statute, you can browse the one-paragraph summaries of written opinions issued by courts that have interpreted that particular statute. You will be looking to see whether a court has addressed your particular issue. If so, you can find and read the entire case in the law library. Reading what a judge has had to say about the statute regarding facts similar to yours is an invaluable guide to understanding how a judge is likely to handle the issue in your case, although when and where the case was decided may be important.

Finding the Federal Rules of Bankruptcy Procedure (FRBP)

The Federal Rules of Bankruptcy Procedure govern what happens if an issue is contested in the bankruptcy court. They also apply to certain routine bankruptcy procedures, such as deadlines for filing paperwork. Because most cases sail through the court without any need for the bankruptcy judge's intervention, you may not need to be familiar with these rules. However, certain types of creditor actions in the bankruptcy court must proceed by way of a regular lawsuit conducted under both these rules and the Federal Rules of Civil Procedure—for example, complaints to determine dischargeability of a debt. If you are representing yourself in such a lawsuit, you'll want to know these rules and look at the cases interpreting them. Any law library will have these rules. Your bankruptcy court's website will also have a link to the rules, as does www.law.cornell.edu.

Finding Local Court Rules

Every bankruptcy court operates under a set of local rules that govern how it does business and what is expected of the parties who use it. Throughout this book, we have cautioned you to read the rules for your particular court so that your dealings with the court will go smoothly—and so you won't end up getting tossed out of court if you become involved in litigation, such as an action to determine the dischargeability of a debt or a creditor's motion to lift the automatic stay.

Your bankruptcy court clerk's office will have the local rules available for you. Most courts also post their local rules on their own websites. To find the website for your court, take these steps:

Step 1: Go to www.uscourts.gov/locator.

Step 2: Select "bankruptcy" and enter your zip code in the "Find a Courthouse" box.

Step 3: Browse the list until you find your court and click on it.

Step 4: Click on the local rules link.

Court websites usually contain other helpful information as well, including case information, official and local bankruptcy forms, court guidelines (in addition to the local rules), information for lawyers and BPPs, information about the court and its judges, and the court calendar.

At the law library, the *Collier Bankruptcy Practice Manual* has the local rules for most (if not all) of the nation's bankruptcy courts.

Finding Federal Court Bankruptcy Cases

Court opinions are vital to understanding how a particular law might apply to your individual case. The following levels of federal courts issue bankruptcy-related opinions:

- the U.S. Supreme Court
- the U.S. Courts of Appeals
- the Bankruptcy Appellate Panels
- the U.S. District Courts, and
- the bankruptcy courts.

Most bankruptcy-related opinions are, not surprisingly, issued by the bankruptcy courts. By comparison, very few bankruptcy opinions come out of the U.S. Supreme Court. The other courts are somewhere in the middle.

The Internet

Depending on the date a case was decided, U.S. Supreme Court decisions and U.S. Court of Appeals decisions are available for free on the Internet. You can also subscribe to VersusLaw (at www.versuslaw.com), which provides U.S. Court of Appeals cases for an earlier period than you can get for free—often back to 1950. VersusLaw doesn't require you to sign a long-term contract and you can try it for free. VersusLaw also publishes many U.S. District Court cases on its website.

Bankruptcy Code Sections (11 U.S.C.)

§ 101   Definitions

§ 109   Who May File for Which Type of Bankruptcy; Credit Counseling Requirements

§ 110   Rules for Bankruptcy Petition Preparers

§ 111   Budget and Credit Counseling Agencies

§ 302   Who Can File Joint Cases

§ 326   How Trustees Are Compensated

§ 332   Consumer Privacy Ombudsmen

§ 341   Meeting of Creditors

§ 342   Notice of Creditors' Meeting; Informational Notice to Debtors; Requirements for Notice by Debtors

§ 343   Examination of Debtor at Creditors' Meeting

§ 348   Converting From One Type of Bankruptcy to Another

§ 349   Dismissing a Case

§ 350   Closing and Reopening a Case

§ 362   The Automatic Stay

§ 365   How Leases and Executory Contracts Are Treated in Bankruptcy

§ 366   Continuing or Reconnecting Utility Service

§ 501   Filing of Creditors' Claims

§ 506   Allowed Secured Claims and Lien Avoidance

§ 507   Priority Claims

§ 521   Paperwork Requirements and Deadlines

§ 522   Exemptions; Residency Requirements for Homestead Exemption; Stripping Liens From Property

§ 523   Nondischargeable Debts

§ 524   Effect of Discharge and Reaffirmation of Debts

§ 525   Prohibited Postbankruptcy Discrimination

§ 526   Restrictions on Debt Relief Agencies

§ 527   Required Disclosures by Debt Relief Agencies

§ 528   Requirements for Debt Relief Agencies

§ 541   What Property Is Part of the Bankruptcy Estate

§ 547   Preferences

§ 548   Fraudulent Transfers

§ 554   Trustee's Abandonment of Property in the Bankruptcy Estate

§ 707   The Means Test; Dismissal for Abuse; Conversion From Chapter 7 to Chapter 13

§ 722   Redemption of Liens on Personal Property

§ 727   Chapter 7 Discharge; Financial Management Counseling Requirements

§ 1301   Stay of Action Against Codebtor

§ 1302   Duties of the Chapter 13 Trustee

§ 1304   Rights of Chapter 13 Debtor Engaged in Business

§ 1305   Property of the Chapter 13 Bankruptcy Estate

§ 1307   Conversion of Chapter 13 to Another Title and Dismissal

§ 1308   Pre-petition Tax Return Filing Requirement

§ 1322   Required Contents of Chapter 13 Plan

§ 1323   Modification of Plan Before Confirmation

§ 1324   Timing of Confirmation Hearing

§ 1325   Requirements for Confirmation of Plan

§ 1326   Chapter 13 Plan Payments

§ 1327   Effect of Confirmation

§ 1328   Requirements for, and Effect of, Chapter 13 Discharge

§ 1329   Modification of Chapter 13 Plan After Confirmation

Opinions by the bankruptcy courts are generally not yet available over the Internet, unless you subscribe to Lexis or Westlaw, both of which are extremely pricey.

U.S. Supreme Court. To find a Supreme Court case, go to www.supremecourt.gov.

U.S. Court of Appeals. Google has federal appeals cases going back to 1925. Go to "Google Scholar." Then simply select "Case Law" and type in a case name.

U.S. District Court and Bankruptcy Court. Cases reported by the bankruptcy courts are generally not available online unless you subscribe to Westlaw or Lexis. However, if you know the name of a particular case and the court that decided it, a Google search might lead you to a court's website, where some judges post their decisions. Still, you will probably have to take a trip to a law library if you want to know what the judges are doing in these courts—where the legal rubber meets the judicial road.

The Law Library

U.S. Supreme Court cases are published in three different book series:

- *Supreme Court Reports*
- *Supreme Court Reporter,* and
- *Supreme Court Lawyer's Edition.*

Some law libraries carry all three of these publications; others have only one. The cases are the same, but each series has different editorial enhancements.

U.S. Court of Appeals cases are published in the *Federal Reporter* (abbreviated simply as "F."). Most law libraries, large and small, carry this series.

Many U.S. District Court cases are published in the *Federal Supplement* (F.Supp.), a series available in most law libraries.

Written opinions of bankruptcy judges, and related appeals, are published in the *Bankruptcy Reporter* (B.R.), available in most mid- to large-sized libraries. To accurately understand how your bankruptcy court is likely to interpret the laws in your particular case, sooner or later you will need access to the *Bankruptcy Reporter.*

State Statutes

The secret to understanding what property you can keep frequently lies in the exemptions that your state allows you to claim. These exemptions are found in your state's statutes.

The Internet

Every state has its statutes online, including its exemption statutes. This means that you can read your state's exemption statutes for yourself. Follow these steps:

Step 1: Go to Appendix A. At the top of your state's exemption table, you'll see a general reference to the collection of laws for your state that contains the exemption statutes.

The Structure of the Court System for Bankruptcy Cases

Bankruptcy court decisions play a role in the overall bankruptcy law. Every state has at least one bankruptcy court and most states have several. Each of these courts is called on to decide contested issues arising in the bankruptcy cases filed in that court. Many of these decisions are published in the *Bankruptcy Reporter*, published by West Publishing Co.

If a party doesn't like the outcome of the bankruptcy court's decision, and can afford it, it can appeal the case (ask a higher court to review the decision) to the U.S District Court in the area where the bankruptcy court is located. In many parts of the country, the party may opt instead to appeal to the Bankruptcy Appellate Panel, or BAP, in the judicial circuit in which the bankruptcy court is located. U.S. District Court decisions do not have to be followed by other courts that decide the same issue, but the opinions by the BAP must be followed by the bankruptcy courts in the same judicial circuit unless

these opinions conflict with a higher circuit court (see below). These decisions are routinely published in volumes covering the U.S. District Court and the U.S. Court of Appeals.

If a party doesn't like a decision issued by a U.S. District Court or BAP, it can appeal the decision to the U.S. Court of Appeals in the appropriate judicial circuit. (This would be the second appeal.) A decision by the Court of Appeals supersedes decisions by the U.S. District Court or BAP and becomes law for that circuit. These decisions are also published alongside other Court of Appeal decisions.

Finally, a party to a U.S. Court of Appeals decision can appeal that decision to the U.S. Supreme Court (called petitioning for certiorari). The U.S. Supreme Court can decide to hear the case, or not. Decisions by the U.S. Supreme Court are the last word on any particular issue. These decisions are published along with other U.S. Supreme Court decisions.

Step 2: Go to www.nolo.com/legal-research/state-law.html.

Step 3: Under "State Law Resources," click on your state.

Step 4: Click on the link to your state's code.

Step 5: Use the exemption citation to the far right of your state's exemption table to search for the statute.

The Law Library

Your law library will have your state's statutes in book form, usually referred to as your state's code, annotated statutes, or compiled laws. Use Appendix A in this book to find a reference to the exemption statute you want to read, then use that reference to locate the exemption statute in the code. Once you find and read the statute, you can browse the summaries of court opinions interpreting the statute and, if you wish, read the cases in their entirety.

Alternatively, if your library has a copy of *Collier on Bankruptcy* (see above), you can find the exemptions for your state, accompanied by annotations summarizing state court interpretations.

State Court Cases

State courts are sometimes called on to interpret exemption statutes. If a court has interpreted the statute in which you are interested, you'll definitely want to chase down the relevant case and read it for yourself.

The Internet

All states make their more recent cases available free on the Internet—usually back to about 1996. To find these cases for your state:

Step 1: Go to www.law.cornell.edu/opinions.html#state.

Step 2: Click on your state.

Step 3: Locate the link to the court opinions for your state. This may be one link, or there may be separate links for your state's supreme court and your state's courts of appeal (the lower trial courts seldom publish their opinions, so you probably won't be able to find them).

If you want to go back to an earlier case, consider subscribing to VersusLaw at www.versuslaw.com. As mentioned earlier, you don't have to sign a long-term contract.

The Law Library

Your law library will have a collection of books that contains opinions issued by your state's courts. If you have a citation, you can go right to the case. If you don't have a citation, you'll need to use a digest to find relevant bankruptcy cases. Finding cases by subject matter is a little too advanced for this brief summary. See *Legal Research: How to Find & Understand the Law*, by Stephen Elias (Nolo), for more help.

Other Helpful Resources

The Office of the United States Trustee's website, at www.justice.gov/ust, provides lists of approved credit and financial management counseling agencies, median income figures for every state, the IRS national, regional, and local expenses you will need to complete the means test, and all of the forms you will need to file, in a fill-in-the-blanks PDF format. You can also download official bankruptcy forms from www.uscourts.gov/forms/bankruptcy-forms. However, this site doesn't include required local forms; for those, you'll have to visit your court or its website.

As part of the bankruptcy process, you are required to give the replacement (retail) value for all of the property you list in Schedule A/B. These figures are also the key to figuring out which of your property is exempt. Here are some tips on finding these values:

- **Cars.** Use the *Kelley Blue Book*, at www.kbb.com, or the website of the National Auto Dealers Association, www.nada.com.

- **Other personal property.** Check prices on eBay, www.ebay.com.
- **Homes.** Check the prices for which comparable homes have sold in the recent past. Information (purchase price, sales date, and address) is available free from sites like www.zillow.com, www.homevalues.com, and realtor.com. ●

Alternatives to Bankruptcy

After reading the previous 11 chapters, you should have a pretty good idea of what filing a consumer Chapter 7 or a Chapter 13 bankruptcy will involve —and what you can hope to get out of it. Before you decide whether either type of bankruptcy is the right solution, however, consider the other options described in this chapter. Although bankruptcy is the only sensible remedy for some people with debt problems, an alternative course of action makes better sense for others.

Do Nothing

Surprisingly, the best approach for some people who are deeply in debt is to take no action at all. You can't be thrown in jail for being unable to pay your debts (except in rare cases in which a court finds you in contempt of a court order), and your creditors can't collect money from you that you just don't have.

Creditors Must Sue to Collect

Except for taxing agencies and student loan creditors, creditors must first sue you in court and get a money judgment before they can go after your income and property. The big exception to this general rule is that a creditor can take back collateral— repossess a car or furniture, for example— when you default on a debt that's secured by that collateral. (If you're worried about foreclosure on a house, see Ch. 5.)

Under the typical security agreement (a contract involving collateral), the creditor can repossess the property without first going to court. But the creditor will not be able to go after your other property and income for any "deficiency" (the difference between what you owe and what the repossessed property fetches at auction) without first going to court for a money judgment.

Much of Your Property Is Protected

Even if creditors get a money judgment against you, they can't take away such essentials as:

- basic clothing
- ordinary household furnishings
- personal effects
- food
- Social Security or SSI payments
- unemployment benefits
- public assistance
- bank accounts with direct deposits from government benefit programs, and
- 75% of your wages (but child support judgments can grab a larger share).

The state exemptions described in Ch. 4 (and listed in Appendix A) apply whether or not you file for bankruptcy. Even creditors who get a money judgment against you can't seize these protected items to satisfy the judgment. (However, neither the federal bankruptcy exemptions nor the California System 2 exemptions described in Ch. 4 apply if a creditor sues you. Those are bankruptcy-only exemptions. And once in a while, a state might have an exemption that applies in bankruptcy but not to judgment creditors.)

What It Means to Be Judgment Proof

If all of the property you own is exempt, you are what is commonly referred to as "judgment proof." Whoever sues you and wins will be holding a useless piece of paper (at least temporarily), simply because you don't have anything that can legally be taken. While money judgments last a long time—typically ten years—and can be renewed, this won't make any difference unless your finances change for the better. If that happens, you might reconsider bankruptcy at that time.

If your creditors know that their chances of collecting a judgment from you any time soon are slim, they probably won't sue you in the first place. Instead, they'll simply write off your debt and treat it as a deductible business loss for income tax purposes. After some years have passed (usually between four and ten), the debt will become legally uncollectable, under state laws known as statutes of limitation.

Even if the creditor sues you in time, lawsuits cost money. If a creditor decides not to go to court at the present time, it is unlikely to seek a judgment at a later date. In short, because creditors are reluctant to throw good money after bad, your poor economic circumstances might shield you from trouble.

> **CAUTION**
>
> **Watch out for later liens, even if you don't currently own real estate.** Even though you may technically be judgment proof because you don't own any real estate, a lien recorded in your county may cause problems later on if you buy a house. This is because in some states (including California) creditors can record liens even if you don't own any property. If you later buy property, the lien will "pop up" and attach to the property, meaning you'll have to deal with it. If this happens after you've completed a bankruptcy, you may be able to reopen the bankruptcy and file a motion to avoid the lien (See Ch. 10).

> **CAUTION**
>
> **Don't restart the clock.** The statute of limitations can be renewed if you revive an old debt by, for example, admitting that you owe it or making a payment. As soon as you acknowledge a debt, the clock starts all over again. Savvy creditors are aware of this loophole and may try to trick you into admitting the debt so they can sue to collect it. Sometimes, it might be a good idea to try to repay a debt, particularly one to a local merchant with whom you wish to continue doing business. But unless you are planning to make good on the debt or try to negotiate a new payment schedule, you should avoid any admissions. (You'll find a sample letter that avoids admitting a debt below.)

Stopping Debt Collector Harassment

Many people are moved to file for bankruptcy to stop their creditors from making harassing telephone calls and writing threatening letters. (See Ch. 1 for more on the automatic stay.) Fortunately, there is another way to get annoying creditors off your back if they are collecting consumer debts. (This law doesn't apply to the collection of business debts.) Federal law forbids collection agencies from threatening you, lying about what they can do to you, or invading your privacy. And many state laws prevent original creditors from taking similar actions.

Under the federal law, you can legally force collection agencies to stop phoning or writing you by simply demanding that they stop, even if you owe them a bundle and can't pay a cent. (The law is the federal Fair Debt Collections Practices Act, 15 U.S.C. §§ 1692 and following.) For more information, see *Solve Your Money Troubles*, by Amy Loftsgordon and Cara O'Neill (Nolo). Below is a sample letter asking a creditor to stop contacting the debtor.

Negotiate With Your Creditors

If you have some income, or you have assets you're willing to sell, you may be better off negotiating with your creditors than filing for bankruptcy. Negotiation may buy you some time to get back on your feet, or you and your creditors may agree to settle your debts for less than the amount you owe.

Sample Letter to Collection Agency

November 11, 20xx
Sasnak Collection Service
49 Pirate Place
Topeka, Kansas 69000

Attn: Marc Mist

Re: Lee Anne Ito

Account No. 88-90-92

Dear Mr. Mist:

For the past three months, I have received several phone calls and letters from you concerning an overdue Rich's Department Store account.

This is my formal notice to you under 15 U.S.C. § 1692c to cease all further communications with me except for the reasons specifically set forth in the federal law.

This letter is not meant in any way to be an acknowledgment that I owe this money.

Very truly yours,

Lee Anne Ito
Lee Anne Ito

Creditors don't like the hassle of instituting collection proceedings, or the fact that these proceedings tend to turn debt-owing customers into former customers. To avoid the collection process and to keep customers, creditors sometimes will reduce the debtor's expected payments, extend the time to pay, drop their demands for late fees, and make similar adjustments. They're most likely to be lenient if they believe you are making an honest effort to deal with your debt problems.

As soon as it becomes clear to you that you're going to have trouble paying a bill, call or write to the creditor. Explain the problem—whether it's an accident, job layoff, divorce, emergency expense for your child, unexpected tax bill, or something else. Mention any development that points to an improving financial condition, such as job prospects. This tells the creditor that you are continuing to be serious about paying the full debt but just can't afford to right now.

Token payments make a big difference, especially to local creditors. And if you want to keep that credit or that business relationship, paying even a small amount might help. On the other hand, if it's been a long time since you've made any payments, you might want to hold off on any payment until you've checked on the "statute of limitations" for that debt (the state time limit after which the debt goes away if no court action has been filed to collect it). Your payment might have the unfortunate effect of starting up a new limitations period. Restarting the statute of limitations period gives the creditor more time to sue you.

Your success in getting creditors to give you time to pay will depend on the types of debts you have, how far behind you are,

and the creditors' policies toward debts that are in arrears.

If you are not yet behind on your bills, be aware that a number of creditors have a policy that requires you to default—and in some cases, become at least 90 days past due—before they will negotiate with you for better repayment terms. If any creditor makes this a condition of negotiating, find out from the creditor if it can keep the default out of your credit report.

Some creditors simply refuse to negotiate with debtors. Despite the fact that creditors get at least something when they negotiate settlements, many ignore debtors' pleas for help, continue to make telephone calls demanding payment (unless you assert your right under federal law to not receive the calls—see "Stopping Bill Collector Harassment," above) and leave debtors with few options other than to file for bankruptcy. In fact, many people who file bankruptcy do so because of the unreasonableness of their creditors or the collection agencies hired by their creditors.

To help your creditors see the benefit of settling with you on reasonable terms, it often won't hurt to mention the fact that you're thinking of filing for bankruptcy. Creditors know that they are very likely to get nothing in a bankruptcy case and may settle for a reasonable discount. This being said, don't be surprised if a creditor tells you to "go ahead and file." More than a few creditors stand on what they take to be principle.

Get Outside Help to Design a Repayment Plan

Many people have trouble negotiating with creditors, either because they don't have the skills and negotiating experience to do a good job or because they find the whole process exceedingly unpleasant. Because the ability to negotiate is an art, many people benefit from outside help.

If you don't want to negotiate with your creditors, you can turn to a lawyer or to a credit counseling agency. These agencies come in two basic varieties: nonprofit and for profit. They all work on the same basic principle: A repayment plan is negotiated with all of your unsecured creditors. You make one monthly payment to the agency, which distributes the payment to your creditors as provided in the plan. As long as you make the payments, the creditors will not take any action against you. And, if you succeed in completing the plan, one or more of your creditors may be willing to offer you new credit on reasonable terms.

The nonprofit agencies tend to be funded primarily by the major creditors (in the form of a commission for each repayment plan they negotiate) and by moderate fees charged to the users. The for-profit agencies are funded by the same sources but tend to charge much higher fees.

The big downside to entering into one of the repayment plans is that if you fail to make a payment, the creditors may pull the plug on the deal and come after you, regardless of how faithful you've been in the past. When that happens, you may find that you would have been better off filing for bankruptcy in the first place.

How Debt Management Typically Works

To use a credit counseling agency to help you pay your debts, you must have some steady income. A counselor will contact your creditors to let them know that you've sought assistance and need more time to pay. Based on your income and debts, the counselor, with your creditors, will decide how much you must pay and for how long. You must then make one payment each month to the counseling agency, which in turn will pay your creditors. The agency will ask the creditors to return a small percentage of the money received to the agency office, in order to fund its work. This arrangement is generally referred to as a "debt management program."

Some creditors will make overtures to help you when you're participating in a debt management program, such as reducing interest, waiving minimum payments, and forgiving late charges. But many creditors will not make interest concessions, such as waiving a portion of the accumulated interest to help you repay the principal

portion of the debt. Even if you successfully complete a debt management program, your credit will still be damaged.

Disadvantages of Debt Management

Participating in a credit counseling agency's debt management program is a little bit like filing for Chapter 13 bankruptcy. But working with a credit or debt counseling agency has one big advantage: No bankruptcy will appear on your credit record. On the other hand, a debt management program has two disadvantages when compared to Chapter 13 bankruptcy. First, if you miss a plan payment in Chapter 13, you will often be provided a way to make it up and continue to protect you from creditors who would otherwise start collection actions. A debt management program has no such protection, so any one creditor can pull the plug on your plan. Also, a debt management program plan usually requires you to pay your unsecured debts in full, over time. In Chapter 13, you often are only required to pay a small fraction of your nonpriority unsecured debts (if any), such as credit card and medical debts.

Critics of credit counseling agencies point out that the counselors tilt toward signing people up for a repayment plan in circumstances where bankruptcy would be in their best interest—so the agency will get a commission from the creditors that isn't available for cases that end up in bankruptcy. However, credit counseling agencies approved by the Office of the U.S. Trustee have a number of requirements placed on them to protect against undue influence by creditors and are required to make a number of disclosures that should prevent you from being ripped off. (See Ch. 2 for more on these rules.)

File for Chapter 11 Bankruptcy

Chapter 11 bankruptcy is ordinarily used by financially struggling businesses to reorganize their affairs. However, it is also available to individuals. Individuals who consider Chapter 11 bankruptcy usually have debts in excess of one or both of the Chapter 13 bankruptcy limits—$394,725 of unsecured debts and $1,184,200 of secured debts—or substantial nonexempt assets, such as several pieces of real estate.

The initial filing fee is currently $1,717 compared to $335 for Chapter 7 or $310 for Chapter 13 bankruptcy. In addition, you must pay a quarterly fee, based on a percentage of the disbursements made to pay your debts. The fee runs from $250 a quarter when the disbursements total less than $15,000, to $10,000 a quarter when disbursements total $5,000,000 or more. The fee must be paid until your reorganization plan is either approved or dismissed, or your case is converted to Chapter 7 bankruptcy. Most attorneys require a minimum $15,000 retainer fee or more to handle a Chapter 11 bankruptcy case. Add to that the Chapter 11 bankruptcy

court fees, which in one year could run from $1,000 to $10,000, and you can see that Chapter 11 isn't for everyone.

You'll need a lawyer to file for Chapter 11 bankruptcy. A Chapter 11 bankruptcy typically turns into a long, expensive mess, and many Chapter 11 filings are converted to Chapter 7 once legal fees gobble up the assets.

However, don't shy away from Chapter 11 bankruptcy only because of the fees and costs. Be sure to consider all factors in order to choose the type of bankruptcy that will work best for your situation.

File for Chapter 12 Bankruptcy

Chapter 12 bankruptcy is like Chapter 13 bankruptcy in many respects. However, only people and entities that meet the definition of family farmer may use it. To qualify as a family farmer, all of the following must be true:

- Your debts cannot exceed $4,153,150.
- Fifty percent or more of your debt must have arisen from the farming operation, not including a purchase money mortgage.
- Fifty percent or more of your income must have been earned from the farming operation in the year preceding the filing of the petition.
- Your income must be "sufficiently stable and regular" to enable payments under a Chapter 12 plan.

Like Chapter 13, you must file a schedule of assets and liabilities and a statement of financial affairs. Even though a trustee is appointed to supervise the plan, the farm debtor remains in possession of the farm assets and actions by creditors are automatically stayed upon filing the petition.

As in Chapter 13, you must file a plan that meets Chapter 12 requirements. The plan must provide that all unsecured debts are paid in full or, alternatively, all disposable income is used to pay down the unsecured debt over the ensuing three-year period (which can be extended to five years with court permission). Plan payments must pay unsecured creditors at least what they would have received in a Chapter 7 bankruptcy. After completion of the plan, all debts are discharged except those that wouldn't be dischargeable in Chapter 7.

Chapter 12 has several advantages over Chapter 13 bankruptcy. The court has unrestricted authority to modify (cram down) secured debts, such as mortgages and car notes, so the debt matches the market value of the property. (See Ch. 6 for more on cramdowns.) This is different from Chapter 13, where cramdowns cannot be used for mortgages on your primary residence and recent car loans. Another advantage of Chapter 12: Secured debts that extend beyond the plan period can be modified without having to pay them all off in the plan. That is, payments can extend beyond the plan until the debt is paid off in the normal course of time. And unlike Chapter 13, priority debts do not have to be paid in full so long as all disposable income over a five-year period is devoted to the plan.

If you are interested in Chapter 12 bankruptcy, consult with a lawyer.

Glossary

341 meeting. See "meeting of creditors."

341 notice. A notice sent to the debtor and the debtor's creditors announcing the date, time, and place for the first meeting of creditors. The 341 notice is sent along with the notice of bankruptcy filing and information about important deadlines by which creditors have to take certain actions, such as filing objections.

342 notice. A notice that the court clerk is required to give to debtors pursuant to Section 342 of the Bankruptcy Code, to inform them of their obligations as bankruptcy debtors and the consequences of not being completely honest in their bankruptcy case.

707(b) action. An action taken by the U.S. Trustee, the regular trustee, or any creditor, under authority of Section 707(b) of the Bankruptcy Code, to dismiss a debtor's Chapter 7 filing on the ground of abuse.

Abuse. Misuse of the Chapter 7 bankruptcy remedy. This term is typically applied to Chapter 7 bankruptcy filings that should have been filed under Chapter 13 because the debtor appears to have enough disposable income to fund a Chapter 13 repayment plan.

Accounts receivable. Money or other property that one person or business owes to another for goods or services. Accounts receivable most often refer to the debts owed to a business by its customers.

Administrative expenses. The trustee's fee, the debtor's attorney's fee, and other costs of bringing a bankruptcy case that a debtor must pay in full in a Chapter 13 repayment plan. Administrative costs are typically 10% of the debtor's total payments under the plan.

Administrative Office of the United States Courts. The federal government agency that issues court rules and forms to be used by the federal courts, including bankruptcy courts.

Adversary action. Any lawsuit that begins with the filing of a formal complaint and formal service of process on the parties being sued. In a bankruptcy case, adversary actions are often brought to determine the dischargeability of a debt or to recover property transferred by the debtor shortly before filing for bankruptcy.

Affidavit. A written statement of facts, signed under oath in front of a notary public.

Allowed secured claim. A debt that is secured by collateral or a lien against the debtor's property, for which the creditor has filed a proof of claim with the bankruptcy court.

The claim is secured only to the extent of the value of the property—for example, if a debtor owes $5,000 on a note for a car that is worth only $3,000, the remaining $2,000 is an unsecured claim.

Amendment. A document filed by the debtor that changes one or more documents previously filed with the court. A debtor often files an amendment because the trustee requires changes to the debtor's paperwork based on the testimony at the meeting of creditors.

Animals. An exemption category in many states. Some states specifically exempt pets or livestock and poultry. If your state simply allows you to exempt "animals," you may include livestock, poultry, or pets. Some states exempt only domestic animals, which are usually considered to be all animals except pets.

Annuity. A type of insurance policy that pays out during the life of the insured, unlike life insurance, which pays out at the insured's death. Once the insured reaches the age specified in the policy, he or she receives monthly payments until death.

Appliance. A household apparatus or machine, usually operated by electricity, gas, or propane. Examples include refrigerators, stoves, washing machines, dishwashers, vacuum cleaners, air conditioners, and toasters.

Arms and accoutrements. Arms are weapons (such as pistols, rifles, and swords); accoutrements are the furnishings of a soldier's outfit, such as a belt or pack, but not clothes or weapons.

Arms-length creditor. A creditor with whom the debtor deals in the normal course of business, as opposed to an insider (a friend, relative, or business partner).

Articles of adornment. See "jewelry."

Assessment benefits. See "stipulated insurance."

Assisted person. Any person contemplating or filing for bankruptcy who receives bankruptcy assistance, whose debts are primarily consumer debts, and whose nonexempt property is valued at less than $192,450. A person or an entity that offers help to an assisted person is called a "debt relief agency."

Automatic stay. An injunction automatically issued by the bankruptcy court when a debtor files for bankruptcy. The automatic stay prohibits most creditor collection activities, such as filing or continuing lawsuits, making written requests for payment, or notifying credit reporting bureaus of an unpaid debt.

Avails. Any amount available to the owner of an insurance policy other than the actual proceeds of the policy. Avails include dividend payments, interest, cash or surrender value (the money you'd get if you sold your policy back to the insurance company), and loan value (the amount of cash you can borrow against the policy).

Bankruptcy Abuse Prevention and Reform Act of 2005. The formal name of the bankruptcy law that took effect on October 17, 2005.

Bankruptcy administrator. The official responsible for supervising the administration of bankruptcy cases, estates, and trustees in Alabama and North Carolina, where there is no U.S. Trustee.

Bankruptcy Appellate Panel. A specialized court that hears appeals of bankruptcy court decisions (available only in some regions).

Bankruptcy assistance. Goods or services provided to an "assisted person" for the purpose of providing information, advice, counsel, document preparation or filing, or attendance at a creditors' meeting; appearing in a case or proceeding on behalf of another person; or providing legal representation.

Bankruptcy Code. The federal law that governs the creation and operation of the bankruptcy courts and establishes bankruptcy procedures. (You can find the Bankruptcy Code in Title 11 of the United States Code.)

Bankruptcy estate. All of the property you own when you file for bankruptcy, except for most pensions and educational trusts. The trustee technically takes control of your bankruptcy estate for the duration of your case.

Bankruptcy lawyer. A lawyer who specializes in bankruptcy and is licensed to practice law in the federal courts.

Bankruptcy petition preparer. Any non-lawyer who helps someone with his or her bankruptcy. Bankruptcy petition preparers (BPPs) are a special type of debt relief agency, regulated by the U.S. Trustee. Because they are not lawyers, BPPs can't represent anyone in bankruptcy court or provide legal advice.

Bankruptcy Petition Preparer Fee Declaration. An official form bankruptcy petition preparers must file with the bankruptcy court to disclose their fees.

Bankruptcy Petition Preparer Notice to Debtor. A written notice that bankruptcy petition preparers must provide to debtors who use their services. The notice explains that bankruptcy petition preparers aren't attorneys and that they are permitted to perform only certain acts, such as entering information in the bankruptcy petition and schedules under the direction of their clients.

Benefit or benevolent society benefits. See "fraternal benefit society benefits."

Building materials. Items, such as lumber, brick, stone, iron, paint, and varnish, that are used to build or improve a structure.

Burial plot. A cemetery plot.

Business bankruptcy. A bankruptcy in which the debts arise primarily from the operation of a business, including bankruptcies filed by corporations, limited liability companies, and partnerships.

Certification. The act of signing a document under penalty of perjury. (The document that is signed is also called a certification.)

Chapter 7 bankruptcy. A liquidation bankruptcy, in which the trustee sells the debtor's nonexempt property and distributes the proceeds to the debtor's creditors. At the end of the case, the debtor receives a discharge of all remaining debts, except those that cannot legally be discharged.

Chapter 7 Means Test Calculation. The means test used to determine whether a Chapter 7 bankruptcy would constitute abuse.

Chapter 7 Statement of Your Current Monthly Income. The official bankruptcy form a debtor must file in a Chapter 7 filing that shows the debtor's current monthly income, calculates whether the debtor's income is higher than the state's median family income.

Chapter 9 bankruptcy. A type of bankruptcy restricted to governmental units.

Chapter 11 bankruptcy. A type of bankruptcy intended to help businesses reorganize their debt load in order to remain in business. A Chapter 11 bankruptcy is typically much more expensive than a Chapter 7 or 13 bankruptcy because all of the lawyers must be paid out of the bankruptcy estate.

Chapter 12 bankruptcy. A type of bankruptcy designed to help small farmers reorganize their debts.

Chapter 13 bankruptcy. A type of consumer bankruptcy designed to help individuals reorganize their debts and pay all or a portion of them over three to five years.

Chapter 13 Calculation of Your Disposable Income. The official bankruptcy form used to calculate the amount of the debtor's projected disposable income that will be available to pay the debtor's unsecured creditors.

Chapter 13 plan. A document filed in a Chapter 13 bankruptcy in which the debtor shows how all of his or her projected disposable income will be used over a three- to five-year period to pay all mandatory debts—for example, back child support, taxes, and mortgage arrearages—as well as some or all unsecured, nonpriority debts, such as medical and credit card bills.

Chapter 13 Statement of Your Current Monthly Income and Calculation of Commitment Period. The official bankruptcy form a debtor must file in a Chapter 13 case, setting out the debtor's current monthly income and required repayment plan length.

Claim. A creditor's assertion that the bankruptcy filer owes it a debt or obligation.

Clothing. As an exemption category, the everyday clothes you and your family need for work, school, household use, and protection from the elements. In many states, luxury items and furs are not included in the clothing exemption category.

Codebtor. A person who assumes an equal responsibility, along with the debtor, to repay a debt or loan.

Collateral. Property pledged by a borrower as security for a loan.

Common law property states. States that don't use a community property system to classify marital property.

Community property. Certain property owned by married couples in Arizona, California, Idaho, Louisiana, New Mexico, Nevada, Texas, Washington, Wisconsin, and, if both spouses agree, Alaska. Very generally, all property acquired during the marriage is considered community property, belonging equally to both spouses, except for gifts and inheritances to one spouse. Similarly, all debts incurred during the marriage are considered community debts, owed equally by both spouses, with limited exceptions.

Complaint. A formal document that initiates a lawsuit.

Complaint to determine dischargeablity. A complaint initiating an adversary action in bankruptcy court that asks the court to decide whether a particular debt should be discharged at the end of the debtor's bankruptcy case.

Condominium. A building or complex in which separate units, such as townhouses or apartments, are owned by individuals, and the common areas (lobby, hallways, stairways, and so on) are jointly owned by the unit owners.

Confirmation. The bankruptcy judge's ruling approving a Chapter 13 plan.

Confirmation hearing. A court hearing conducted by a bankruptcy judge in which the judge decides whether a debtor's proposed Chapter 13 plan appears to be feasible and meets all applicable legal requirements.

Consumer bankruptcy. A bankruptcy in which a preponderance of the debt was incurred for personal, family, or household purposes.

Consumer debt. A debt incurred by an individual for personal, family, or household purposes.

Contingent debts. Debts that may be owed if certain events happen or conditions are satisfied.

Contingent interests in the estate of a decedent. The right to inherit property if one or more conditions to the inheritance are satisfied. For example, a debtor who will inherit property only if he survives his brother has a contingent interest.

Conversion. When a debtor who has filed one type of bankruptcy switches to another type—as when a Chapter 7 debtor converts to a Chapter 13 bankruptcy, or vice versa.

Cooperative housing. A building or another residential structure that is owned by a corporation formed by the residents. In exchange for purchasing stock in the corporation, the residents have the right to live in particular units.

Cooperative insurance. Compulsory employment benefits provided by a state or federal government, such as old age, survivors, disability, and health insurance, to ensure a minimum standard of living for lower- and middle-income people. Also called social insurance.

Court clerk. The court employee who is responsible for accepting filings and other documents, and generally maintaining an accurate and efficient flow of paper and information in the court.

Cramdown. In a Chapter 13 bankruptcy, the act of reducing a secured debt to the replacement value of the collateral securing the debt.

Credit counseling. Counseling that explores the possibility of repaying debts outside of bankruptcy and educates the debtor about credit, budgeting, and financial management. Under the new bankruptcy law, a debtor must undergo credit counseling with an approved provider before filing for bankruptcy.

Credit insurance. An insurance policy that covers a borrower for an outstanding loan. If the borrower dies or becomes disabled before paying off the loan, the policy will pay off the balance due.

Creditor. A person or an institution to whom money is owed.

Creditor committee. In a Chapter 11 bankruptcy, a committee that represents the unsecured debtors in reorganization proceedings.

Creditor matrix. A specially formatted list of creditors that a debtor must file with the bankruptcy petition. The matrix helps the court notify creditors of the bankruptcy filing and the date and time set for the first meeting of creditors.

Creditors' meeting. See "meeting of creditors."

Crops. Products of the soil or earth that are grown and raised annually and gathered in a single season. Thus, oranges (on the tree or harvested) are crops; an orange tree isn't.

Current market value. What property could be sold for. This is how a debtor's property was previously valued for purposes of determining whether the property is protected by an applicable exemption. Under the new bankruptcy law, property must be valued at its "replacement cost."

Current monthly income. As defined by the new bankruptcy law, a bankruptcy filer's total gross income (whether taxable or not), averaged over the six-month period immediately preceding the month in which the bankruptcy is filed. The current monthly income is used to determine whether the debtor can file for Chapter 7 bankruptcy, among other things.

Debt. An obligation of any type, including a loan, credit, or promise to perform a contract or lease.

Debt relief agency. An umbrella term for any person or agency—including lawyers and bankruptcy petition preparers, but excluding banks, nonprofit and government agencies, and employees of debt relief agencies—that provides "bankruptcy assistance" to an "assisted person."

Debtor. Someone who owes money to another person or business. Also, the generic term used to refer to anyone who files for bankruptcy.

Declaration. A written statement that is made under oath but not witnessed by a notary public.

Declaration of homestead. A form filed with the county recorder's office to put on record your right to a homestead exemption. In most states, the homestead exemption is automatic—that is, you are not required to record a homestead declaration in order to claim the homestead exemption. A few states do require such a recording, however.

Disability benefits. Payments made under a disability insurance or retirement plan when the insured is unable to work (or retires early) because of disability, accident, or sickness.

Discharge. A court order, issued at the conclusion of a Chapter 7 or Chapter 13 bankruptcy case, which legally relieves the debtor of personal liability for debts that can be discharged in that type of bankruptcy.

Discharge exceptions. Debts that are not discharged in a bankruptcy case. The debtor continues to owe these debts even after the bankruptcy is concluded.

Discharge hearing. A hearing conducted by a bankruptcy court to explain the discharge, urge the debtor to stay out of debt, and review reaffirmation agreements to make sure they are feasible and fair.

Dischargeability action. An adversary action brought by a party who asks the court to determine whether a particular debt qualifies for discharge.

Dischargeable debt. A debt that is wiped out at the conclusion of a bankruptcy case, unless the judge decides that it should not be.

Dismissal. When the court orders a case to be closed without providing the relief available under the bankruptcy laws. For example, a Chapter 13 case might be dismissed because the debtor fails to propose a feasible plan; a Chapter 7 case might be dismissed for abuse.

Disposable income. The difference between a debtor's "current monthly income" and allowable expenses. This is the amount that the bankruptcy law deems available to pay into a Chapter 13 plan.

Domestic animals. See "animals."

Domestic support obligation. An obligation to pay alimony or child support to a spouse, child, or government entity pursuant to an order by a court or another governmental unit.

Doubling. The ability of married couples to double the amount of certain property exemptions when filing for bankruptcy together. The federal bankruptcy exemptions allow doubling. State laws vary—some permit doubling and some do not.

Education Individual Retirement Account. A type of account to which a person can contribute a certain amount of tax-deferred funds every year for the educational benefit of the debtor or certain relatives. Such an account is not part of the debtor's bankruptcy estate.

Emergency bankruptcy filing. An initial bankruptcy filing that includes only the petition and the creditor matrix, filed right away because the debtor needs the protection of the automatic stay to prevent a creditor from taking certain action, such as a foreclosure. An emergency filing case will be dismissed if the other required documents and forms are not filed in a timely manner.

Endowment insurance. An insurance policy that gives an insured who lives for a specified time (the endowment period) the right to receive the face value of the policy (the amount paid at death). If the insured dies sooner, the beneficiary named in the policy receives the proceeds.

Equity. The amount you get to keep if you sell property—typically the property's market value, less the costs of sale and the value of any liens on the property.

ERISA-qualified benefits. Pensions that meet the requirements of the Employee Retirement Income Security Act (ERISA), a federal law that sets minimum standards for such plans and requires beneficiaries to receive certain notices.

Executory contract. A contract in which one or both parties still have a duty to carry out one or more of the contract's terms.

Exempt property. Property described by state and federal laws (exemptions) that a debtor is entitled to keep in a Chapter 7 bankruptcy. Exempt property cannot be taken and sold by the trustee for the benefit of the debtor's unsecured creditors.

Exemptions. State and federal laws specifying the types of property creditors are not entitled to take to satisfy a debt, and the bankruptcy trustee is not entitled to take and sell for the benefit of the debtor's unsecured creditors.

Farm tools. Tools used by a person whose primary occupation is farming. Some states limit farm tools of the trade to items that can be held in the hand, such as hoes, axes, pitchforks, shovels, scythes, and the like. In other states, farm tools also include plows, harnesses, mowers, reapers, and so on.

Federal exemptions. A list of exemptions contained in the federal Bankruptcy Code. Some states give debtors the option of using the federal exemptions rather than the state exemptions.

Federal Rules of Bankruptcy Procedure. A set of rules issued by the Administrative Office of the United States Courts, which govern bankruptcy court procedures.

Filing date. The date a bankruptcy petition in a particular case is filed. With few exceptions, debts incurred after the filing date are not discharged. Similarly, property owned before the filing date is part of the bankruptcy estate, while property acquired after the filing date is not.

Fines, penalties, and restitution. Debts owed to a court or a victim as a result of a sentence in a criminal matter. These debts are generally not dischargeable in bankruptcy.

Foreclosure. The process by which a creditor with a lien on real estate forces a sale of the property in order to collect on the lien. Foreclosure typically occurs when a homeowner defaults on a mortgage.

Fraternal benefit society benefits. Benefits, often group life insurance, paid for by fraternal societies, such as the Elks, Masons, Knights of Columbus, or the Knights of Maccabees, for their members. Also called benefit society, benevolent society, or mutual aid association benefits.

Fraud. Generally, an act that is intended to mislead another for the purpose of financial gain. In a bankruptcy case, fraud is any writing or representation intended to mislead creditors for the purpose of obtaining a loan or credit, or any act intended to mislead the bankruptcy court or the trustee.

Fraudulent transfer. In a bankruptcy case, a transfer of property to another for less than the property's value regardless of intent. Fraudulently transferred property can be recovered and sold by the trustee for the benefit of the creditors to recover the difference between the real value of the property and the amount received by the debtor.

Fraudulently concealed assets. Property that a bankruptcy debtor deliberately fails to disclose as required by the bankruptcy rules.

Furnishings. An exemption category recognized in many states, which includes furniture, fixtures in your home (such as a heating unit, furnace, or built-in lighting), and other items with which a home is furnished, such as carpets and drapes.

Good faith. In a Chapter 13 case, when a debtor files for bankruptcy with the sincere purpose of paying off debts over the period of time required by law rather than for manipulative purposes—such as to prevent a foreclosure that by all rights should be allowed to proceed.

Goods and chattels. See "personal property."

Group life or group health insurance. A single insurance policy covering individuals in a group (for example, employees) and their dependents.

Head of household. A person who supports and maintains, in one household, one or more people who are closely related to the person by blood, marriage, or adoption. Also referred to as "head of family."

Health aids. Items needed to maintain their owner's health, such as a wheelchair, crutches, prosthesis, or a hearing aid. Many states require that health aids be prescribed by a physician.

Health benefits. Benefits paid under health insurance plans, such as Blue Cross/Blue Shield, to cover the costs of health care.

Heirloom. An item with special monetary or sentimental value, which is passed down from generation to generation.

Home equity loan. A loan made to a homeowner on the basis of the equity in the home—and secured by the home in the same manner as a mortgage.

Homestead. A state or federal exemption applicable to property where the debtor lives when he or she files bankruptcy—usually including boats and mobile homes.

Homestead declaration. See "declaration of homestead."

Household good. As an exemption category, an item of permanent nature (as opposed to items consumed, like food or cosmetics) used in or about the house. This includes linens, dinnerware, utensils, pots and pans, and small electronic equipment like radios. Many state laws specifically list the types of household goods that fall within this exemption, as do the federal bankruptcy laws.

Householder. A person who supports and maintains a household, with or without other people. Also called a "housekeeper."

Impairs an exemption. When a lien, in combination with any other liens on the property and the amount the debtor is entitled to claim as exempt, exceeds the value of the property the debtor could claim in the absence of any liens. For example, if property is worth $15,000, there are $5,000 worth of liens on the property, and the debtor is entitled to a $5,000 exemption in the property, a lien that exceeded $5,000 would impair the debtor's exemption. Certain types of liens that impair an exemption may be removed (avoided) by the debtor if the court so orders.

Implement. As an exemption category, an instrument, tool, or utensil used by a person to accomplish his or her job.

In lieu of homestead (or burial) exemption. Designates an exemption that is available only if you don't claim the homestead (or burial) exemption.

Injunction. A court order prohibiting a person or an entity from taking specified actions—for example, the automatic stay (in reality an automatic injunction), which prevents most creditors from trying to collect their debts.

Insider creditor. A creditor with whom the debtor has a personal relationship, such as a relative, friend, or business partner.

Intangible property. Property that cannot be physically touched, such as an ownership share in a corporation or a copyright. Documents—such as a stock certificate—may provide evidence of intangible property.

Involuntary dismissal. When a bankruptcy judge dismisses a case because the debtor fails to carry out his or her duties—such as filing papers in a timely manner and cooperating with the trustee—or because the debtor files the bankruptcy in bad faith or engages in abuse by wrongfully filing for Chapter 7 when he or she should have filed for Chapter 13.

Involuntary lien. A lien that is placed on the debtor's property without the debtor's consent—for instance, when the IRS places a lien on property for back taxes.

IRS expenses. A table of national and regional expense estimates published by the IRS.

Debtors whose "current monthly income" is more than their state's "median family income" must use the IRS expenses to calculate their average net income in a Chapter 7 case, or their disposable income in a Chapter 13 case.

Jewelry. Items created for personal adornment; usually includes watches. Also called "articles of adornment."

Joint debtors. Married people who file for bankruptcy together and pay a single filing fee.

Judgment proof. A description of a person whose income and property are such that a creditor can't (or won't) seize them to enforce a money judgment—for example, a dwelling protected by a homestead exemption or a bank account containing only a few dollars.

Judicial lien. A lien created by the recording of a court money judgment against the debtor's property—usually real estate.

Lease. A contract that governs the relationship between an owner of property and a person who wishes to use the property for a specific period of time—as in car and real estate leases.

Lien. A legal claim against property that must be paid before title to the property can be transferred. Liens can also often be collected through repossession (personal property) or foreclosure (real estate), depending on the type of lien.

Lien avoidance. A bankruptcy procedure in which certain types of liens can be removed from certain types of property. Liens that are not avoided survive the bankruptcy even though the underlying debt may be cancelled—for instance, a lien remains on a car even if the debt evidenced by the car note is discharged in the bankruptcy.

Life estate. The right to live in, but not own, a specific home until your death.

Life insurance. A policy that provides for the payment of money to an individual (called the beneficiary) in the event of the death of another (called the insured). The policy matures (becomes payable) only when the insured dies.

Lifting the stay. When a bankruptcy court allows a creditor to continue with debt collection or other activities that are otherwise banned by the automatic stay. For instance, the court might allow a landlord to proceed with an eviction or a lender to repossess a car because the debtor has defaulted on the note.

Liquid assets. Cash or items that are easily convertible into cash, such as a money market account, stock, U.S. Treasury bill, or bank deposit.

Liquidated debt. An existing debt for a specified amount arising out of a contract or court judgment. In contrast, an unliquidated debt is a claim for an as-yet uncertain amount, such as for injuries suffered in a car accident before the case goes to court.

Lost future earnings. The portion of a lawsuit judgment intended to compensate an injured person for the money he or she won't be able to earn in the future because of the injury. Also called lost earnings payments or recoveries.

Luxuries. In bankruptcy, goods or services purchased by the debtor that a court decides were not appropriate in light of the debtor's insolvency. This might include vacations, jewelry, costly cars, or frequent meals at expensive restaurants.

Mailing matrix. See "creditor matrix."

Marital debts. Debts owed jointly by a married couple.

Marital property. Property owned jointly by a married couple.

Marital settlement agreement. An agreement between a divorcing couple that sets out who gets what percentage (or what specific items) of the marital property, who pays what marital debts, and who gets custody and pays child support if there are children of the marriage.

Materialmen's and mechanics' liens. Liens imposed by statute on real estate when suppliers of materials, labor, and contracting services used to improve the real estate are not properly compensated.

Matured life insurance benefits. Insurance benefits that are currently payable because the insured person has died.

Means test. A formula that uses predefined income and expense categories to determine whether a debtor whose income is more than the median family income for his or her state should be allowed to file a Chapter 7 bankruptcy.

Median family income. An annual income figure for which there are as many families with incomes below that level as there are above that level. The U.S. Census Bureau publishes median family income figures for each state and for different family sizes. In bankruptcy, the median family income is used as a basis for determining whether a debtor must pass the means test to file Chapter 7 bankruptcy, and whether a debtor filing a Chapter 13 bankruptcy must commit all his or her projected disposable income to a five-year repayment plan.

Meeting of creditors. A meeting that the debtor is required to attend in a bankruptcy case, at which the trustee and creditors may ask the debtor questions about his or her property, information in the documents and forms he or she filed, and his or her debts.

Mortgage. A contract in which a loan is made with real estate as collateral. If the borrower defaults on loan payments, the lender can foreclose on the property.

Motion. A formal legal procedure in which the bankruptcy judge is asked to rule on a dispute in the bankruptcy case. To bring a motion, a party must file a document explaining what relief is requested, the facts of the dispute, and the legal reasons why the court should grant the relief. The party bringing the motion must mail these documents to all affected parties and let them know when the court will hear argument on the motion.

Motion to avoid judicial lien on real estate. A motion brought by a bankruptcy debtor that asks the bankruptcy court to remove a judicial lien on real estate because the lien impairs the debtor's homestead exemption.

Motion to lift stay. A motion in which a creditor asks the court for permission to continue a court action or collection activities in spite of the automatic stay.

Motor vehicle. A self-propelled vehicle suitable for use on a street or road. This includes a car, truck, motorcycle, van, and moped. See also "tools of the trade."

Musical instrument. An instrument having the capacity, when properly operated, to produce a musical sound. Pianos, guitars, drums, drum machines, synthesizers, and harmonicas are all musical instruments.

Mutual aid association benefits. See "fraternal benefit society benefits."

Mutual assessment or mutual life. See "stipulated insurance."

Necessities. Articles needed to sustain life, such as food, clothing, medical care, and shelter.

Newly discovered creditors. Creditors who the debtor discovers after the bankruptcy is filed. If the case is still open, the debtor can amend the list to include the creditors; if the case is closed, it usually can be reopened to accommodate the amendment.

Nonbankruptcy federal exemptions. Federal laws that allow a debtor who has not filed for bankruptcy to keep creditors away from certain property. The debtor can also use these exemptions in bankruptcy if the debtor is using a state exemption system.

Nondischargeable debt. Debt that survives bankruptcy, such as back child support and most student loans.

Nonexempt property. Property in the bankruptcy estate that is unprotected by the exemption system available to the debtor (this is typically—but not always—the exemption system in the state where the debtor files bankruptcy). In a Chapter 7 bankruptcy, the trustee may sell it for the benefit of the debtor's unsecured creditors. In a Chapter 13 bankruptcy, debtors must propose a plan that pays their unsecured creditors at least the value of their unsecured property.

Nonpossessory, nonpurchase money lien. A lien placed on property that is already owned by the debtor and is used as collateral for the loan without being possessed by the lender. In contrast, a nonpurchase money, possessory lien exists on collateral that is held by a pawnshop.

Nonpriority debt. A type of debt that is not entitled to be paid first in bankruptcy, as priority debts are. Nonpriority debts do not have to be paid in full in a Chapter 13 case.

Nonpriority, unsecured claim. A claim that is not for a priority debt (such as child support) and is not secured by collateral or other property. Typical examples include credit card debt, medical bills, and student loans. In a Chapter 13 repayment plan, nonpriority, unsecured claims are paid only after all other debts are paid.

Notice of appeal. A form that must be filed with a court when a party wishes to appeal a judgment or an order issued by the court. Often, the notice of appeal must be filed within ten days of the date the order or judgment is entered in the court's records.

Objection. A document one party files to oppose a proposed action by another party—for instance, when a creditor or trustee files an objection to a bankruptcy debtor's claim of exemption.

Order for relief. The court's automatic injunction against certain collection and other activities that might negatively affect the bankruptcy estate. Another name for the "automatic stay."

Oversecured debt. A debt that is secured by collateral that is worth more than the amount of the debt.

PACER. An online, fee-based database containing bankruptcy court dockets (records of proceedings in bankruptcy cases) and federal court documents, such as court rules and recent appellate court decisions.

Pain and suffering damages. The portion of a court judgment intended to compensate for past, present, and future mental and physical pain, suffering, impairment of ability to work, and mental distress caused by an injury.

Partially secured debt. A debt secured by collateral that is worth less than the debt itself—for instance, when a person owes $15,000 on a car that is worth only $10,000.

Party in interest. Any person or entity that has a financial interest in the outcome of a bankruptcy case, including the trustee, the debtor, and all creditors.

Pension. A fund into which payments are made to provide an employee income after retirement. Typically, the beneficiary can't access the account without incurring a significant penalty, usually a tax. There are many types of pensions, including defined benefit pensions provided by many large corporations and individual pensions (such as 401(k)s and IRAs). In bankruptcy, most pensions are not considered part of a bankruptcy estate and are therefore not affected by a bankruptcy filing.

Personal financial responsibility counseling. Under the new bankruptcy law, a two-hour class intended to teach good budget management. Every consumer bankruptcy filer must attend such a class in order to obtain a discharge in Chapter 7, Chapter 12, or Chapter 13 bankruptcy.

Personal injury cause of action. The right to seek compensation for physical and mental suffering, including injury to body, reputation, or both. For example, someone who is hit and injured by a car might have a personal injury cause of action against the driver.

Personal injury recovery. The portion of a lawsuit judgment or insurance settlement that is intended to compensate someone for physical and mental suffering, including physical injury, injury to reputation, or both. Bankruptcy exemptions usually do not apply to compensation for pain or suffering or punitive damages—in other words, that part of the recovery can be taken by the trustee in a Chapter 7 case.

Personal property. All property not classified as real property, including tangible items such as cars and jewelry, and intangible property such as stocks, pensions, royalties, and residuals.

Petition. The document a debtor files to officially begin a bankruptcy case and ask for relief. Other documents and schedules must be filed to support the petition at the time it is filed, or shortly afterwards.

Pets. See "animals."

Preference. A payment made by a debtor to a creditor within a defined period prior to filing for bankruptcy—within three months for arms-length creditors (regular commercial creditors) and one year for insider creditors (close family and business associates). Because a preference gives that debtor an edge over other debtors in the bankruptcy case, the trustee can recover the preference and distribute it among all of the creditors.

Prepetition. Any time prior to the moment the bankruptcy petition is filed.

Prepetition counseling. Debt or credit counseling that occurs before the bankruptcy petition is filed—as opposed to personal financial management counseling, which occurs after the petition is filed.

Presumed abuse. In a Chapter 7 bankruptcy, when the debtor has a current monthly income in excess of the family median income for the state where the debtor lives, and has sufficient income to propose a Chapter 13 plan under the "means test." If abuse is presumed, the debtor has to prove that his or her Chapter 7 filing is not abusive in order to proceed further.

Primarily business debts. When the majority of debt owed by a bankruptcy debtor—in dollar terms—arises from debts incurred to operate a business.

Primarily consumer debts. When the majority of debt owed by a bankruptcy debtor—in dollar terms—arises from debts incurred for personal or family purposes.

Priority claim. See "priority debt."

Priority creditor. A creditor who has filed a Proof of Claim showing that the debtor owes it a priority debt.

Priority debt. A type of debt that is paid first if there are distributions to be made from the bankruptcy estate. Priority debts include alimony and child support, fees owed to the trustee and attorneys in the case, and wages owed to employees. With one exception (back child support obligations assigned to government entities), priority claims must be paid in full in a Chapter 13 bankruptcy.

Proceeds for damaged exempt property. Money received through insurance coverage, arbitration, mediation, settlement, or a lawsuit to pay for exempt property that has been damaged or destroyed. For example, if a debtor had the right to use a $30,000 homestead exemption, but his or her home was destroyed by fire, the debtor can instead exempt $30,000 of the insurance proceeds.

Projected disposable income. The amount of income a debtor will have left over each month, after deducting allowable expenses, payments on mandatory debts, and administrative expenses from his or her current monthly income. This is the amount the debtor must pay toward his or her unsecured nonpriority debts in a Chapter 13 plan.

Proof of Claim. A formal document filed by bankruptcy creditors in a bankruptcy case to assert their right to payments from the bankruptcy estate, if any payments are made.

Proof of service. A document signed under penalty of perjury by the person serving a document showing how the service was made, who made it, and when.

Property of the estate. See "bankruptcy estate."

Purchase money loans. Loans that are made to purchase specific property items, and that use the property as collateral to assure repayment, such as car loans and mortgages.

Purchase money security interest. A claim on property owned by the holder of a loan that was used to purchase the property and that is secured by the property (as collateral).

Reaffirmation. An agreement entered into after a bankruptcy filing (postpetition) between the debtor and a creditor in which the debtor agrees to repay all or part of a prepetition debt after the bankruptcy is over. For instance, a debtor makes an agreement with the holder of a car note that the debtor can keep the car and must continue to pay the debt after bankruptcy. A reaffirmation agreement restores the original contract to what it was prior to the bankruptcy case.

Real property. Real estate (land and buildings on the land, usually including mobile homes attached to a foundation).

Reasonable investigation. A bankruptcy attorney's obligation, under the new bankruptcy law, to look into the information provided to him or her by a client.

Redemption. In a Chapter 7 bankruptcy, when the debtor obtains legal title to collateral for a secured debt by paying the secured creditor the replacement value of the collateral in a lump sum. For example, a debtor may redeem a car note by paying the lender the replacement value of the car (what a retail vendor would charge for the car, considering its age and condition).

Reopen a case. To open a closed bankruptcy case—usually for the purpose of adding an overlooked creditor or filing a motion to avoid an overlooked lien. A debtor must request that the court reopen the case.

Repayment plan. An informal plan to repay creditors most or all of what they are owed outside of bankruptcy. Also refers to the plan proposed by a debtor in a Chapter 13 case.

Replacement cost. What it would cost to replace a particular item by buying it from a retail vendor, considering its age and condition—for instance, when buying a car from a used car dealer, furniture from a used furniture shop, or electronic equipment on eBay.

Repossession. When a secured creditor takes property used as collateral because the debtor has defaulted on the loan secured by the collateral.

Request to lift the stay. A written request filed in bankruptcy court by a creditor, which seeks permission to engage in debt collection activity otherwise prohibited by the automatic stay.

Schedule A/B. The official bankruptcy form a debtor must file to describe all of his or her property, including real estate and personal property owned by the debtor,

such as jewelry and vehicles, and tangible property, such as investments and accounts receivable.

Schedule C. The official bankruptcy form a debtor must file to describe the property the debtor is claiming as exempt, and the legal basis for the claims of exemption.

Schedule D. The official bankruptcy form a debtor must file to describe all secured debts owed by the debtor, such as car notes and mortgages.

Schedule E/F. The official bankruptcy form a debtor must file to describe all unsecured debts, including priority debts, such as back child support and taxes, and nonpriority debts, such as most credit card balances, medical bills, and student loans.

Schedule G. The official bankruptcy form a debtor must file to describe any leases and executory contracts (contracts under which one or both parties still have obligations) to which the debtor is a party.

Schedule H. The official bankruptcy form a debtor must file to describe all codebtors that might be affected by the bankruptcy.

Schedule I. The official bankruptcy form a debtor must file to describe the debtor's income.

Schedule J. The official bankruptcy form a debtor must file to describe the debtor's actual monthly expenses.

Schedules. Official bankruptcy forms a debtor must file, detailing the debtor's property, debts, income, and expenses.

Second deed of trust. A loan against real estate made after the original mortgage (or first deed of trust). Most home equity loans are second deeds of trust.

Secured claim. A debt secured by collateral under a written agreement (for instance, a mortgage or car note) or by operation of law—such as a tax lien.

Secured creditor. The owner of a secured claim.

Secured debt. A debt secured by collateral.

Secured interest. A claim to property used as collateral. For instance, a lender on a car note retains legal title to the car until the loan is paid off.

Secured property. Property that is collateral for a secured debt.

Serial bankruptcy filing. A practice used by some debtors to file and dismiss one bankruptcy after another to obtain the protection of the automatic stay, even though the bankruptcies themselves offer no debt relief—for instance, when a debtor files successive Chapter 13 cases to prevent foreclosure of his or her home even though there are no debts to repay.

Sickness benefits. See "disability benefits."

State exemptions. State laws that specify the types of property creditors are not entitled to take to satisfy a debt, and the bankruptcy trustee is not entitled to take and sell for the benefit of the debtor's unsecured creditors.

Statement About Your Social Security Numbers. The official bankruptcy form a debtor must file to disclose the debtor's complete Social Security number.

Statement of Financial Affairs for Individuals Filing for Bankruptcy. The official bankruptcy form a debtor must file to describe the debtor's legal, economic, and business transactions for the several years prior to filing, including gifts, preferences, income, closing of deposit accounts, lawsuits, and other information that the trustee needs to assess the legitimacy of the bankruptcy and the true extent of the bankruptcy estate.

Statement of Intention for Individuals Filing Under Chapter 7. The official bankruptcy form a debtor must file in a Chapter 7 case to tell the court and secured creditors how the debtor plans to treat his or her secured debts—that is, reaffirm the debt, redeem the debt, or surrender the property and discharge the debt.

Statutory lien. A lien imposed on property by law, such as tax liens and mechanics' liens, as opposed to voluntary liens (such as mortgages) and liens arising from court judgments (judicial liens).

Stay. See "automatic stay."

Stipulated insurance. An insurance policy that allows the insurance company to assess an amount on the insured, above the standard premium payments, if the company experiences losses worse than had been calculated into the standard premium. Also called assessment, mutual assessment, or mutual life insurance.

Stock options. A contract between a corporation and an employee that gives the employee the right to purchase corporate stock at a specific price mentioned in the contract (the strike price).

Stripdown of lien. In a Chapter 13 bankruptcy, when the amount of a lien on collateral is reduced to the collateral's replacement value. See "cramdown."

Student loan. A type of loan made for educational purposes by nonprofit or commercial lenders with repayment and interest terms dictated by federal law. Student loans are not dischargeable in bankruptcy unless the debtor can show that repaying the loan would impose an "undue hardship."

Substantial abuse. Under the old bankruptcy law, filing a Chapter 7 bankruptcy when a Chapter 13 bankruptcy was feasible.

Suits, executions, garnishments, and attachments. Activities engaged in by creditors to enforce money judgments, typically involving the seizure of wages and bank accounts.

Summary of Your Assets and Liabilities and Certain Statistical Information. The official bankruptcy form a debtor must file to summarize the property and debt information contained in a debtor's schedules.

Surrender value. See "avails."

Surrendering collateral. In Chapter 7 bankruptcy, the act of returning collateral to a secured lender in order to discharge the underlying debt—for example, returning a car to discharge the car note.

Tangible personal property. See "tangible property" and "personal property."

Tangible property. Property that may be physically touched. Examples include money, furniture, cars, jewelry, artwork, and houses. Compare "intangible property."

Tax lien. A statutory lien imposed on property to secure payment of back taxes —typically income and property taxes.

Tenancy by the entirety. A way that married couples can hold title to property in about half of the states. When one spouse dies, the surviving spouse automatically owns 100% of the property. In most cases, this type of property is not part of the bankruptcy estate if only one spouse files.

To ___ acres. A limitation on the size of a homestead that may be exempted.

Tools of the trade. Items needed to perform a line of work that you are currently doing and relying on for support. For a mechanic, plumber, or carpenter, for example, tools of trade are the implements used to repair, build, and install. Traditionally, tools of the trade were limited to items that could be held in the hand. Most states, however, now embrace a broader definition, and a debtor may be able to fit many items under a tool of trade exemption.

Transcript of tax return. A summary of a debtor's tax return provided by the IRS upon the debtor's request, usually acceptable as a substitute for the return in the instances when a return must be filed under the new bankruptcy law.

Trustee. An official appointed by the bankruptcy court to carry out the administrative tasks associated with a bankruptcy and to seize and sell nonexempt property in the bankruptcy estate for the benefit of the debtor's unsecured creditors.

U.S. Trustee. An official employed by the Office of the U.S. Trustee (a division of the U.S. Department of Justice) who is responsible for overseeing bankruptcy trustees, regulating credit and personal financial management counselors, regulating bankruptcy petition preparers, auditing bankruptcy cases, ferreting out fraud, and generally making sure that the bankruptcy laws are obeyed.

Undersecured debt. A debt secured by collateral that is worth less than the debt.

Undue hardship. The conditions under which a debtor may discharge a student loan—for example, when the debtor has no income and little chance of earning enough to repay the loan in the future.

Unexpired lease. A lease that is still in effect as of the filing date of the bankruptcy case.

Unmatured life insurance. A policy that is not yet payable because the insured is still alive.

Unscheduled debt. A debt that is not included in the schedules accompanying a bankruptcy filing, perhaps because it was overlooked or intentionally left out.

Unsecured priority claims. Priority claims that aren't secured by collateral, such as back child support or taxes for which no lien has been placed on the debtor's property.

Valuation of property. The act of determining the replacement value of property for the purpose of describing it in the bankruptcy schedules, determining whether it is protected by an applicable exemption, redeeming secured property, or cramming down a lien in Chapter 13 bankruptcy.

Voluntary dismissal. When a bankruptcy debtor dismisses his or her Chapter 7 or Chapter 13 case on his or her own, without coercion by the court.

Voluntary lien. A lien agreed to by the debtor, as when the debtor signs a mortgage, car note, or second deed of trust.

Weekly net earnings. The earnings a debtor has left after mandatory deductions, such as income tax, mandatory union dues, and Social Security contributions, have been subtracted from his or her gross income.

Wildcard exemption. A dollar value that the debtor can apply to any type of property to make it—or more of it—exempt. In some states, filers may use the unused portion of a homestead exemption as a wildcard exemption.

Willful and malicious act. An act done with the intent to cause harm. In a Chapter 7 bankruptcy, a debt arising from the debtor's willful and malicious act is not discharged if the victim proves to the bankruptcy court's satisfaction that the act occurred.

Willful or malicious act resulting in a civil judgment. A bad act that was careless or reckless, but was not necessarily intended to cause harm. In a Chapter 13 case, a debt arising from the debtor's act that was either willful or malicious is not discharged if it is part of a civil judgment.

Wrongful death cause of action. The right to seek compensation for having to live without a deceased person. Usually only the spouse and children of the deceased have a wrongful death cause of action.

Wrongful death recoveries. The portion of a lawsuit judgment intended to compensate a plaintiff for having to live without a deceased person. The compensation is intended to cover the earnings and the emotional comfort and support the deceased would have provided.

Federal and State Exemption Tables

The charts in this appendix are divided into categories of property, such as insurance, personal property, and wages. Following each exemption, we provide the numerical citation to the state statute that includes the exemption.

The states are listed alphabetically, followed by the federal exemptions. We also note which states allow you to choose between the federal and state bankruptcy exemptions.

RELATED TOPIC

Need help understanding a term? Many of the categories, types of property, and other terms used in these charts are defined in the Glossary, which you'll find right before this appendix.

Doubling

When a married couple files for bankruptcy jointly, federal law and the laws of some states allow them each to claim the full amount of an exemption. (11 U.S.C. § 522.) Because a couple gets to claim twice the amount available to those who file alone, this practice is informally known as "doubling."

Not all states allow doubling, however. And some states allow married filers to double only certain exemptions (for example, they might be allowed to double personal property exemptions but not the homestead exemption). In the charts that follow, we indicate exemptions that cannot be doubled and states that don't allow doubling at all. Unless you see a note stating that you cannot double, assume that you can.

Wage Garnishment Laws and Exemptions in Bankruptcy

Almost all states have a wage garnishment law that applies to judgment creditors, limiting how much they can take from your paycheck. In most states, you can use the wage garnishment law as an exemption in bankruptcy. Some states, however, don't allow this. If your state doesn't let bankruptcy filers use the wage garnishment law as an exemption, we indicate that on the chart. Some states have a specific statute that exempts a certain portion of wages in bankruptcy—obviously, you can use this in bankruptcy.

The federal bankruptcy exemptions do not have a separate exemption for wages. If you use the federal exemptions (assuming your state gives you the choice), the only way you can protect wages is by using the wildcard exemption.

What Income Is Exempt?

In most states, you can use the wage garnishment law to protect income that was already earned but not yet received on the day you filed for bankruptcy—called "earned but unpaid wages."

In some states, the wage garnishment exemption also protects wages you received before you filed for bankruptcy (it's easiest to claim the exemption if these wages are not mixed with other funds). In other states, the wage garnishment exemption does not protect wages that you received prior to filing for bankruptcy.

Some state exemptions protect all kinds of "earnings," regardless of type, while others protect only wages for the "performance of services," and exclude other kinds of income.

Checking the Law in Your State

Before relying on a wage garnishment statute to protect your wages, make sure that the judge in your jurisdiction agrees that the garnishment statute creates an exemption that can be used in bankruptcy. Often, the best way to do this is to ask a local bankruptcy attorney. (Many provide free initial consultations.)

Retirement Accounts

Virtually all types of tax-exempt retirement accounts are exempt in bankruptcy, whether you use the state or federal exemptions. You can exempt 401(k)s, 403(b)s, profit-sharing and money purchase plans, IRAs (including Roth, SEP, and SIMPLE IRAs), and defined-benefit plans.

These exemptions are unlimited—that is, the entire account is exempt, regardless of how much money is in it—except in the case of traditional and Roth IRAs. For these types of IRAs only, the exemption is limited to a total value of $1,283,025 per person (this figure will be adjusted every three years for inflation). If you have more than one traditional or Roth IRA, you don't get to exempt $1,283,025 per account: Your total exemption, no matter how many accounts you have, is $1,283,025.

If you are using the federal bankruptcy exemptions, you can find this new retirement account provision at 11 U.S.C. § 522(d)(12). If you are using state exemptions, cite 11 U.S.C. § 522(b)(3)(C) as the applicable exemption when you complete your bankruptcy papers.

Confirm the Exemptions Before Relying on Them

The exemptions in the following charts were current when this book went to press, but your state may have changed the law since then. In addition, states often carve out exceptions to the exemptions, which are far too detailed to list here. For instance, even if an item is listed as exempt in one of these charts, you might have to give it up to pay child support or a tax debt.

Before relying on any particular exemption, consider reading the exemption statute yourself, using the research information in Ch. 11. Last, but certainly not least, consult with a bankruptcy lawyer.

> **CAUTION**
>
> **These charts provide general information only.** There are exceptions to state exemption laws that are much too detailed to include here. Consider doing further legal research or consulting an attorney about the exemptions you plan to claim, particularly if you anticipate—or are facing—a challenge to your exemption claims.

Alabama

Federal bankruptcy exemptions not available. All law references are to Alabama Code unless otherwise noted.

ASSET	EXEMPTION	LAW
homestead	Real property or mobile home to $15,000; property cannot exceed 160 acres	6-10-2
	Must record homestead declaration before attempted sale of home	6-10-20
insurance	Annuity proceeds or avails to $250 per month	27-14-32
	Disability proceeds or avails to an average of $250 per month	27-14-31
	Fraternal benefit society benefits	27-34-27
	Life insurance proceeds or avails	6-10-8; 27-14-29
	Life insurance proceeds or avails if clause prohibits proceeds from being used to pay beneficiary's creditors	27-15-26
	Mutual aid association benefits	27-30-25
pensions	Tax-exempt retirement accounts, including 401(k)s, 403(b)s, profit-sharing and money purchase plans, SEP and SIMPLE IRAs, and defined-benefit plans	11 U.S.C. § 522(b)(3)(C)
	Traditional and Roth IRAs to $1,283,025 per person	11 U.S.C. § 522(b)(3)(C); (n)
	IRAs, Roth IRAs & other retirement accounts	19-3B-508
	Judges (only payments being received)	12-18-10(a),(b)
	Law enforcement officers	36-21-77
	Spendthrift trusts (with exceptions)	19-3B-501 to 503
	State employees	36-27-28
	Teachers	16-25-23
personal property	Books of debtor & family	6-10-6
	Burial place for self & family	6-10-5
	Church pew for self & family	6-10-5
	Clothing of debtor & family	6-10-6
	Family portraits or pictures	6-10-6
public benefits	Aid to blind, aged, disabled & other public assistance, including earned income tax credit(In re James, 406 F. 3d 1340 (11th Cir 2005))	38-4-8; 38-5-5
	Crime victims' compensation	15-23-15(e)
	Southeast Asian War POWs' benefits	31-7-1; 31-7-2
	Unemployment compensation	25-4-140
	Workers' compensation	25-5-86
tools of trade	Arms, uniforms, equipment that state military personnel are required to keep	31-2-78
wages	With respect to consumer loans, consumer credit sales & consumer leases, 75% of weekly net earnings or 30 times the federal minimum hourly wage; all other cases, 75% of earned but unpaid wages; bankruptcy judge may authorize more for low-income debtors	5-19-15; 6-10-7
wildcard	$7,500 of any personal property, except wages	6-10-6; 6-10-126

Alaska

Alaska exemption amounts are adjusted regularly by administrative order. Current amounts are found at 8 Alaska Admin. Code tit. 8, § 95.030. Amounts reflect adjustment as of 10/1/2012.

ASSET	EXEMPTION	LAW
homestead	$72,900 (joint owners may each claim a portion, but total can't exceed $72,900)	09.38.010(a)
insurance	Disability benefits	09.38.015(b); 09.38.030(e)(1),(5)
	Fraternal benefit society benefits	21.84.240
	Life insurance or annuity contracts, total avails to $500,000	09.38.025
	Medical, surgical, or hospital benefits	09.38.015(a)(3)
miscellaneous	Alimony, to extent wages exempt	09.38.030(e)(2)
	Child support payments made by collection agency	09.38.015(b)
	Liquor licenses	09.38.015(a)(7)
	Property of business partnership	09.38.100(b)
pensions	Tax-exempt retirement accounts, including 401(k)s, 403(b)s, profit-sharing and money purchase plans, SEP and SIMPLE IRAs, and defined-benefit plans	11 U.S.C. § 522(b)(3)(C)
	Traditional and Roth IRAs to $1,283,025 per person	11 U.S.C. § 522(b)(3)(C); (n)
	Elected public officers (only benefits building up)	09.38.015(b)
	ERISA-qualified benefits deposited more than 120 days before filing bankruptcy	09.38.017
	Judicial employees (only benefits building up)	09.38.015(b)
	Public employees (only benefits building up)	09.38.015(b); 39.35.505
	Roth & traditional IRAs, medical savings accounts	09.38.017(e)(3)
	Teachers (only benefits building up)	09.38.015(b)
	Other pensions, to extent wages exempt (only payments being received)	09.38.030(e)(5)
personal property	Books, musical instruments, clothing, family portraits, household goods & heirlooms to $4,050 total	09.38.020(a)
	Building materials	34.35.105
	Burial plot	09.38.015(a)(1)
	Cash or other liquid assets to $1,890; for sole wage earner in household, $2,970 (restrictions apply—see *wages*)	09.38.030(b)
	Deposit in apartment or condo owners' association	09.38.010(e)
	Health aids needed	09.38.015(a)(2)
	Jewelry to $1,350	09.38.020(b)
	Money held in mortgage escrow accounts after July 1, 2008	09.38.015(e)
	Motor vehicle to $4,050; vehicle's market value can't exceed $27,000	09.38.020(e)
	Personal injury recoveries, to extent wages exempt	09.38.030(e)(3)
	Pets to $1,350	09.38.020(d)
	Proceeds for lost, damaged, or destroyed exempt property	09.38.060
	Tuition credits under an advance college tuition payment contract	09.38.015(a)(8)
	Wrongful death recoveries, to extent wages exempt	09.38.030(e)(3)
public benefits	Adult assistance to elderly, blind, disabled	47.25.550
	Alaska benefits for low-income seniors	09.38.015(a)(11)
	Alaska longevity bonus	09.38.015(a)(5)
	Crime victims' compensation	09.38.015(a)(4)
	Federally exempt public benefits paid or due	09.38.015(a)(6)
	General relief assistance	47.25.210
	Senior care (prescription drug) benefits	09.38.015(a)(10)
	20% of permanent fund dividends	43.23.065
	Unemployment compensation	09.38.015(b); 23.20.405
	Workers' compensation	23.30.160

tools of trade	Implements, books & tools of trade to $3,780	09.38.020(c)
wages	Weekly net earnings to $473; for sole wage earner in a household, $743; if you don't receive weekly or semimonthly pay, you can claim $1,890 in cash or liquid assets paid any month; for sole wage earner in household, $2,970	9.38.030(a),(b); 9.38.050(b)
wildcard	None	

Arizona

Federal bankruptcy exemptions not available. All law references are to Arizona Revised Statutes unless otherwise noted.

ASSET	EXEMPTION	LAW
homestead	Real property, an apartment, or mobile home you occupy to $150,000; sale proceeds exempt 18 months after sale or until new home purchased, whichever occurs first (spouses may not double)	33-1101(A)
	May record homestead declaration to clarify which one of multiple eligible parcels is being claimed as homestead	33-1102
insurance	Fraternal benefit society benefits	20-877
	Group life insurance policy or proceeds	20-1132
	Health, accident, or disability benefits	33-1126(A)(4)
	Life insurance cash value or proceeds, or annuity contract if owned at least two years and beneficiary is dependent family member	33-1126(A)(6); 20-1131(D)
	Life insurance proceeds to $20,000 if beneficiary is spouse or child	33-1126(A)(1)
miscellaneous	Alimony, child support needed for support	33-1126(A)(3)
	Minor child's earnings, unless debt is for child	33-1126(A)(2)
pensions *see also wages*	Tax-exempt retirement accounts, including 401(k)s, 403(b)s, profit-sharing and money purchase plans, SEP and SIMPLE IRAs, and defined-benefit plans	11 U.S.C. § 522(b)(3)(C)
	Traditional and Roth IRAs to $1,283,025 per person	11 U.S.C. § 522(b)(3)(C); (n)
	Board of regents members, faculty, & administrative officers under board's jurisdiction	15-1628(I)
	District employees	48-227
	ERISA-qualified benefits deposited over 120 days before filing	33-1126(B)
	IRAs & Roth IRAs (*In re Herrscher*, 121 B.R. 29 (D. Ariz. 1989))	33-1126(B)
	Firefighters	9-968
	Police officers	9-931
	Public Safety Personnel Retirement System	38-850(c)
	Rangers	41-955
	State employees' retirement & disability	38-792; 38-797.11
personal property *spouses may double all personal property*	Household furniture & appliances not covered by other exemptions to $6,000 total	33-1123
	Bank deposit to $300 in one account	33-1126(A)(9)
	Bible; bicycle; sewing machine; typewriter; computer; burial plot; rifle, pistol, or shotgun to $1,000 total	33-1125
	Books to $250; clothing to $500; wedding & engagement rings to $2,000; watch to $150; pets, horses, milk cows & poultry to $800; musical instruments to $400	33-1125
	Food & fuel to last 6 months	33-1124
	Funeral deposits to $5,000	32-1391.05(4)
	Health aids	33-1125(9)
	Motor vehicle to $6,000 ($12,000, if debtor is physically disabled)	33-1125(8)
	Prepaid rent or security deposit to $2,000 or 1½ times your rent, whichever is less, in lieu of homestead	33-1126(C)
	Proceeds for sold or damaged exempt property	33-1126(A)(5),(8)
	Wrongful death awards	12-592
public benefits	Unemployment compensation	23-783(A)
	Welfare benefits	46-208
	Workers' compensation	23-1068(B)

tools of trade *husband & wife may double*	Arms, uniforms, & accoutrements of profession or office required by law	33-1130(3)
	Farm machinery, utensils, seed, instruments of husbandry, feed, grain, & animals to $5,000 total	33-1130(2)
	Library & teaching aids of teacher	33-1127
	Tools, equipment, instruments, & books to $2,500	33-1130(1)
wages	75% of earned but unpaid weekly net earnings or 30 times the federal minimum hourly wage; 50% of wages for support orders; bankruptcy judge may authorize more for low-income debtors	33-1131
wildcard	None	

Arkansas

Federal bankruptcy exemptions available. All law references are to Arkansas Code Annotated unless otherwise noted.

Note: In 1990, the 8th Circuit Court of Appeals declared Arkansas' bankruptcy exemption statute (found at Ark. Code Ann. § 16-66-218) unconstitutional for bankruptcy purposes as it relates to personal property. (*In re Holt*, 894 F.2d 1005 (8th Cir. 1990).) The court said that the Arkansas Constitution's provision of a $200 exemption for any personal property ($500 if married) acted as a cap and overrode the more generous exemption amounts in the statute. The personal property exemptions may be used in a nonbankruptcy context, however.

ASSET	EXEMPTION	LAW
homestead *choose* *Option 1 or 2*	1. For married person or head of family: unlimited exemption on real or personal property used as residence to ¼ acre in city, town, or village, or 80 acres elsewhere; if property is between ¼ and 1 acre in city, town, or village, or 80 to 160 acres elsewhere, additional limit is $2,500; homestead may not exceed 1 acre in city, town, or village, or 160 acres elsewhere (spouses may not double)	Constitution 9-3; 9-4, 9-5; 16-66-210;16-66-218(b)(3), (4); *In re Stevens*, 829 F.2d 693 (8th Cir. 1987)
	2. Real or personal property used as residence to $800 if single; $1,250 if married	16-66-218(a)(1)
insurance	Annuity contract	23-79-134
	Disability benefits	23-79-133
	Fraternal benefit society benefits	23-74-403
	Group life insurance	23-79-132
	Life, health, accident, or disability cash value or proceeds paid or due to $500	16-66-209; Constitution 9-1, 9-2; *In re Holt*, 894 F.2d 1005 (8th Cir. 1990)
	Life insurance proceeds if clause prohibits proceeds from being used to pay beneficiary's creditors	23-79-131
	Life insurance proceeds or avails if beneficiary isn't the insured	23-79-131
	Mutual assessment life or disability benefits to $1,000	23-72-114
	Stipulated insurance premiums	23-71-112
pensions	Tax-exempt retirement accounts, including 401(k)s, 403(b)s, profit-sharing and money purchase plans, SEP and SIMPLE IRAs, and defined-benefit plans	11 U.S.C. § 522(b)(3)(C)
	Traditional and Roth IRAs to $1,283,025 per person	11 U.S.C. § 522(b)(3)(C); (n)
	Disabled firefighters	24-11-814
	Disabled police officers	24-11-417
	Firefighters	24-10-616
	IRA deposits to $20,000 if deposited over 1 year before filing for bankruptcy	16-66-218(b)(16)
	Police officers	24-10-616
	School employees	24-7-715
	State police officers	24-6-205; 24-6-223
personal property	Burial plot to 5 acres, if choosing federal homestead exemption (Option 2)	16-66-207; 16-66-218(a)(1)
	Clothing	Constitution 9-1, 9-2
	Prepaid funeral trusts	23-40-117
public benefits	Crime victims' compensation	16-90-716(e)
	Unemployment compensation	11-10-109
	Workers' compensation	11-9-110
tools of trade	Implements, books & tools of trade to $750	16-66-218(a)(4)
wages	Earned but unpaid wages due for 60 days; in no event less than $25 per week	16-66-208; 16-66-218(b)(6)
wildcard	$500 of any personal property if married or head of family; $200 if not married	Constitution 9-1, 9-2

California—System 1

Federal bankruptcy exemptions not available. California has two systems; you must select one or the other. All law references are to California Code of Civil Procedure unless otherwise noted. Many exemptions do not apply to claims for child support.

Note: California's exemption amounts are no longer updated in the statutes themselves. California Code of Civil Procedure Section 740.150 deputized the California Judicial Council to update the exemption amounts every three years. As a result, the amounts listed in this chart will not match the amounts that appear in the cited statutes. The current exemption amounts can be found on the California Judicial Council website, www.courts.ca.gov/forms.htm.

ASSET	EXEMPTION	LAW
homestead	Real or personal property you occupy including mobile home, boat, stock cooperative, community apartment, planned development, or condo to $75,000 if single & not disabled; $100,000 for families if no other member has a homestead (if only one spouse files, may exempt one-half of amount if home held as community property & all of amount if home held as tenants in common); $175,000 if 65 or older, or physically or mentally disabled; $175,000 if 55 or older, single & earn gross annual income under $25,000 or married & earn gross annual income under $35,000 & creditors seek to force the sale of your home; forced sale proceeds received exempt for 6 months after (spouses may not double); separated married debtor may claim homestead in community property homestead occupied by other spouse	704.710; 704.720; 704.730; *In re McFall*, 112 B.R. 336 (9th Cir. B.A.P. 1990)
	May file homestead declaration to protect exemption amount from attachment of judicial liens and to protect proceeds of voluntary sale for 6 months	704.920
insurance	Disability or health benefits	704.130
	Fidelity bonds	Labor 404
	Fraternal benefit society benefits	704.170
	Fraternal unemployment benefits	704.120
	Homeowners' insurance proceeds for 6 months after received, to homestead exemption amount	704.720(b)
	Life insurance proceeds if clause prohibits proceeds from being used to pay beneficiary's creditors	Ins. 10132; Ins. 10170; Ins. 10171
	Matured life insurance benefits needed for support	704.100(c)
	Unmatured life insurance policy cash surrender value completely exempt; loan value exempt to $12,800	704.100(b)
miscellaneous	Business or professional licenses	695.060
	Inmates' trust funds to $1,600 (spouses may not double)	704.090
	Property of business partnership	Corp. 16501-04
pensions	Tax-exempt retirement accounts, including 401(k)s, 403(b)s, profit-sharing and money purchase plans, SEP and SIMPLE IRAs, and defined-benefit plans	11 U.S.C. § 522(b)(3)(C)
	Traditional and Roth IRAs to $1,283,025 per person	11 U.S.C. § 522(b)(3)(C); (n)
	County employees	Gov't 31452
	County firefighters	Gov't 32210
	County peace officers	Gov't 31913
	Private retirement benefits, including IRAs & Keoghs	704.115
	Public employees	Gov't 21255
	Public retirement benefits	704.110

personal property	Appliances, furnishings, clothing, & food	704.020
	Bank deposits from Social Security Administration to $3,200 ($4,800 for husband & wife); unlimited if SS funds are not commingled with other funds. Bank deposits of other public benefits to $1,600 ($2,375 for husband & wife)	704.080
	Building materials to repair or improve home to $3,200 (spouses may not double)	704.030
	Burial plot	704.200
	Funds held in escrow	Fin. 17410
	Health aids	704.050
	Jewelry, heirlooms, & art to $8,000 total (spouses may not double)	704.040
	Motor vehicles to $3,050, or $3,050 in auto insurance for loss or damages (spouses may not double)	704.010
	Personal injury & wrongful death causes of action	704.140(a); 704.150(a)
	Personal injury & wrongful death recoveries needed for support; if receiving installments, at least 75%	704.140(b), (c), (d); 704.150(b), (c)
public benefits	Aid to blind, aged, disabled; public assistance	704.170
	Financial aid to students	704.190
	Relocation benefits	704.180
	Unemployment benefits	704.120
	Union benefits due to labor dispute	704.120(b)(5)
	Workers' compensation	704.160
tools of trade	Tools, implements, materials, instruments, uniforms, one commercial vehicle, books, furnishings, & equipment to $8,000 total ($15,975 total if used by both spouses in same occupation)	704.060
	Commercial vehicle (Vehicle Code § 260) to $4,850 ($9,700 total if used by both spouses in same occupation) (this counts toward total tools of trade exemption)	704.060
wages	Minimum 75% of wages paid within 30 days prior to filing	704.070
	Public employees' vacation credits; if receiving installments, at least 75%	704.113
wildcard	None	

California—System 2

Refer to the notes for California—System 1, above.

Note: Married couples may not double any exemptions. (*In re Talmadge*, 832 F.2d 1120 (9th Cir. 1987); *In re Baldwin*, 70 B.R. 612 (9th Cir. B.A.P 1987).)

ASSET	EXEMPTION	LAW
homestead	Real or personal property, including co-op, used as residence to $26,800; unused portion of homestead may be applied to any property	703.140(b)(1)
insurance	Disability benefits	703.140(b)(10)(C)
	Life insurance proceeds needed for support of family	703.140(b)(11)(C)
	Unmatured life insurance contract accrued avails to $14,325	703.140(b)(8)
	Unmatured life insurance policy other than credit	703.140(b)(7)
miscellaneous	Alimony, child support needed for support	703.140(b)(10)(D)
pensions	Tax-exempt retirement accounts, including 401(k)s, 403(b)s, profit-sharing and money purchase plans, SEP and SIMPLE IRAs, and defined-benefit plans	11 U.S.C. § 522(b)(3)(C)
	Traditional and Roth IRAs to $1,283,025 per person	11 U.S.C. § 522(b)(3)(C); (n)
	ERISA-qualified benefits needed for support	703.140(b)(10)(E)
personal property	Animals, crops, appliances, furnishings, household goods, books, musical instruments, & clothing to $675 per item	703.140(b)(3)
	Burial plot to $26,800, in lieu of homestead	703.140(b)(1)
	Health aids	703.140(b)(9)
	Jewelry to $1,600	703.140(b)(4)
	Motor vehicles to $5,350	703.140(b)(2)
	Personal injury recoveries to $26,800	703.140(b)(11)(D), (E)
	Wrongful death recoveries needed for support	703.140(b)(11)(B)
public benefits	Crime victims' compensation	703.140(b)(11)(A)
	Public assistance	703.140(b)(10)(A)
	Social Security	703.140(b)(10)(A)
	Unemployment compensation	703.140(b)(10)(A)
	Veterans benefits	703.140(b)(10)(B)
tools of trade	Implements, books & tools of trade to $8,000	703.140(b)(6)
wages	None	
wildcard	$1,425 of any property	703.140(b)(5)
	Unused portion of homestead or burial exemption of any property	703.140(b)(5)

Colorado

Federal bankruptcy exemptions not available. All law references are to Colorado Revised Statutes unless otherwise noted.

ASSET	EXEMPTION	LAW
homestead	Real property, mobile home, manufactured home, or house trailer you occupy to $75,000; $105,000 if owner, spouse, or dependent is disabled or at least 60 years old; sale proceeds exempt 2 years after received	38-41-201; 38-41-201.6; 38-41-203; 38-41-207; *In re Pastrana*, 216 B.R. 948 (D. Colo., 1998)
	Spouse or child of deceased owner may claim homestead exemption	38-41-204
insurance	Disability benefits to $200 per month; if lump sum, entire amount exempt	10-16-212
	Fraternal benefit society benefits	10-14-403
	Group life insurance policy or proceeds	10-7-205
	Homeowners' insurance proceeds for 1 year after received, to homestead exemption amount	38-41-209
	Life insurance cash surrender value to $100,000, except contributions to policy within past 48 months	13-54-102(1)(l)
	Life insurance proceeds if clause prohibits proceeds from being used to pay beneficiary's creditors	10-7-106
miscellaneous	Child support or domestic support obligation	13-54-102(u); 13-54-102.5
	Property of business partnership	7-60-125
pensions *see also wages*	Tax-exempt retirement accounts, including 401(k)s, 403(b)s, profit-sharing and money purchase plans, SEP and SIMPLE IRAs, and defined-benefit plans	11 U.S.C. § 522(b)(3)(C)
	Traditional and Roth IRAs to $1,283,025 per person	11 U.S.C. § 522(b)(3)(C); (n)
	ERISA-qualified benefits, including IRAs & Roth IRAs	13-54-102(1)(s)
	Firefighters & police officers	31-30.5-208; 31-31-203
	Public employees' pensions, deferred compensation & defined contribution plans	24-51-212
	Veterans pension for veteran, spouse, or dependents if veteran served in war or armed conflict	13-54-102(1)(h); 13-54-104
personal property	1 burial plot per family member	13-54-102(1)(d)
	Clothing to $2,000	13-54-102(1)(a)
	Food & fuel to $600	13-54-102(1)(f)
	Health aids	13-54-102(1)(p)
	Household goods to $3,000	13-54-102(1)(e)
	Jewelry & articles of adornment to $2,500	13-54-102(1)(b)
	Motor vehicles or bicycles used for work to $7,500; $12,500 if used by a debtor or by a dependent who is disabled or 60 or over	13-54-102(j)(I), (II)
	Personal injury recoveries	13-54-102(1)(n)
	Family pictures & books to $2,000	13-54-102(1)(c)
	Proceeds for damaged exempt property	13-54-102(1)(m)
	Security deposits	13-54-102(1)(r)
public benefits	Aid to blind, aged, disabled; public assistance	26-2-131
	Crime victims' compensation	13-54-102(1)(q); 24-4.1-114
	Disability benefits to $3,000	13-54-102(v)
	Earned income tax credit or refund	13-54-102(1)(o)
	Unemployment compensation	8-80-103
	Veterans benefits for veteran, spouse, or child if veteran served in war or armed conflict	13-54-102(1)(h)
	Workers' compensation	8-42-124

tools of trade	Livestock or other animals, machinery, tools, equipment, & seed of person engaged in agriculture, to $50,000 total	13-54-102(1)(g)
	Professional's library to $3,000 (if not claimed under other tools of trade exemption)	13-54-102(1)(k)
	Stock in trade, supplies, fixtures, tools, machines, electronics, equipment, books & other business materials, to $30,000 total	13-54-102(1)(i)
	Military equipment personally owned by members of the National Guard	13-54-102(1)(h.5)
wages	Minimum 75% of weekly net earnings or 30 times the federal or state minimum wage, whichever is greater, including pension & insurance payments. *In re Nye*, 210 B.R. 857 (D. Colo. 1997); *In re Kobemusz*, 160 B.R. 844 (D. Colo. 1993)	13-54-104
wildcard	None	

Connecticut

Federal bankruptcy exemptions available. All law references are to Connecticut General Statutes Annotated unless otherwise noted.

ASSET	EXEMPTION	LAW
homestead	Owner-occupied real property, including co-op or mobile manufactured home, to $75,000; applies only to claims arising after 1993, but to $125,000 in the case of a money judgment arising out of services provided at a hospital	52-352a(e); 52-352b(t)
insurance	Disability benefits paid by association for its members	52-352b(p)
	Fraternal benefit society benefits	38a-637
	Health or disability benefits	52-352b(e)
	Life insurance proceeds if clause prohibits proceeds from being used to pay beneficiary's creditors	38a-454
	Life insurance proceeds or avails	38a-453
	Unmatured life insurance policy avails to $4,000 if beneficiary is dependent	52-352b(s)
miscellaneous	Alimony, to extent wages exempt	52-352b(n)
	Child support	52-352b(h)
	Farm partnership animals & livestock feed reasonably required to run farm where at least 50% of partners are members of same family	52-352d
pensions	Tax-exempt retirement accounts, including 401(k)s, 403(b)s, profit-sharing and money purchase plans, SEP and SIMPLE IRAs, and defined-benefit plans	11 U.S.C. § 522(b)(3)(C)
	Traditional and Roth IRAs to $1,283,025 per person	11 U.S.C. § 522(b)(3)(C); (n)
	ERISA-qualified benefits, including IRAs, Roth IRAs & Keoghs, to extent wages exempt	52-321a; 52-352b(m)
	Medical savings account	52-321a
	Municipal employees	7-446
	State employees	5-171; 5-192w
	Teachers	10-183q
personal property	Appliances, food, clothing, furniture, bedding	52-352b(a)
	Burial plot	52-352b(c)
	Health aids needed	52-352b(f)
	Motor vehicle to $3,500	52-352b(j)
	Proceeds for damaged exempt property	52-352b(q)
	Residential utility & security deposits for 1 residence	52-352b(l)
	Spendthrift trust funds required for support of debtor & family	52-321(d)
	Transfers to a licensed debt adjuster	52-352b(u)
	Tuition savings accounts	52-321a(E)
	Wedding & engagement rings	52-352b(k)
public benefits	Crime victims' compensation	52-352b(o); 54-213
	Public assistance	52-352b(d)
	Social Security	52-352b(g)
	Unemployment compensation	31-272(c); 52-352b(g)
	Veterans benefits	52-352b(g)
	Workers' compensation	52-352b(g)
tools of trade	Arms, military equipment, uniforms, musical instruments of military personnel	52-352b(i)
	Tools, books, instruments, & farm animals needed	52-352b(b)
wages	Minimum 75% of earned but unpaid weekly disposable earnings, or 40 times the state or federal hourly minimum wage, whichever is greater	52-361a(f)
wildcard	$1,000 of any property	52-352b(r)

Delaware

Federal bankruptcy exemptions not available. All law references are to Delaware Code Annotated (in the form "title number-section number") unless otherwise noted.

Note: A single person may exempt no more than $25,000 total in all exemptions (not including retirement plans and principal residence); a husband and wife may exempt no more than $50,000 total (10-4914).

ASSET	EXEMPTION	LAW
homestead	Real property or manufactured home used as principal residence to $125,000 in 2012; $125,000 for working or married persons where one spouse is 65 or older (spouses may not double)	10-4914(c)
	Property held as tenancy by the entirety may be exempt against debts owed by only one spouse	*In re Kelley,* 289 B.R. 38 (Bankr. D. Del. 2003)
insurance	Annuity contract proceeds to $350 per month	18-2728
	Fraternal benefit society benefits	18-6218
	Group life insurance policy or proceeds	18-2727
	Health or disability benefits	18-2726
	Life insurance proceeds if clause prohibits proceeds from being used to pay beneficiary's creditors	18-2729
	Life insurance proceeds or avails	18-2725
pensions	Tax-exempt retirement accounts, including 401(k)s, 403(b)s, profit-sharing and money purchase plans, SEP and SIMPLE IRAs, and defined-benefit plans	11 U.S.C. § 522(b)(3)(C)
	Traditional and Roth IRAs to $1,283,025 per person	11 U.S.C. § 522(b)(3)(C); (n)
	IRAs, Roth IRAs & any other retirement plans	10-4915
	Kent County employees	9-4316
	Police officers	11-8803
	State employees	29-5503
	Volunteer firefighters	16-6653
personal property	Bible, books, & family pictures	10-4902(a)
	Burial plot	10-4902(a)
	Church pew or any seat in public place of worship	10-4902(a)
	Clothing, includes jewelry	10-4902(a)
	College investment plan account (limit for year before filing is $5,000 or average of past two years' contribution, whichever is more)	10-4916
	Principal and income from spendthrift trusts	12-3536
	Pianos & leased organs	10-4902(d)
	Sewing machines	10-4902(c)
public benefits	Aid to blind	31-2309
	Aid to aged, disabled; general assistance	31-513
	Crime victims' compensation	11-9011
	Unemployment compensation	19-3374
	Workers' compensation	19-2355
tools of trade	Tools of trade and/or vehicle necessary for employment to $15,000 each	10-4914(c)
	Tools, implements & fixtures to $75 in New Castle & Sussex Counties; to $50 in Kent County	10-4902(b)
wages	85% of earned but unpaid wages	10-4913
wildcard	$500 of any personal property, except tools of trade, if head of family	10-4903

District of Columbia

Federal bankruptcy exemptions available. All law references are to District of Columbia Code unless otherwise noted.

ASSET	EXEMPTION	LAW
homestead	Any property used as a residence or co-op that debtor or debtor's dependent uses as a residence	15-501(a)(14)
	Property held as tenancy by the entirety may be exempt against debts owed by only one spouse	*Estate of Wall*, 440 F.2d 215 (D.C. Cir. 1971)
insurance	Disability benefits	15-501(a)(7); 31-4716.01
	Fraternal benefit society benefits	31-5315
	Group life insurance policy or proceeds	31-4717
	Life insurance payments	15-501(a)(11)
	Life insurance proceeds if clause prohibits proceeds from being used to pay beneficiary's creditors	31-4719
	Life insurance proceeds or avails	31-4716
	Other insurance proceeds to $200 per month, maximum 2 months, for head of family; else $60 per month	15-503
	Unmatured life insurance contract other than credit life insurance	15-501(a)(5)
miscellaneous	Alimony or child support	15-501(a)(7)
pensions *see also wages*	Tax-exempt retirement accounts, including 401(k)s, 403(b)s, profit-sharing and money purchase plans, SEP and SIMPLE IRAs, and defined-benefit plans	11 U.S.C. § 522(b)(3)(C)
	Traditional and Roth IRAs to $1,283,025 per person	11 U.S.C. § 522(b)(3)(C); (n)
	ERISA-qualified benefits, IRAs, Keoghs, etc. to maximum deductible contribution	15-501(b)(9)
	Any stock bonus, annuity, pension, or profit-sharing plan	15-501(a)(7)
	Judges	11-1570(f)
	Public school teachers	38-2001.17; 38-2021.17
personal property	Appliances, books, clothing, household furnishings, goods, musical instruments, pets to $425 per item or $8,625 total	15-501(a)(2)
	Cemetery & burial funds	43-111
	Cooperative association holdings to $500	29-928
	Food for 3 months	15-501(a)(12)
	Health aids	15-501(a)(6)
	Higher education tuition savings account	47-4510
	Residential condominium deposit	42-1904.09
	All family pictures; all the family library to $400	15-501(a)(8)
	Motor vehicle to $2,575	15-501(a)(1)
	Payment, including pain & suffering, for loss of debtor or person depended on	15-501(a)(11)
	Uninsured motorist benefits	31-2408.01(h)
	Wrongful death damages	15-501(a)(11); 16-2703
public benefits	Aid to blind, aged, disabled; general assistance	4-215.01
	Crime victims' compensation	4-507(e); 15-501(a)(11)
	Social Security	15-501(a)(7)
	Unemployment compensation	51-118
	Veterans benefits	15-501(a)(7)
	Workers' compensation	32-1517

tools of trade	Library, furniture, tools of professional or artist to $300	15-501(a)(13)
	Tools of trade or business to $1,625	15-501(a)(5)
	Mechanic's tools to $200	15-503(b)
	Seal & documents of notary public	1-1206
wages	Minimum 75% of earned but unpaid wages, pension payments; bankruptcy judge may authorize more for low-income debtors	16-572
	Nonwage (including pension & retirement) earnings to $200 per month for head of family; else $60 per month for a maximum of two months	15-503
	Payment for loss of future earnings	15-501(e)(11)
wildcard	Up to $850 in any property, plus up to $8,075 if you don't use the homestead exemption	15-501(a)(3)

Florida

Federal bankruptcy exemptions not available. All law references are to Florida Statutes Annotated unless otherwise noted.

ASSET	EXEMPTION	LAW
homestead	Real or personal property including mobile or modular home to unlimited value; cannot exceed half acre in municipality or 160 acres elsewhere; spouse or child of deceased owner may claim homestead exemption	222.01; 222.02; 222.03; 222.05; Constitution 10-4; *In re Colwell*, 196 F.3d 1225 (11th Cir. 1999)
	May file homestead declaration	222.01
	Property held as tenancy by the entirety may be exempt against debts owed by only one spouse	*Havoco of America, Ltd. v. Hill*, 197 F.3d 1135 (11th Cir. 1999)
insurance	Annuity contract proceeds; does not include lottery winnings	222.14; *In re Pizzi*, 153 B.R. 357 (S.D. Fla. 1993)
	Death benefits payable to a specific beneficiary, not the deceased's estate	222.13
	Disability or illness benefits	222.18
	Fraternal benefit society benefits	632.619
	Life insurance cash surrender value	222.14
miscellaneous	Alimony, child support needed for support	222.201
	Damages to employees for injuries in hazardous occupations	769.05
pensions *see also wages*	Tax-exempt retirement accounts, including 401(k)s, 403(b)s, profit-sharing and money purchase plans, SEP and SIMPLE IRAs, and defined-benefit plans	11 U.S.C. § 522(b)(3)(C)
	Traditional and Roth IRAs to $1,283,025 per person	11 U.S.C. § 522(b)(3)(C); (n)
	County officers, employees	122.15
	ERISA-qualified benefits, including IRAs & Roth IRAs	222.21(2)
	Firefighters	175.241
	Police officers	185.25
	State officers, employees	121.131
	Teachers	238.15
personal property	Any personal property to $1,000 (husband & wife may double); to $4,000 if no homestead claimed	222.25(4) Const. Art. X. § 4(a)(2)
	Health aids	222.25(2)
	Motor vehicle to $1,000	222.25(1)
	Preneed funeral contract deposits	497.56(8)
	Prepaid college education trust deposits	222.22(1)
	Prepaid hurricane savings accounts	222.22(4)
	Prepaid medical savings account & health savings account deposits	222.22(2)
public benefits	Crime victims' compensation, unless seeking to discharge debt for treatment of injury incurred during the crime	960.14
	Earned income tax credit	222.25(3)
	Public assistance	222.201
	Social Security	222.201
	Reemployment assistance	222.201; 443.051(2), (3)
	Veterans benefits	222.201; 744.626
	Workers' compensation	440.22
tools of trade	None	
wages	100% of wages for heads of family up to $750 per week either unpaid or paid & deposited into bank account for up to 6 months	222.11
	Federal government employees' pension payments needed for support & received 3 months prior	222.21
wildcard	See personal property	

Georgia

Federal bankruptcy exemptions not available. All law references are to the Official Code of Georgia Annotated unless otherwise noted.

ASSET	EXEMPTION	LAW
homestead	Real or personal property, including co-op, used as residence to $21,500 (to $43,000 if married and debtor spouse is sole owner); up to $5,000 of unused portion of homestead may be applied to any property	44-13-100(a)(1); 44-13-100(a)(6); *In re Burnett*, 303 B.R. 684 (M.D. Ga. 2003)
insurance	Annuity & endowment contract benefits	33-28-7
	Disability or health benefits to $250 per month	33-29-15
	Fraternal benefit society benefits	33-15-62
	Group insurance	33-30-10
	Proceeds & avails of life insurance	33-26-5; 33-25-11
	Life insurance proceeds if policy owned by someone you depended on, needed for support	44-13-100(a)(11)(C)
	Unmatured life insurance contract	44-13-100(a)(8)
	Unmatured life insurance dividends, interest, loan value, or cash value to $2,000 if beneficiary is you or someone you depend on	44-13-100(a)(9)
miscellaneous	Alimony, child support needed for support	44-13-100(a)(2)(D)
pensions	Tax-exempt retirement accounts, including 401(k)s, 403(b)s, profit-sharing and money purchase plans, SEP and SIMPLE IRAs, and defined-benefit plans	11 U.S.C. § 522(b)(3)(C)
	Traditional and Roth IRAs to $1,283,025 per person	11 U.S.C. § 522(b)(3)(C); (n)
	Employees of nonprofit corporations	44-13-100(a)(2.1)(B)
	ERISA-qualified benefits & IRAs	18-4-22
	Public employees	44-13-100(a)(2.1)(A); 47-2-332
	Payments from IRA necessary for support	44-13-100(a)(2)(F)
	Other pensions needed for support	18-4-22; 44-13-100(a)(2)(E); 44-13-100(a)(2.1)(C)
personal property	Animals, crops, clothing, appliances, books, furnishings, household goods, musical instruments to $300 per item, $5,000 total	44-13-100(a)(4)
	Burial plot, in lieu of homestead	44-13-100(a)(1)
	Compensation for lost future earnings needed for support to $7,500	44-13-100(a)(11)(E)
	Health aids	44-13-100(a)(10)
	Jewelry to $500	44-13-100(a)(5)
	Motor vehicles to $5,000	44-13-100(a)(3)
	Personal injury recoveries to $10,000	44-13-100(a)(11)(D)
	Wrongful death recoveries needed for support	44-13-100(a)(11)(B)
public benefits	Aid to blind	49-4-58
	Aid to disabled	49-4-84
	Crime victims' compensation	44-13-100(a)(11)(A)
	Local public assistance	44-13-100(a)(2)(A)
	Old age assistance	49-4-35
	Social Security	44-13-100(a)(2)(A)
	Unemployment compensation	44-13-100(a)(2)(A)
	Veterans benefits	44-13-100(a)(2)(B)
	Workers' compensation	34-9-84
tools of trade	Implements, books & tools of trade to $1,500	44-13-100(a)(7)
wages	Minimum 75% of earned but unpaid weekly disposable earnings, or 30 times the state or federal hourly minimum wage, whichever is greater, for private & federal workers; bankruptcy judge may authorize more for low-income debtors	18-4-20; 18-4-21
wildcard	$600 of any property	44-13-100(a)(6)
	Unused portion of homestead exemption to $5,000	44-13-100(a)(6)

Hawaii

Federal bankruptcy exemptions available. All law references are to Hawaii Revised Statutes unless otherwise noted.

ASSET	EXEMPTION	LAW
homestead	Head of family or over 65 to $30,000; all others to $20,000; property cannot exceed 1 acre; sale proceeds exempt for 6 months after sale (spouses may not double)	651-91; 651-92; 651-96
	Property held as tenancy by the entirety may be exempt against debts owed by only one spouse or reciprocal beneficiary	509-2; *Security Pacific Bank v. Chang*, 818 F.Supp. 1343 (D. Haw. 1993)
insurance	Annuity contract or endowment policy proceeds if beneficiary is insured's spouse, child, or parent	431:10-232(b)
	Accident, health, or sickness benefits	431:10-231
	Fraternal benefit society benefits	432:2-403
	Group life insurance policy or proceeds	431:10-233
	Life insurance proceeds if clause prohibits proceeds from being used to pay beneficiary's creditors	431:10D-112
	Life or health insurance policy for spouse or child	431:10-234
miscellaneous	Property of business partnership	425-125
pensions	Tax-exempt retirement accounts, including 401(k)s, 403(b)s, profit-sharing and money purchase plans, SEP and SIMPLE IRAs, and defined-benefit plans	11 U.S.C. § 522(b)(3)(C)
	Traditional and Roth IRAs to $1,283,025 per person	11 U.S.C. § 522(b)(3)(C); (n)
	IRAs, Roth IRAs, and ERISA-qualified benefits deposited over 3 years before filing bankruptcy	651-124
	Firefighters	88-169
	Police officers	88-169
	Public officers & employees	88-91; 653-3
personal property	Appliances & furnishings	651-121(1)
	Books	651-121(1)
	Burial plot to 250 sq. ft. plus tombstones, monuments, & fencing	651-121(4)
	Clothing	651-121(1)
	Jewelry, watches, & articles of adornment to $1,000	651-121(1)
	Motor vehicle to wholesale value of $2,575	651-121(2)
	Proceeds for sold or damaged exempt property; sale proceeds exempt for 6 months after sale	651-121(5)
public benefits	Crime victims' compensation & special accounts created to limit commercial exploitation of crimes	351-66; 351-86
	Public assistance paid by Department of Health Services for work done in home or workshop	346-33
	Temporary disability benefits	392-29
	Unemployment compensation	383-163
	Unemployment work relief funds to $60 per month	653-4
	Workers' compensation	386-57
tools of trade	Tools, implements, books, instruments, uniforms, furnishings, fishing boat, nets, motor vehicle, & other property needed for livelihood	651-121(3)
wages	Prisoner's wages held by Department of Public Safety (except for restitution, child support, & other claims)	353-22.5
	Unpaid wages due for services of past 31 days	651-121(6)
wildcard	None	

Idaho

Federal bankruptcy exemptions not available. All law references are to Idaho Code unless otherwise noted.

ASSET	EXEMPTION	LAW
homestead	Real property or mobile home to $100,000; sale proceeds exempt for 6 months (spouses may not double)	55-1003; 55-1113
	Must record homestead exemption for property that is not yet occupied	55-1004
insurance	Annuity contract proceeds to $1,250 per month; if not yet receiving payments from the annuity, cash surrender value to amount of premiums paid during 6 months before bankruptcy petition	41-1836
	Death or disability benefits	11-604(1)(a); 41-1834
	Fraternal benefit society benefits	41-3218
	Group life insurance benefits	41-1835
	Homeowners' insurance proceeds to amount of homestead exemption	55-1008
	Life insurance proceeds if clause prohibits proceeds from being used to pay beneficiary's creditors	41-1930
	Life insurance proceeds or avails for beneficiary other than the insured	11-604(d); 41-1833
	Medical, surgical, or hospital care benefits & amount in medical savings account	11-603(5)
	Unmatured life insurance contract, other than credit life insurance, owned by debtor	11-605(9)
	Unmatured life insurance contract interest or dividends to $5,000 owned by debtor or person debtor depends on	11-605(10)
miscellaneous	Alimony, child support	11-604(1)(b)
	Liquor licenses	23-514
pension *see also wages*	Tax-exempt retirement accounts, including 401(k)s, 403(b)s, profit-sharing and money purchase plans, SEP and SIMPLE IRAs, and defined-benefit plans	11 U.S.C. § 522(b)(3)(C)
	Traditional and Roth IRAs to $1,283,025 per person	11 U.S.C. § 522(b)(3)(C); (n)
	ERISA-qualified benefits	55-1011
	Firefighters	72-1422
	Government & private pensions, retirement plans, IRAs, Roth IRAs, Keoghs, etc.	11-604A
	Police officers	50-1517
	Public employees	59-1317
personal property	Appliances, furnishings, books, clothing, pets, musical instruments, family portraits, & sentimental heirlooms to $750 per item, $7,500 total	11-605(1)
	Building materials	45-514
	Burial plot	11-603(1)
	College savings program account	11-604A(4)(b)
	Crops cultivated on maximum of 50 acres, to $1,000; water rights to 160 inches	11-605(6) and (7)
	Firearm (1) to $750	11-605(8)
	Health aids	11-603(2)
	Jewelry to $1,000	11-605(2)
	Motor vehicle to $7,000	11-605(3)
	Personal injury recoveries	11-604(1)(c)
	Proceeds for damaged exempt property for 3 months after proceeds received	11-606
	Provisions (food, water, and storage equipment) sufficient for up to 12 months	11-605(4)
	Wrongful death recoveries	11-604(1)(c)

public benefits	Aid to blind, aged, disabled	56-223
	Federal, state & local public assistance, including earned income tax credit (but not child or education tax credit) (*In re Jones*, 107 B.R. 751 (Bankr. D. Idaho 1989; *In re Steinmetz*, 261 B.R. 32 (Bankr. D. Idaho 2001); *In re Crampton*, 249 B.R. 215 (Bankr.D. Idaho 2000))	11-603(4)
	General assistance	56-223
	Social Security	11-603(3)
	Unemployment compensation	11-603(6)
	Veterans benefits	11-603(3)
	Workers' compensation	72-802
tools of trade	Arms, uniforms & accoutrements that peace officer, National Guard, or military personnel is required to keep	11-605(6)
	Implements, books & tools of trade to $2,500	11-605(3)
wages	Minimum 75% of earned but unpaid weekly disposable earnings, or 30 times the federal hourly minimum wage, whichever is greater but not more than $1,500 in a calendar year; pension payments; bankruptcy judge may authorize more for low-income debtors	11-207; 11-605-12; 11-206
wildcard	$800 in any tangible personal property	11-605(11)

Illinois

Federal bankruptcy exemptions not available. All law references are to Illinois Compiled Statutes Annotated unless otherwise noted.

Note: Although one court has held that the Illinois Wage Deduction Act creates a bankruptcy exemption, *In re Mayer*, 288 B.R. 869 (Bankr. N.D. Ill. 2008) (Wedoff, J.), most other Illinois courts addressing the issue have found that it does not. (*In re Radzilowsky*, 448 B.R. 767 (Bankr. N.D. Ill. May 6, 2011); *In re Kapusta*, 2011 WL 2173675 (C.D. Ill. June 2, 2011); *In re Koeneman*, 410 B.R. 820 (C.D. Ill. 2009); *In re Thum*, 329 B.R. 848 (Bankr. C.D. Ill. 2005).)

ASSET	EXEMPTION	LAW
homestead	Real or personal property including a farm, lot & buildings, condo, co-op, or mobile home to $15,000; sale proceeds exempt for 1 year	735-5/12-901; 735-5/12-906
	Spouse or child of deceased owner may claim homestead exemption	735-5/12-902
	Illinois recognizes tenancy by the entirety, with limitations	750-65/22; 765-1005/1c; *In re Gillissie*, 215 B.R. 370 (Bankr. N.D. Ill. 1998); *Great Southern Co. v. Allard*, 202 B.R. 938 (N.D. Ill. 1996)
insurance	Fraternal benefit society benefits	215-5/299.1a
	Health or disability benefits	735-5/12-1001 (g)(3)
	Homeowners' proceeds if home destroyed, to $15,000	735-5/12-907
	Life insurance, annuity proceeds, or cash value if beneficiary is insured's child, parent, spouse, or other dependent	215-5/238; 735-5/12-1001(f)
	Life insurance proceeds to a spouse or dependent of debtor to extent needed for support	735-5/12-1001(f), (g)(3)
miscellaneous	Alimony, child support	735-5/12-1001 (g)(4)
	Property of business partnership	805-205/25
pensions	Tax-exempt retirement accounts, including 401(k)s, 403(b)s, profit-sharing and money purchase plans, SEP and SIMPLE IRAs, and defined-benefit plans	11 U.S.C. § 522(b)(3)(C)
	Traditional and Roth IRAs to $1,283,025 per person	11 U.S.C. § 522 (b)(3)(C); (n)
	Civil service employees	40-5/11-223
	County employees	40-5/9-228
	Disabled firefighters; widows & children of firefighters	40-5/22-230
	IRAs and ERISA-qualified benefits	735-5/12-1006
	Firefighters	40-5/4-135; 40-5/6-213
	General Assembly members	40-5/2-154
	House of correction employees	40-5/19-117
	Judges	40-5/18-161
	Municipal employees	40-5/7-217(a); 40-5/8-244
	Park employees	40-5/12-190
	Police officers	40-5/3-144.1; 40-5/5-218
	Public employees	735-5/12-1006
	Public library employees	40-5/19-218
	Sanitation district employees	40-5/13-805
	State employees	40-5/14-147
	State university employees	40-5/15-185
	Teachers	40-5/16-190; 40-5/17-151

personal property	Bible, family pictures, schoolbooks & clothing	735-5/12-1001(a)
	Health aids	735-5/12-1001(e)
	Illinois College Savings Pool accounts invested more than 1 year before filing if below federal gift tax limit, or 2 years before filing if above	735-5/12-1001(j)
	Motor vehicle to $2,400	735-5/12-1001(c)
	Personal injury recoveries to $15,000	735-5/12-1001 (h)(4)
	Preneed cemetery sales funds, care funds & trust funds	235-5/6-1; 760-100/4; 815-390/16
	Prepaid tuition trust fund	110-979/45(g)
	Proceeds of sold exempt property	735-5/12-1001
	Wrongful death recoveries	735-5/12-1001 (h)(2)
public benefits	Aid to aged, blind, disabled; public assistance, including earned income tax credit and child tax credit (applies to future payments but not funds already received) (*In re Fish*, 224 B.R. 82 (Bankr. S.D. Ill 1998); *In re Vazquez*, No. 13-32174 (Bankr. N.D. Ill 2014); *In re Frueh*, No. 14-B-81029 (Bankr. W.D. Ill 2014))	305-5/11-3; 735-5/12-1001 (g)(1)
	Crime victims' compensation	735-5/12-1001 (h)(1)
	Restitution payments on account of WWII relocation of Aleuts & Japanese Americans	735-5/12-1001 (12)(h)(5)
	Social Security	735-5/12-1001 (g)(1)
	Unemployment compensation	735-5/12-1001 (g)(1), (3)
	Veterans benefits	735-5/12-1001 (g)(2)
	Workers' compensation	820-305/21
	Workers' occupational disease compensation	820-310/21
tools of trade	Implements, books, & tools of trade to $1,500	735-5/12-1001(d)
wages	Minimum 85% of earned but unpaid weekly wages or 45 times the federal minimum hourly wage (or state minimum hourly wage, if higher); bankruptcy judge may authorize more for low-income debtors (some judges may not allow this exemption). See note at beginning of Illinois chart.	735-5/12-803
wildcard	$4,000 of any personal property (does not include wages)	735-5/12-1001(b)

Indiana

Federal bankruptcy exemptions not available. All law references are to Indiana Statutes Annotated unless otherwise noted.

ASSET	EXEMPTION	LAW
homestead *see also wildcard*	Real or personal property used as residence to $19,300	34-55-10-2(c)(1)
	Property held as tenancy by the entirety may be exempt against debts incurred by only one spouse	34-55-10-2(c)(5); 32-17-3-1
insurance	Employer's life insurance policy on employee	27-1-12-17.1
	Fraternal benefit society benefits	27-11-6-3
	Group life insurance policy	27-1-12-29
	Life insurance policy, proceeds, cash value, or avails if beneficiary is insured's spouse or dependent	27-1-12-14
	Life insurance proceeds if clause prohibits proceeds to be used to pay beneficiary's creditors	27-2-5-1
	Mutual life or accident proceeds needed for support	27-8-3-23; *In re Stinnet*, 321 B.R. 477 (S.D. Ind. 2005)
miscellaneous	Property of business partnership	23-4-1-25
pensions	Tax-exempt retirement accounts, including 401(k)s, 403(b)s, profit-sharing and money purchase plans, SEP and SIMPLE IRAs, and defined-benefit plans	11 U.S.C. § 522(b)(3)(C)
	Traditional and Roth IRAs to $1,283,025 per person	11 U.S.C. § 522(b)(3)(C); (n)
	Firefighters	36-8-7-22; 36-8-8-17
	Police officers	36-8-8-17; 10-12-2-10
	Public employees	5-10.3-8-9
	Public or private retirement benefits & contributions	34-55-10-2(c)(6)
	Sheriffs	36-8-10-19
	State teachers	5-10.4-5-14
personal property	Education savings account (529 and Coverdell) contributions made more than 2 years prior to filing; contributions made more than 1 but less than 2 years prior to filing to $5,000; no exemption for contributions made less than 1 year prior to filing	34-55-10-2(c)(9), (10)
	Health aids	34-55-10-2(c)(4)
	Money in medical care savings account or health savings account	34-55-10-2(c)(7), (8)
	Spendthrift trusts	30-4-3-2
	$400 of any intangible personal property, except money owed to you	34-55-10-2(c)(3)
public benefits	Crime victims' compensation, unless seeking to discharge the debts for which the victim was compensated	5-2-6.1-38
	Earned income tax credit (but not child tax credit) (*In re King*, 508 B.R. 71 (Bankr. N.D. Ind. 2014); *In re Jackson*, No. 12–9635–RLM–7A (Bankr. S.D. In. 2013))	34-55-10-2(c)(11)
	Supplemental state fair relief fund	34-13-8; 34-55-102(c)(13)
	Unemployment compensation	22-4-33-3
	Veterans disability benefits	34-55-10-2(c)(12)
	Workers' compensation	22-3-2-17
tools of trade	National Guard uniforms, arms & equipment	10-16-10-3
wages	Minimum 75% of earned but unpaid weekly disposable earnings, or 30 times the federal hourly minimum wage; bankruptcy judge may authorize more for low-income debtors. (*In re Haraughty*, 403 B.R. 607 (Bankr. S.D. Indiana 2009).)	24-4.5-5-105
wildcard	$10,250 of any real estate or tangible personal property	34-55-10-2(c)(2)

Iowa

Federal bankruptcy exemptions not available. All law references are to Iowa Code Annotated unless otherwise noted.

ASSET	EXEMPTION	LAW
homestead	May record homestead declaration	561.4
	Real property or an apartment to an unlimited value; property cannot exceed ½ acre in town or city, 40 acres elsewhere (spouses may not double)	499A.18; 561.2; 561.16
insurance	Accident, disability, health, illness, or life proceeds or avails	627.6(6)
	Disability or illness benefit	627.6(8)(c)
	Employee group insurance policy or proceeds	509.12
	Fraternal benefit society benefits	512B.18
	Life insurance proceeds if clause prohibits proceeds from being used to pay beneficiary's creditors	508.32
	Life insurance proceeds paid to spouse, child, or other dependent (limited to $10,000 if acquired within 2 years of filing for bankruptcy)	627.6(6)
	Upon death of insured, up to $15,000 total proceeds from all matured life, accident, health, or disability policies exempt from beneficiary's debts contracted before insured's death	627.6(6)(c)
miscellaneous	Alimony, child support needed for support	627.6(8)(d)
	Liquor licenses	123.38
pensions *see also wages*	Tax-exempt retirement accounts, including 401(k)s, 403(b)s, profit-sharing and money purchase plans, SEP and SIMPLE IRAs, and defined-benefit plans	11 U.S.C. § 522(b)(3)(C)
	Traditional and Roth IRAs to $1,283,025 per person	11 U.S.C. § 522(b)(3)(C); (n)
	Disabled firefighters, police officers (only payments being received)	410.11
	Federal government pension	627.8
	Firefighters	411.13
	Other pensions, annuities & contracts fully exempt; however, contributions made within 1 year prior to filing for bankruptcy not exempt to the extent they exceed normal & customary amounts	627.6(8)(e)
	Peace officers	97A.12
	Police officers	411.13
	Public employees	97B.39
	Retirement plans, Keoghs, IRAs, Roth IRAs, ERISA-qualified benefits	627.6(8)(f)
personal property	Bibles, books, portraits, pictures & paintings to $1,000 total	627.6(3)
	Burial plot to 1 acre	627.6(4)
	Clothing & its storage containers, household furnishings, appliances, musical instruments, and other personal property to $7,000	627.6(5)
	Health aids	627.6(7)
	Jewelry to $2,000	627.6(1)(6)
	Residential security or utility deposit, or advance rent, to $500	627.6(14)
	Rifle or musket; shotgun	627.6(2)
	One motor vehicle to $7,000	627.6(9)
	Wedding or engagement rings, limited to $7,000 (minus any amounts used under the jewelry exemption) if purchased after marriage and within last two years	627.6(1)(a)
	Wrongful death proceeds and awards needed for support of debtor and dependents	627.6(15)

public benefits	Adopted child assistance		627.19
	Aid to dependent children		239B.6
	Any public assistance benefit, including earned income tax credit and child tax credit (*In re Hatch*, 13-03342-als7 (Bankr. N.D. Iowa 2014); *In re Longstreet*, 246 B.R. 611 (Bankr. S.D. Iowa 2000))		627.6(8)(a)
	Social Security		627.6(8)(a)
	Unemployment compensation		627.6(8)(a)
	Veterans benefits		627.6(8)(b)
	Workers' compensation		627.13
tools of trade	Farming equipment; includes livestock, feed to $10,000		627.6(11)
	National Guard articles of equipment		29A.41
	Nonfarming equipment to $10,000		627.6(10)
wages	Expected annual earnings	Amount NOT exempt per year	642.21
	$0 to $11,999	$250	
	$12,000 to $15,999	$400	
	$16,000 to $23,999	$800	
	$24,000 to $34,999	$1,000	
	$35,000 to $49,999	$2,000	
	More than $50,000	10%	
	In re Irish, 311 B.R. 63 (8th Cir. B.A.P. 2004) Not exempt from spousal or child support		
	Wages or salary of a prisoner		356.29
wildcard	$1,000 of any personal property, including cash		627.6(14)

Kansas

Federal bankruptcy exemptions not available. Although Kansas has opted out of the federal exemptions, it does allow debtors to use exemptions in 11 U.S.C.A. § 522(d)(10). See K.S.A. 60-2312(b). All law references are to Kansas Statutes Annotated unless otherwise noted.

ASSET	EXEMPTION	LAW
homestead	Real property or mobile home you occupy or intend to occupy to unlimited value; property cannot exceed 1 acre in town or city, 160 acres on farm	60-2301; Constitution 15-9
insurance	Cash value of life insurance; not exempt if obtained within 1 year prior to bankruptcy with fraudulent intent	60-2313(a)(7); 40-414(b)
	Disability & illness benefits	60-2313(a)(1)
	Fraternal life insurance benefits	60-2313(a)(8)
	Life insurance proceeds	40-414(a)
miscellaneous	Alimony, maintenance & support	60-2312(b)
	Liquor licenses	60-2313(a)(6); 41-326
pensions	Tax-exempt retirement accounts, including 401(k)s, 403(b)s, profit-sharing and money purchase plans, SEP and SIMPLE IRAs, and defined-benefit plans	11 U.S.C. § 522(b)(3)(C)
	Traditional and Roth IRAs to $1,283,025 per person	11 U.S.C. § 522(b)(3)(C); (n)
	Elected & appointed officials in cities with populations between 120,000 & 200,000	13-14a10
	ERISA-qualified benefits	60-2308(b)
	Federal government pension needed for support & paid within 3 months of filing for bankruptcy (only payments being received)	60-2308(a)
	Firefighters	12-5005(e); 14-10a10
	Judges	20-2618
	Police officers	12-5005(e); 13-14a10
	Public employees	74-4923; 74-49,105
	State highway patrol officers	74-4978g
	State school employees	72-5526
	Payment under a stock bonus, pension, profit-sharing, annuity, or similar plan or contract on account of illness, disability, death, age, or length of service, to the extent reasonably necessary for support	60-2312(b)
personal property	Burial plot or crypt	60-2304(d)
	Clothing to last 1 year	60-2304(a)
	Earned income tax credit	60-2315
	Food & fuel to last 1 year	60-2304(a)
	Funeral plan prepayments	60-2313(a)(10); 16-310(d)
	Furnishings & household equipment	60-2304(a)
	Jewelry & articles of adornment to $1,000	60-2304(b)
	Motor vehicle to $20,000; if designed or equipped for disabled person, no limit	60-2304(c)
public benefits	Crime victims' compensation	60-2313(a)(7); 74-7313(d)
	Earned income tax credit	60-2315
	General assistance	39-717(c)
	Social Security	60-2312(b)
	Unemployment compensation	60-2313(a)(4); 44-718(c)
	Veterans benefits	60-2312(b)
	Workers' compensation	60-2313(a)(3); 44-514

tools of trade	Books, documents, furniture, instruments, equipment, breeding stock, seed, grain & stock to $7,500 total	60-2304(e)
	National Guard uniforms, arms & equipment	48-245
wages	Minimum 75% of disposable weekly wages or 30 times the federal minimum hourly wage per week, whichever is greater; bankruptcy judge may authorize more for low-income debtors; *In re Urban* 262 B.R. 865 (Bankr. D. Kan. 2001)	60-2310
wildcard	None	

Kentucky

Federal bankruptcy exemptions available. All law references are to Kentucky Revised Statutes unless otherwise noted.

ASSET	EXEMPTION	LAW
homestead	Real or personal property used as residence to $5,000; sale proceeds exempt	427.060; 427.090
insurance	Annuity contract proceeds to $350 per month	304.14-330
	Cooperative life or casualty insurance benefits	427.110(1)
	Fraternal benefit society benefits	427.110(2)
	Group life insurance proceeds	304.14-320
	Health or disability benefits	304.14-310
	Life insurance policy if beneficiary is a married woman	304.14-340
	Life insurance proceeds if clause prohibits proceeds from being used to pay beneficiary's creditors	304.14-350
	Life insurance proceeds or cash value if beneficiary is someone other than insured	304.14-300
miscellaneous	Alimony, child support needed for support	427.150(1)
pensions	Tax-exempt retirement accounts, including 401(k)s, 403(b)s, profit-sharing and money purchase plans, SEP and SIMPLE IRAs, and defined-benefit plans	11 U.S.C. § 522(b)(3)(C)
	Traditional and Roth IRAs to $1,283,025 per person	11 U.S.C. § 522(b)(3)(C); (n)
	ERISA-qualified benefits, including IRAs, SEPs & Keoghs deposited more than 120 days before filing	427.150
	Firefighters	67A.620; 95.878
	Police officers	427.120; 427.125
	State employees	61.690
	Teachers	161.700
	Urban county government employees	67A.350
personal property	Burial plot to $5,000, in lieu of homestead	427.060
	Clothing, jewelry, articles of adornment & furnishings to $3,000 total	427.010(1)
	Health aids	427.010(1)
	Lost earnings payments needed for support	427.150(2)(d)
	Medical expenses paid & reparation benefits received under motor vehicle reparation law	304.39-260
	Motor vehicle to $2,500	427.010(1)
	Personal injury recoveries to $7,500 (not to include pain & suffering or pecuniary loss)	427.150(2)(c)
	Prepaid tuition payment fund account	164A.707(3)
	Wrongful death recoveries for person you depended on, needed for support	427.150(2)(b)
public benefits	Aid to blind, aged, disabled; public assistance, includes earned income tax credit if eligible for Kentucky benefits (*In re Beltz*, 263 B.R. 525 (Bankr. W.D. Ky. 2001))	205.220(c)
	Crime victims' compensation	427.150(2)(a)
	Unemployment compensation	341.470(4)
	Workers' compensation	342.180
tools of trade	Library, office equipment, instruments & furnishings of minister, attorney, physician, surgeon, chiropractor, veterinarian, or dentist to $1,000	427.040
	Motor vehicle of auto mechanic, mechanical, or electrical equipment servicer, minister, attorney, physician, surgeon, chiropractor, veterinarian, or dentist to $2,500	427.030
	Tools, equipment, livestock & poultry of farmer to $3,000	427.010(1)
	Tools of nonfarmer to $300	427.030
wages	Minimum 75% of disposable weekly earnings or 30 times the federal minimum hourly wage per week, whichever is greater; bankruptcy judge may authorize more for low-income debtors	427.010(2), (3)
wildcard	$1,000 of any property	427.160

Louisiana

Federal bankruptcy exemptions not available. All law references are to Louisiana Revised Statutes Annotated unless otherwise noted.

ASSET	EXEMPTION	LAW
homestead	Property you occupy to $35,000 (if debt is result of catastrophic or terminal illness or injury, limit is full value of property as of 1 year before filing); cannot exceed 5 acres in city or town, 200 acres elsewhere (spouses may not double)	20:1(A)(1),(2),(3)
	Spouse or child of deceased owner may claim homestead exemption; spouse given home in divorce gets homestead	20:1(B)
insurance	Annuity contract proceeds & avails	22:912
	Fraternal benefit society benefits	22:298
	Group insurance policies or proceeds	22:944
	Health, accident, or disability proceeds or avails	22:1015
	Life insurance proceeds or avails; if policy issued within 9 months of filing, exempt only to $35,000	22:912
miscellaneous	Property of minor child	13:3881(A)(3); Civil Code Art. 223
pensions	Tax-exempt retirement accounts, including 401(k)s, 403(b)s, profit-sharing and money purchase plans, SEP and SIMPLE IRAs, and defined-benefit plans	11 U.S.C. § 522(b)(3)(C)
	Traditional and Roth IRAs to $1,283,025 per person	11 U.S.C. § 522(b)(3)(C); (n)
	Assessors	11:1403
	Court clerks	11:1526
	District attorneys	11:1583
	ERISA-qualified benefits, including IRAs, Roth IRAs & Keoghs, if contributions made over 1 year before filing for bankruptcy	13:3881; 20:33(1)
	Firefighters	11:2263
	Gift or bonus payments from employer to employee or heirs whenever paid	20:33(2)
	Judges	11:1378
	Louisiana University employees	11:952.3
	Municipal employees	11:1735
	Parochial employees	11:1905
	Police officers	11:3513
	School employees	11:1003
	Sheriffs	11:2182
	State employees	11:405
	Teachers	11:704
	Voting registrars	11:2033
personal property	Military accoutrements; bedding; dishes, glassware, utensils, silverware (nonsterling); clothing, family portraits, musical instruments; bedroom, living room & dining room furniture; poultry, 1 cow, household pets; heating & cooling equipment, refrigerator, freezer, stove, washer & dryer, iron, sewing machine	13:3881(A)(4)
	Firearms, arms, and ammunition for any purpose to $2,500	13:3881(A)(4)(g)
	Cemetery plot, monuments	8:313
	Disaster relief insurance proceeds	13:3881(A)(7)
	Engagement & wedding rings to $5,000	13:3881(A)(5)
	Motor vehicle to $7,500	13:3881(A)(7)
	Motor vehicle modified for disability to $7,500	13:3881(A)(8)
	Spendthrift trusts	9:2004

public benefits	Aid to blind, aged, disabled; public assistance	46:111
	Crime victims' compensation	46:1811
	Earned income tax credit	13:3881(A)(6)
	Unemployment compensation	23:1693
	Workers' compensation	23:1205
tools of trade	Tools, instruments, books, $7,500 of equity in a motor vehicle, one firearm to $500, needed to work	13:3881(A)(2)
wages	Minimum 75% of disposable weekly earnings or 30 times the federal minimum hourly wage per week, whichever is greater; bankruptcy judge may authorize more for low-income debtors	13:3881(A)(1)
wildcard	None	

Maine

Federal bankruptcy exemptions not available. All law references are to Maine Revised Statutes Annotated, in the form "title number-section number," unless otherwise noted.

ASSET	EXEMPTION	LAW
homestead	Real or personal property (including cooperative) used as residence to $47,500; if debtor has minor dependents in residence, to $95,000; if debtor over age 60 or physically or mentally disabled, $95,000; proceeds of sale exempt for six months	14-4422(1)
insurance	Annuity proceeds to $450 per month	24-A-2431
	Death benefit for police, fire, or emergency medical personnel who die in the line of duty	25-1612
	Disability or health proceeds, benefits, or avails	14-4422(13)(A), (C); 24-A-2429
	Fraternal benefit society benefits	24-A-4118
	Group health or life policy or proceeds	24-A-2430
	Life, endowment, annuity, or accident policy, proceeds or avails	14-4422(14)(C); 24-A-2428
	Life insurance policy, interest, loan value, or accrued dividends for policy from person you depended on, to $4,000	14-4422(11)
	Unmatured life insurance policy, except credit insurance policy	14-4422(10)
miscellaneous	Alimony & child support needed for support	14-4422(13)(D)
pensions	Tax-exempt retirement accounts, including 401(k)s, 403(b)s, profit-sharing and money purchase plans, SEP and SIMPLE IRAs, and defined-benefit plans	11 U.S.C. § 522(b)(3)(C)
	Traditional and Roth IRAs to $1,283,025 per person	11 U.S.C. § 522(b)(3)(C); (n)
	ERISA-qualified benefits needed for support	14-4422(13)(E)
	Judges	4-1203
	Legislators	3-703
	State employees	5-17054
personal property	Animals, crops, musical instruments, books, clothing, furnishings, household goods, appliances to $200 per item	14-4422(3)
	Balance due on repossessed goods; total amount financed can't exceed $2,000	9-A-5-103
	Burial plot in lieu of homestead exemption	14-4422(1)
	Cooking stove; furnaces & stoves for heat	14-4422(6)(A), (B)
	Food to last 6 months	14-4422(7)(A)
	Fuel not to exceed 10 cords of wood, 5 tons of coal, or 1,000 gal. of heating oil	14-4422(6)(C)
	Health aids	14-4422(12)
	Jewelry to $750	14-4422(4)
	Lost earnings payments needed for support	14-4422(14)(E)
	Military clothes, arms & equipment	37-B-262
	Motor vehicle to $5,000	14-4422(2)
	Personal injury recoveries to $12,500	14-4422(14)(D)
	Seeds, fertilizers & feed to raise & harvest food for 1 season	14-4422(7)(B)
	Tools & equipment to raise & harvest food	14-4422(7)(C)
	Wrongful death recoveries needed for support	14-4422(14)(B)
public benefits	Maintenance under the Rehabilitation Act	26-1411-H
	Crime victims' compensation	14-4422(14)(A)
	Federal, state, or local public assistance benefits; earned income and child tax credits (but see In re Tetrault, No. 12-21373 (Bankr. D. Maine 2013) (child tax credit not exempt if no refund))	14-4422(13)(A); 22-3180, 22-3766
	Social Security	14-4422(13)(A)
	Unemployment compensation	14-4422(13)(A), (C)
	Veterans benefits	14-4422(13)(B)
	Workers' compensation	39-A-106

tools of trade	Books, materials & stock to $5,000	14-4422(5)
	Commercial fishing boat, 5-ton limit	14-4422(9)
	One of each farm implement (& its maintenance equipment needed to harvest & raise crops)	14-4422(8)
wages	None	
wildcard	Unused portion of exemption in homestead to $6,000; to be used for animals, crops, musical instruments, books, clothing, furnishings, household goods, appliances, jewelry, tools of the trade & personal injury recoveries	14-4422(16)
	$400 of any property	14-4422(15)

Maryland

Federal bankruptcy exemptions not available. All law references are to Maryland Code of Courts & Judicial Proceedings unless otherwise noted. New Maryland homestead exemption is indexed for inflation by matching the federal homestead amount.

ASSET	EXEMPTION	LAW
homestead	Owner-occupied residential property or co-op or condo to $22,975 (spouses may double). Includes manufactured home that has been converted to real property pursuant to Real Property Art. 8B-201. Property held as tenancy by the entirety is exempt against debts owed by only one spouse	11-504(f); *In re Birney*, 200 F.3d 225 (4th Cir. 1999)
insurance	Disability or health benefits, including court awards, arbitrations & settlements	11-504(b)(2)
	Fraternal benefit society benefits	Ins. 8-431; Estates & Trusts 8-115
	Life insurance or annuity contract proceeds or avails if beneficiary is insured's dependent, child, or spouse	Ins. 16-111(a); Estates & Trusts 8-115
	Medical insurance benefits deducted from wages plus medical insurance payments to $145 per week or 75% of disposable wages	Commercial Law 15-601.1(3)
miscellaneous	Child support	11-504(b)(6)
	Alimony to same extent wages are exempt	11-504(b)(7)
pensions	Tax-exempt retirement accounts, including 401(k)s, 403(b)s, profit-sharing and money purchase plans, SEP and SIMPLE IRAs, and defined-benefit plans	11 U.S.C. § 522(b)(3)(C)
	Traditional and Roth IRAs to $1,283,025 per person	11 U.S.C. § 522(b)(3)(C); (n)
	ERISA-qualified benefits, including IRAs, Roth IRAs & Keoghs	11-504(h)(1), (4)
	State employees	State Pers. & Pen. 21-502
personal property	Appliances, furnishings, household goods, books, pets & clothing to $1,000 total	11-504(b)(4)
	Burial plot	Bus. Reg. 5-503
	Health aids	11-504(b)(3)
	Perpetual care trust funds	Bus. Reg. 5-603
	Prepaid college trust funds	Educ. 18-1913
	Lost future earnings recoveries	11-504(b)(2)
public benefits	Baltimore Police death benefits	Code of 1957 art. 24, 16-103
	Crime victims' compensation	Crim. Proc. 11-816(b)
	Public assistance benefits	Human Services § 5-407(a)(1), (2)
	Unemployment compensation	Labor & Employment 8-106
	Workers' compensation	Labor & Employment 9-732
tools of trade	Clothing, books, tools, instruments & appliances to $5,000	11-504(b)(1)
wages	Earned but unpaid wages, the greater of 75% or $145 per week; in Kent, Caroline, Queen Anne's & Worcester Counties, the greater of 75% or 30 times federal minimum hourly wage. *In re Stine*, 360 F.3d 455 (4th Cir. 2004); *Bank of America v. Stine*, 379 Md. 76, 839 A.2d 727, 729 (2003)	Commercial Law 15-601.1
wildcard	$6,000 in cash or any property	11-504(b)(5)
	An additional $5,000 personal property	11-504(f)

Massachusetts

Federal bankruptcy exemptions available. All law references are to Massachusetts General Laws Annotated, in the form "title number-section number," unless otherwise noted.

ASSET	EXEMPTION	LAW
homestead	Property held as tenancy by the entirety may be exempt against debt for nonnecessity owed by only one spouse	209-1
	Automatic homestead for principal residence (including mobile home) to $125,000; to $500,000 if homestead declaration is recorded and complies with Massachusetts law; spouses may not double; trust beneficiaries are eligible for exemption; owners with a disability or 62 or older may each exempt up to $500,000, but aggregate cannot be more than $1,000,000. *In re Peirce*, 467 B.R. 260 (Bankr. D. Mass.)	188-1, 2, 5
	Spouse or children of deceased owner may claim homestead exemption	188-2
insurance	Disability benefits to $400 per week	175-110A, 175-36B
	Fraternal benefit society benefits	176-22
	Group annuity policy or proceeds	175-132C
	Group life insurance policy	175-135; 175-36
	Life insurance or annuity contract proceeds if clause prohibits proceeds from being used to pay beneficiary's creditors. *In re Sloss*, 279 B.R. 6 (Bankr. D. Mass. 2002)	175-119A
	Life insurance policy if beneficiary is a married woman. *In re Sloss*, 279 B.R. 6 (Bankr. D. Mass. 2002)	175-126
	Life or endowment policy, proceeds, or cash value. *In re Sloss*, 279 B.R. 6 (Bankr. D. Mass. 2002)	175-125
	Medical malpractice self-insurance	175F-15
miscellaneous	Property of business partnership	108A-25
pensions *see also wages*	Tax-exempt retirement accounts, including 401(k)s, 403(b)s, profit-sharing and money purchase plans, SEP and SIMPLE IRAs, and defined-benefit plans	11 U.S.C. § 522(b)(3)(C)
	Traditional and Roth IRAs to $1,283,025 per person	11 U.S.C. § 522(b)(3)(C); (n)
	Credit union employees	171-84
	ERISA-qualified benefits, including IRAs & Keoghs to specified limits	235-34A; 246-28
	Private retirement benefits	32-41
	Public employees	32-19
	Savings bank employees	168-41; 168-44
personal property	2 cows, 12 sheep, 2 swine, 4 tons of hay	235-34(4)
	Beds & bedding; heating unit, stove, refrigerator, freezer & hot water heater; clothing	235-34(1)
	Bibles & books to $500 total	235-34(3)
	Burial plots, tombs & church pew	235-34(11),(8)
	Cash for fuel, heat, water, or light to $500 per month	235-34(1)
	Cash to $2,500/month for rent, in lieu of homestead	235-34(14)
	Cooperative association shares to $100	235-34(13)
	Food or cash for food to $600	235-34(7)
	Household furnishings to $15,000	235-34(2)
	Jewelry to $1,225	235-34(18)
	Motor vehicle to $7,500; to $15,000 if used by elderly or disabled debtor	235-34(16)
	Moving expenses for eminent domain	79-6A
	Sewing machine, computer, TV to $300	235-34(12)
	Trust company, bank, or credit union deposits to $2,500	235-34(15); 235-28A

public benefits	Public assistance	235-34(15)
	Temporary assistance for needy families	118-10
	Unemployment compensation	151A-36
	Veterans benefits	115-5
	Workers' compensation	152-47
tools of trade	Arms, accoutrements & uniforms required	235-34(10)
	Fishing boats, tackle & nets to $1,500	235-34(9)
	Materials you designed & procured to $5,000	235-34(6)
	Tools, implements & fixtures to $5,000 total	235-34(5)
wages	Earned but unpaid wages to 85% or 50x minimum wage per week	235-34(15)
wildcard	$1,000 plus up to $5,000 of unused automobile, tools of the trade, and household furniture exemptions	235-34(17)

Michigan

Federal bankruptcy exemptions available. All law references are to Michigan Compiled Laws Annotated unless otherwise noted.

Under Michigan law, bankruptcy exemption amounts are adjusted for inflation every three years (starting in 2005) by the Michigan Department of Treasury. You can find the current amounts at www.michigan.gov/documents/BankruptcyExemptions2005_141050_7.pdf or by searching Google for "Property Debtor in Bankruptcy May Exempt, Inflation Adjusted Amounts."

ASSET	EXEMPTION	LAW
homestead	Property held as tenancy by the entirety may be exempt against debts owed by only one spouse	600.5451(1)(n)
	Real property including condo to $38,225 ($57,350 if over 65 or disabled); property cannot exceed 1 lot in town, village, city, or 40 acres elsewhere; spouse or children of deceased owner may claim homestead exemption; spouses or unmarried co-owners may not double	600.5451(1)(m); *Vinson v. Dakmak*, 347 B.R. 620 (E.D. Mich. 2006)
insurance	Disability, mutual life, or health benefits	600.5451(1)(j)
	Employer-sponsored life insurance policy or trust fund	500.2210
	Fraternal benefit society benefits	500.8181
	Life, endowment, or annuity proceeds if clause prohibits proceeds from being used to pay beneficiary's creditors	500.4054
	Life insurance	500.2207
miscellaneous	Property of business partnership	449.25
pensions	Tax-exempt retirement accounts, including 401(k)s, 403(b)s, profit-sharing and money purchase plans, SEP and SIMPLE IRAs, and defined-benefit plans	11 U.S.C. § 522(b)(3)(C)
	Traditional and Roth IRAs to $1,283,025 per person	11 U.S.C. § 522(b)(3)(C); (n)
	ERISA-qualified benefits, except contributions within last 120 days	600.5451(1)(l)
	Firefighters, police officers	38.559(6); 38.1683
	IRAs & Roth IRAs, except contributions within last 120 days	600.5451(1)(k)
	Judges and probate judges	38.2308; 38.1683
	Legislators	38.1057; 38.1683
	Public school employees	38.1346; 38.1683
	State employees	38.40; 38.1683
personal property	Appliances, utensils, books, furniture, jewelry & household goods to $600 each, $3,825 total	600.5451(1)(c)
	Burial plots, cemeteries	600.5451(1)(a)(vii)
	Church pew, slip, seat for entire family to $650	600.5451(1)(d)
	Clothing; family pictures	600.5451(1)(a)
	Food & fuel to last family for 6 months	600.5451(1)(b)
	Crops, animals, and feed to $2,550	600.5451(1)(e)
	1 motor vehicle to $3,525	600.5451(1)(g)
	Computer & accessories to $650	600.5451(1)(h)
	Household pets to $650	600.5451(1)(f)
	Professionally prescribed health aids	600.5451(a)
public benefits	Crime victims' compensation	18.362
	Social welfare benefits	400.63
	Unemployment compensation	421.30
	Veterans benefits for Korean War veterans	35.977
	Veterans benefits for Vietnam veterans	35.1027
	Veterans benefits for WWII veterans	35.926
	Workers' compensation	418.821

tools of trade	Arms & accoutrements required	600.6023(1)(a)
	Tools, implements, materials, stock, apparatus, or other things needed to carry on occupation to $2,550 total	600.5451(1)(i)
wages	Head of household may keep 60% of earned but unpaid wages (no less than $15/week), plus $2/week per nonspouse dependent; if not head of household may keep 40% (no less than $10/week)	600.5311
wildcard	None	

Minnesota

Federal bankruptcy exemptions available. All law references are to Minnesota Statutes Annotated, unless otherwise noted.

Note: Section 550.37(4)(a) requires certain exemptions to be adjusted for inflation on July 1 of even-numbered years; this table includes all changes made through July 1, 2018. Exemptions are published on or before the May 1 issue of the Minnesota State Register. Go to http://mn.gov. In the search box, type "dollar amount adjustments."

Note: In cases of suspected fraud, the Minnesota constitution permits courts to cap exemptions that would otherwise be unlimited. (*In re Tveten*, 402 N.W.2d 551 (Minn. 1987); *In re Medill*, 119 B.R. 685 (Bankr. D. Minn. 1990); *In re Sholdan*, 217 F.3d 1006 (8th Cir. 2000).)

ASSET	EXEMPTION	LAW
homestead	Home & land on which it is situated to $390,000; if homestead is used for agricultural purposes, $975,000; cannot exceed ½ acre in city, 160 acres elsewhere (spouses may not double)	510.01; 510.02
	Manufactured home to an unlimited value	550.37 subd. 12
insurance	Accident or disability proceeds	550.39
	Fraternal benefit society benefits	64B.18
	Life insurance proceeds to $46,000 if beneficiary is spouse or child of insured, plus $11,500 per dependent	550.37 subd. 10
	Police, fire, or beneficiary association benefits	550.37 subd. 11
	Unmatured life insurance contract dividends, interest, or loan value to $9,200 if insured is debtor or person debtor depends on	550.37 subd. 23
miscellaneous	Earnings of minor child	550.37 subd. 15
pensions	Tax-exempt retirement accounts, including 401(k)s, 403(b)s, profit-sharing and money purchase plans, SEP and SIMPLE IRAs, and defined-benefit plans	11 U.S.C. § 522(b)(3)(C)
	Traditional and Roth IRAs to $1,283,025 per person	11 U.S.C. § 522(b)(3)(C); (n)
	ERISA-qualified benefits if needed for support, up to $69,000 in present value	550.37 subd. 24
	IRAs or Roth IRAs needed for support, up to $69,000 in present value	550.37 subd. 24
	Public employees	353.15; 356.401
	State employees	352.965 subd. 8; 356.401
	State troopers	352B.071; 356.401
personal property	Appliances, furniture, radio, phonographs & TV to $10,350 total	550.37 subd. 4(b)
	Bible & books	550.37 subd. 2
	Burial plot; church pew or seat	550.37 subd. 3
	Clothing, one watch, food & utensils for family	550.37 subd. 4(a)
	Motor vehicle to $4,600 (up to $46,000 if vehicle has been modified for disability)	550.37 subd. 12(a)
	Personal injury recoveries	550.37 subd. 22
	Proceeds for damaged exempt property	550.37 subds. 9, 16
	Wedding rings to $2,817.50	550.37 subd. 4(c)
	Wrongful death recoveries	550.37 subd. 22
public benefits	Crime victims' compensation	611A.60
	Public benefits, including earned income tax credit, child tax credit, education tax credit (*In re Tomczyk*, 295 B.R. 894 (Bankr. D. Minn. 2003); *In re Dmitruk*, 517 B.R. 921 (Bankr. 8th Cir. 2014))	550.37 subd. 14
	Unemployment compensation	268.192 subd. 2
	Veterans benefits	550.38
	Workers' compensation	176.175

tools of trade *total (except teaching materials) can't exceed $13,000*	Farm machines, implements, livestock, produce & crops	550.37 subd. 5
	Teaching materials of college, university, public school, or public institution teacher	550.37 subd. 8
	Tools, machines, instruments, stock in trade, furniture & library to $11,500 total	550.37 subd. 6
wages	Minimum 75% of weekly disposable earnings or 40 times federal minimum hourly wage, whichever is greater	571.922
	Wages deposited into bank accounts for 20 days after depositing	550.37 subd. 13
	Wages paid within 6 months of returning to work after receiving welfare or after incarceration; includes earnings deposited in a financial institution in the last 60 days	550.37 subd. 14
wildcard	None	

Mississippi

Federal bankruptcy exemptions not available. All law references are to Mississippi Code unless otherwise noted.

ASSET	EXEMPTION	LAW
homestead	May file homestead declaration	85-3-27; 85-3-31
	Mobile home does not qualify as homestead unless you own land on which it is located (see *personal property*)	*In re Cobbins*, 234 B.R. 882 (S.D. Miss. 1999)
	Property you own & occupy to $75,000; if over 60 & married or widowed may claim a former residence; property cannot exceed 160 acres; sale proceeds exempt	85-3-1(b)(i); 85-3-21; 85-3-23
insurance	Disability benefits	85-3-1(b)(ii)
	Fraternal benefit society benefits	83-29-39
	Homeowners' insurance proceeds to $75,000	85-3-23
	Life insurance proceeds if clause prohibits proceeds from being used to pay beneficiary's creditors	83-7-5; 85-3-11; 85-3-13, 85-3-15
pensions	Tax-exempt retirement accounts, including 401(k)s, 403(b)s, profit-sharing and money purchase plans, SEP and SIMPLE IRAs, and defined-benefit plans	11 U.S.C. § 522(b)(3)(C)
	Traditional and Roth IRAs to $1,283,025 per person	11 U.S.C. § 522(b)(3)(C); (n)
	ERISA-qualified benefits, IRAs, Keoghs deposited over 1 year before filing bankruptcy	85-3-1(e)
	Firefighters (includes death benefits)	21-29-257; 45-2-1
	Highway patrol officers	25-13-31
	Law enforcement officers' death benefits	45-2-1
	Police officers (includes death benefits)	21-29-257; 45-2-1
	Private retirement benefits to extent tax deferred	71-1-43
	Public employees retirement & disability benefits	25-11-129
	State employees	25-14-5
	Teachers	25-11-201(1)(d)
	Volunteer firefighters' death benefits	45-2-1
personal property	Mobile home to $30,000	85-3-1(d)
	Personal injury judgments to $10,000	85-3-17
	Sale or insurance proceeds for exempt property	85-3-1(b)(i)
	State health savings accounts	85-3-1(g)
	Tangible personal property to $10,000: any items worth less than $200 each; furniture, dishes, kitchenware, household goods, appliances, 1 radio, 1 TV, 1 firearm, 1 lawnmower, clothing, wedding rings, motor vehicles, tools of the trade, books, crops, health aids, domestic animals, cash on hand (does not include works of art, antiques, jewelry, or electronic entertainment equipment)	85-3-1(a)
	Tax-qualified § 529 education savings plans, including those under the Mississippi Prepaid Affordable College Tuition Program	85-3-1(f)
public benefits	Assistance to aged	43-9-19
	Assistance to blind	43-3-71
	Assistance to disabled	43-29-15
	Crime victims' compensation	99-41-23(7)
	Federal income tax refund to $5,000; earned income tax credit to $5,000; state tax refunds to $5,000	85-3-1(h); (i); (j); (k)
	Social Security	25-11-129
	Unemployment compensation	71-5-539
	Workers' compensation	71-3-43

tools of trade	*See personal property*	
wages	Earned but unpaid wages owed for 30 days; after 30 days, minimum 75% of earned but unpaid weekly disposable earnings or 30 times the federal hourly minimum wage, whichever is greater; bankruptcy judge may authorize more for low-income debtors	85-3-4
wildcard	$50,000 of any property, including deposits of money, available to Mississippi resident who is at least 70 years old; *also see personal property*	85-3-1(h)

Missouri

Federal bankruptcy exemptions not available. All law references are to Annotated Missouri Statutes unless otherwise noted.

Note: Federal bankruptcy courts have held that under *Benn v. Cole* (*In re Benn*), 491 F.3d 811, 814 (8th Cir. 2007) exemption statutes in Missouri must use the word "exempt" for property to be exempt in bankruptcy. Lower courts have interpreted this to mean that the words "not subject to execution or attachment" do *not* create an exemption for bankruptcy purposes.

Many pension exemption statutes in Missouri do not have the words required to create an exemption in bankruptcy. However, Missouri courts, interpreting the same law, point out that Missouri has long held otherwise—that such Missouri statutes do create an exemption in bankruptcy. See *Russell v. Healthmont of Missouri, LLC*, 348 S.W. 3d 784 (Missouri Court of Appeals, Western District 2011).

The Missouri wage garnishment statute may not be a valid bankruptcy exemption under *In re Benn*, because the word "exempt" does not appear in the wage garnishment statute. See *In re Parsons*, 437 B.R. 854 (Bankr. E.D. Mo. 2010).

ASSET	EXEMPTION	LAW
homestead	Property held as tenancy by the entirety may be exempt against debts owed by only one spouse	*In re Eads*, 271 B.R. 371 (Bankr. W.D. Mo. 2002)
	Real property to $15,000 or mobile home to $5,000 (joint owners may not double)	513.430(6); 513.475; *In re Smith*, 254 B.R. 751 (Bankr. W.D. Mo. 2000)
insurance	Assessment plan or life insurance proceeds	377.090
	Disability or illness benefits	513.430(10)(c)
	Fraternal benefit society benefits to $5,000, bought over 6 months before filing	513.430(8)
	Life insurance dividends, loan value, or interest to $150,000, bought over 6 months before filing	513.430(8)
	Stipulated insurance premiums	377.330
	Unmatured life insurance policy	513.430(7)
miscellaneous	Alimony, child support to $750 per month	513.430(10)(d)
	Property of business partnership	358.250
pensions	Tax-exempt retirement accounts, including 401(k)s, 403(b)s, profit-sharing and money purchase plans, SEP and SIMPLE IRAs, and defined-benefit plans	11 U.S.C. § 522(b)(3)(C)
	Traditional and Roth IRAs to $1,283,025 per person	11 U.S.C. § 522(b)(3)(C); (n)
	Employee benefit spendthrift trust	456.014
	Employees of cities with 100,000 or more people	71.207
	ERISA-qualified benefits, IRAs, Roth IRAs & other retirement accounts needed for support	513.430(10)(e), (f)
	Firefighters	87.090; 87.365; 87.485
	Highway & transportation employees	104.250
	Inherited retirement accounts	513.040(f)
	Police department employees	86.190; 86.353; 86.1430
	Public officers & employees	70.695; 70.755
	State employees	104.540
	Teachers. But see *In re Smith*, 10-60388 (W.D. Mo. 2010). See note at beginning of Missouri chart	169.090

personal property	Appliances, household goods, furnishings, clothing, books, crops, animals & musical instruments to $3,000 total	513.430(1)
	Burial grounds to 1 acre or $100	214.190
	Health aids	513.430(9)
	Health savings accounts	513.040(10)(f)
	Motor vehicles to $3,000 in aggregate	513.430(5)
	Wedding or engagement ring to $1,500 & other jewelry to $500. *In re Urie*, 2006 WL 533514 (Bankr. W.D. Mo. 2006)	513.430(2)
	Wrongful death recoveries for person you depended on	513.430(11)
	Firearms, including accessories and ammunition to $1,500	513.430(12)
public benefits	Crime victims' compensation	595.025
	Public assistance, including earned income tax credit, but not child tax credit (*In re Corbett*, No. 13–60042 (Bankr. W.D. Mo. 2013); *In re Hardy*, 495 BR 440 (Bankr. W.D. Mo. 2013))	513.430(10)(a)
	Social Security	513.430(10)(a)
	Unemployment compensation	288.380(10)(l); 513.430(10)(c)
	Veterans benefits	513.430(10)b)
	Workers' compensation	287.260
tools of trade	Implements, books & tools of trade to $3,000	513.430(4)
wages	Minimum 75% of weekly earnings (90% of weekly earnings for head of family), or 30 times the federal minimum hourly wage, whichever is more; bankruptcy judge may authorize more for low-income debtors. See note at beginning of Missouri chart.	525.030
	See note at beginning of Missouri chart. Wages of servant or common laborer to $90	513.470
wildcard	$600 of any property; an additional $1,250 if head of family, plus another $350 per child under age 21	513.430(3); 513.440

Montana

Federal bankruptcy exemptions not available. All law references are to Montana Code Annotated unless otherwise noted.

ASSET	EXEMPTION	LAW
homestead	Must record homestead declaration before filing for bankruptcy	70-32-105
	Real property or mobile home you occupy to $250,000; sale, condemnation, or insurance proceeds exempt for 18 months	70-32-104; 70-32-201; 70-32-213
insurance	Annuity contract proceeds to $350 per month	33-15-514
	Disability or illness proceeds, avails, or benefits	25-13-608(1)(d); 33-15-513
	Fraternal benefit society benefits	33-7-522
	Group life insurance policy or proceeds	33-15-512
	Hail insurance benefits	80-2-245
	Life insurance proceeds if clause prohibits proceeds from being used to pay beneficiary's creditors	33-20-120
	Medical, surgical, or hospital care benefits	25-13-608(1)(f)
	Unmatured life insurance contracts	25-13-608(1)(k)
miscellaneous	Alimony, child support	25-13-608(1)(g)
pensions	Tax-exempt retirement accounts, including 401(k)s, 403(b)s, profit-sharing and money purchase plans, SEP and SIMPLE IRAs, and defined-benefit plans	11 U.S.C. § 522(b)(3)(C)
	Traditional and Roth IRAs to $1,283,025 per person	11 U.S.C. § 522(b)(3)(C); (n)
	IRAs & ERISA-qualified benefits deposited over 1 year before filing bankruptcy or up to 15% of debtor's gross annual income	31-2-106
	Firefighters	19-18-612(1)
	IRA & Roth IRA contributions & earnings made before judgment filed	25-13-608(1)(e)
	Police officers	19-19-504(1)
	Public employees	19-2-1004; 25-13-608(i)
	Teachers	19-20-706(2); 25-13-608(j)
	University system employees	19-21-212
personal property	Appliances, household furnishings, goods, animals with feed, crops, musical instruments, books, firearms, sporting goods, clothing & jewelry to $600 per item, $4,500 total	25-13-609(1)
	Burial plot	25-13-608(1)(h)
	Cooperative association shares to $500 value	35-15-404
	Health aids	25-13-608(1)(a)
	Motor vehicle to $2,500	25-13-609(2)
	Proceeds from sale or for damage or loss of exempt property for 6 months after received	25-13-610
public benefits	Aid to aged, disabled needy persons	53-2-607
	Crime victims' compensation	53-9-129
	Local public assistance	25-13-608(1)(b)
	Silicosis benefits	39-73-110
	Social Security	25-13-608(1)(b)
	Subsidized adoption payments to needy persons	53-2-607
	Unemployment compensation	31-2-106(2); 39-51-3105
	Veterans benefits	25-13-608(1)(c)
	Vocational rehabilitation to blind needy persons	53-2-607
	Workers' compensation	39-71-743
tools of trade	Implements, books & tools of trade to $3,000	25-13-609(3)
	Uniforms, arms & accoutrements needed to carry out government functions	25-13-613(b)

wages	Minimum 75% of earned but unpaid weekly disposable earnings, or 30 times the federal hourly minimum wage, whichever is greater; bankruptcy judge may authorize more for low-income debtors	25-13-614
wildcard	None	

Nebraska

Federal bankruptcy exemptions not available. All law references are to Revised Statutes of Nebraska unless otherwise noted.

ASSET	EXEMPTION	LAW
homestead	$60,000 for head of family or an unmarried person age 65 or older; cannot exceed 2 lots in city or village, 160 acres elsewhere; sale proceeds exempt 6 months after sale (spouses may not double)	40-101; 40-111; 40-113
	May record homestead declaration	40-105
insurance	Fraternal benefit society benefits to $100,000 loan value unless beneficiary convicted of a crime related to benefits	44-1089
	Life insurance proceeds and avails to $100,000	44-371
pensions *see also wages*	Tax-exempt retirement accounts, including 401(k)s, 403(b)s, profit-sharing and money purchase plans, SEP and SIMPLE IRAs, and defined-benefit plans	11 U.S.C. § 522(b)(3)(C)
	Traditional and Roth IRAs to $1,283,025 per person	11 U.S.C. § 522(b)(3)(C); (n)
	County employees	23-2322
	Deferred compensation of public employees	48-1401
	ERISA-qualified benefits including IRAs & Roth IRAs needed for support	25-1563.01
	Military disability benefits	25-1559
	School employees	79-948
	State employees	84-1324
personal property	Burial plot	12-517
	Clothing	25-1556(2)
	Crypts, lots, tombs, niches, vaults	12-605
	Furniture, household goods & appliances, household electronics, personal computers, books & musical instruments to $1,500	25-1556(3)
	Health aids	25-1556(5)
	Medical or health savings accounts to $25,000	8-1, 131(2)(b)
	Perpetual care funds	12-511
	Personal injury recoveries	25-1563.02
	Personal possessions	25-1556
public benefits	Aid to disabled, blind, aged; public assistance	68-1013
	Earned income tax credit	25-1553
	General assistance to poor persons	68-148
	Unemployment compensation	48-647
	Workers' compensation	48-149
tools of trade	Equipment or tools including a vehicle used in or for commuting to principal place of business to $2,400 (husband & wife may double)	25-1556(4); *In re Keller,* 50 B.R. 23 (D. Neb. 1985)
wages	Minimum 85% of earned but unpaid weekly disposable earnings or pension payments for head of family; minimum 75% of earned but unpaid weekly disposable earnings or 30 times the federal hourly minimum wage, whichever is greater, for all others; bankruptcy judge may authorize more for low-income debtors	25-1558
wildcard	$2,500 of any personal property except wages	25-1552

Nevada

Federal bankruptcy exemptions not available. All law references are to Nevada Revised Statutes Annotated unless otherwise noted.

ASSET	EXEMPTION	LAW
homestead	Must record homestead declaration before filing for bankruptcy	115.020
	Real property or mobile home to $550,000. Spouses may not double	115.010; 21.090(1)(m)
insurance	Annuity contract proceeds	687B.290
	Fraternal benefit society benefits	695A.220
	Group life or health policy or proceeds	687B.280
	Health proceeds or avails	687B.270
	Life insurance policy or proceeds	21.090(1)(k); *In re Bower*, 234 B.R. 109 (Nev. 1999)
	Life insurance proceeds if you're not the insured	687B.260
	Private disability insurance proceeds	21.090(1)(ee)
miscellaneous	Alimony & child support	21.090(1)(s)
	Property of some business partnerships	87.250
	Security deposits for a rental residence, except landlord may enforce terms of lease or rental agreement	21.090(1)(n)
pensions	Tax-exempt retirement accounts, including 401(k)s, 403(b)s, profit-sharing and money purchase plans, SEP and SIMPLE IRAs, and defined-benefit plans	11 U.S.C. § 522(b)(3)(C)
	Traditional and Roth IRAs to $1,283,025 per person	11 U.S.C. § 522(b)(3)(C); (n)
	ERISA-qualified benefits, deferred compensation, SEP IRA, Roth IRA, or IRA to $500,000	21.090(1)(r)
	Public employees	286.670; 21.090(1)(ii)
personal property	Appliances, household goods, furniture, wearing apparel, home & yard equipment to $12,000 total	21.090(1)(b)
	Books, works of art, musical instruments & jewelry to $5,000	21.090(1)(a)
	Burial plot purchase money held in trust	689.700; 21.090(1)(ff)
	Funeral service contract money held in trust	689.700
	Health aids	21.090(1)(q)
	Interests in qualifying trusts	21.090(1)(cc)
	Keepsakes & pictures	21.090(1)(a)
	Metal-bearing ores, geological specimens, art curiosities, or paleontological remains; must be arranged, classified, cataloged & numbered in reference books	21.100
	Mortgage impound accounts	645B.180
	Motor vehicle to $15,000; no limit on vehicle equipped for disabled person	21.090(1)(f), (o)
	1 gun	21.090(1)(i)
	Personal injury compensation to $16,150	21.090(1)(u)
	Restitution received for criminal act	21.090(1)(x)
	Stock in certain closely held corporations	21.090(1)(bb); 78.764
	Tax refunds derived from the state or federal earned income credit	21.090(1)(aa)
	Wrongful death awards to survivors	21.090(1)(v)

public benefits	Aid to blind, aged, disabled; public assistance	422.291; 21.090(1)(kk); 422A.325
	Crime victims' compensation	21.090
	Earned income tax credit (state or federal)	21.090(1)(bb)
	Industrial insurance (workers' compensation)	616C.205; 21.090(1)(gg)
	Public assistance for children	432.036; 21.090(1)(ll)
	Social Security retirement, disability, SSI, survivor benefits	21.090(1)(y)
	Unemployment compensation	612.710; 21.090(1)(hh)
	Vocational rehabilitation benefits	615.270; 21.090(1)(jj)
tools of trade	Arms, uniforms & accoutrements you're required to keep	21.090(1)(j)
	Cabin or dwelling of miner or prospector; mining claim, cars, implements & appliances to $4,500 total (for working claim only)	21.090(1)(e)
	Farm trucks, stock, tools, equipment & seed to $4,500	21.090(1)(c)
	Library, equipment, supplies, tools, inventory & materials to $10,000	21.090(1)(d)
wages	Minimum 75% of disposable weekly earnings or 50 times the federal minimum hourly wage per week, whichever is more; bankruptcy judge may authorize more for low-income debtors. *In re Christensen*, 149 P.3d 40 (2006)	21.090(1)(g)
wildcard	$1,000 of any personal property	21.090(1)(z)

New Hampshire

Federal bankruptcy exemptions available. All law references are to New Hampshire Revised Statutes Annotated unless otherwise noted.

ASSET	EXEMPTION	LAW
homestead	Real property or manufactured housing (& the land it's on if you own it) to $120,000	480:1
insurance	Firefighters' aid insurance	402:69
	Fraternal benefit society benefits	418:17
	Homeowners' insurance proceeds to $5,000	512:21(VIII)
miscellaneous	Jury, witness fees	512:21(VI)
	Property of business partnership	304-A:25
	Wages of minor child	512:21(III)
pensions	Tax-exempt retirement accounts, including 401(k)s, 403(b)s, profit-sharing and money purchase plans, SEP and SIMPLE IRAs, and defined-benefit plans	11 U.S.C. § 522(b)(3)(C)
	Traditional and Roth IRAs to $1,283,025 per person	11 U.S.C. § 522(b)(3)(C); (n)
	ERISA-qualified retirement accounts including IRAs & Roth IRAs	512:2 (XIX)
	Federally created pension (only benefits building up)	512:21(IV)
	Firefighters	102:23
	Police officers	103:18
	Public employees	100-A:26
personal property	Beds, bedding & cooking utensils	511:2(II)
	Bibles & books to $800	511:2(VIII)
	Burial plot, lot	511:2(XIV)
	Church pew	511:2(XV)
	Clothing	511:2(I)
	Cooking & heating stoves, refrigerator	511:2(IV)
	Domestic fowl to $300	511:2(XIII)
	Food & fuel to $400	511:2(VI)
	Furniture to $3,500	511:2(III)
	Jewelry to $500	511:2(XVII)
	Motor vehicle to $4,000	511:2(XVI)
	Proceeds for lost or destroyed exempt property	512:21(VIII)
	Sewing machine	511:2(V)
	1 cow, 6 sheep & their fleece, 4 tons of hay	511:2(XI); (XII)
	1 hog or pig or its meat (if slaughtered)	511:2(X)
public benefits	Aid to blind, aged, disabled; public assistance	167:25
	Unemployment compensation	282-A:159
	Workers' compensation	281-A:52
tools of trade	Tools of your occupation to $5,000	511:2(IX)
	Uniforms, arms & equipment of military member	511:2(VII)
	Yoke of oxen or horse needed for farming or teaming	511:2(XII)
wages	50 times the federal minimum hourly wage per week	512:21(II)
	Deposits in any account designated a payroll account	512:21(XI)
	Earned but unpaid wages of spouse	512:21(III)
	Note: Wage exemptions cannot be used in bankruptcy. See *In re Damast*, 136 B.R. 11 (Bankr. D. N.H. 1991)	
wildcard	$1,000 of any property	511:2(XVIII)
	Unused portion of bibles & books, food & fuel, furniture, jewelry, motor vehicle & tools of trade exemptions to $7,000	511:2(XVIII)

New Jersey

Federal bankruptcy exemptions available. All law references are to New Jersey Statutes Annotated unless otherwise noted.

ASSET	EXEMPTION	LAW
homestead	None, but survivorship interest of a spouse in property held as tenancy by the entirety is exempt from creditors of a single spouse	*Freda v. Commercial Trust Co. of New Jersey*, 570 A.2d 409 (N.J. 1990)
insurance	Annuity contract proceeds to $500 per month	17B:24-7
	Disability benefits	17:18-12
	Disability, death, medical, or hospital benefits for civil defense workers	App. A:9-57.6
	Disability or death benefits for military member	38A:4-8
	Group life or health policy or proceeds	17B:24-9
	Health or disability benefits	17:18-12; 17B:24-8
	Life insurance proceeds if clause prohibits proceeds from being used to pay beneficiary's creditors	17B:24-10
	Life insurance proceeds or avails if you're not the insured	17B:24-6b
pensions	Tax-exempt retirement accounts, including 401(k)s, 403(b)s, profit-sharing and money purchase plans, SEP and SIMPLE IRAs, and defined-benefit plans	11 U.S.C. § 522(b)(3)(C)
	Traditional and Roth IRAs to $1,283,025 per person	11 U.S.C. § 522(b)(3)(C); (n)
	Alcohol beverage control officers	43:8A-20
	City boards of health employees	43:18-12
	Civil defense workers	App. A:9-57.6
	County employees	43:10-57; 43:10-105
	ERISA-qualified benefits for city employees	43:13-9
	Firefighters, police officers, traffic officers	43:16-7; 43:16A-17
	IRAs	*In re Yuhas*, 104 F.3d 612 (3d Cir. 1997)
	Judges	43:6A-41
	Municipal employees	43:13-44
	Prison employees	43:7-13
	Public employees	43:15A-53
	School district employees	18A:66-116
	State police	53:5A-45
	Street & water department employees	43:19-17
	Teachers	18A:66-51
	Trust containing personal property created pursuant to federal tax law, including 401(k) plans, IRAs, Roth IRAs & higher education (529) savings plans	25:2-1; *In re Yuhas*, 104 F.3d 612 (3d Cir. 1997)
personal property	Burial plots	45:27-21
	Clothing	2A:17-19
	Furniture & household goods to $1,000	2A:26-4
	Personal property & possessions of any kind, stock or interest in corporations to $1,000 total	2A:17-19
public benefits	Old age, permanent disability assistance	44:7-35
	Unemployment compensation	43:21-53
	Workers' compensation	34:15-29
tools of trade	None	
wages	90% of earned but unpaid wages if annual income is less than 250% of federal poverty level; 75% if annual income is higher	2A:17-56
	Wages or allowances received by military personnel	38A:4-8
wildcard	None	

New Mexico

Federal bankruptcy exemptions available. All law references are to New Mexico Statutes Annotated unless otherwise noted.

ASSET	EXEMPTION	LAW
homestead	$60,000	42-10-9
insurance	Benevolent association benefits to $5,000	42-10-4
	Fraternal benefit society benefits	59A-44-18
	Life, accident, health, or annuity benefits, withdrawal or cash value, if beneficiary is a New Mexico resident	42-10-3
	Life insurance proceeds	42-10-5
miscellaneous	Ownership interest in unincorporated association	53-10-2
	Property of business partnership	54-1A-501
pensions	Tax-exempt retirement accounts, including 401(k)s, 403(b)s, profit-sharing and money purchase plans, SEP and SIMPLE IRAs, and defined-benefit plans	11 U.S.C. § 522(b)(3)(C)
	Traditional and Roth IRAs to $1,283,025 per person	11 U.S.C. § 522(b)(3)(C); (n)
	Pension or retirement benefits	42-10-1; 42-10-2
	Public school employees	22-11-42A
personal property	Books & furniture	42-10-1; 42-10-2
	Building materials	48-2-15
	Clothing	42-10-1; 42-10-2
	Cooperative association shares, minimum amount needed to be member	53-4-28
	Health aids	42-10-1; 42-10-2
	Jewelry to $2,500	42-10-1; 42-10-2
	Materials, tools & machinery to dig, drill, complete, operate, or repair oil line, gas well, or pipeline	70-4-12
	Motor vehicle to $4,000	42-10-1; 42-10-2
public benefits	Crime victims' compensation	31-22-15
	General assistance	27-2-21
	Occupational disease disablement benefits	52-3-37
	Unemployment compensation	51-1-37
	Workers' compensation	52-1-52
tools of trade	$1,500	42-10-1; 42-10-2
wages	Minimum 75% of disposable earnings or 40 times the federal hourly minimum wage, whichever is more; bankruptcy judge may authorize more for low-income debtors	35-12-7
wildcard	$500 of any personal property	42-10-1
	$5,000 of any real or personal property, in lieu of homestead	42-10-10

New York

Federal bankruptcy exemptions are available. All references are to Consolidated Laws of New York unless otherwise noted; Civil Practice Law & Rules are abbreviated C.P.L.R.

ASSET	EXEMPTION	LAW
homestead	Real property including co-op, condo, or mobile home, to $82,775, $137,950, or $165,550, depending on the county	C.P.L.R. 5206(a); *In re Pearl*, 723 F.2d 193 (2nd Cir. 1983)
insurance	Annuity contract benefits due the debtor, if debtor paid for the contract; $5,000 limit if purchased within 6 months prior to filing & not tax deferred	Ins. 3212(d); Debt. & Cred. 283(1)
	Disability or illness benefits to $400 per month	Ins. 3212(c)
	Life insurance proceeds & avails if the beneficiary is not the debtor, or if debtor's spouse has taken out policy	Ins. 3212(b)
	Life insurance proceeds left at death with the insurance company, if clause prohibits proceeds from being used to pay beneficiary's creditors	Est. Powers & Trusts 7-1.5(a)(2)
miscellaneous	Alimony, child support	C.P.L.R. 5205 (d)(3); Debt. & Cred. 282(2)(d)
	Property of business partnership	Partnership 51
pensions	Tax-exempt retirement accounts, including 401(k)s, 403(b)s, profit-sharing and money purchase plans, SEP and SIMPLE IRAs, and defined-benefit plans	11 U.S.C. § 522(b)(3)(C)
	Traditional and Roth IRAs to $1,283,025 per person	11 U.S.C. § 522(b)(3)(C); (n)
	ERISA-qualified benefits, IRAs, Roth IRAs & Keoghs & income needed for support	C.P.L.R. 5205(c); Debt. & Cred. 282(2)(e)
	Public retirement benefits	Ins. 4607
	State employees	Ret. & Soc. Sec. 10
	Teachers	Educ. 524
	Village police officers	Unconsolidated 5711-o
	Volunteer ambulance workers' benefits	Vol. Amb. Wkr. Ben. 23
	Volunteer firefighters' benefits	Vol. Firefighter Ben. 23
personal property	Religious texts, schoolbooks, other books to $550; pictures; clothing; church pew or seat; sewing machine, refrigerator, TV, radio; furniture, cooking utensils & tableware, dishes; food to last 120 days; stoves with fuel to last 120 days; domestic animal with food to last 120 days, to $1,100; wedding ring; watch, jewelry, art to $1,100; exemptions may not exceed $11,025 total (including tools of trade & limited annuity)	C.P.L.R. 5205(a)(1)-(6); Debt. & Cred. 283(1)
	Burial plot without structure to ¼ acre	C.P.L.R. 5206(f)
	Cash (including savings bonds, tax refunds, bank & credit union deposits) to $5,525, or to $11,050 after exemptions for personal property taken, whichever amount is less (for debtors who do not claim homestead)	Debt. & Cred. 283(2)
	College tuition savings program trust fund	C.P.L.R. 5205(j)
	Electronic deposits of exempt property into bank account in last 45 days	C.P.L.R. 5205(l)(1)
	Health aids, including service animals with food	C.P.L.R. 5205(h)
	Lost future earnings recoveries needed for support	Debt. & Cred. 282(3)(iv)
	Motor vehicle to $4,425; $11,025 if equipped for disabled person (except if municipality is creditor)	Debt. & Cred. 282(1); *In re Miller*, 167 B.R. 782 (S.D. N.Y. 1994)
	Personal injury recoveries up to 1 year after receiving	Debt. & Cred. 282(3)(iii)
	Recovery for injury to exempt property up to 1 year after receiving	C.P.L.R. 5205(b)
	Savings & loan savings to $600	Banking 407
	Security deposit to landlord, utility company	C.P.L.R. 5205(g)
	Spendthrift trust fund principal, 90% of income if not created by debtor	C.P.L.R. 5205(c), (d)
	Wrongful death to $8,275 recoveries for person you depended on	Debt. & Cred. 282(3)(ii)

public benefits	Aid to blind, aged, disabled	Debt. & Cred. 282(2)(c)
	Crime victims' compensation	Debt. & Cred. 282(3)(i)
	Home relief, local public assistance	Debt. & Cred. 282(2)(a)
	Public assistance, does not include earned income tax credit (*In re Fasarakis*, 423 B.R. 34 (E.D.N.Y. 2010)) but might include rent-controlled lease (*In re Santiago-Monteverde*, 2014 N.Y. Slip Op. 08051 (Ct. App. N.Y. 2014))	Soc. Serv. 137
	Social Security	Debt. & Cred. 282(2)(a)
	Unemployment compensation	Debt. & Cred. 282(2)(a)
	Veterans benefits	Debt. & Cred. 282(2)(b)
	Workers' compensation	Debt. & Cred. 282(2)(c); Work. Comp. 33, 218
tools of trade	Farm machinery, team & food for 60 days; professional furniture, books & instruments to $3,300 total	C.P.L.R. 5205(a),(b)
	Uniforms, medal, emblem, equipment, horse, arms & sword of member of military	C.P.L.R. 5205(e)
wages	90% of earned but unpaid wages received within 60 days before & anytime after filing	C.P.L.R. 5205(d); 5231
	90% of earnings from dairy farmer's sales to milk dealers	C.P.L.R. 5205(f)
	100% of pay of noncommissioned officer, private, or musician in U.S. or N.Y. state armed forces. *In re Wiltsie*, 443 B.R. 223 (Bankr. N.D. N.Y. 2011)	C.P.L.R. 5205(e)
wildcard	$1,100 of personal property, bank account, or cash in lieu of homestead	C.P.L.R. 5205(a)(9)

North Carolina

Federal bankruptcy exemptions not available. All law references are to General Statutes of North Carolina unless otherwise noted.

ASSET	EXEMPTION	LAW
homestead	Property held as tenancy by the entirety may be exempt against debts owed by only one spouse	*In re Chandler*, 148 B.R. 13 (E.D. N.C. 1992)
	Real or personal property, including co-op, used as residence to $35,000; $60,000 if 65 or older; property owned with spouse as tenants by the entirety or joint tenants with right of survivorship, and spouse has died; up to $5,000 of unused portion of homestead may be applied to any property	1C-1601(a)(1),(2)
insurance	Employee group life policy or proceeds	58-58-165
	Fraternal benefit society benefits	58-24-85
	Life insurance on spouse or children	1C-1601(a)(6); Const. Art. X § 5
miscellaneous	Alimony, support, separate maintenance, and child support necessary for support of debtor and dependents	1C-1601(a)(12)
	Property of business partnership	59-55
	Support received by a surviving spouse for 1 year, up to $10,000	30-15
pensions	Tax-exempt retirement accounts, including 401(k)s, 403(b)s, profit-sharing and money purchase plans, SEP and SIMPLE IRAs, and defined-benefit plans	11 U.S.C. § 522(b)(3)(C)
	Traditional and Roth IRAs to $1,283,025 per person	11 U.S.C. § 522(b)(3)(C); (n)
	Firefighters & rescue squad workers	58-86-90
	IRAs & Roth IRAs	1C-1601(a)(9)
	Law enforcement officers	143-166.30(g)
	Legislators	120-4.29
	Municipal, city & county employees	128-31
	Retirement benefits from another state to extent exempt in that state	1C-1601(a)(11)
	Teachers & state employees	135-9; 135-95
personal property	Animals, crops, musical instruments, books, wearing apparel, appliances, household goods & furnishings to $5,000 total; may add $1,000 per dependent, up to $4,000 total additional (all property must have been purchased at least 90 days before filing)	1C-1601(a)(4)
	Burial plot to $18,500, in lieu of homestead	1C-1601(a)(1)
	College savings account established under 26 U.S.C. § 529 to $25,000, excluding certain contributions within prior year	1C-1601(a)(10)
	Health aids	1C-1601(a)(7)
	Motor vehicle to $3,500	1C-1601(a)(3)
	Personal injury & wrongful death recoveries for person you depended on	1C-1601(a)(8)
public benefits	Aid to blind	111-18
	Crime victims' compensation	15B-17
	Public adult assistance under work first program	108A-36
	Unemployment compensation	96-17
	Workers' compensation	97-21
tools of trade	Implements, books & tools of trade to $2,000	1C-1601(a)(5)
wages	Earned but unpaid wages received 60 days before filing for bankruptcy, needed for support	1-362
wildcard	$5,000 of unused homestead or burial exemption	1C-1601(a)(2)
	$500 of any personal property	Constitution Art. X § 1

North Dakota

Federal bankruptcy exemptions not available. All law references are to North Dakota Century Code unless otherwise noted.

ASSET	EXEMPTION	LAW
homestead	Real property, house trailer, or mobile home to $100,000 (spouses may not double)	28-22-02(10); 47-18-01
insurance	Fraternal benefit society benefits	26.1-15.1-18; 26.1-33-40;
	Any unmatured life insurance contract, other than credit life insurance	28-22-03.1(4)
	Life insurance proceeds payable to deceased's estate, not to a specific beneficiary	26.1-33-40
	Life insurance surrender value to $8,000 per policy, if beneficiary is insured's dependent & policy was owned over 1 year before filing for bankruptcy; limit does not apply if more needed for support	28-22-03.1(5)
miscellaneous	Child support payments	14-09-09.31; 28-22-03.1(8)(d)
pensions	Tax-exempt retirement accounts, including 401(k)s, 403(b)s, profit-sharing and money purchase plans, SEP and SIMPLE IRAs, and defined-benefit plans	11 U.S.C. § 522(b)(3)(C)
	Traditional and Roth IRAs to $1,283,025 per person	11 U.S.C. § 522(b)(3)(C); (n)
	Disabled veterans' benefits, except military retirement pay	28-22-03.1(4)(d)
	ERISA-qualified benefits, IRAs, Roth IRAs & Keoghs to $100,000 per plan; no limit if more needed for support; total of all accounts cannot exceed $200,000	28-22-03.1(7)
	Public employees' deferred compensation	54-52.2-06
	Public employees' pensions	28-22-19(1)
personal property	One Bible or other religious text; schoolbooks; other books	28-22-02(4)
	Burial plots, church pew	28-22-02(2), (3)
	Wearing apparel to $5,000 and all clothing & family pictures	28-22-02(1), (5)
	Crops or grain raised by debtor on 160 acres where debtor resides	28-22-02(8)
	Food & fuel to last 1 year	28-22-02(6)
	Health aids	28-22-03.1(6)
	Insurance proceeds for exempt property	28-22-02(9)
	One motor vehicle to $2,950 (or $32,000 for vehicle that has been modified to accommodate owner's disability)	28-22-03.1(2)
	Personal injury recoveries to $15,000	28-22-03.1(4)(b)
	Wrongful death recoveries to $15,000	28-22-03.1(4)(a)
public benefits	Crime victims' compensation	28-22-03.1(4); 28-22-19(2)
	Old age & survivor insurance program benefits	52-09-22
	Public assistance	28-22-19(3)
	Social Security	28-22-03.1(8)(a)
	Unemployment compensation	52-06-30
	Veterans disability benefits	28-22-03.1(8)(b)
	Workers' compensation	65-05-29
tools of trade	Books, tools & implements of trade to $1,500	28-22-03.1(3)
wages	Minimum 75% of disposable weekly earnings or 40 times the federal minimum wage, whichever is more; bankruptcy judge may authorize more for low-income debtors. Note: Wage exemption cannot be used in bankruptcy.	32-09.1-03
wildcard	$10,000 of any property in lieu of homestead	28-22-03.1(1)
	Head of household not claiming crops or grain may claim $7,500 of any personal property	28-22-03
	Unmarried with no dependents not claiming crops or grain may claim $3,750 of any personal property	28-22-05

Ohio

Federal bankruptcy exemptions not available. All law references are to Ohio Revised Code unless otherwise noted. Amounts are adjusted for inflation by tracking federal exemption amounts.

ASSET	EXEMPTION	LAW
homestead	Property held as tenancy by the entirety may be exempt against debts owed by only one spouse	*In re Pernus*, 143 B.R. 856 (N.D. Ohio 1992)
	Real or personal property used as residence to $136,925	2329.66(A)(1)(b)
insurance	Benevolent society benefits to $5,000	2329.63; 2329.66(A)(6)(a)
	Disability benefits needed for support	2329.66(A)(6)(e); 3923.19
	Fraternal benefit society benefits	2329.66(A)(6)(d); 3921.18
	Group life insurance policy or proceeds	2329.66(A)(6)(c); 3917.05
	Life, endowment, or annuity contract avails for your spouse, child, or dependent	2329.66(A)(6)(b); 3911.10
	Life insurance proceeds for a spouse	3911.12
	Life insurance proceeds if clause prohibits proceeds from being used to pay beneficiary's creditors	3911.14
miscellaneous	Alimony, child support needed for support	2329.66(A)(11)
	Property of business partnership	1775.24; 2329.66(A)(14)
pensions	Tax-exempt retirement accounts, including 401(k)s, 403(b)s, profit-sharing and money purchase plans, SEP and SIMPLE IRAs, and defined-benefit plans	11 U.S.C. § 522(b)(3)(C)
	Traditional and Roth IRAs to $1,283,025 per person	11 U.S.C. § 522(b)(3)(C); (n)
	ERISA-qualified benefits needed for support	2329.66(A)(10)(b)
	Firefighters, police officers	742.47
	IRAs, Roth IRAs & Keoghs needed for support	2329.66(A)(10)(c), (a)
	Public employees	145.56
	Public safety officers' death benefit	2329.66(A)(10)(a)
	Public school employees	3309.66
	State highway patrol employees	5505.22
	Volunteer firefighters' dependents	146.13
personal property	Animals, crops, books, musical instruments, appliances, household goods, furnishings, wearing apparel, firearms, hunting & fishing equipment to $600 per item; jewelry to $1,600 in the aggregate; $12,625 total	2329.66(A)(4)(b), (c), (d); *In re Szydlowski*, 186 B.R. 907 (N.D. Ohio 1995)
	Burial plot	517.09; 2329.66(A)(8)
	Cash, money due within 90 days, tax refund, bank, security & utility deposits to $475	2329.66(A)(3); *In re Szydlowski*, 186 B.R. 907 (N.D. Ohio 1995)
	Compensation for lost future earnings needed for support, received during 12 months before filing	2329.66(A)(12)(d)
	Health aids (professionally prescribed)	2329.66(A)(7)
	Motor vehicle to $3,775	2329.66(A)(2)(b)
	Personal injury recoveries to $23,700, received during 12 months before filing	2329.66(A)(12)(c)
	Tuition credit or payment	2329.66(A)(16)
	Wrongful death recoveries for person debtor depended on, needed for support, received during 12 months before filing	2329.66(A)(12)(b)
public benefits	Crime victims' compensation, received during 12 months before filing	2329.66(A)(12)(a); 2743.66(D)
	Disability assistance payments	2329.66(A)(9)(f); 5115.07
	Child tax credit and earned income tax credit	2329.66(A)(9)(g)
	Public assistance	2329.66(A)(9)(d), (e); 5107.75; 5108.08
	Unemployment compensation	2329.66(A)(9)(c); 4141.32
	Vocational rehabilitation benefits	2329.66(A)(9)(a); 3304.19
	Workers' compensation	2329.66(A)(9)(b); 4123.67

tools of trade	Implements, books & tools of trade to $2,400	2329.66(A)(5)
wages	Minimum 75% of disposable weekly earnings or 30 times the federal hourly minimum wage, whichever is higher; bankruptcy judge may authorize more for low-income debtors. *In re Jones*, 318 B.R. 841 (Bankr. S.D. Ohio 2005)	2329.66(A)(13)
wildcard	$1,250 of any property	2329.66(A)(18)

Oklahoma

Federal bankruptcy exemptions not available. All law references are to Oklahoma Statutes Annotated (in the form "title number-section number"), unless otherwise noted.

ASSET	EXEMPTION	LAW
homestead	Real property or manufactured home to unlimited value; property cannot exceed 1 acre in city, town, or village, or 160 acres elsewhere; $5,000 limit if more than 25% of total sq. ft. area used for business purposes; okay to rent homestead as long as no other residence is acquired	31-1(A)(1); 31-1(A)(2); 31-2
insurance	Annuity benefits & cash value	36-3631.1
	Assessment or mutual benefits	36-2410
	Fraternal benefit society benefits	36-2718.1
	Funeral benefits prepaid & placed in trust	36-6125
	Group life policy or proceeds	36-3632
	Life, health, accident & mutual benefit insurance proceeds & cash value, if clause prohibits proceeds from being used to pay beneficiary's creditors	36-3631.1
	Limited stock insurance benefits	36-2510
miscellaneous	Alimony, child support	31-1(A)(19)
	Beneficiary's interest in a statutory support trust	6-3010
	Liquor license	37-532
	Property of business partnership	54-1-504
pensions	Tax-exempt retirement accounts, including 401(k)s, 403(b)s, profit-sharing and money purchase plans, SEP and SIMPLE IRAs, and defined-benefit plans	11 U.S.C. § 522(b)(3)(C)
	Traditional and Roth IRAs to $1,283,025 per person	11 U.S.C. § 522(b)(3)(C); (n)
	County employees	19-959
	Disabled veterans	31-7
	ERISA-qualified benefits, IRAs, Roth IRAs, Education IRAs & Keoghs	31-1(A)(20), (24)
	Firefighters	11-49-126
	Judges	20-1111
	Law enforcement employees	47-2-303.3
	Police officers	11-50-124
	Public employees	74-923
	Tax-exempt benefits	60-328
	Teachers	70-17-109
personal property	Books, portraits & pictures	31-1(A)(6)
	Burial plots	31-1(A)(4); 8-7
	Clothing to $4,000	31-1(A)(7)
	College savings plan interest	31-1A(24)
	Deposits in an IDA (Individual Development Account)	31-1A(22)
	Food & seed for growing to last 1 year	31-1(A)(17)
	Guns for household use to $2,000	31-1A(14)
	Health aids (professionally prescribed)	31-1(A)(9)
	Household & kitchen furniture; personal computer and related equipment	31-1(A)(3)
	Livestock for personal or family use: 5 dairy cows & calves under 6 months; 100 chickens; 20 sheep; 10 hogs; 2 horses, bridles & saddles; forage & feed to last 1 year	31-1(A)(10), (11), (12), (15), (16), (17)
	Motor vehicle to $7,500	31-1(A)(13)
	Personal injury & wrongful death recoveries to $50,000	31-1(A)(21)
	Prepaid funeral benefits	36-6125(H)
	War bond payroll savings account	51-42
	Wedding and anniversary rings to $3,000	31-1(A)(8)

public benefits	Crime victims' compensation	21-142.13
	Public assistance	56-173
	Federal earned income tax credit	31-1(A)(23)
	Social Security	56-173
	Unemployment compensation	40-2-303
	Workers' compensation	85-48
tools of trade	Implements needed to farm homestead; tools, books & apparatus to $10,000 total	31-1(A)(5); 31-1(C)
wages	75% of wages earned in 90 days before filing bankruptcy; bankruptcy judge may allow more if you show hardship	12-1171.1; 31-1(A)(18); 31-1.1
wildcard	None	

Oregon

Federal bankruptcy exemptions available. All law references are to Oregon Revised Statutes unless otherwise noted.

ASSET	EXEMPTION	LAW
homestead	Prepaid rent & security deposit for renter's dwelling	*In re Casserino*, 379 F.3d 1069 (9th Cir. 2004)
	Real property of a soldier or sailor during time of war	408.440
	Real property you occupy or intend to occupy to $40,000 ($50,000 for joint owners); property cannot exceed 1 block in town or city or 160 acres elsewhere; sale proceeds exempt 1 year from sale if you intend to purchase another home or use sale proceeds for rent	18.395; 18.402; *In re Wynn*, 369 B.R. 605 (D. Or. 2007)
	Tenancy by entirety not exempt, but subject to survivorship rights of nondebtor spouse	*In re Pletz*, 225 B.R. 206 (D. Or. 1997)
insurance	Annuity contract benefits to $500 per month	743.049
	Fraternal benefit society benefits to $7,500	748.207; 18.348
	Group life policy or proceeds not payable to insured	743.047
	Health or disability proceeds or avails	743.050
	Life insurance proceeds or cash value if you are not the insured	743.046; 743.047
miscellaneous	Alimony, child support needed for support	18.345(1)(i)
	Liquor licenses	471.292 (1)
pensions	Tax-exempt retirement accounts, including 401(k)s, 403(b)s, profit-sharing and money purchase plans, SEP and SIMPLE IRAs, and defined-benefit plans	11 U.S.C. § 522(b)(3)(C)
	Traditional and Roth IRAs to $1,283,025 per person	11 U.S.C. § 522(b)(3)(C); (n)
	ERISA-qualified benefits, including IRAs & SEPs & payments to $7,500	18.358; 18.348
	Public officers', employees' pension payments to $7,500	237.980; 238.445; 18.348(2)
personal property	Books, pictures & musical instruments to $600 total	18.345(1)(a)
	Building materials for construction of an improvement	87.075
	Burial plot	65.870
	Clothing, jewelry & other personal items to $1,800 total	18.345(1)(b)
	Compensation for lost earnings payments for debtor or someone debtor depended on, to extent needed	18.345(1)(L),(3)
	Domestic animals, poultry & pets to $1,000 plus food to last 60 days (no doubling)	18.345(1)(e)
	Food & fuel to last 60 days if debtor is householder	18.345(1)(f)
	Furniture, household items, utensils, radios & TVs to $3,000 total (no doubling)	18.345(1)(f)
	Health aids	18.345(1)(h)
	Health savings accounts & medical savings accounts	18.345(1)(o)
	Higher education savings account to $7,500	348.863; 18.348(1)
	Motor vehicle to $3,000	18.345(1)(d),(3)
	Personal injury recoveries to $10,000	18.345(1)(k),(3)
	Pistol, rifle or shotgun (owned by person over 16) to $1,000	18.362
	Wages deposited into a bank account to $7,500; cash for sold exempt property	18.348; 18.385

public benefits	Aid to blind to $7,500	411.706; 411.760; 18.348
	Aid to disabled to $7,500	411.706; 411.760; 18.348
	Civil defense & disaster relief to $7,500	18.348
	Crime victims' compensation	18.345(1)(j),(3); 147.325
	Federal earned income tax credit	18.345(1)(n)
	General assistance to $7,500	411.760; 18.348
	Injured inmates' benefits to $7,500	655.530; 18.348
	Medical assistance to $7,500	414.095; 18.348
	Old-age assistance to $7,500	411.706; 411.760; 18.348
	Unemployment compensation to $7,500	657.855; 18.348
	Veterans benefits & proceeds of Veterans loans	407.125; 407.595; 18.348(m)
	Vocational rehabilitation to $7,500	344.580; 18.348
	Workers' compensation to $7,500	656.234; 18.348
tools of trade	Tools, library, team with food to last 60 days, to $5,000	18.345(1)(c), (3)
wages	75% of disposable wages or $170 per week, whichever is greater; bankruptcy judge may authorize more for low-income debtors	18.385
	Wages withheld in state employee's bond savings accounts. *In re Robinson*, 241 B.R. 447 (9th Cir. B.A.P. 1999)	292.070
wildcard	$400 of any personal property not already covered by existing exemption	18.345(1)(p)

Pennsylvania

Federal bankruptcy exemptions available. All law references are to Pennsylvania Consolidated Statutes Annotated unless otherwise noted.

ASSET	EXEMPTION	LAW
homestead	None; however, property held as tenancy by the entirety may be exempt against debts owed by only one spouse	*In re Martin*, 269 B.R. 119 (M.D. Pa. 2001)
insurance	Accident or disability benefits	42-8124(c)(7)
	Fraternal benefit society benefits	42-8124(c)(1), (8)
	Group life policy or proceeds	42-8124(c)(5)
	Insurance policy or annuity contract payments where insured is the beneficiary, cash value or proceeds to $100 per month	42-8124(c)(3)
	Life insurance & annuity proceeds if clause prohibits proceeds from being used to pay beneficiary's creditors	42-8214(c)(4)
	Life insurance annuity policy cash value or proceeds if beneficiary is insured's dependent, child or spouse	42-8124(c)(6)
	No-fault automobile insurance proceeds	42-8124(c)(9)
miscellaneous	Property of business partnership	15-8342
pensions	Tax-exempt retirement accounts, including 401(k)s, 403(b)s, profit-sharing and money purchase plans, SEP and SIMPLE IRAs, and defined-benefit plans	11 U.S.C. § 522(b)(3)(C)
	Traditional and Roth IRAs to $1,283,025 per person	11 U.S.C. § 522(b)(3)(C); (n)
	City employees	53-13445; 53-23572; 53-39383; 42-8124(b)(1)(iv)
	County employees	16-4716
	Municipal employees	53-881.115; 42-8124(b)(1)(vi)
	Police officers	53-764; 53-776; 53-23666; 42-8124(b)(1)(iii)
	Private retirement benefits to extent tax-deferred, if clause prohibits proceeds from being used to pay beneficiary's creditors; exemption limited to deposits of $15,000 per year made at least 1 year before filing (limit does not apply to rollovers from other exempt funds or accounts)	42-8124(b)(1)(vii), (viii), (ix)
	Public school employees	24-8533; 42-8124(b)(1)(i)
	State employees	71-5953; 42-8124(b)(1)(ii)
personal property	Bibles & schoolbooks	42-8124(a)(2)
	Clothing	42-8124(a)(1)
	Military uniforms & accoutrements	42-8124(a)(4); 51-4103
	Sewing machines	42-8124(a)(3)
public benefits	Crime victims' compensation	18-11.708
	Korean conflict veterans benefits	51-20098
	Unemployment compensation	42-8124(a)(10); 43-863
	Veterans benefits	51-20012; 20048; 20098; 20127
	Workers' compensation	42-8124(c)(2)
tools of trade	Seamstress's sewing machine	42-8124(a)(3)
wages	Earned but unpaid wages	42-8127
	Wages of victims of abuse	42-8127(f)
wildcard	$300 of any property, including cash, real property, securities, or proceeds from sale of exempt property	42-8123

Rhode Island

Federal bankruptcy exemptions available. All law references are to General Laws of Rhode Island unless otherwise noted.

ASSET	EXEMPTION	LAW
homestead	$500,000 in land & buildings you occupy or intend to occupy as a principal residence (spouse may not double)	9-26-4.1
insurance	Accident or sickness proceeds, avails, or benefits	27-18-24
	Fraternal benefit society benefits	27-25-18
	Life insurance proceeds if clause prohibits proceeds from being used to pay beneficiary's creditors	27-4-12
	Temporary disability insurance	28-41-32
miscellaneous	Earnings of a minor child	9-26-4(9)
	Property of business partnership	7-12-36
pensions	Tax-exempt retirement accounts, including 401(k)s, 403(b)s, profit-sharing and money purchase plans, SEP and SIMPLE IRAs, and defined-benefit plans	11 U.S.C. § 522(b)(3)(C)
	Traditional and Roth IRAs to $1,283,025 per person	11 U.S.C. § 522(b)(3)(C); (n)
	ERISA-qualified benefits	9-26-4(12)
	Firefighters	9-26-5
	IRAs & Roth IRAs	9-26-4(11)
	Police officers	9-26-5
	Private employees	28-17-4
	State & municipal employees	36-10-34
personal property	Beds, bedding, furniture, household goods & supplies, to $9,600 total (spouses may not double)	9-26-4(3); In re Petrozella, 247 B.R. 591 (R.I. 2000)
	Bibles & books to $300	9-26-4(4)
	Burial plot	9-26-4(5)
	Clothing	9-26-4(1)
	Consumer cooperative association holdings to $50	7-8-25
	Debt secured by promissory note or bill of exchange	9-26-4(7)
	Jewelry to $2,000	9-26-4 (14)
	Motor vehicles to $12,000	9-26-4 (13)
	Prepaid tuition program or tuition savings account	9-26-4 (15)
public benefits	Aid to blind, aged, disabled; general assistance	40-6-14
	Crime victims' compensation	12-25.1-3(b)(2)
	State disability benefits	28-41-32
	Unemployment compensation	28-44-58
	Veterans disability or survivors death benefits	30-7-9
	Workers' compensation	28-33-27
tools of trade	Library of practicing professional	9-26-4(2)
	Working tools to $2,000	9-26-4(2)
wages	Earned but unpaid wages due military member on active duty	30-7-9
	Earned but unpaid wages due seaman	9-26-4(6)
	Earned but unpaid wages to $50	9-26-4(8)(iii)
	Wages of any person who had been receiving public assistance are exempt for 1 year after going off of relief	9-26-4(8)(ii)
	Wages of spouse & minor children	9-26-4(9)
	Wages paid by charitable organization or fund providing relief to the poor	9-26-4(8)(i)
wildcard	$6,500 in any assets	9-26-4(16)

South Carolina

Federal bankruptcy exemptions not available. All law references are to Code of Laws of South Carolina unless otherwise noted. (Amounts adjusted for inflation in 2014 (15-41-30(B).)

ASSET	EXEMPTION	LAW
homestead	Real property, including co-op, to $59,100 (single owner); $118,200 (multiple owners)	15-41-30(A)(1)
insurance	Accident & disability benefits	38-63-40(D)
	Benefits accruing under life insurance policy after death of insured, where proceeds left with insurance company pursuant to agreement; benefits not exempt from action to recover necessaries if parties agree	38-63-50
	Disability or illness benefits	15-41-30(A)(11)(C)
	Dividend, interest/loan value of unmatured life insurance contract to $4,725	15-41-30(A)(9)
	Fraternal benefit society benefits	38-38-330
	Group life insurance proceeds; cash value to $50,000	38-63-40(C); 38-65-90
	Life insurance avails from policy for person you depended on to $4,725	15-41-30(A)(9)
	Life insurance proceeds from policy for person you depended on, needed for support	15-41-30(A)(12)(c)
	Proceeds & cash surrender value of life insurance payable to beneficiary other than insured's estate & for the express benefit of insured's spouse, children, or dependents (must be purchased 2 years before filing) to $50,000	38-63-90
	Proceeds of life insurance or annuity contract	38-63-40(B)
	Unmatured life insurance contract, except credit insurance policy	15-41-30(A)(8)
miscellaneous	Alimony, child support	15-41-30(A)(11)(d)
	Property of business partnership	33-41-720
pensions	Tax-exempt retirement accounts, including 401(k)s, 403(b)s, profit-sharing and money purchase plans, SEP and SIMPLE IRAs, and defined-benefit plans	11 U.S.C. § 522(b)(3)(C)
	Traditional and Roth IRAs to $1,283,025 per person	11 U.S.C. § 522(b)(3)(C); (n)
	ERISA-qualified benefits; your share of the pension plan fund	15-41-30(10)(E), (14)
	Firefighters	9-13-230
	General assembly members	9-9-180
	IRAs & Roth IRAs	15-41-30(A)(13)
	Judges, solicitors	9-8-190
	Police officers	9-11-270
	Public employees	9-1-1680
personal property	Animals, crops, appliances, books, clothing, household goods, furnishings, musical instruments to $4,725 total	15-41-30(A)(3)
	Burial plot to $59,100, in lieu of homestead	15-41-30(1)
	Cash & other liquid assets to $5,900, in lieu of burial or homestead exemption	15-41-30(A)(5)
	College investment program trust fund	59-2-140
	Health aids	15-41-30(A)(10)
	Jewelry to $1,175	15-41-30(A)(4)
	Motor vehicle to $5,900	15-41-30(A)(2)
	Personal injury & wrongful death recoveries for person you depended on for support	15-41-30(A)(12)
public benefits	Crime victims' compensation	15-41-30(A)(12); 16-3-1300
	General relief; aid to aged, blind, disabled	43-5-190
	Local public assistance	15-41-30(A)(11)
	Social Security	15-41-30(A)(11)
	Unemployment compensation	15-41-30(A)(11)
	Veterans benefits	15-41-30(A)(11)
	Workers' compensation	42-9-360
tools of trade	Implements, books & tools of trade to $1,775	15-41-30(A)(6)
wages	None (use federal nonbankruptcy wage exemption)	15-41-30(A)(7)
wildcard	Up to $5,900 for any property from unused exemption amounts	15-41-30(A)(7)

South Dakota

Federal bankruptcy exemptions not available. All law references are to South Dakota Codified Law unless otherwise noted.

ASSET	EXEMPTION	LAW
homestead	Gold or silver mine, mill, or smelter not exempt	43-31-5
	May file homestead declaration	43-31-6
	Real property to unlimited value or mobile home (larger than 240 sq. ft. at its base & registered in state at least 6 months before filing) to unlimited value; property cannot exceed 1 acre in town or 160 acres elsewhere; sale proceeds to $60,000 ($170,000 if over age 70 or widow or widower who hasn't remarried) exempt for 1 year after sale (spouses may not double)	43-31-1; 43-31-2; 43-31-3; 43-31-4; 43-45-3
	Spouse or child of deceased owner may claim homestead exemption	43-31-13
insurance	Annuity contract proceeds to $250 per month	58-12-6; 58-12-8
	Endowment, life insurance, policy proceeds to $20,000; if policy issued by mutual aid or benevolent society, cash value to $20,000	58-12-4
	Fraternal benefit society benefits	58-37A-18
	Health benefits to $20,000	58-12-4
	Life insurance proceeds, if clause prohibits proceeds from being used to pay beneficiary's creditors	58-15-70
	Life insurance proceeds to $10,000, if beneficiary is surviving spouse or child	43-45-6
miscellaneous	Court-ordered alimony or support if not lump sum, up to $750 per month	43-45-2(9)
pensions	Tax-exempt retirement accounts, including 401(k)s, 403(b)s, profit-sharing and money purchase plans, SEP and SIMPLE IRAs, and defined-benefit plans	11 U.S.C. § 522(b)(3)(C)
	Traditional and Roth IRAs to $1,283,025 per person	11 U.S.C. § 522(b)(3)(C); (n)
	City employees	9-16-47
	ERISA-qualified benefits, limited to income & distribution on $1,000,000	43-45-16
	Public employees	3-12-115
personal property	Bible, schoolbooks; other books to $200	43-45-2(4)
	Burial plots, church pew	43-45-2(2), (3)
	Cemetery association property	47-29-25
	Clothing	43-45-2(5)
	Family pictures	43-45-2(1)
	Food & fuel to last 1 year	43-45-2(6)
	Health aids professionally prescribed	43-45-2(8)
public benefits	Crime victims' compensation	23A-28B-24
	Public assistance	28-7A-18
	Unemployment compensation	61-6-28
	Workers' compensation	62-4-42
tools of trade	None	
wages	Earned wages owed 60 days before filing bankruptcy, needed for support of family	15-20-12
	Wages of prisoners in work programs	24-8-10
wildcard	Head of family may claim $7,000, or nonhead of family may claim $5,000 of any personal property	43-45-4

Tennessee

Federal bankruptcy exemptions not available. All law references are to Tennessee Code Annotated unless otherwise noted.

ASSET	EXEMPTION	LAW
homestead	$5,000; $7,500 for joint owners; $25,000 if at least one dependent is a minor child (if 62 or older, $12,500 if single; $20,000 if married; $25,000 if spouse is also 62 or older)	26-2-301
	2–15-year lease	26-2-303
	Life estate	26-2-302
	Property held as tenancy by the entirety may be exempt against debts owed by only one spouse, but survivorship right is not exempt	In re Arango, 136 B.R. 740 aff'd, 992 F.2d 611 (6th Cir. 1993); In re Arwood, 289 B.R. 889 (Bankr. E.D. Tenn. 2003)
	Spouse or child of deceased owner may claim homestead exemption	26-2-301
insurance	Accident, health, or disability benefits for resident & citizen of Tennessee	26-2-110
	Disability or illness benefits	26-2-111(1)(C)
	Fraternal benefit society benefits	56-25-1403
	Life insurance or annuity	56-7-203
miscellaneous	Alimony, child support owed for 30 days before filing for bankruptcy	26-2-111(1)(E)
	Educational scholarship trust funds & prepayment plans	49-4-108; 49-7-822
pensions	Tax-exempt retirement accounts, including 401(k)s, 403(b)s, profit-sharing and money purchase plans, SEP and SIMPLE IRAs, and defined-benefit plans	11 U.S.C. § 522(b)(3)(C)
	Traditional and Roth IRAs to $1,283,025 per person	11 U.S.C. § 522(b)(3)(C); (n)
	ERISA-qualified benefits, IRAs & Roth IRAs	26-2-111(1)(D)
	Public employees	8-36-111
	State & local government employees	26-2-105
	Teachers	49-5-909
personal property	Bible, schoolbooks, family pictures & portraits	26-2-104
	Burial plot to 1 acre	26-2-305; 46-2-102
	Clothing & storage containers	26-2-104
	Health aids	26-2-111(5)
	Health savings accounts	26-2-105
	Lost future earnings payments for you or person you depended on	26-2-111(3)
	Personal injury recoveries to $7,500; wrongful death recoveries to $10,000 ($15,000 total for personal injury, wrongful death & crime victims' compensation)	26-2-111(2)(B), (C)
	Wages of debtor deserting family, in hands of family	26-2-109
public benefits	Aid to blind	71-4-117
	Aid to disabled	71-4-1112
	Crime victims' compensation to $5,000 (see personal property)	26-2-111(2)(A); 29-13-111
	Local public assistance	26-2-111(1)(A)
	Old-age assistance	71-2-216
	Relocation assistance payments	13-11-115
	Social Security	26-2-111(1)(A)
	Unemployment compensation	26-2-111(1)(A)
	Veterans benefits	26-2-111(1)(B)
	Workers' compensation	50-6-223
tools of trade	Implements, books & tools of trade to $1,900	26-2-111(4)
wages	Minimum 75% of disposable weekly earnings or 30 times the federal minimum hourly wage, whichever is more, plus $2.50 per week per child; bankruptcy judge may authorize more for low-income debtors. Note: In re Lawrence, 219 B.R. 786 (E.D. Tenn. 1998) ruled that wage garnishment is not an exemption in bankruptcy.	26-2-106, 107
wildcard	$10,000 of any personal property including deposits on account with any bank or financial institution	26-2-103

Texas

Federal bankruptcy exemptions available. All law references are to Texas Revised Civil Statutes Annotated unless otherwise noted.

ASSET	EXEMPTION	LAW
homestead	Unlimited; property cannot exceed 10 acres in town, village, city or 100 acres (200 for families) elsewhere; sale proceeds exempt for 6 months after sale (renting okay if another home not acquired, Prop. 41.003)	Prop. 41.001; 41.002; Const. Art. 16 §§ 50, 51
	If property acreage is larger than what is covered by homestead exemption, may have to file homestead declaration	Prop. 41.005; 41.021 to 41.023
insurance	Fraternal benefit society benefits	Ins. 885.316
	Life, health, accident, or annuity benefits, monies, policy proceeds & cash values due or paid to beneficiary or insured	Ins. 1108.051
	Texas employee uniform group insurance	Ins. 1551.011
	Texas public school employees group insurance	Ins. 1575.006
	Texas state college or university employee benefits	Ins. 1601.008
miscellaneous	Alimony & child support	Prop. 42.001(b)(3)
	Higher education savings plan trust account	Educ. 54.709(e)
	Liquor licenses & permits	Alco. Bev. Code 11.03
	Prepaid tuition plans	Educ. 54.639
pensions	Tax-exempt retirement accounts, including 401(k)s, 403(b)s, profit-sharing and money purchase plans, SEP and SIMPLE IRAs, and defined-benefit plans	11 U.S.C. § 522(b)(3)(C)
	Traditional and Roth IRAs to $1,283,025 per person	11 U.S.C. § 522(b)(3)(C); (n)
	County & district employees	Gov't. 811.006
	ERISA-qualified government or church benefits, including Keoghs, IRAs, & Roth IRAs	Prop. 42.0021
	Firefighters	6243e(5); 6243a-1(8.03); 6243b(15); 6243e(5); 6243e.1(1.04)
	Judges	Gov't. 831.004
	Law enforcement officers, firefighters, emergency medical personnel survivors	Gov't. 615.005
	Municipal employees & elected officials, state employees	6243h(22); Gov't. 811.005
	Police officers	6243d-1(17); 6243j(20); 6243a-1(8.03); 6243b(15); 6243d-1(17)
	Retirement benefits to extent tax-deferred	Prop. 42.0021
	Teachers	Gov't. 821.005
personal property to $100,000 total for family, $50,000 for single adult (include tools of trade in these aggregate limits)	Athletic & sporting equipment, including bicycles	Prop. 42.002(a)(8)
	Bible or other book containing sacred writings of a religion (doesn't count toward $30,000 or $60,000 total)	Prop. 42.001(b)(4)
	Burial plots (exempt from total)	Prop. 41.001
	Clothing & food	Prop. 42.002(a)(2), (5)
	Health aids (exempt from total)	Prop. 42.001(b)(2)
	Health savings accounts	Prop. 42.0021
	Home furnishings including family heirlooms	Prop. 42.002(a)(1)
	Jewelry (limited to 25% of total exemption)	Prop. 42.002(a)(6)
	Pets & domestic animals plus their food: 2 horses, mules, or donkeys & tack; 12 head of cattle; 60 head of other livestock; 120 fowl	Prop. 42.002(a)(10), (11)
	1 two-, three- or four-wheeled motor vehicle per family member or per single adult who holds a driver's license; or, if not licensed, who relies on someone else to operate vehicle	Prop. 42.002(a)(9)
	2 firearms	Prop. 42.002(a)(7)

public benefits	Crime victims' compensation	Crim. Proc. 56.49
	Medical assistance	Hum. Res. 32.036
	Public assistance	Hum. Res. 31.040
	Unemployment compensation	Labor 207.075
	Workers' compensation	Labor 408.201
tools of trade *included in aggregate dollar limits for personal property*	Farming or ranching vehicles & implements	Prop. 42.002(a)(3)
	Tools, equipment (includes boat & motor vehicles used in trade) & books	Prop. 42.002(a)(4)
wages	Earned but unpaid wages	Prop. 42.001(b)(1)
	Unpaid commissions not to exceed 25% of total personal property exemptions	Prop. 42.001(d)
wildcard	None	

Utah

Federal bankruptcy exemptions not available. All law references are to Utah Code unless otherwise noted.

ASSET	EXEMPTION	LAW
homestead	Must file homestead declaration before attempted sale of home	78B-5-504
	Real property, mobile home, or water rights to $30,000 if primary residence; $5,000 if not primary residence	78B-5-504
	Sale proceeds exempt for 1 year	78B-5-503(5)(b)
insurance	Disability, illness, medical, or hospital benefits	78B-5-505(1)(a)(iii)
	Fraternal benefit society benefits	31A-9-603
	Life insurance policy cash surrender value, excluding payments made on the contract within the prior year	78B-5-505(i)(a)(xiii)
	Life insurance proceeds if beneficiary is insured's spouse or dependent, as needed for support	78B-5-505(i)(a)(xi)
	Medical, surgical & hospital benefits	78B-5-505(1)(a)(iv)
miscellaneous	Alimony needed for support	78B-5-505(a)(vi), (vii)
	Child support	78B-5-505(1) (f), (k)
pensions	Tax-exempt retirement accounts, including 401(k)s, 403(b)s, profit-sharing and money purchase plans, SEP and SIMPLE IRAs, and defined-benefit plans	11 U.S.C. § 522(b)(3)(C)
	Traditional and Roth IRAs to $1,283,025 per person	11 U.S.C. § 522(b)(3)(C); (n)
	ERISA-qualified benefits, IRAs, Roth IRAs & Keoghs (benefits that have accrued & contributions that have been made at least 1 year prior to filing)	78B-5-505(1)(a)(xiv)
	Other pensions & annuities needed for support	78-23-6(3)
	Public employees	49-11-612
personal property	Animals, books & musical instruments to $1,000	78B-5-506(1)(c)
	Artwork depicting, or done by, a family member	78B-5-505(1)(a)(Ix)
	Bed, bedding, carpets	78B-5-505(1)(a)(viii)
	Burial plot	78B-5-505(1)(a)(i)
	Clothing (cannot claim furs or jewelry)	78B-5-505(1)(a)(viii)
	Dining & kitchen tables & chairs to $1,000	78B-5-505(1)(b)
	Firearms to $250	78B-5-506(1)(e)
	Food to last 12 months	78B-5-505(1)(a)(viii)
	Health aids	78B-5-505(1)(a)(ii)
	Heirlooms to $1,000	78B-5-506(1)(d)
	Motor vehicle to $3,000	78B-5-506(3)
	Personal injury, wrongful death recoveries for you or person you depended on	78B-5-505(1)(a)(x)
	Proceeds for sold, lost, or damaged exempt property	78B-5-507
	Refrigerator, freezer, microwave, stove, sewing machine, washer & dryer	78B-5-505(1)(a)(viii)
	Sofas, chairs & related furnishings to $1,000	78B-5-506(1)(a)
public benefits	Crime victims' compensation	63-25a-421(4)
	General assistance	35A-3-112
	Occupational disease disability benefits	34A-3-107
	Unemployment compensation	35A-4-103(4)(b)
	Veterans benefits	78B-5-505(1)(a)(v)
	Workers' compensation	34A-2-422
tools of trade	Implements, books & tools of trade to $5,000	78B-5-506(2)
	Military property of National Guard member	39-1-47
wages	Unpaid earnings due as of the bankruptcy filing date in an amount equal to 1/24 of the median Utah annual income if paid more than once per month and 1/12 if paid monthly	78B-5-505(1)(a)(xvi)
wildcard	None	

Vermont

Federal bankruptcy exemptions available. All law references are to Vermont Statutes Annotated unless otherwise noted.

ASSET	EXEMPTION	LAW
homestead	Property held as tenancy by the entirety may be exempt against debts owed by only one spouse	*In re McQueen*, 21 B.R. 736 (D. Ver. 1982)
	Real property or mobile home to $125,000; may also claim rents, issues, profits & out-buildings (spouses may not double); *D'Avignon v. Palmisano*, 34 B.R. 796 (D.Vt. 1982)	27-101
	Spouse of deceased owner may claim homestead exemption	27-105
insurance	Annuity contract benefits to $350 per month	8-3709
	Disability benefits that supplement life insurance or annuity contract	8-3707
	Disability or illness benefits needed for support	12-2740(19)(C)
	Fraternal benefit society benefits	8-4478
	Group life or health benefits	8-3708
	Health benefits to $200 per month	8-4086
	Life insurance proceeds for person you depended on	12-2740(19)(H)
	Life insurance proceeds if clause prohibits proceeds from being used to pay beneficiary's creditors	8-3705
	Life insurance proceeds if beneficiary is not the insured	8-3706
	Unmatured life insurance contract other than credit	12-2740(18)
miscellaneous	Alimony, child support	12-2740(19)(D)
pensions	Tax-exempt retirement accounts, including 401(k)s, 403(b)s, profit-sharing and money purchase plans, SEP and SIMPLE IRAs, and defined-benefit plans	11 U.S.C. § 522(b)(3)(C)
	Traditional and Roth IRAs to $1,283,025 per person	11 U.S.C. § 522(b)(3)(C); (n)
	Municipal employees	24-5066
	Other pensions	12-2740(19)(J)
	Self-directed accounts (IRAs, Roth IRAs, Keoghs); contributions must be made 1 year before filing	12-2740(16)
	State employees	3-476
	Teachers	16-1946
personal property	Appliances, furnishings, goods, clothing, books, crops, animals, musical instruments to $2,500 total	12-2740(5)
	Bank deposits to $700	12-2740(15)
	Cow, 2 goats, 10 sheep, 10 chickens & feed to last 1 winter; 3 swarms of bees plus honey; 5 tons coal or 500 gal. heating oil; 10 cords of firewood; 500 gal. bottled gas; growing crops to $5,000; yoke of oxen or steers, plow & ox yoke; 2 horses with harnesses, halters & chains	12-2740(6), (9)–(14)
	Health aids	12-2740(17)
	Jewelry to $500; wedding ring unlimited	12-2740(3), (4)
	Motor vehicles to $2,500	12-2740(1)
	Personal injury, lost future earnings, wrongful death recoveries for you or person you depended on	12-2740(19)(F), (G), (I)
	Stove, heating unit, refrigerator, freezer, water heater & sewing machines	12-2740(8)
public benefits	Aid to blind, aged, disabled; general assistance	33-124
	Crime victims' compensation needed for support	12-2740(19)(E)
	Social Security needed for support	12-2740(19)(A)
	Unemployment compensation	21-1367
	Veterans benefits needed for support	12-2740(19)(B)
	Workers' compensation	21-681
tools of trade	Books & tools of trade to $5,000	12-2740(2)
wages	Entire wages, if you received welfare during 2 months before filing	12-3170

	Minimum 75% of weekly disposable earnings or 30 times the federal minimum hourly wage, whichever is greater; bankruptcy judge may authorize more for low-income debtors. Note: The court in *In re Riendeau*, 293 B.R. 832 (D. Vt. 2002) held that Vermont's wage garnishment law does not create an exemption that can be used in bankruptcy.	12-3170
wildcard	Unused exemptions for motor vehicle, tools of trade, jewelry, household furniture, appliances, clothing & crops to $7,000	12-2740(7)
	$400 of any property	12-2740(7)

Virginia

Federal bankruptcy exemptions not available. All law references are to Code of Virginia unless otherwise noted.

ASSET	EXEMPTION	LAW
homestead	$5,000 plus $500 per dependent; rents & profits; sale proceeds exempt to $5,000 (unused portion of homestead may be applied to any personal property); exemption is $10,000 if over 65	*Cheeseman v. Nachman,* 656 F.2d 60 (4th Cir. 1981); 34-4; 34-18; 34-20
	May include mobile home	*In re Goad,* 161 B.R. 161 (W.D. Va. 1993)
	Must file homestead declaration before filing for bankruptcy	34-6
	Property held as tenancy by the entirety may be exempt against debts owed by only one spouse	*In re Bunker,* 312 F.3d 145 (4th Cir. 2002)
	Surviving spouse may claim $20,000; if no surviving spouse, minor children may claim exemption	64.2-311
insurance	Accident or sickness benefits	38.2-3406
	Burial society benefits	38.2-4021
	Cooperative life insurance benefits	38.2-3811
	Fraternal benefit society benefits	38.2-4118
	Group life or accident insurance for government officials	51.1-510
	Group life insurance policy or proceeds	38.2-3339
	Industrial sick benefits	38.2-3549
	Life insurance proceeds	38.2-3122
miscellaneous	Property of business partnership	50-73.108
	Unpaid spousal or child support	34-26(10)
pensions *see also wages*	Tax-exempt retirement accounts, including 401(k)s, 403(b)s, profit-sharing and money purchase plans, SEP and SIMPLE IRAs, and defined-benefit plans	11 U.S.C. § 522(b)(3)(C)
	Traditional and Roth IRAs to $1,283,025 per person	11 U.S.C. § 522(b)(3)(C); (n)
	City, town & county employees	51.1-802
	ERISA-qualified benefits to same extent permitted by federal bankruptcy law	34-34
	Judges	51.1-300
	State employees	51.1-124.4(A)
	State police officers	51.1-200
personal property	Bible	34-26(1)
	Burial plot	34-26(3)
	Clothing to $1,000	34-26(4)
	Family portraits & heirlooms to $5,000 total	34-26(2)
	Firearms to $3,000	34-26(4b)
	Health aids	34-26(6)
	Health savings accounts & medical savings accounts	38.2-5604
	Household furnishings to $5,000	34-26(4a)
	Motor vehicles to $6,000	34-26(8)
	Personal injury causes of action & recoveries	34-28.1
	Pets	34-26(5)
	Prepaid tuition contracts	23-38.81(E)
	Wedding & engagement rings	34-26(1a)
public benefits	Aid to blind, aged, disabled; general relief	63.2-506
	Crime victims' compensation unless seeking to discharge debt for treatment of injury incurred during crime	19.2-368.12
	Earned income tax credit or child tax credit	34-26(9)
	Payments to tobacco farmers	3.1-1111.1
	Unemployment compensation	60.2-600
	Workers' compensation	65.2-531

tools of trade	For farmer, pair of horses, or mules with gear; one wagon or cart, one tractor to $3,000; 2 plows & wedges; one drag, harvest cradle, pitchfork, rake; fertilizer to $1,000	34-27
	Tools, books & instruments of trade, including motor vehicles, to $10,000, needed in your occupation or education	34-26(7)
	Uniforms, arms, equipment of military member	44-96
wages	Minimum 75% of weekly disposable earnings or 40 times the federal minimum hourly wage, whichever is greater; bankruptcy judge may authorize more for low-income debtors	34-29
wildcard	Unused portion of homestead exemption	34-13
	$10,000 of any property for disabled veterans	34-4.1

Washington

Federal bankruptcy exemptions available. All law references are to Revised Code of Washington Annotated unless otherwise noted.

ASSET	EXEMPTION	LAW
homestead	Must record homestead declaration before sale of home if property unimproved or home unoccupied	6.15.040
	Real property or manufactured home to $125,000; unimproved property intended for residence to $15,000 (spouses may not double)	6.13.010; 6.13.030
insurance	Annuity contract proceeds to $2,500 per month	48.18.430
	Disability proceeds, avails, or benefits	48.36A.180
	Fraternal benefit society benefits	48.18.400
	Group life insurance policy or proceeds	48.18.420
	Life insurance proceeds or avails if beneficiary is not the insured	48.18.410
miscellaneous	Child support payments	6.15.010(1)(c)(iv)
pensions	Tax-exempt retirement accounts, including 401(k)s, 403(b)s, profit-sharing and money purchase plans, SEP and SIMPLE IRAs, and defined-benefit plans	11 U.S.C. § 522(b)(3)(C)
	Traditional and Roth IRAs to $1,283,025 per person	11 U.S.C. § 522(b)(3)(C); (n)
	City employees	41.28.200; 41.44.240
	ERISA-qualified benefits, IRAs, Roth IRAs & Keoghs	6.15.020
	Judges	2.10.180; 2.12.090
	Law enforcement officials & firefighters	41.26.053
	Police officers	41.20.180
	Public & state employees	41.40.052
	State patrol officers	43.43.310
	Teachers	41.32.052
	Volunteer firefighters	41.24.240
personal property	Appliances, furniture, household goods, home & yard equipment to $6,500 total for individual ($13,000 for community)	6.15.010(1)(c)(i)
	Books and electronic media to $3,500	6.15.010(1)(b)
	Burial ground	68.24.220
	Burial plots sold by nonprofit cemetery association	68.20.120
	Clothing, but no more than $3,500 in furs, jewelry, ornaments	6.15.010(1)(a)
	Fire insurance proceeds for lost, stolen, or destroyed exempt property	6.15.030
	Food & fuel for comfortable maintenance	6.15.010(1)(c)(i)
	Health aids prescribed	6.15.010(1)(c)(v)
	Health savings account & medical savings account deposits	6.15.020
	Keepsakes & family pictures	6.15.010(1)(b)
	Motor vehicle to $3,250 total for individual (two vehicles to $6,500 for community)	6.15.010(1)(c)(iii)
	Personal injury recoveries to $20,000	6.15.010(1)(c)(vi)
	Tuition units purchased more than 2 years before	6.15.010(1)(e)
public benefits	Child welfare	74.13.070
	Crime victims' compensation	7.68.070(10)
	General assistance	74.04.280
	Industrial insurance (workers' compensation)	51.32.040
	Old-age assistance	74.08.210
	Unemployment compensation	50.40.020

tools of trade	Farmer's trucks, stock, tools, seed, equipment & supplies to $10,000 total	6.15.010(1)(d)(i)
	Library, office furniture, office equipment & supplies of physician, surgeon, attorney, clergy, or other professional to $10,000 total	6.15.010(1)(d)(ii)
	Tools & materials used in any other trade to $10,000	6.15.010(1)(d)(iii)
wages	Minimum 75% of weekly disposable earnings or 30 times the federal minimum hourly wage, whichever is greater; bankruptcy judge may authorize more for low-income debtors	6.27.150
wildcard	$3,000 of any personal property (no more than $1,500 in cash, bank deposits, bonds, stocks & securities)	6.15.010(1)(c)(ii)

West Virginia

Federal bankruptcy exemptions not available. All law references are to West Virginia Code unless otherwise noted.

ASSET	EXEMPTION	LAW
homestead	Real or personal property used as residence to $25,000; unused portion of homestead may be applied to any property	38-10-4(a)
insurance	Fraternal benefit society benefits	33-23-21
	Group life insurance policy or proceeds	33-6-28
	Health or disability benefits	38-10-4(j)(3)
	Life insurance payments from policy for person you depended on, needed for support	38-10-4(k)(3)
	Unmatured life insurance contract, except credit insurance policy	38-10-4(g)
	Unmatured life insurance contract's accrued dividend, interest, or loan value to $8,000, if debtor owns contract & insured is either debtor or a person on whom debtor is dependent	38-10-4(h)
miscellaneous	Alimony, child support needed for support	38-10-4(j)(4)
pensions	Tax-exempt retirement accounts, including 401(k)s, 403(b)s, profit-sharing and money purchase plans, SEP and SIMPLE IRAs, and defined-benefit plans	11 U.S.C. § 522(b)(3)(C)
	Traditional and Roth IRAs to $1,283,025 per person	11 U.S.C. § 522(b)(3)(C); (n)
	ERISA-qualified benefits, IRAs needed for support	38-10-4(j)(5)
	Public employees	5-10-46
	Teachers	18-7A-30
personal property	Animals, crops, clothing, appliances, books, household goods, furnishings, musical instruments to $400 per item, $8,000 total	38-10-4(c)
	Burial plot to $25,000, in lieu of homestead	38-10-4(a)
	Health aids	38-10-4(i)
	Jewelry to $1,000	38-10-4(d)
	Lost earnings payments needed for support	38-10-4(k)(5)
	Motor vehicle to $2,400	38-10-4(b)
	Personal injury recoveries to $15,000	38-10-4(k)(4)
	Prepaid higher education tuition trust fund & savings plan payments	38-10-4(k)(6)
	Wrongful death recoveries for person you depended on, needed for support	38-10-4(k)(2)
public benefits	Aid to blind, aged, disabled; general assistance	9-5-1
	Crime victims' compensation	38-10-4(k)(1)
	Social Security	38-10-4(j)(1)
	Unemployment compensation	38-10-4(j)(1)
	Veterans benefits	38-10-4(j)(2)
	Workers' compensation	23-4-18
tools of trade	Implements, books & tools of trade to $1,500	38-10-4(f)
wages	Minimum 30 times the federal minimum hourly wage per week; bankruptcy judge may authorize more for low-income debtors	38-5A-3
wildcard	$800 plus unused portion of homestead or burial exemption, of any property	38-10-4(e)

Wisconsin

Federal bankruptcy exemptions available. All law references are to Wisconsin Statutes Annotated unless otherwise noted.

ASSET	EXEMPTION	LAW
homestead	Property you occupy or intend to occupy to $75,000; $150,000 for married couples filing jointly; sale proceeds exempt for 2 years if you intend to purchase another home (spouses may not double)	815.20
insurance	Federal disability insurance benefits	815.18(3)(ds)
	Fire and casualty insurance (2 years from receipt)	815.18(e)
	Fraternal benefit society benefits	614.96
	Life insurance proceeds for someone debtor depended on, needed for support	815.18(3)(i)(a)
	Life insurance proceeds held in trust by insurer, if clause prohibits proceeds from being used to pay beneficiary's creditors	632.42
	Unmatured life insurance contract (except credit insurance contract) if debtor owns contract & insured is debtor or dependents, or someone debtor is dependent on	815.18(3)(f)
	Unmatured life insurance contract's accrued dividends, interest, or loan value to $150,000 total, if debtor owns contract & insured is debtor or dependents, or someone debtor is dependent on (to $4,000 if issued less than 2 years prior)	815.18(3)(f)
miscellaneous	Alimony, child support needed for support	815.18(3)(c)
	Property of business partnership	178.21(3)(c)
pensions	Tax-exempt retirement accounts, including 401(k)s, 403(b)s, profit-sharing and money purchase plans, SEP and SIMPLE IRAs, and defined-benefit plans	11 U.S.C. § 522(b)(3)(C)
	Traditional and Roth IRAs to $1,283,025 per person	11 U.S.C. § 522 (b)(3)(C); (n)
	Certain municipal employees	62.63(4)
	Firefighters, police officers who worked in city with population over 100,000	815.18(3)(ef)
	Military pensions	815.18(3)(n)
	Private or public retirement benefits	815.18(3)(j)
	Public employees	40.08(1)
personal property	Burial plot, tombstone, coffin	815.18(3)(a)
	College savings account or tuition trust fund	815.18(3)(o)(p)
	Deposit accounts to $5,000	815.18(3)(o)(p)
	Fire & casualty proceeds for destroyed exempt property for 2 years from receiving	815.18(3)(e)
	Household goods & furnishings, clothing, keepsakes, jewelry, appliances, books, musical instruments, firearms, sporting goods, animals & other tangible personal property to $12,000 total	815.18(3)(d)
	Lost future earnings recoveries, needed for support	815.18(3)(i)(d)
	Motor vehicles to $4,000; unused portion of $12,000 personal property exemption may be added	815.18(3)(g)
	Personal injury recoveries to $50,000	815.18(3)(i)(c)
	Tenant's lease or stock interest in housing co-op, to homestead amount	182.004(6)
	Wages used to purchase savings bonds	20.921(1)(e)
	Wrongful death recoveries, needed for support	815.18(3)(i)(b)
public benefits	Crime victims' compensation	949.07
	Social services payments	49.96
	Unemployment compensation	108.13
	Veterans benefits	45.03(8)(b)
	Workers' compensation	102.27
tools of trade	Equipment, inventory, farm products, books & tools of trade to $15,000 total	815.18(3)(b)

wages	75% of weekly net income or 30 times the greater of the federal or state minimum hourly wage; bankruptcy judge may authorize more for low-income debtors	815.18(3)(h)
	Wages of county jail prisoners	303.08(3)
	Wages of county work camp prisoners	303.10(7)
	Wages of inmates under work-release plan	303.065(4)(b)
wildcard	None	

Wyoming

Federal bankruptcy exemptions not available. All law references are to Wyoming Statutes Annotated unless otherwise noted.

ASSET	EXEMPTION	LAW
homestead	Property held as tenancy by the entirety may be exempt against debts owed by only one spouse	*In re Anselmi*, 52 B.R. 479 (D. Wy. 1985)
	Real property or a house trailer you occupy to $20,000	1-20-101; 102; 104
	Spouse or child of deceased owner may claim homestead exemption	1-20-103
insurance	Annuity contract proceeds to $350 per month	26-15-132
	Disability benefits if clause prohibits proceeds from being used to pay beneficiary's creditors	26-15-130
	Fraternal benefit society benefits	26-29-218
	Group life or disability policy or proceeds, cash surrender & loan values, premiums waived & dividends	26-15-131
	Individual life insurance policy proceeds, cash surrender & loan values, premiums waived & dividends	26-15-129
	Life insurance proceeds held by insurer, if clause prohibits proceeds from being used to pay beneficiary's creditors	26-15-133
miscellaneous	Liquor licenses & malt beverage permits	12-4-604
pensions	Tax-exempt retirement accounts, including 401(k)s, 403(b)s, profit-sharing and money purchase plans, SEP and SIMPLE IRAs, and defined-benefit plans	11 U.S.C. § 522(b)(3)(C)
	Traditional and Roth IRAs to $1,283,025 per person	11 U.S.C. § 522 (b)(3)(C); (n)
	Criminal investigators, highway officers	9-3-620
	Firefighters' death benefits	15-5-209
	Game & fish wardens	9-3-620
	Police officers	15-5-313(c)
	Private or public retirement funds & accounts including IRAs, Roth IRAs and SFP IRAs	1-20-110
	Public employees	9-3-426
personal property	Bedding, furniture, household articles & food to $4,000 per person in the home	1-20-106(a)(iii)
	Bible, schoolbooks & pictures	1-20-106(a)(i)
	Burial plot	1-20-106(a)(ii)
	Clothing & wedding rings to $2,000	1-20-105
	Medical savings account contributions	1-20-111
	Motor vehicle to $5,000	1-20-106(a)(iv)
	3 firearms and ammunition (1,000 rounds per firearm) to $3,000	1-20-106(a)(v)
	Prepaid funeral contracts	26-32-102
public benefits	Crime victims' compensation	1-40-113
	General assistance	42-2-113(b)
	Unemployment compensation	27-3-319
	Workers' compensation	27-14-702
tools of trade	Library & implements of profession to $4,000 or tools, motor vehicle, implements, team & stock in trade to $4,000	1-20-106(b)
wages	Earnings of National Guard members	19-9-401
	Minimum 75% of disposable weekly earnings or 30 times the federal hourly minimum wage, whichever is more	1-15-511; 1-15-408; 40-14-505
	Wages of inmates in adult community corrections program	7-18-114
	Wages of inmates in correctional industries program	25-13-107
	Wages of inmates on work release	7-18-308
wildcard	None	

Federal Bankruptcy Exemptions

Spouses filing jointly may double all exemptions. All references are to 11 U.S.C. § 522. These exemptions were last adjusted in 2016. Every three years ending on April 1, these amounts will be adjusted to reflect changes in the Consumer Price Index. Debtors in the following states may select the federal bankruptcy exemptions:

Alaska	Kentucky	New Jersey	Rhode Island
Arkansas	Massachusetts	New Mexico	Texas
Connecticut	Michigan	New York	Vermont
District of Columbia	Minnesota	Oregon	Washington
Hawaii	New Hampshire	Pennsylvania	Wisconsin

ASSET	EXEMPTION	SUBSECTION
homestead	Real property, including co-op or mobile home, or burial plot to $23,675; unused portion of homestead to $11,850 may be applied to any property	(d)(1); (d)(5)
insurance	Disability, illness, or unemployment benefits	(d)(10)(C)
	Life insurance payments from policy for person you depended on, needed for support	(d)(11)(C)
	Life insurance policy with loan value, in accrued dividends or interest, to $12,625	(d)(8)
	Unmatured life insurance contract, except credit insurance policy	(d)(7)
miscellaneous	Alimony, child support needed for support	(d)(10)(D)
pensions	Tax exempt retirement accounts (including 401(k)s, 403(b)s, profit-sharing and money purchase plans, SEP and SIMPLE IRAs, and defined-benefit plans)	(b)(3)(C)
	IRAs and Roth IRAs to $1,283,025 per person	(b)(3)(C)(n)
personal property	Animals, crops, clothing, appliances, books, furnishings, household goods, musical instruments to $600 per item, $12,625 total	(d)(3)
	Health aids	(d)(9)
	Jewelry to $1,600	(d)(4)
	Lost earnings payments	(d)(11)(E)
	Motor vehicle to $3,775	(d)(2)
	Personal injury recoveries to $23,675 (not to include pain & suffering or pecuniary loss)	(d)(11)(D)
	Wrongful death recoveries for person you depended on	(d)(11)(B)
public benefits	Crime victims' compensation	(d)(11)(A)
	Public assistance	(d)(10)(A)
	Social Security	(d)(10)(A)
	Unemployment compensation	(d)(10)(A)
	Veterans benefits	(d)(10)(A)
tools of trade	Implements, books & tools of trade to $2,375	(d)(6)
wages	None	
wildcard	$1,250 of any property	(d)(5)
	Up to $11,850 of unused homestead exemption amount, for any property	(d)(5)

Federal Nonbankruptcy Exemptions

These exemptions are available only if you select your state exemptions. You may use them for any exemptions in addition to those allowed by your state, but they cannot be claimed if you file using federal bankruptcy exemptions. All law references are to the United States Code.

ASSET	EXEMPTION	LAW
death & disability benefits	Government employees	5 § 8130
	Longshoremen & harbor workers	33 § 916
	War risk, hazard, death, or injury compensation	42 § 1717
miscellaneous	Debts of seaman incurred while on a voyage	46 § 11111
	Indian lands or homestead sales or lease proceeds	25 § 410; 412a
	Klamath Indian tribe benefits for Indians residing in Oregon; agricultural or grazing lands to $5,000	25 §§ 543; 545
	Life insurance benefits for serviceman's Group Life Ins. or Veteran's Group Life Ins.	38 § 1970(g)
	Military deposits in savings accounts while on permanent duty outside U.S.	10 § 1035
	Military group life insurance	38 § 1970(g)
	Railroad workers' unemployment insurance	45 § 352(e)
	Seamen's clothing	46 § 11110
	Seamen's wages (except for spousal and child support)	46 § 11109
	Minimum 75% of disposable weekly earnings or 30 times the federal minimum hourly wage, whichever is more; bankruptcy judge may authorize more for low-income debtors	15 § 1673
retirement	CIA employees	50 § 403
	Civil service employees	5 § 8346
	Foreign Service employees	22 § 4060
	Military Medal of Honor roll pensions	38 § 1562(c)
	Military service employees	10 § 1440
	Railroad workers	45 § 231m
	Social Security	42 § 407
	Veterans benefits	38 § 5301
survivors benefits	Judges, U.S. court & judicial center directors, administrative assistants to U.S. Supreme Court Chief Justice	28 § 376
	Lighthouse workers	33 § 775
	Military service	10 § 1450

Charts and Worksheets

Download Worksheets, Get Updates, and More Online

You can download the worksheets in this appendix at:

www.nolo.com/back-of-book/FIBA.html

You'll find other useful information there, too, including legal updates and author blogs.

Median Family Income Chart (Effective May 1, 2017)			
State	Family Size		
	1 Earner	2 People	3 People	4 People *
Alabama	$43,476	$52,970	$60,367	$70,940
Alaska	$62,326	$85,281	$86,944	$97,831
Arizona	$46,779	$58,684	$62,227	$72,052
Arkansas	$39,265	$48,602	$55,175	$67,486
California	$52,416	$70,245	$75,160	$84,059
Colorado	$55,858	$72,037	$81,496	$95,117
Connecticut	$62,929	$80,974	$91,867	$113,409
Delaware	$51,703	$68,041	$77,862	$93,811
DC	$51,907	$99,046	$99,046	$113,478
Florida	$44,576	$55,344	$60,636	$72,382
Georgia	$43,274	$56,301	$62,483	$73,202
Hawaii	$61,057	$73,656	$85,099	$98,059
Idaho	$46,779	$55,532	$57,240	$71,195
Illinois	$50,765	$66,487	$76,406	$91,216
Indiana	$46,412	$57,558	$66,148	$77,566
Iowa	$47,147	$63,760	$70,989	$83,522
Kansas	$47,591	$63,327	$72,981	$83,528
Kentucky	$42,589	$51,524	$57,696	$72,863
Louisiana	$43,063	$53,080	$59,303	$71,957
Maine	$48,842	$60,398	$67,690	$81,950
Maryland	$63,401	$81,507	$92,819	$112,685
Massachusetts	$61,102	$76,414	$93,755	$113,651
Michigan	$47,088	$57,366	$68,192	$82,985
Minnesota	$52,785	$70,889	$85,033	$101,762
Mississippi	$37,051	$46,712	$50,614	$61,182
Missouri	$44,994	$57,288	$65,260	$81,172

* Add $8,400 for each individual in excess of 4.

Median Family Income Chart (Effective May 1, 2017) (continued)

State	Family Size			
	1 Earner	2 People	3 People	4 People *
Montana	$47,675	$58,348	$64,970	$79,929
Nebraska	$47,071	$66,165	$71,939	$83,719
Nevada	$47,057	$61,609	$61,983	$72,918
New Hampshire	$62,357	$75,367	$89,188	$108,702
New Jersey	$62,933	$75,305	$93,656	$114,886
New Mexico	$43,104	$57,704	$57,704	$60,256
New York	$51,408	$66,056	$75,870	$91,998
North Carolina	$42,946	$55,722	$64,521	$72,830
North Dakota	$53,523	$71,100	$81,166	$96,473
Ohio	$46,242	$57,938	$68,361	$83,040
Oklahoma	$43,986	$56,532	$61,386	$69,061
Oregon	$50,333	$61,553	$70,877	$80,170
Pennsylvania	$51,138	$61,271	$75,018	$90,821
Rhode Island	$50,318	$68,303	$77,079	$100,468
South Carolina	$43,256	$55,598	$61,453	$71,876
South Dakota	$42,245	$63,684	$66,535	$81,509
Tennessee	$43,270	$53,887	$60,042	$69,160
Texas	$46,709	$61,704	$65,713	$76,842
Utah	$56,638	$62,903	$71,047	$79,710
Vermont	$54,121	$67,202	$80,415	$92,951
Virginia	$56,456	$71,871	$82,395	$97,731
Washington	$59,154	$72,460	$79,754	$92,727
West Virginia	$45,401	$48,325	$56,781	$71,399
Wisconsin	$48,407	$62,914	$76,179	$89,245
Wyoming	$59,974	$71,971	$80,219	$82,871

* Add $8,400 for each individual in excess of 4.

Median Family Income Chart (Effective May 1, 2017) (continued)				
Commonwealth or U.S. Territory	Family Size			
	1 Earner	2 People	3 People	4 People *
Guam	$40,152	$48,008	$54,708	$66,204
Northern Mariana Islands	$26,964	$26,964	$31,370	$46,139
Puerto Rico	$23,758	$23,758	$23,758	$29,502
Virgin Islands	$31,857	$38,288	$40,824	$44,725

* Add $8,400 for each individual in excess of 4.

Worksheet A: Current Monthly Income

Use this worksheet to calculate your current monthly income; use figures for you and your spouse if you plan to file jointly.

Line 1. Calculate your total income over the last six months before any deductions from wages, salary, tips, bonuses, overtime, and so on.

A.	Month 1	$ _____
B.	Month 2	_____
C.	Month 3	_____
D.	Month 4	_____
E.	Month 5	_____
F.	Month 6	_____
G.	TOTAL WAGES (add Lines 1A–1F)	$ _____

Line 2. Add up all other income for the last six months.

A.	Net business, profession, or farm income	_____
B.	Interest, dividends, and royalties	_____
C.	Net income from rents and real property	_____
D.	Pension and retirement income	_____
E.	Alimony or family support	_____
F.	Spousal contributions (if not filing jointly)	_____
G.	Unemployment compensation	_____
H.	Workers' compensation	_____
I.	State disability insurance	_____
J.	Annuity payments	_____
K.	Other	_____
L.	TOTAL OTHER INCOME (add Lines 2A–2K)	$ _____

Line 3. Calculate total income over the six months prior to filing.

A.	Enter total wages (Line 1G)	_____
B.	Enter total other income (Line 2L)	_____
C.	TOTAL INCOME OVER THE SIX MONTHS PRIOR TO FILING. Add Lines 3A and 3B together.	$ _____

Line 4. Average monthly income over the six months prior to filing. This is called your "current monthly income."

A.	Enter total six-month income (Line 3C).	_____
B.	CURRENT MONTHLY INCOME. Divide Line 4A by 6.	$ _____

Worksheet B: Allowable Monthly Expenses

Use this worksheet to calculate the monthly expenses allowed by the IRS.

Calculate total allowable monthly expenses.

A.	Food, clothing, and so on	$ _____
B.	Transportation	_____
C.	Housing and utilities	_____
D.	Domestic support	_____
E.	Dependent care	_____
F.	Education	_____
G.	Taxes	_____
H.	Mandatory payroll deductions	_____
I.	Insurance	_____
J.	Court-ordered payments	_____
K.	Charitable contributions	_____
L.	Child care	_____
M.	Health care	_____
N.	Communications	_____
O.	Total allowable monthly expenses. Add lines A–N together	$ _____

Current Monthly Income (from Worksheet A, Line 4B). $ _____

Total Allowable Monthly Expenses (from Line O above).   _____

Net monthly income. $ _____

- If net monthly income is less than $124.50, you have passed the means test and you do not need to continue.

- If net monthly income is $124.50 or more, complete Worksheet C.

Worksheet C: Monthly Disposable Income

Use this worksheet to find out how much income you would have left over, after paying the IRS expenses calculated in Worksheet B, your secured and priority debts, any arrearages on your secured debts, and the administrative costs associated with a Chapter 13 bankruptcy, to devote to your unsecured, nonpriority debts.

Line 1. Figure out what you would have to pay each month over the next five years on your secured debts.

    A.   Total amount due over the next five years for a mortgage or second deed of trust $ _____

    B.   Total amount due over the next five years on a car note   _____

    C.   Total amount due over the next five years on all other secured debts   _____

    D.   Add Lines 1A–1C together to figure out the total amount you owe on all secured debts for the next five years.   _____

    E.   Divide Line 1D by 60 to determine how much you would have to pay each month on these debts for the next five years.   _____

Line 2. Figure out what you would have to pay each month over the next five years to make up your arrearages (missed payments) on secured debts.

    A.   Total arrearage on mortgage or second deed of trust $ _____

    B.   Total arrearage on car note   _____

    C.   Total arrearage on all other secured debts   _____

    D.   Add Lines 2A–2C together to figure out your total arrearage on secured debts.   _____

    E.   Divide Line 2D by 60 to determine how much you would have to pay each month to pay off these arrearages over the next five years.   _____

Line 3. Figure out how much you will owe on your priority debts for the next five years.

    A.   Back child support and alimony you owe $ _____

    B.   Priority income taxes you owe   _____

    C.   Other priority debts you owe   _____

    D.   Add Lines 3A–3C together to figure out the total priority debt you owe.   _____

    E.   Divide Line 3D by 60 to determine how much you would have to pay each month to pay off these priority debts over the next five years.   _____

Line 4. Calculate the total amount you would have left over each month after paying allowable expenses and the debts you would have to pay in full in a Chapter 13 plan.

A. Enter your current monthly income (from Line 4B on Worksheet A). $ _____

B. Enter your allowable monthly expenses (from Line O) on Worksheet B). _____

C. Subtract Line 4B from Line 4A to calculate your net income, after allowable expenses. _____

D. Enter your total monthly payments for secured debts, arrearages on secured debts, and priority debts (the sum of Lines 1E, 2E, and 3E, above). _____

E. Subtract Line 4D from Line 4C to calculate how much you would have left over each month, after paying your allowable expenses and your monthly payments on the debts you would have to pay in full in a Chapter 13 plan. _____

Line 5. Calculate your monthly disposable income.

A. Enter your leftover monthly income from Line 4E, above. $ _____

B. Multiply Line 5A by the administrative expense multiplier for your judicial district to calculate how much you would have to pay each month for administrative costs. _____

C. MONTHLY DISPOSABLE INCOME. Subtract Line 5B from Line 5A.

$ _____

- If your monthly disposable income (Line 5C) is less than $128.33, you have passed the means test and you do not need to continue.

- If your monthly disposable income (Line 5C) is $128.33 or more, complete Worksheet D.

Worksheet D: The Means Test

Use this worksheet to figure out whether you will be allowed to file for Chapter 7 bankruptcy, or whether you will be limited to Chapter 13.

Line 1. Figure out how much disposable income you will have over the next five years.

    A. Enter your monthly disposable income (from Line 5C of Worksheet C). $ _____

    B. Multiply Line 1A by 60 to calculate your monthly disposable income for the next five years. $ _____

- If Line 1B is more than $12,850, you have failed the means test. Do not continue.

- If Line 1B is less than $7,700, you have passed the means test. Do not continue.

- If Line 1B at least $7,700 but not more than $12,850, continue to Line 2.

Line 2. Add up your unsecured, nonpriority debts.

    A. Back rent $ _____

    B. Medical bills   _____

    C. Alimony and child support   _____

    D. Student loans   _____

    E. Utility bills   _____

    F. Loans from friends or relatives   _____

    G. Health club dues   _____

    H. Lawyer and accountant bills   _____

    I. Union dues   _____

    J. Church or synagogue dues   _____

    K. Money judgments arising out of contract disputes   _____

    L. Money judgments arising out of negligent behavior   _____

M. Deficiency judgments from secured loans   _____

N. Credit and charge card purchases and cash advances   _____

O. Department store credit card purchases   _____

P. Other   _____

Q. TOTAL UNSECURED, NONPRIORITY DEBT.
    Add Lines 2A–2P.   _____

R. Divide Line 2Q by four to calculate 25% of your total unsecured,
    nonpriority debt. $ _____

- If Line 2R is larger than Line 1B, you have passed the means test and you do not need to continue.

- If Line 1B is equal or larger than Line 2R, you have failed the means test unless you can prove special circumstances.

Worksheet E: Personal Property Checklist

Cash on hand (include sources)
- ☐ In your home
- ☐ In your wallet
- ☐ Under your mattress

Deposits of money (include sources)
- ☐ Bank account
- ☐ Brokerage account (with stockbroker)
- ☐ Certificates of deposit (CDs)
- ☐ Credit union deposit
- ☐ Escrow account
- ☐ Money market account
- ☐ Money in a safe deposit box
- ☐ Savings and loan deposit

Security deposits
- ☐ Electric
- ☐ Gas
- ☐ Heating oil
- ☐ Security deposit on a rental unit
- ☐ Prepaid rent
- ☐ Rented furniture or equipment
- ☐ Telephone
- ☐ Water

Household goods, supplies, and furnishings
- ☐ Antiques
- ☐ Appliances
- ☐ Carpentry tools
- ☐ China and crystal
- ☐ Clocks
- ☐ Dishes
- ☐ Food (total value)

- ☐ Furniture (list every item; go from room to room so you don't miss anything)
- ☐ Gardening tools
- ☐ Home computer (for personal use)
- ☐ Iron and ironing board
- ☐ Lamps
- ☐ Lawn mower or tractor
- ☐ Microwave oven
- ☐ Patio or outdoor furniture
- ☐ Radios
- ☐ Rugs
- ☐ Sewing machine
- ☐ Silverware and utensils
- ☐ Small appliances
- ☐ Snow blower
- ☐ Stereo system
- ☐ Telephone and answering machines
- ☐ Televisions
- ☐ Vacuum cleaner
- ☐ Video equipment (VCR, camcorder)

Books, pictures, and other art objects; stamp, coin, and other collections
- ☐ Art prints
- ☐ Bibles
- ☐ Books
- ☐ Coins
- ☐ Collectibles (such as political buttons, baseball cards)
- ☐ Family portraits
- ☐ Figurines
- ☐ Original artworks

- [ ] Photographs
- [ ] Records, CDs, and audiotapes
- [ ] Stamps
- [ ] Videotapes, DVDs

Apparel

- [ ] Clothing
- [ ] Furs

Jewelry

- [ ] Engagement and wedding rings
- [ ] Gems
- [ ] Precious metals
- [ ] Watches

Firearms, sports equipment, and other hobby equipment

- [ ] Board games
- [ ] Bicycle
- [ ] Camera equipment
- [ ] Electronic musical equipment
- [ ] Exercise machine
- [ ] Fishing gear
- [ ] Guns (rifles, pistols, shotguns, and muskets)
- [ ] Model or remote-controlled cars or planes
- [ ] Musical instruments
- [ ] Scuba diving equipment
- [ ] Ski equipment
- [ ] Other sports equipment
- [ ] Other weapons (swords and knives)

Interests in insurance policies

- [ ] Credit insurance
- [ ] Disability insurance
- [ ] Health insurance

- [ ] Homeowners' or renters' insurance
- [ ] Term life insurance
- [ ] Whole life insurance

Annuities

Pension or profit-sharing plans

- [ ] IRA
- [ ] Keogh
- [ ] Pension or retirement plan
- [ ] 401(k) plan

Stock and interests in incorporated and unincorporated companies

Interests in partnerships

- [ ] Limited partnership interest
- [ ] General partnership interest

Government and corporate bonds and other investment instruments

- [ ] Corporate bonds
- [ ] Municipal bonds
- [ ] Promissory notes
- [ ] U.S. savings bonds

Accounts receivable

- [ ] Accounts receivable from business
- [ ] Commissions already earned

Family support

- [ ] Alimony (spousal support, and maintenance) due under court order
- [ ] Child support payments due under court order
- [ ] Payments due under divorce property settlement

Other debts for which the amount owed is known and definite

- ☐ Disability benefits due
- ☐ Disability insurance due
- ☐ Judgments obtained against third parties you haven't yet collected
- ☐ Sick pay earned
- ☐ Social Security benefits due
- ☐ Tax refund due under returns already filed
- ☐ Vacation pay earned
- ☐ Wages due
- ☐ Workers' compensation due

Any special powers that you or another person can exercise for your benefit, other than those listed under "real estate"

- ☐ A right to receive, at some future time, cash, stock, or other personal property placed in an irrevocable trust
- ☐ Current payments of interest or principal from a trust
- ☐ General power of appointment over personal property

An interest in property due to another person's death

- ☐ Any interest as the beneficiary of a living trust, if the trustor has died
- ☐ Expected proceeds from a life insurance policy where the insured has died
- ☐ Inheritance from an existing estate in probate (the owner has died and the court is overseeing the distribution of the property), even if the final amount is not yet known
- ☐ Inheritance under a will that is contingent on one or more events occurring, but only if the owner has died

All other contingent claims and claims where the amount owed you is not known, including tax refunds, counterclaims, and rights to setoff claims (claims you think you have against a person, government, or corporation, but you haven't yet sued on)

- ☐ Claims against a corporation, government entity, or individual
- ☐ Potential tax refund on a return that is not yet filed

Patents, copyrights, and other intellectual property

- ☐ Copyrights
- ☐ Patents
- ☐ Trade secrets
- ☐ Trademarks
- ☐ Trade names

Licenses, franchises, and other general intangibles

- ☐ Building permits
- ☐ Cooperative association holdings
- ☐ Exclusive licenses
- ☐ Liquor licenses
- ☐ Nonexclusive licenses
- ☐ Patent licenses
- ☐ Professional licenses

Automobiles and other vehicles

- ☐ Car
- ☐ Minibike or motor scooter
- ☐ Mobile or motor home, if on wheels
- ☐ Motorcycle
- ☐ Recreational vehicle (RV)
- ☐ Trailer
- ☐ Truck
- ☐ Van

Boats, motors, and accessories

☐ Boat (canoe, kayak, rowboat, shell, sailboat, pontoon, and yacht)

☐ Boat radar, radio, or telephone

☐ Outboard motor

Aircraft and accessories

☐ Aircraft

☐ Aircraft radar, radio, and other accessories

Office equipment, furnishings, and supplies

☐ Artwork in your office

☐ Computers, software, modems, and printers

☐ Copier

☐ Fax machine

☐ Furniture

☐ Rugs

☐ Supplies

☐ Telephones

☐ Typewriters

Machinery, fixtures, equipment, and supplies used in business

☐ Military uniforms and accoutrements

☐ Tools of your trade

Business inventory

Livestock, poultry, and other animals

☐ Birds

☐ Cats

☐ Dogs

☐ Fish and aquarium equipment

☐ Horses

☐ Other pets

☐ Livestock and poultry

Crops—growing or harvested

Farming equipment and implements

Farm supplies, chemicals, and feed

Other personal property of any kind not already listed

☐ Church pew

☐ Health aids (such as a wheelchair or crutches)

☐ Hot tub or portable spa

☐ Season tickets

Anything else

☐ _____

☐ _____

☐ _____

Worksheet F: Property Value Schedule

List the total replacement value of each item in your Personal Property Checklist.

Item	Replacement Value
1. Cash	$ _____
2. Bank accounts	_____
3. Security deposits	_____
4. Household goods and furniture	_____
5. Books, pictures, etc.	_____
6. Clothing	_____
7. Furs and jewelry	_____
8. Sports and hobby equipment	_____
9. Interest in insurance	_____
10. Annuities	_____
11. Pensions and profit-sharing plans	_____
12. Stock and interest in business	_____
13. Interest in partnership and ventures	_____
14. Bonds	_____
15. Accounts receivable	_____
16. Alimony and family support	_____
17. Other liquidated debts, tax refund	_____
18. Future interests and life estates	_____
19. Interests due to another's death	_____
20. Other contingent claims	_____
21. Intellectual property rights	_____
22. Licenses and franchises	_____
23. Vehicles	_____
24. Boats, motors, and accessories	_____
25. Aircraft and accessories	_____
26. Office equipment, furniture, and supplies	_____
27. Machinery, fixtures, etc.	_____
28. Inventory	_____
29. Animals	_____
30. Crops—growing or harvested	_____
31. Farm equipment	_____
32. Farm supplies, chemicals, and feed	_____
33. Anything not listed above	_____
TOTAL	$ _____

Sample Bankruptcy Forms

Fill in this information to identify your case:

United States Bankruptcy Court for the:

EASTERN DISTRICT OF CALIFORNIA

Case number *(if known)* _____

Chapter you are filing under:

■ Chapter 7

☐ Chapter 11

☐ Chapter 12

☐ Chapter 13

☐ Check if this an amended filing

Official Form 101

Voluntary Petition for Individuals Filing for Bankruptcy

12/15

The bankruptcy forms use you and Debtor 1 to refer to a debtor filing alone. A married couple may file a bankruptcy case together—called a *joint case*—and in joint cases, these forms use you to ask for information from both debtors. For example, if a form asks, "Do you own a car," the answer would be yes if either debtor owns a car. When information is needed about the spouses separately, the form uses *Debtor 1* and *Debtor 2* to distinguish between them. In joint cases, one of the spouses must report information as *Debtor 1* and the other as *Debtor 2*. The same person must be *Debtor 1* in all of the forms.

Be as complete and accurate as possible. If two married people are filing together, both are equally responsible for supplying correct information. If more space is needed, attach a separate sheet to this form. On the top of any additional pages, write your name and case number (if known). Answer every question.

Part 1:	Identify Yourself

	About Debtor 1:	About Debtor 2 (Spouse Only in a Joint Case):
1. Your full name Write the name that is on your government-issued picture identification (for example, your driver's license or passport). Bring your picture identification to your meeting with the trustee.	**Carrie** First name **Anne** Middle name **Edwards** Last name and Suffix (Sr., Jr., II, III)	First name Middle name Last name and Suffix (Sr., Jr., II, III)
2. All other names you have used in the last 8 years Include your married or maiden names.		
3. Only the last 4 digits of your Social Security number or federal Individual Taxpayer Identification number (ITIN)	xxx-xx-6287	

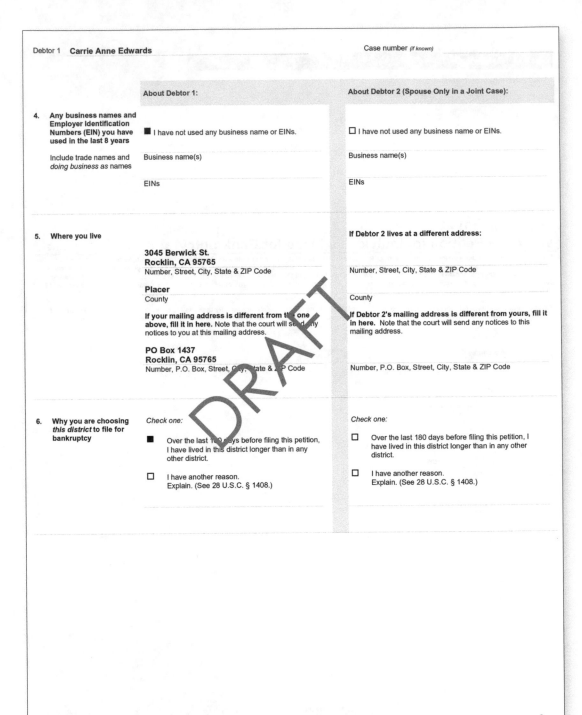

Debtor 1   **Carrie Anne Edwards**

Case number *(if known)*

	About Debtor 1:	About Debtor 2 (Spouse Only in a Joint Case):
4. Any business names and Employer Identification Numbers (EIN) you have used in the last 8 years Include trade names and *doing business as* names	■ I have not used any business name or EINs. Business name(s) EINs	☐ I have not used any business name or EINs. Business name(s) EINs
5. Where you live	**3045 Berwick St.** **Rocklin, CA 95765** Number, Street, City, State & ZIP Code **Placer** County **If your mailing address is different from the one above, fill it in here.** Note that the court will send any notices to you at this mailing address. **PO Box 1437** **Rocklin, CA 95765** Number, P.O. Box, Street, City, State & ZIP Code	**If Debtor 2 lives at a different address:** Number, Street, City, State & ZIP Code County **If Debtor 2's mailing address is different from yours, fill it in here.** Note that the court will send any notices to this mailing address. Number, P.O. Box, Street, City, State & ZIP Code
6. Why you are choosing *this district* to file for bankruptcy	*Check one:* ■ Over the last 180 days before filing this petition, I have lived in this district longer than in any other district. ☐ I have another reason. Explain. (See 28 U.S.C. § 1408.)	*Check one:* ☐ Over the last 180 days before filing this petition, I have lived in this district longer than in any other district. ☐ I have another reason. Explain. (See 28 U.S.C. § 1408.)

Debtor 1	**Carrie Anne Edwards**		Case number *(if known)*

Part 2: **Tell the Court About Your Bankruptcy Case**

7. The chapter of the Bankruptcy Code you are choosing to file under

Check one. (For a brief description of each, see *Notice Required by 11 U.S.C. § 342(b) for Individuals Filing for Bankruptcy (Form 2010)).* Also, go to the top of page 1 and check the appropriate box.

- ■ Chapter 7
- ☐ Chapter 11
- ☐ Chapter 12
- ☐ Chapter 13

8. How you will pay the fee

- ■ **I will pay the entire fee when I file my petition.** Please check with the clerk's office in your local court for more details about how you may pay. Typically, if you are paying the fee yourself, you may pay with cash, cashier's check, or money order. If your attorney is submitting your payment on your behalf, your attorney may pay with a credit card or check with a pre-printed address.
- ☐ **I need to pay the fee in installments.** If you choose this option, sign and attach the *Application for Individuals to Pay The Filing Fee in Installments* (Official Form 103A).
- ☐ **I request that my fee be waived** (You may request this option only if you are filing for Chapter 7. By law, a judge may, but is not required to, waive your fee, and may do so only if your income is less than 150% of the official poverty line that applies to your family size and you are unable to pay the fee in installments). If you choose this option, you must fill out the *Application to Have the Chapter 7 Filing Fee Waived* (Official Form 103B) and file it with your petition.

9. Have you filed for bankruptcy within the last 8 years?

- ■ No.
- ☐ Yes.

District	When	Case number
District	When	Case number
District	When	Case number

10. Are any bankruptcy cases pending or being filed by a spouse who is not filing this case with you, or by a business partner, or by an affiliate?

- ■ No
- ☐ Yes.

Debtor	Relationship to you
District	When	Case number, if known
Debtor	Relationship to you
District	When	Case number, if known

11. Do you rent your residence?

- ■ No. Go to line 12.
- ☐ Yes. Has your landlord obtained an eviction judgment against you and do you want to stay in your residence?
  - ☐ No. Go to line 12.
  - ☐ Yes. Fill out *Initial Statement About an Eviction Judgment Against You* (Form 101A) and file it with this bankruptcy petition.

Official Form 101   **Voluntary Petition for Individuals Filing for Bankruptcy**   page 3

Debtor 1   **Carrie Anne Edwards**   Case number *(if known)*

Part 3:   **Report About Any Businesses You Own as a Sole Proprietor**

12. Are you a sole proprietor of any full- or part-time business?

■ No.   Go to Part 4.

☐ Yes.   Name and location of business

A sole proprietorship is a business you operate as an individual, and is not a separate legal entity such as a corporation, partnership, or LLC.

Name of business, if any

If you have more than one sole proprietorship, use a separate sheet and attach it to this petition.

Number, Street, City, State & ZIP Code

Check the appropriate box to describe your business:

☐   Health Care Business (as defined in 11 U.S.C. § 101(27A))

☐   Single Asset Real Estate (as defined in 11 U.S.C. § 101(51B))

☐   Stockbroker (as defined in 11 U.S.C. § 101(53A))

☐   Commodity Broker (as defined in 11 U.S.C. § 101(6))

☐   None of the above

13. Are you filing under Chapter 11 of the Bankruptcy Code and are you a *small business debtor*?

If you are filing under Chapter 11, the court must know whether you are a small business debtor so that it can set appropriate deadlines. If you indicate that you are a small business debtor, you must attach your most recent balance sheet, statement of operations, cash-flow statement, and federal income tax return or if any of these documents do not exist, follow the procedure in 11 U.S.C. 1116(1)(B).

For a definition of *small business debtor*, see 11 U.S.C. § 101(51D).

■ No.   I am not filing under Chapter 11.

☐ No.   I am filing under Chapter 11, but I am NOT a small business debtor according to the definition in the Bankruptcy Code.

☐ Yes.   I am filing under Chapter 11 and I am a small business debtor according to the definition in the Bankruptcy Code.

Part 4:   **Report if You Own or Have Any Hazardous Property or Any Property That Needs Immediate Attention**

14. Do you own or have any property that poses or is alleged to pose a threat of imminent and identifiable hazard to public health or safety? Or do you own any property that needs immediate attention?

■ No.

☐ Yes.   What is the hazard?

If immediate attention is needed, why is it needed?

For example, do you own perishable goods, or livestock that must be fed, or a building that needs urgent repairs?

Where is the property?

Number, Street, City, State & Zip Code

Debtor 1   **Carrie Anne Edwards**   Case number *(if known)*

Part 5:	Explain Your Efforts to Receive a Briefing About Credit Counseling

About Debtor 1:

About Debtor 2 (Spouse Only in a Joint Case):

15. Tell the court whether you have received a briefing about credit counseling.

The law requires that you receive a briefing about credit counseling before you file for bankruptcy. You must truthfully check one of the following choices. If you cannot do so, you are not eligible to file.

If you file anyway, the court can dismiss your case, you will lose whatever filing fee you paid, and your creditors can begin collection activities again.

You must check one:

☑ **I received a briefing from an approved credit counseling agency within the 180 days before I filed this bankruptcy petition, and I received a certificate of completion.**

Attach a copy of the certificate and the payment plan, if any, that you developed with the agency.

☐ **I received a briefing from an approved credit counseling agency within the 180 days before I filed this bankruptcy petition, but I do not have a certificate of completion.**

Within 14 days after you file this bankruptcy petition, you MUST file a copy of the certificate and payment plan, if any.

☐ **I certify that I asked for credit counseling services from an approved agency, but was unable to obtain those services during the 7 days after I made my request, and exigent circumstances merit a 30-day temporary waiver of the requirement.**

To ask for a 30-day temporary waiver of the requirement, attach a separate sheet explaining what efforts you made to obtain the briefing, why you were unable to obtain it before you filed for bankruptcy, and what exigent circumstances required you to file this case.

Your case may be dismissed if the court is dissatisfied with your reasons for not receiving a briefing before you filed for bankruptcy. If the court is satisfied with your reasons, you must still receive a briefing within 30 days after you file. You must file a certificate from the approved agency, along with a copy of the payment plan you developed, if any. If you do not do so, your case may be dismissed.

Any extension of the 30-day deadline is granted only for cause and is limited to a maximum of 15 days.

☐ **I am not required to receive a briefing about credit counseling because of:**

     ☐ **Incapacity.**
         I have a mental illness or a mental deficiency that makes me incapable of realizing or making rational decisions about finances.

     ☐ **Disability.**
         My physical disability causes me to be unable to participate in a briefing in person, by phone, or through the internet, even after I reasonably tried to do so.

     ☐ **Active duty.**
         I am currently on active military duty in a military combat zone.

If you believe you are not required to receive a briefing about credit counseling, you must file a motion for waiver credit counseling with the court.

You must check one:

☐ **I received a briefing from an approved credit counseling agency within the 180 days before I filed this bankruptcy petition, and I received a certificate of completion.**

Attach a copy of the certificate and the payment plan, if any, that you developed with the agency.

☐ **I received a briefing from an approved credit counseling agency within the 180 days before I filed this bankruptcy petition, but I do not have a certificate of completion.**

Within 14 days after you file this bankruptcy petition, you MUST file a copy of the certificate and payment plan, if any.

☐ **I certify that I asked for credit counseling services from an approved agency, but was unable to obtain those services during the 7 days after I made my request, and exigent circumstances merit a 30-day temporary waiver of the requirement.**

To ask for a 30-day temporary waiver of the requirement, attach a separate sheet explaining what efforts you made to obtain it before you filed for bankruptcy, and what exigent circumstances required you to file this case.

Your case may be dismissed if the court is dissatisfied with your reasons for not receiving a briefing before you filed for bankruptcy.

If the court is satisfied with your reasons, you must still receive a briefing within 30 days after you file. You must file a certificate from the approved agency, along with a copy of the payment plan you developed, if any. If you do not do so, your case may be dismissed.

Any extension of the 30-day deadline is granted only for cause and is limited to a maximum of 15 days.

☐ **I am not required to receive a briefing about credit counseling because of:**

     ☐ **Incapacity.**
         I have a mental illness or a mental deficiency that makes me incapable of realizing or making rational decisions about finances.

     ☐ **Disability.**
         My physical disability causes me to be unable to participate in a briefing in person, by phone, or through the internet, even after I reasonably tried to do so.

     ☐ **Active duty.**
         I am currently on active military duty in a military combat zone.

If you believe you are not required to receive a briefing about credit counseling, you must file a motion for waiver of credit counseling with the court.

Official Form 101   **Voluntary Petition for Individuals Filing for Bankruptcy**   page 5

Debtor 1 **Carrie Anne Edwards**   Case number *(if known)*

Part 6:	Answer These Questions for Reporting Purposes

16. What kind of debts do you have?

16a. **Are your debts primarily consumer debts?** *Consumer debts* are defined in 11 U.S.C. § 101(8) as "incurred by an individual primarily for a personal, family, or household purpose."

☐ No. Go to line 16b.

■ Yes. Go to line 17.

16b. **Are your debts primarily business debts?** *Business debts* are debts that you incurred to obtain money for a business or investment or through the operation of the business or investment.

☐ No. Go to line 16c.

☐ Yes. Go to line 17.

16c. State the type of debts you owe that are not consumer debts or business debts

17. Are you filing under Chapter 7?

☐ No. I am not filing under Chapter 7. Go to line 18.

Do you estimate that after any exempt property is excluded and administrative expenses are paid that funds will be available for distribution to unsecured creditors?

■ Yes. I am filing under Chapter 7. Do you estimate that after any exempt property is excluded and administrative expenses are paid that funds will be available to distribute to unsecured creditors?

■ No

☐ Yes

18. How many Creditors do you estimate that you owe?

■ 1-49
☐ 50-99
☐ 100-199
☐ 200-999

☐ 1,000-5,000
☐ 5,001-10,000
☐ 10,001-25,000

☐ 25,001-50,000
☐ 50,001-100,000
☐ More than 100,000

19. How much do you estimate your assets to be worth?

☐ $0 - $50,000
☐ $50,001 - $100,000
■ $100,001 - $500,000
☐ $500,001 - $1 million

☐ $1,000,001 - $10 million
☐ $10,000,001 - $50 million
☐ $50,000,001 - $100 million
☐ $100,000,001 - $500 million

☐ $500,000,001 - $1 billion
☐ $1,000,000,001 - $10 billion
☐ $10,000,000,001 - $50 billion
☐ More than $50 billion

20. How much do you estimate your liabilities to be?

☐ $0 - $50,000
☐ $50,001 - $100,000
■ $100,001 - $500,000
☐ $500,001 - $1 million

☐ $1,000,001 - $10 million
☐ $10,000,001 - $50 million
☐ $50,000,001 - $100 million
☐ $100,000,001 - $500 million

☐ $500,000,001 - $1 billion
☐ $1,000,000,001 - $10 billion
☐ $10,000,000,001 - $50 billion
☐ More than $50 billion

Part 7:	Sign Below

For you

I have examined this petition, and I declare under penalty of perjury that the information provided is true and correct.

If I have chosen to file under Chapter 7, I am aware that I may proceed, if eligible, under Chapter 7, 11, 12, or 13 of title 11, United States Code. I understand the relief available under each chapter, and I choose to proceed under Chapter 7.

If no attorney represents me and I did not pay or agree to pay someone who is not an attorney to help me fill out this document, I have obtained and read the notice required by 11 U.S.C. § 342(b).

I request relief in accordance with the chapter of title 11, United States Code, specified in this petition.

I understand making a false statement, concealing property, or obtaining money or property by fraud in connection with a bankruptcy case can result in fines up to $250,000, or imprisonment for up to 20 years, or both. 18 U.S.C. §§ 152, 1341, 1519, and 3571.

/s/ Carrie Anne Edwards

Carrie Anne Edwards
Signature of Debtor 1

Signature of Debtor 2

Executed on **September 1, 2017**
            MM / DD / YYYY

Executed on
            MM / DD / YYYY

Debtor 1   **Carrie Anne Edwards**   Case number *(if known)*

For your attorney, if you are represented by one	I, the attorney for the debtor(s) named in this petition, declare that I have informed the debtor(s) about eligibility to proceed under Chapter 7, 11, 12, or 13 of title 11, United States Code, and have explained the relief available under each chapter for which the person is eligible. I also certify that I have delivered to the debtor(s) the notice required by 11 U.S.C. § 342(b) and, in a case in which § 707(b)(4)(D) applies, certify that I have no knowledge after an inquiry that the information in the schedules filed with the petition is incorrect.
If you are not represented by an attorney, you do not need to file this page.	

Date   **September 1, 2017**

Signature of Attorney for Debtor   MM / DD / YYYY

Printed name

Firm name

Number, Street, City, State & ZIP Code

Contact phone   Email address

Bar number & State

Debtor 1   **Carrie Anne Edwards**   Case number *(if known)*

For you if you are filing this bankruptcy without an attorney **If you are represented by an attorney, you do not need to file this page.**	The law allows you, as an individual, to represent yourself in bankruptcy court, but **you should understand that many people find it extremely difficult to represent themselves successfully. Because bankruptcy has long-term financial and legal consequences, you are strongly urged to hire a qualified attorney.** To be successful, you must correctly file and handle your bankruptcy case. The rules are very technical, and a mistake or inaction may affect your rights. For example, your case may be dismissed because you did not file a required document, pay a fee on time, attend a meeting or hearing, or cooperate with the court, case trustee, U.S. trustee, bankruptcy administrator, or audit firm if your case is selected for audit. If that happens, you could lose your right to file another case, or you may lose protections, including the benefit of the automatic stay. You must list all your property and debts in the schedules that you are required to file with the court. Even if you plan to pay a particular debt outside of your bankruptcy, you must list that debt in your schedules. If you do not list a debt, the debt may not be discharged. If you do not list property or properly claim it as exempt, you may not be able to keep the property. The judge can also deny you a discharge of all your debts if you do something dishonest in your bankruptcy case, such as destroying or hiding property, falsifying records, or lying. Individual bankruptcy cases are randomly audited to determine if debtors have been accurate, truthful, and complete. **Bankruptcy fraud is a serious crime; you could be fined and imprisoned.** If you decide to file without an attorney, the court expects you to follow the rules as if you had hired an attorney. The court will not treat you differently because you are filing for yourself. To be successful, you must be familiar with the United States Bankruptcy Code, the Federal Rules of Bankruptcy Procedure, and the local rules of the court in which your case is filed. You must also be familiar with any state exemption laws that apply.

Are you aware that filing for bankruptcy is a serious action with long-term financial and legal consequences?

☐ No

■ Yes

Are you aware that bankruptcy fraud is a serious crime and that if your bankruptcy forms are inaccurate or incomplete, you could be fined or imprisoned?

☐ No

■ Yes

Did you pay or agree to pay someone who is not an attorney to help you fill out your bankruptcy forms?

■ No

☐ Yes   Name of Person

Attach *Bankruptcy Petition Preparer's Notice, Declaration, and Signature* (Official Form 119).

By signing here, I acknowledge that I understand the risks involved in filing without an attorney. I have read and understood this notice, and I am aware that filing a bankruptcy case without an attorney may cause me to lose my rights or property if I do not properly handle the case.

/s/ Carrie Anne Edwards	
Carrie Anne Edwards	Signature of Debtor 2
Signature of Debtor 1	
Date **September 1, 2017**	Date
MM / DD / YYYY	MM / DD / YYYY
Contact phone	Contact phone
Cell phone	Cell phone
Email address	Email address

Fill in this information to identify your case:

Debtor 1	**Carrie Anne Edwards**		
	First Name	Middle Name	Last Name
Debtor 2			
(Spouse if, filing)	First Name	Middle Name	Last Name

United States Bankruptcy Court for the: EASTERN DISTRICT OF CALIFORNIA

Case number
(if known)

☐ Check if this is an amended filing

Official Form 106Sum
Summary of Your Assets and Liabilities and Certain Statistical Information   12/15

Be as complete and accurate as possible. If two married people are filing together, both are equally responsible for supplying correct information. Fill out all of your schedules first; then complete the information on this form. If you are filing amended schedules after you file your original forms, you must fill out a new *Summary* and check the box at the top of this page.

Part 1:   Summarize Your Assets

		Your assets Value of what you own
1.	**Schedule A/B: Property** (Official Form 106A/B)	
	1a. Copy line 55, Total real estate, from Schedule A/B	$ 130,000.00
	1b. Copy line 62, Total personal property, from Schedule A/B	$ 65,125.00
	1c. Copy line 63, Total of all property on Schedule A/B	$ 195,125.00

Part 2:   Summarize Your Liabilities

		Your liabilities Amount you owe
2.	*Schedule D: Creditors Who Have Claims Secured by Property* (Official Form 106D)	
	2a. Copy the total you listed in Column A, *Amount of claim*, at the bottom of the last page of Part 1 of *Schedule D*...	$ 169,300.00
3.	*Schedule E/F: Creditors Who Have Unsecured Claims* (Official Form 106E/F)	
	3a. Copy the total claims from Part 1 (priority unsecured claims) from line 6e of *Schedule E/F*	$ 7,500.00
	3b. Copy the total claims from Part 2 (nonpriority unsecured claims) from line 6j of *Schedule E/F*	$ 80,815.00
	Your total liabilities	$ 257,615.00

Part 3:   Summarize Your Income and Expenses

4.	*Schedule I: Your Income* (Official Form 106I) Copy your combined monthly income from line 12 of *Schedule I*	$ 4,721.00
5.	*Schedule J: Your Expenses* (Official Form 106J) Copy your monthly expenses from line 22c of *Schedule J*	$ 4,689.00

Part 4:   Answer These Questions for Administrative and Statistical Records

6. **Are you filing for bankruptcy under Chapters 7, 11, or 13?**

   ☐ No. You have nothing to report on this part of the form. Check this box and submit this form to the court with your other schedules.

   ■ Yes

7. **What kind of debt do you have?**

   ■ **Your debts are primarily consumer debts.** *Consumer debts* are those "incurred by an individual primarily for a personal, family, or household purpose." 11 U.S.C. § 101(8). Fill out lines 8-9g for statistical purposes. 28 U.S.C. § 159.

   ☐ **Your debts are not primarily consumer debts.** You have nothing to report on this part of the form. *Check this box* and submit this form to the court with your other schedules.

Official Form 106Sum   **Summary of Your Assets and Liabilities and Certain Statistical Information**   page 1 of 2

Debtor 1   **Carrie Anne Edwards**   Case number *(if known)* _____

8.   From the *Statement of Your Current Monthly Income*: Copy your total current monthly income from Official Form 122A-1 Line 11; **OR**, Form 122B Line 11; **OR**, Form 122C-1 Line 14. $ **5,676.00**

9.   **Copy the following special categories of claims from Part 4, line 6 of *Schedule E/F*:**

From Part 4 on *Schedule E/F*, copy the following:	Total claim
9a. Domestic support obligations (Copy line 6a.)	$ 4,500.00
9b. Taxes and certain other debts you owe the government. (Copy line 6b.)	$ 3,000.00
9c. Claims for death or personal injury while you were intoxicated. (Copy line 6c.)	$ 0.00
9d. Student loans. (Copy line 6f.)	$ 10,000.00
9e. Obligations arising out of a separation agreement or divorce that you did not report as priority claims. (Copy line 6g.)	$ 0.00
9f. Debts to pension or profit-sharing plans, and other similar debts. (Copy line 6h.)	+$ 0.00

9g. **Total.** Add lines 9a through 9f. $ **17,500.00**

Fill in this information to identify your case and this filing:

Debtor 1	**Carrie Anne Edwards**		
	First Name	Middle Name	Last Name
Debtor 2			
(Spouse, if filing)	First Name	Middle Name	Last Name

United States Bankruptcy Court for the: EASTERN DISTRICT OF CALIFORNIA

Case number _____

☐ Check if this is an amended filing

Official Form 106A/B
Schedule A/B: Property
12/15

In each category, separately list and describe items. List an asset only once. If an asset fits in more than one category, list the asset in the category where you think it fits best. Be as complete and accurate as possible. If two married people are filing together, both are equally responsible for supplying correct information. If more space is needed, attach a separate sheet to this form. On the top of any additional pages, write your name and case number (if known). Answer every question.

Part 1: Describe Each Residence, Building, Land, or Other Real Estate You Own or Have an Interest In

1. Do you own or have any legal or equitable interest in any residence, building, land, or similar property?

☐ No. Go to Part 2.

■ Yes. Where is the property?

1.1

045 Berwick St.
Street address, if available, or other description

Rocklin   CA   95765-0000
City   State   ZIP Code

Placer
County

What is the property? Check all that apply

■ Single-family home
☐ Duplex or multi-unit building
☐ Condominium or cooperative
☐ Manufactured or mobile home
☐ Land
☐ Investment property
☐ Timeshare
☐ Other _____

Who has an interest in the property? Check one

■ Debtor 1 only
☐ Debtor 2 only
☐ Debtor 1 and Debtor 2 only
☐ At least one of the debtors and another

Do not deduct secured claims or exemptions. Put the amount of any secured claims on *Schedule D: Creditors Who Have Claims Secured by Property.*

Current value of the entire property?	Current value of the portion you own?
$130,000.00	**$130,000.00**

Describe the nature of your ownership interest (such as fee simple, tenancy by the entireties, or a life estate), if known.

Fee simple

☐ Check if this is community property (see instructions)

Other information you wish to add about this item, such as local property identification number:

Residence is in foreclosure. Sale of property has been scheduled for July 19, 20xx. I am still living in the house and am hoping to modify the mortgage.

2. Add the dollar value of the portion you own for all of your entries from Part 1, including any entries for pages you have attached for Part 1. Write that number here...=>

$130,000.00

Part 2: Describe Your Vehicles

Do you own, lease, or have legal or equitable interest in any vehicles, whether they are registered or not? Include any vehicles you own that someone else drives. If you lease a vehicle, also report it on *Schedule G: Executory Contracts and Unexpired Leases.*

Debtor 1   **Carrie Anne Edwards**   Case number *(if known)* _____

3. Cars, vans, trucks, tractors, sport utility vehicles, motorcycles

☐ No
☑ Yes

3.1 Make: **Toyota**

Model: **Camry**

Year: **2014**

Approximate mileage: **45,000**

Other information:

Fully loaded, good condition (fair market value - nada.com) Location: 3045 Berwick St., Rocklin, CA

Who has an interest in the property? Check one

☑ Debtor 1 only
☐ Debtor 2 only
☐ Debtor 1 and Debtor 2 only
☐ At least one of the debtors and another

☐ Check if this is community property (see instructions)

Do not deduct secured claims or exemptions. Put the amount of any secured claims on *Schedule D: Creditors Who Have Claims Secured by Property.*

Current value of the entire property? **Current value of the portion you own?**

$14,075.00   **$14,075.00**

4. Watercraft, aircraft, motor homes, ATVs and other recreational vehicles, other vehicles, and accessories
Examples: Boats, trailers, motors, personal watercraft, fishing vessels, snowmobiles, motorcycle accessories

☐ No
☑ Yes

4.1 Make: **Coachmen**

Model: **Captiva**

Year: **2003**

Other information:

23 foot Travel Trailer Location: 3045 Berwick St., Rocklin, CA

Who has an interest in the property? Check one

☑ Debtor 1 only
☐ Debtor 2 only
☐ Debtor 1 and Debtor 2 only
☐ At least one of the debtors and another
☐ Check if this is community property (see instructions)

Do not deduct secured claims or exemptions. Put the amount of any secured claims on *Schedule D: Creditors Who Have Claims Secured by Property.*

Current value of the entire property? **Current value of the portion you own?**

$11,000.00   **$11,000.00**

5 Add the dollar value of the portion you own for all of your entries from Part 2, including any entries for pages you have attached for Part 2. Write that number here..=>

$25,075.00

Part 3: Describe Your Personal and Household Items

Do you own or have any legal or equitable interest in any of the following items?

Current value of the portion you own?
Do not deduct secured claims or exemptions.

6. Household goods and furnishings
Examples: Major appliances, furniture, linens, china, kitchenware
☐ No
☑ Yes. Describe.....

All items at fair market value **Washer dryer set (200), refrigerator (400), electric stove (250), misc. furniture (couch, 2 chairs) (450), minor appliances (blender, toaster, mixer) (125), vacuum (50), lawnmower (200), swing set and children's toys (240), snowblower (160) Location: 3045 Berwick St., Rocklin, CA**	**$2,075.00**
End table (700), rolltop desk (700), bed and bedding (800), oriental rug (2500) Location: 3045 Berwick St., Rocklin, CA	**$4,700.00**

Debtor 1   __Carrie Anne Edwards__   Case number *(if known)* _____

7. Electronics

Examples: Televisions and radios; audio, video, stereo, and digital equipment; computers, printers, scanners; music collections; electronic devices including cell phones, cameras, media players, games

☐ No

■ Yes. Describe.....

Stereo system (300), 20" TV (75) **Location: 3045 Berwick St., Rocklin, CA**	$375.00

8. Collectibles of value

Examples: Antiques and figurines; paintings, prints, or other artwork; books, pictures, or other art objects; stamp, coin, or baseball card collections; other collections, memorabilia, collectibles

☐ No

■ Yes. Describe.....

First edition encyclopedia at rare book store price **Location: 3045 Berwick St., Rocklin, CA**	$1,250.00

9. Equipment for sports and hobbies

Examples: Sports, photographic, exercise, and other hobby equipment; bicycles, pool tables, golf clubs, skis; canoes and kayaks; carpentry tools; musical instruments

☐ No

■ Yes. Describe.....

Mountain bike at used bicycle store price (250), digital camera **priced at eBay (200), sword collection priced at antique store (800)** **Location: 3045 Berwick St., Rocklin, CA**	$1,250.00

10. Firearms

Examples: Pistols, rifles, shotguns, ammunition, and related equipment

■ No

☐ Yes. Describe.....

11. Clothes

Examples: Everyday clothes, furs, leather coats, designer wear, shoes, accessories

☐ No

■ Yes. Describe.....

Normal clothing at fair market value (used clothing store prices) **Location: 3045 Berwick St., Rocklin, CA**	$800.00

12. Jewelry

Examples: Everyday jewelry, costume jewelry, engagement rings, wedding rings, heirloom jewelry, watches, gems, gold, silver

☐ No

■ Yes. Describe.....

Diamond necklace (800), watch (75) **Location: 3045 Berwick St., Rocklin, CA**	$875.00

13. Non-farm animals

Examples: Dogs, cats, birds, horses

☐ No

■ Yes. Describe.....

Six-year-old rescue cat **Location: 3045 Berwick St., Rocklin, CA**	$25.00

Debtor 1   Carrie Anne Edwards   Case number *(if known)* _____

14. **Any other personal and household items you did not already list, including any health aids you did not list**

  ■ No

  ☐ Yes. Give specific information.....

15. **Add the dollar value of all of your entries from Part 3, including any entries for pages you have attached for Part 3. Write that number here** ....

$11,350.00

Part 4:	Describe Your Financial Assets

Do you own or have any legal or equitable interest in any of the following?

                                                                                 Current value of the portion you own? Do not deduct secured claims or exemptions.

16. **Cash**

    Examples: Money you have in your wallet, in your home, in a safe deposit box, and on hand when you file your petition

  ☐ No

  ■ Yes..

                                                    Cash in wallet   **$50.00**

17. **Deposits of money**

    Examples: Checking, savings, or other financial accounts; certificates of deposit; shares in credit unions, brokerage houses, and other similar institutions. If you have multiple accounts with the same institution, list each.

  ☐ No

  ■ Yes.......................   Institution name:

                                     Bank of America Checking Account

            17.1.   **Rocklin, California**   **$150.00**

                                     WestAmerica Bank Savings Account

            17.2.   **Rocklin, California**   **$300.00**

18. **Bonds, mutual funds, or publicly traded stocks**

    Examples: Bond funds, investment accounts with brokerage firms, money market accounts

  ■ No

  ☐ Yes.................   Institution or issuer name:

19. **Non-publicly traded stock and interests in incorporated and unincorporated businesses, including an interest in an LLC, partnership, and joint venture**

  ☐ No

  ■ Yes. Give specific information about them....................

                       Name of entity: % of ownership:

                       5,000 shares in BLP Document Services, Inc., a close corporation

                       Location of certificates: 3045 Berwick St., Rocklin, CA (valued at $.10 a share)   %   **$500.00**

20. **Government and corporate bonds and other negotiable and non-negotiable instruments**

    Negotiable instruments include personal checks, cashiers' checks, promissory notes, and money orders.

    Non-negotiable instruments are those you cannot transfer to someone by signing or delivering them.

  ☐ No

  ■ Yes. Give specific information about them

                       Issuer name:

                       Negotiable promissory note from Jonathan Edwards, Carrie's brother, dated 11/3/2013

                       Location: 3045 Berwick St., Rocklin, CA   **$500.00**

Debtor 1   **Carrie Anne Edwards**   Case number *(if known)* _____

21. Retirement or pension accounts
  Examples: Interests in IRA, ERISA, Keogh, 401(k), 403(b), thrift savings accounts, or other pension or profit-sharing plans
  ☐ No
  ■ Yes. List each account separately.

Type of account:	Institution name:	
	TIAA/CREF (ERISA Qualified Pension)	**Unknown**
	IRA, Bank of America, Rocklin, CA (25,000)	**$25,000.00**

22. Security deposits and prepayments
  Your share of all unused deposits you have made so that you may continue service or use from a company
  Examples: Agreements with landlords, prepaid rent, public utilities (electric, gas, water), telecommunications companies, or others
  ■ No
  ☐ Yes. ....   Institution name or individual:

23. Annuities (A contract for a periodic payment of money to you, either for life or for a number of years)
  ■ No
  ☐ Yes............   Issuer name and description.

24. Interests in an education IRA, in an account in a qualified ABLE program, or under a qualified state tuition program.
  26 U.S.C. §§ 530(b)(1), 529A(b), and 529(b)(1).
  ■ No
  ☐ Yes............   Institution name and description. Separately file the records of any interests. 11 U.S.C. § 521(c):

25. Trusts, equitable or future interests in property (other than anything listed in line 1), and rights or powers exercisable for your benefit
  ■ No
  ☐ Yes. Give specific information about them...

26. Patents, copyrights, trademarks, trade secrets, and other intellectual property
  Examples: Internet domain names, websites, proceeds from royalties and licensing agreements
  ☐ No
  ■ Yes. Give specific information about them...

Copyright to book published by Nolo Press (Independent Paralegal's Handbook)	**$1,000.00**

27. Licenses, franchises, and other general intangibles
  Examples: Building permits, exclusive licenses, cooperative association holdings, liquor licenses, professional licenses
  ■ No
  ☐ Yes. Give specific information about them...

Money or property owed to you?	**Current value of the portion you own?** Do not deduct secured claims or exemptions.

28. Tax refunds owed to you
  ☐ No
  ■ Yes. Give specific information about them, including whether you already filed the returns and the tax years.......

Refund for 2016 taxes (expected but not yet received)	**$600.00**

29. Family support
  Examples: Past due or lump sum alimony, spousal support, child support, maintenance, divorce settlement, property settlement
  ■ No
  ☐ Yes. Give specific information......

Debtor 1   Carrie Anne Edwards   Case number *(if known)* _____

30. **Other amounts someone owes you**
    Examples: Unpaid wages, disability insurance payments, disability benefits, sick pay, vacation pay, workers' compensation, Social Security
            benefits; unpaid loans you made to someone else
    ■ No
    ☐ Yes. Give specific information..

31. **Interests in insurance policies**
    Examples: Health, disability, or life insurance; health savings account (HSA); credit, homeowner's, or renter's insurance
    ■ No
    ☐ Yes. Name the insurance company of each policy and list its value.

             Company name: Beneficiary: Surrender or refund
                                                                              value:

32. **Any interest in property that is due you from someone who has died**
    If you are the beneficiary of a living trust, expect proceeds from a life insurance policy, or are currently entitled to receive property because
    someone has died.
    ■ No
    ☐ Yes. Give specific information..

33. **Claims against third parties, whether or not you have filed a lawsuit or made a demand for payment**
    Examples: Accidents, employment disputes, insurance claims, or rights to sue
    ■ No
    ☐ Yes. Describe each claim.........

34. **Other contingent and unliquidated claims of every nature, including counterclaims of the debtor and rights to set off claims**
    ■ No
    ☐ Yes. Describe each claim.........

35. **Any financial assets you did not already list**
    ■ No
    ☐ Yes. Give specific information..

36. **Add the dollar value of all of your entries from Part 4, including any entries for pages you have attached
    for Part 4. Write that number here**..   **$28,100.00**

Part 5:   Describe Any Business-Related Property You Own or Have an Interest In. List any real estate in Part 1.

37. **Do you own or have any legal or equitable interest in any business-related property?**
    ☐ No. Go to Part 6.
    ■ Yes. Go to line 38.

                                                                       **Current value of the
portion you own?**
Do not deduct secured
claims or exemptions.

38. **Accounts receivable or commissions you already earned**
    ■ No
    ☐ Yes. Describe.....

39. **Office equipment, furnishings, and supplies**
    Examples: Business-related computers, software, modems, printers, copiers, fax machines, rugs, telephones, desks, chairs, electronic devices
    ☐ No
    ■ Yes. Describe.....

Used computer used in business	$300.00

Copier (used Xerox), used in business	$300.00

Official Form 106A/B   Schedule A/B: Property   page 6

Debtor 1   **Carrie Anne Edwards**   Case number *(if known)* _____

40. Machinery, fixtures, equipment, supplies you use in business, and tools of your trade
- ■ No
- ☐ Yes. Describe.....

41. Inventory
- ■ No
- ☐ Yes. Describe.....

42. Interests in partnerships or joint ventures
- ■ No
- ☐ Yes. Give specific information about them...................
  -          Name of entity: % of ownership:

43. Customer lists, mailing lists, or other compilations
- ■ No.
- ☐ Do your lists include personally identifiable information (as defined in 11 U.S.C. § 101(41A))?
  - ■ No
  - ☐ Yes. Describe.....

44. Any business-related property you did not already list
- ■ No
- ☐ Yes. Give specific information........

45. Add the dollar value of all of your entries from Part 5, including any entries for pages you have attached for Part 5. Write that number here..

	$600.00

Part 6:   Describe Any Farm- and Commercial Fishing-Related Property You Own or Have an Interest In.
            If you own or have an interest in farmland, list in Part 1.

46. Do you own or have any legal or equitable interest in any farm- or commercial fishing-related property?
- ■ No. Go to Part 7.
- ☐ Yes. Go to line 47.

Part 7:   Describe All Property You Own or Have an Interest in That You Did Not List Above

53. Do you have other property of any kind you did not already list?
Examples: Season tickets, country club membership
- ■ No
- ☐ Yes. Give specific information........

54. Add the dollar value of all of your entries from Part 7. Write that number here ....

	$0.00

Debtor 1   **Carrie Anne Edwards**   Case number *(If known)* _____

| Part 8: | List the Totals of Each Part of this Form |

55. **Part 1: Total real estate, line 2** $130,000.00

56. **Part 2: Total vehicles, line 5** $25,075.00

57. **Part 3: Total personal and household items, line 15** $11,350.00

58. **Part 4: Total financial assets, line 36** $28,100.00

59. **Part 5: Total business-related property, line 45** $600.00

60. **Part 6: Total farm- and fishing-related property, line 52** $0.00

61. **Part 7: Total other property not listed, line 54**   + $0.00

62. **Total personal property.** Add lines 56 through 61... $65,125.00   Copy personal property total $65,125.00

63. **Total of all property on Schedule A/B**. Add line 55 + line 62 $195,125.00

DRAFT

Fill in this information to identify your case:

Debtor 1	**Carrie Anne Edwards**		
	First Name	Middle Name	Last Name
Debtor 2			
(Spouse if, filing)	First Name	Middle Name	Last Name
United States Bankruptcy Court for the:	EASTERN DISTRICT OF CALIFORNIA		
Case number (if known)			

☐ Check if this is an amended filing

Official Form 106C
Schedule C: The Property You Claim as Exempt

4/16

Be as complete and accurate as possible. If two married people are filing together, both are equally responsible for supplying correct information. Using the property you listed on *Schedule A/B: Property* (Official Form 106A/B) as your source, list the property that you claim as exempt. If more space is needed, fill out and attach to this page as many copies of *Part 2: Additional Page* as necessary. On the top of any additional pages, write your name and case number (if known).

For each item of property you claim as exempt, you must specify the amount of the exemption you claim. One way of doing so is to state a specific dollar amount as exempt. Alternatively, you may claim the full fair market value of the property being exempted up to the amount of any applicable statutory limit. Some exemptions—such as those for health aids, rights to receive certain benefits, and tax-exempt retirement funds—may be unlimited in dollar amount. However, if you claim an exemption of 100% of fair market value under a law that limits the exemption to a particular dollar amount and the value of the property is determined to exceed that amount, your exemption would be limited to the applicable statutory amount.

Part 1: Identify the Property You Claim as Exempt

1. **Which set of exemptions are you claiming?** *Check one only, even if your spouse is filing with you.*

   ■ You are claiming state and federal nonbankruptcy exemptions. 11 U.S.C. § 522(b)(3)

   ☐ You are claiming federal exemptions. 11 U.S.C. § 522(b)(2)

2. **For any property you list on** *Schedule A/B* **that you claim as exempt, fill in the information below.**

Brief description of the property and line on *Schedule A/B* that lists this property	Current value of the portion you own Copy the value from *Schedule A/B*	Amount of the exemption you claim *Check only one box for each exemption.*	Specific laws that allow exemption
2003 Coachmen Captiva 23 foot Travel Trailer Location: 3045 Berwick St., Rocklin, CA Line from *Schedule A/B*: **4.1**	$11,000.00	■ $11,000.00 ☐ 100% of fair market value, up to any applicable statutory limit	C.C.P. § 703.140(b)(5)
All items at fair market value **Washer dryer set (200), refrigerator (400), electric stove (250), misc. furniture (couch, 2 chairs) (450), minor appliances (blender, toaster, mixer) (125), vacuum (50), lawnmower (200), swing set and children's toys (240)** Line from *Schedule A/B*: **6.1**	$2,075.00	■ $2,075.00 ☐ 100% of fair market value, up to any applicable statutory limit	C.C.P. § 703.140(b)(3)
End table (700), rolltop desk (700), bed and bedding (800), oriental rug (2500) Location: 3045 Berwick St., Rocklin, CA Line from *Schedule A/B*: **6.2**	$4,700.00	■ $4,700.00 ☐ 100% of fair market value, up to any applicable statutory limit	C.C.P. § 703.140(b)(3)

Debtor 1 **Carrie Anne Edwards**   Case number (if known) _____

Brief description of the property and line on *Schedule A/B* that lists this property	Current value of the portion you own Copy the value from *Schedule A/B*	Amount of the exemption you claim *Check only one box for each exemption.*	Specific laws that allow exemption
Stereo system (300), 20" TV (75) **Location: 3045 Berwick St., Rocklin, CA** Line from *Schedule A/B*: **7.1**	$375.00	■ $375.00 ☐ 100% of fair market value, up to any applicable statutory limit	C.C.P. § 703.140(b)(3)
First edition encyclopedia at rare book store price **Location: 3045 Berwick St., Rocklin, CA** Line from *Schedule A/B*: **8.1**	$1,250.00	■ $1,250.00 ☐ 100% of fair market value, up to any applicable statutory limit	C.C.P. § 703.140(b)(5)
Mountain bike at used bicycle store price (250), Digital camera priced at eBay (200), sword collection priced at antique store (800) **Location: 3045 Berwick St., Rocklin, CA** Line from *Schedule A/B*: **9.1**	$1,250.00	■ $1,250.00 ☐ 100% of fair market value, up to any applicable statutory limit	C.C.P. § 703.140(b)(5)
Normal clothing at fair market value (used clothing store prices) **Location: 3045 Berwick St., Rocklin, CA** Line from *Schedule A/B*: **11.1**	$800.00	■ $800.00 ☐ 100% of fair market value, up to any applicable statutory limit	C.C.P. § 703.140(b)(3)
Diamond necklace (800), watch (75) **Location: 3045 Berwick St., Rocklin, CA** Line from *Schedule A/B*: **12.1**	$875.00	■ $875.00 ☐ 100% of fair market value, up to any applicable statutory limit	C.C.P. § 703.140(b)(4)
Six-year-old rescue cat **Location: 3045 Berwick St., Rocklin, CA** Line from *Schedule A/B*: **13.1**	$25.00	■ $25.00 ☐ 100% of fair market value, up to any applicable statutory limit	C.C.P. § 703.140(b)(3)
Cash in wallet Line from *Schedule A/B*: **16.1**	$50.00	■ $50.00 ☐ 100% of fair market value, up to any applicable statutory limit	C.C.P. § 703.140(b)(5)
Bank of America Checking Account **Rocklin, California** Line from *Schedule A/B*: **17.1**	$150.00	■ $150.00 ☐ 100% of fair market value, up to any applicable statutory limit	C.C.P. § 703.140(b)(5)
WestAmerica Bank Savings Account **Rocklin, California** Line from *Schedule A/B*: **17.2**	$300.00	■ $300.00 ☐ 100% of fair market value, up to any applicable statutory limit	C.C.P. § 703.140(b)(5)
5,000 shares in BLP Document Services, Inc., a close corporation **Location of certificates: 3045 Berwick St., Rocklin, CA (valued at $.10 a share)** Line from *Schedule A/B*: **19.1**	$500.00	■ $500.00 ☐ 100% of fair market value, up to any applicable statutory limit	C.C.P. § 703.140(b)(5)

DRAFT

Debtor 1 **Carrie Anne Edwards**   Case number (if known) _____

Brief description of the property and line on *Schedule A/B* that lists this property	Current value of the portion you own Copy the value from *Schedule A/B*	Amount of the exemption you claim *Check only one box for each exemption.*	Specific laws that allow exemption
Negotiable promissory note from Jonathan Edwards, Carrie's brother, dated 11/3/2013 **Location: 3045 Berwick St., Rocklin, CA** Line from *Schedule A/B*: **20.1**	$500.00	■ $500.00 ☐ 100% of fair market value, up to any applicable statutory limit	C.C.P. § 703.140(b)(5)
TIAA/CREF (ERISA Qualified Pension) Line from *Schedule A/B*: **21.1**	Unknown	☐ ■ 100% of fair market value, up to any applicable statutory limit	C.C.P. § 703.140(b)(10)(E)
IRA, Bank of America, Rocklin, CA (25,000) Line from *Schedule A/B*: **21.2**	$25,000.00	■ $25,000.00 ☐ 100% of fair market value, up to any applicable statutory limit	C.C.P. § 703.140(b)(10)(E)
Copyright in book published by Nolo Press (Independent Paralegal's Handbook) Line from *Schedule A/B*: **26.1**	$1,000.00	■ $1,000.00 ☐ 100% of fair market value, up to applicable statutory limit	C.C.P. § 703.140(b)(5)
Refund for 2016 taxes (expected but not yet received) Line from *Schedule A/B*: **28.1**	$600.00	■ $600.00 ☐ 100% of fair market value, up to any applicable statutory limit	C.C.P. § 703.140(b)(5)
Used computer used in business Line from *Schedule A/B*: **39.1**	$300.00	■ $300.00 ☐ 100% of fair market value, up to any applicable statutory limit	C.C.P. § 703.140(b)(6)
Copier (used Xerox), used in business Line from *Schedule A/B*: **39.2**	$300.00	■ $300.00 ☐ 100% of fair market value, up to any applicable statutory limit	C.C.P. § 703.140(b)(6)

3. **Are you claiming a homestead exemption of more than $160,375?**
    (Subject to adjustment on 4/01/19 and every 3 years after that for cases filed on or after the date of adjustment.)

    ■ No

    ☐ Yes. Did you acquire the property covered by the exemption within 1,215 days before you filed this case?

        ☐ No

        ☐ Yes

Fill in this information to identify your case:

Debtor 1	**Carrie Anne Edwards**		
	First Name	Middle Name	Last Name
Debtor 2			
(Spouse if, filing)	First Name	Middle Name	Last Name
United States Bankruptcy Court for the:	EASTERN DISTRICT OF CALIFORNIA		
Case number (if known)			

☐ Check if this is an amended filing

Official Form 106D

Schedule D: Creditors Who Have Claims Secured by Property   12/15

Be as complete and accurate as possible. If two married people are filing together, both are equally responsible for supplying correct information. If more space is needed, copy the Additional Page, fill it out, number the entries, and attach it to this form. On the top of any additional pages, write your name and case number (if known).

1. Do any creditors have claims secured by your property?

    ☐ No. Check this box and submit this form to the court with your other schedules. You have nothing else to report on this form.

    ■ Yes. Fill in all of the information below.

Part 1:   List All Secured Claims

2. List all secured claims. If a creditor has more than one secured claim, list the creditor separately for each claim. If more than one creditor has a particular claim, list the other creditors in Part 2. As much as possible, list the claims in alphabetical order according to the creditor's name.

	Column A Amount of claim Do not deduct the value of collateral.	Column B Value of collateral that supports this claim	Column C Unsecured portion If any

2.1 Fannie's Furniture
Creditor's Name

55544 Grove St.
Berkeley, CA 94710
Number, Street, City, State & Zip Code

Who owes the debt? Check one.
☐ Debtor 1 only
☐ Debtor 2 only
☐ Debtor 1 and Debtor 2 only
■ At least one of the debtors and another
☐ Check if this claim relates to a community debt

Describe the property that secures the claim:

Used bedroom set

As of the date you file, the claim is Check all that apply.
☐ Contingent
☐ Unliquidated
☐ Disputed

Nature of lien. Check all that apply.
■ An agreement you made (such as mortgage or secured loan)
☐ Statutory lien (such as tax lien, mechanic's lien)
☐ Judgment lien from a lawsuit
☐ Other (including a right to offset) _____

Column A: $1,300.00   Column B: $500.00   Column C: $1,300.00

Date debt was incurred **12/2015**   Last 4 digits of account number **2366**

2.2 GMAC
Creditor's Name

PO Box 23567
Duchesne, UT 84021
Number, Street, City, State & Zip Code

Who owes the debt? Check one.
■ Debtor 1 only
☐ Debtor 2 only
☐ Debtor 1 and Debtor 2 only
☐ At least one of the debtors and another
☐ Check if this claim relates to a community debt

Describe the property that secures the claim:

2014 Toyota Camry 45,000 miles good condition (fair market value - nada.com)
Location: 3045 Berwick St., Rocklin, CA

As of the date you file, the claim is: Check all that apply.
☐ Contingent
☐ Unliquidated
☐ Disputed

Nature of lien. Check all that apply.
■ An agreement you made (such as mortgage or secured car loan)
☐ Statutory lien (such as tax lien, mechanic's lien)
☐ Judgment lien from a lawsuit
■ Other (including a right to offset) **Purchase Money Security**

Column A: $15,000.00   Column B: $14,075.00   Column C: $925.00

Debtor 1   **Carrie Anne Edwards**   Case number (if know) _____

         First Name   Middle Name   Last Name

Date debt was incurred   **1/2016**   Last 4 digits of account number   **8696**

2.3	**Grand Junction Mortgage**			

Creditor's Name

Describe the property that secures the claim: **$135,000.00**   **$130,000.00**   **$5,000.00**

3045 Berwick St. Rocklin, CA 95765

3456 Eighth St
Clearlake, CA 95422

Number, Street, City, State & Zip Code

As of the date you file, the claim is: Check all that apply.
- ☐ Contingent
- ☐ Unliquidated
- ☐ Disputed

Who owes the debt? Check one.
- ■ Debtor 1 only
- ☐ Debtor 2 only
- ☐ Debtor 1 and Debtor 2 only
- ☐ At least one of the debtors and another
- ☐ Check if this claim relates to a community debt

Nature of lien. Check all that apply.
- ■ An agreement you made (such as mortgage or secured car loan)
- ☐ Statutory lien (such as tax lien, mechanic's lien)
- ☐ Judgment lien from a lawsuit
- ■ Other (including a right to offset)   **First Mortgage**

Date debt was incurred   **12/2009**   Last 4 digits of account number   **5555**

2.4	**Lending Tree**			

Creditor's Name

Describe the property that secures the claim: **$18,000.00**   **$130,000.00**   **$18,000.00**

3045 Berwick St. Rocklin, CA 95765

PO Box 3333
Palo Alto, CA 94310

Number, Street, City, State & Zip Code

As of the date you file, the claim is: Check all that apply.
- ☐ Contingent
- ☐ Unliquidated
- ☐ Disputed

Who owes the debt? Check one.
- ■ Debtor 1 only
- ☐ Debtor 2 only
- ☐ Debtor 1 and Debtor 2 only
- ☐ At least one of the debtors and another
- ☐ Check if this claim relates to a community debt

Nature of lien. Check all that apply.
- ■ An agreement you made (such as mortgage or secured car loan)
- ☐ Statutory lien (such as tax lien, mechanic's lien)
- ☐ Judgment lien from a lawsuit
- ■ Other (including a right to offset)   **Second Mortgage**

Date debt was incurred   **12/2009**   Last 4 digits of account number   **5555**

Add the dollar value of your entries in Column A on this page. Write that number here:	**$169,300.00**
If this is the last page of your form, add the dollar value totals from all pages. Write that number here:	**$169,300.00**

Part 2:   **List Others to Be Notified for a Debt That You Already Listed**

Use this page only if you have others to be notified about your bankruptcy for a debt that you already listed in Part 1. For example, if a collection agency is trying to collect from you for a debt you owe to someone else, list the creditor in Part 1, and then list the collection agency here. Similarly, if you have more than one creditor for any of the debts that you listed in Part 1, list the additional creditors here. If you do not have additional persons to be notified for any debts in Part 1, do not fill out or submit this page.

Fill in this information to identify your case:

Debtor 1	**Carrie Anne Edwards**
	First Name · Middle Name · Last Name
Debtor 2	
(Spouse if, filing)	First Name · Middle Name · Last Name
United States Bankruptcy Court for the:	EASTERN DISTRICT OF CALIFORNIA
Case number (if known)	

☐ Check if this is an amended filing

Official Form 106E/F
Schedule E/F: Creditors Who Have Unsecured Claims   12/15

Be as complete and accurate as possible. Use Part 1 for creditors with PRIORITY claims and Part 2 for creditors with NONPRIORITY claims. List the other party to any executory contracts or unexpired leases that could result in a claim. Also list executory contracts on Schedule A/B: Property (Official Form 106A/B) and on Schedule G: Executory Contracts and Unexpired Leases (Official Form 106G). Do not include any creditors with partially secured claims that are listed in Schedule D: Creditors Who Have Claims Secured by Property. If more space is needed, copy the Part you need, fill it out, number the entries in the boxes on the left. Attach the Continuation Page to this page. If you have no information to report in a Part, do not file that Part. On the top of any additional pages, write your name and case number (if known).

Part 1:   List All of Your PRIORITY Unsecured Claims

1. **Do any creditors have priority unsecured claims against you?**

    ☐ No. Go to Part 2.

    ■ Yes.

2. **List all of your priority unsecured claims.** If a creditor has more than one priority unsecured claim, list the creditor separately for each claim. For each claim listed, identify what type of claim it is. If a claim has both priority and nonpriority amounts, list that claim here and show both priority and nonpriority amounts. As much as possible, list the claims in alphabetical order according to the creditor's name. If you have more than two priority unsecured claims, fill out the Continuation Page of Part 1. If more than one creditor holds a particular claim, list the other creditors in Part 3.

    (For an explanation of each type of claim, see the instructions for this form in the instruction booklet.)

			Total claim	Priority amount	Nonpriority amount

2.1 | **IRS**
Priority Creditor's Name

Columbus, OH 43266
Number Street City State Zip Code

Who incurred the debt? Check one.

■ Debtor 1 only

☐ Debtor 2 only

☐ Debtor 1 and Debtor 2 only

☐ At least one of the debtors and another

☐ Check if this claim is for a community debt

Is the claim subject to offset?

■ No

☐ Yes

Last 4 digits of account number 5532 — **$3,000.00** — **$3,000.00** — **$0.00**

When was the debt incurred? April 15, 2015

As of the date you file, the claim is: Check all that apply

☐ Contingent

☐ Unliquidated

☐ Disputed

Type of PRIORITY unsecured claim:

☐ Domestic support obligations

■ Taxes and certain other debts you owe the government

☐ Claims for death or personal injury while you were intoxicated

☐ Other. Specify _____

2.2 | **Jon Edwards**
Priority Creditor's Name
900 Grand View
Jackson, WY 83001
Number Street City State Zip Code

Who incurred the debt? Check one.

■ Debtor 1 only

☐ Debtor 2 only

☐ Debtor 1 and Debtor 2 only

☐ At least one of the debtors and another

☐ Check if this claim is for a community debt

Is the claim subject to offset?

■ No

☐ Yes

Last 4 digits of account number _____ — **$4,500.00** — **$4,500.00** — **$0.00**

When was the debt incurred? 2015 - 2016

As of the date you file, the claim is: Check all that apply

☐ Contingent

☐ Unliquidated

☐ Disputed

Type of PRIORITY unsecured claim:

■ Domestic support obligations

☐ Taxes and certain other debts you owe the government

☐ Claims for death or personal injury while you were intoxicated

☐ Other. Specify _____

Debtor 1 **Carrie Anne Edwards**   Case number (if know) _____

Part 2: **List All of Your NONPRIORITY Unsecured Claims**

3. **Do any creditors have nonpriority unsecured claims against you?**

☐ No. You have nothing to report in this part. Submit this form to the court with your other schedules.

■ Yes.

4. List all of your nonpriority unsecured claims in the alphabetical order of the creditor who holds each claim. If a creditor has more than one nonpriority unsecured claim, list the creditor separately for each claim. For each claim listed, identify what type of claim it is. Do not list claims already included in Part 1. If more than one creditor holds a particular claim, list the other creditors in Part 3. If you have more than three nonpriority unsecured claims fill out the Continuation Page of Part 2.

		Total claim

4.1	**Alan Accountant**	Last 4 digits of account number **C356**	**$500.00**

Nonpriority Creditor's Name
5 Green St.
Cleveland, OH 44118
Number Street City State Zip Code

When was the debt incurred? **4/2015**

Who incurred the debt? Check one.

As of the date you file, the claim is: Check all that apply

■ Debtor 1 only   ☐ Contingent
☐ Debtor 2 only   ☐ Unliquidated
☐ Debtor 1 and Debtor 2 only   ☐ Disputed
☐ At least one of the debtors and another   **Type of NONPRIORITY unsecured claim:**
☐ Check if this claim is for a community debt   ☐ Student loans
                                     ☐ Obligations arising out of a separation agreement or divorce that you did not report as priority claims
Is the claim subject to offset?   ☐ Debts to pension or profit-sharing plans, and other similar debts
■ No   ■ Other. Specify **Tax preparation**
☐ Yes

4.2	**American Allowance**	Last 4 digits of account number **8899**	**$5,600.00**

Nonpriority Creditor's Name
PO Box 1
New York, NY 10001
Number Street City State Zip Code

When was the debt incurred? **1/2009 to 12/2016**

Who incurred the debt? Check one.

As of the date you file, the claim is: Check all that apply

■ Debtor 1 only   ☐ Contingent
☐ Debtor 2 only   ☐ Unliquidated
☐ Debtor 1 and Debtor 2 only   ☐ Disputed
☐ At least one of the debtors and another   **Type of NONPRIORITY unsecured claim:**
☐ Check if this claim is for a community debt   ☐ Student loans
                                     ☐ Obligations arising out of a separation agreement or divorce that you did not report as priority claims
Is the claim subject to offset?   ☐ Debts to pension or profit-sharing plans, and other similar debts
■ No   ■ Other. Specify **Credit card charges**
☐ Yes

Debtor 1 __Carrie Anne Edwards__ Case number (if know) _____

4.3	**Angel of Mercy Hospital**	

Nonpriority Creditor's Name
4444 Elevisior St.
Belmont, CA 94003
Number Street City State Zip Code

Who incurred the debt? Check one.

■ Debtor 1 only
☐ Debtor 2 only
☐ Debtor 1 and Debtor 2 only
☐ At least one of the debtors and another
☐ **Check if this claim is for a community debt**

Is the claim subject to offset?

■ No
☐ Yes

Last 4 digits of account number __7582__

When was the debt incurred? __12/2014__

As of the date you file, the claim is: Check all that apply

☐ Contingent
☐ Unliquidated
☐ Disputed

Type of NONPRIORITY unsecured claim:

☐ Student loans
☐ Obligations arising out of a separation agreement or divorce that you did not report as priority claims
☐ Debts to pension or profit-sharing plans, and other similar debts
■ Other. Specify __Uninsured surgery and medical treatment__

$34,000.00

4.4	**Bob Jones III**	

Nonpriority Creditor's Name
4566 Fifth Ave.
New York, NY 10020
Number Street City State Zip Code

Who incurred the debt? Check one.

■ Debtor 1 only
☐ Debtor 2 only
☐ Debtor 1 and Debtor 2 only
☐ At least one of the debtors and another
☐ **Check if this claim is for a community debt**

Is the claim subject to offset?

■ No
☐ Yes

Last 4 digits of account number __6656__

When was the debt incurred? __7/2017__

As of the date you file, the claim is: Check all that apply

■ Contingent
■ Unliquidated
■ Disputed

Type of NONPRIORITY unsecured claim:

☐ Student loans
☐ Obligations arising out of a separation agreement or divorce that you did not report as priority claims
☐ Debts to pension or profit-sharing plans, and other similar debts
■ Other. Specify __Auto accident--negligence claim__

Unknown

4.5	**Bonnie Johnson**	

Nonpriority Creditor's Name
3335 Irving St.
Clearlake, CA 95422
Number Street City State Zip Code

Who incurred the debt? Check one.

■ Debtor 1 only
☐ Debtor 2 only
☐ Debtor 1 and Debtor 2 only
☐ At least one of the debtors and another
☐ **Check if this claim is for a community debt**

Is the claim subject to offset?

■ No
☐ Yes

Last 4 digits of account number _____

When was the debt incurred? __8/2015__

As of the date you file, the claim is: Check all that apply

☐ Contingent
☐ Unliquidated
☐ Disputed

Type of NONPRIORITY unsecured claim:

☐ Student loans
☐ Obligations arising out of a separation agreement or divorce that you did not report as priority claims
☐ Debts to pension or profit-sharing plans, and other similar debts
■ Other. Specify __Personal loan__

$5,500.00

Debtor 1 __Carrie Anne Edwards__   Case number (if know) _____

| 4.6 | __Cal State Central Credit Union__ | Last 4 digits of account number __2345__ | $8,765.00 |

Nonpriority Creditor's Name
__1205 N. Dutton Ave.__
__Santa Rosa, CA 95401__
Number Street City State Zip Code

Who incurred the debt? Check one.

When was the debt incurred? __1/2010 to 3/2017__

As of the date you file, the claim is: Check all that apply

■ Debtor 1 only

□ Debtor 2 only

□ Debtor 1 and Debtor 2 only

□ At least one of the debtors and another

□ **Check if this claim is for a community debt**

Is the claim subject to offset?

■ No

□ Yes

□ Contingent

□ Unliquidated

□ Disputed

Type of NONPRIORITY unsecured claim:

□ Student loans

□ Obligations arising out of a separation agreement or divorce that you did not report as priority claims

□ Debts to pension or profit-sharing plans, and other similar debts

■ Other. Specify __Misc. charges__

| 4.7 | __Citibank__ | Last 4 digits of account number __1863__ | $10,000.00 |

Nonpriority Creditor's Name
__200 East North St.__
__Columbus, OH 43266__
Number Street City State Zip Code

Who incurred the debt? Check one.

When was the debt incurred? __2010__

As of the date you file, the claim is: Check all that apply

■ Debtor 1 only

□ Debtor 2 only

□ Debtor 1 and Debtor 2 only

□ At least one of the debtors and another

□ **Check if this claim is for a community debt**

Is the claim subject to offset?

■ No

□ Yes

□ Contingent

□ Unliquidated

□ Disputed

Type of NONPRIORITY unsecured claim:

■ Student loans

□ Obligations arising out of a separation agreement or divorce that you did not report as priority claims

□ Debts to pension or profit-sharing plans, and other similar debts

□ Other. Specify _____

__Student loan__

| 4.8 | __Dr. Dennis Dentist__ | Last 4 digits of account number __4401__ | $1,050.00 |

Nonpriority Creditor's Name
__45 Superior Way__
__Cleveland, OH 44118__
Number Street City State Zip Code

Who incurred the debt? Check one.

When was the debt incurred? __12/2015 to 6/2016__

As of the date you file, the claim is: Check all that apply

■ Debtor 1 only

□ Debtor 2 only

□ Debtor 1 and Debtor 2 only

□ At least one of the debtors and another

□ **Check if this claim is for a community debt**

Is the claim subject to offset?

■ No

□ Yes

□ Contingent

□ Unliquidated

□ Disputed

Type of NONPRIORITY unsecured claim:

□ Student loans

□ Obligations arising out of a separation agreement or divorce that you did not report as priority claims

□ Debts to pension or profit-sharing plans, and other similar debts

■ Other. Specify __Dental work__

Debtor 1   **Carrie Anne Edwards**   Case number (if know)

4.9

Dr. Helen Jones
Nonpriority Creditor's Name
443 First St.
Soledad, CA 94750
Number Street City State ZIp Code

Who incurred the debt? Check one.

- ☑ Debtor 1 only
- ☐ Debtor 2 only
- ☐ Debtor 1 and Debtor 2 only
- ☐ At least one of the debtors and another
- ☐ **Check if this claim is for a community debt**

Is the claim subject to offset?

- ☑ No
- ☐ Yes

Last 4 digits of account number   **5671**   **$5,000.00**

When was the debt incurred?   **4/2016 to 8/2016**

As of the date you file, the claim is: Check all that apply

- ☐ Contingent
- ☐ Unliquidated
- ☐ Disputed

Type of NONPRIORITY unsecured claim:

- ☐ Student loans
- ☐ Obligations arising out of a separation agreement or divorce that you did not report as priority claims
- ☐ Debts to pension or profit-sharing plans, and other similar debts
- ☑ Other. Specify   **Pediatric care**

4.10

Illuminating Co.
Nonpriority Creditor's Name
20245 Old Hwy 53
Clearlake, CA 95422
Number Street City State ZIp Code

Who incurred the debt? Check one.

- ☑ Debtor 1 only
- ☐ Debtor 2 only
- ☐ Debtor 1 and Debtor 2 only
- ☐ At least one of the debtors and another
- ☐ **Check if this claim is for a community debt**

Is the claim subject to offset?

- ☑ No
- ☐ Yes

Last 4 digits of account number   **794**   **$750.00**

When was the debt incurred?   **3/2017 to 4/2017**

As of the date you file, the claim is: Check all that apply

- ☐ Contingent
- ☐ Unliquidated
- ☐ Disputed

Type of NONPRIORITY unsecured claim:

- ☐ Student loans
- ☐ Obligations arising out of a separation agreement or divorce that you did not report as priority claims
- ☐ Debts to pension or profit-sharing plans, and other similar debts
- ☑ Other. Specify   **Electrical work on house**

4.11

Jess Allen Pest Control
Nonpriority Creditor's Name
1770 N. Loop Avenue
Sacramento, CA 95814
Number Street City State ZIp Code

Who incurred the debt? Check one.

- ☑ Debtor 1 only
- ☐ Debtor 2 only
- ☐ Debtor 1 and Debtor 2 only
- ☐ At least one of the debtors and another
- ☐ **Check if this claim is for a community debt**

Is the claim subject to offset?

- ☑ No
- ☐ Yes

Last 4 digits of account number   **4590**   **$1,200.00**

When was the debt incurred?   **2/2017**

As of the date you file, the claim is: Check all that apply

- ☐ Contingent
- ☐ Unliquidated
- ☐ Disputed

Type of NONPRIORITY unsecured claim:

- ☐ Student loans
- ☐ Obligations arising out of a separation agreement or divorce that you did not report as priority claims
- ☐ Debts to pension or profit-sharing plans, and other similar debts
- ☑ Other. Specify   **Ongoing contract for pest extermination services**

Debtor 1   **Carrie Anne Edwards**   Case number (if know) _____

4.12

John White, Esq.	Last 4 digits of account number **153**	**$3,450.00**

Nonpriority Creditor's Name
PO Box 401
Finley, CA 95435
Number Street City State Zip Code

When was the debt incurred?   **2/2011 to 8/2012**

As of the date you file, the claim is: Check all that apply

Who incurred the debt? Check one.

■ Debtor 1 only

☐ Debtor 2 only

☐ Debtor 1 and Debtor 2 only

☐ At least one of the debtors and another

☐ **Check if this claim is for a community debt**

Is the claim subject to offset?

■ No

☐ Yes

☐ Contingent

☐ Unliquidated

☐ Disputed

Type of NONPRIORITY unsecured claim:

☐ Student loans

☐ Obligations arising out of a separation agreement or divorce that you did not report as priority claims

☐ Debts to pension or profit-sharing plans, and other similar debts

■ Other. Specify   **Legal representation in lawsuit against neighbor for incursion on property**

4.13

PG&E	Last 4 digits of account number **0550**	**$1,200.00**

Nonpriority Creditor's Name
315 North Forbes St.
Rocklin, CA 95765
Number Street City State Zip Code

When was the debt incurred?   **12/2016 to 6/2017**

As of the date you file, the claim is: Check all that apply

Who incurred the debt? Check one.

■ Debtor 1 only

☐ Debtor 2 only

☐ Debtor 1 and Debtor 2 only

☐ At least one of the debtors and another

☐ **Check if this claim is for a community debt**

Is the claim subject to offset?

■ No

☐ Yes

☐ Contingent

☐ Unliquidated

☐ Disputed

Type of NONPRIORITY unsecured claim:

☐ Student loans

☐ Obligations arising out of a separation agreement or divorce that you did not report as priority claims

☐ Debts to pension or profit-sharing plans, and other similar debts

■ Other. Specify   **Gas and electric service**

4.14

Sears	Last 4 digits of account number **0097**	**$3,800.00**

Nonpriority Creditor's Name
PO Box 11
Chicago, IL 60619
Number Street City State Zip Code

When was the debt incurred?   **1/2009 to 12/2016**

As of the date you file, the claim is: Check all that apply

Who incurred the debt? Check one.

■ Debtor 1 only

☐ Debtor 2 only

☐ Debtor 1 and Debtor 2 only

☐ At least one of the debtors and another

☐ **Check if this claim is for a community debt**

Is the claim subject to offset?

■ No

☐ Yes

☐ Contingent

☐ Unliquidated

☐ Disputed

Type of NONPRIORITY unsecured claim:

☐ Student loans

☐ Obligations arising out of a separation agreement or divorce that you did not report as priority claims

☐ Debts to pension or profit-sharing plans, and other similar debts

■ Other. Specify   **Dept. store and catalog charges**

Part 3:   **List Others to Be Notified About a Debt That You Already Listed**

5. Use this page only if you have others to be notified about your bankruptcy, for a debt that you already listed in Parts 1 or 2. For example, if a collection agency is trying to collect from you for a debt you owe to someone else, list the original creditor in Parts 1 or 2, then list the collection agency here. Similarly, if you have more than one creditor for any of the debts that you listed in Parts 1 or 2, list the additional creditors here. If you do not have additional persons to be notified for any debts in Parts 1 or 2, do not fill out or submit this page.

Name and Address   On which entry in Part 1 or Part 2 did you list the original creditor?

Debtor 1 **Carrie Anne Edwards**   Case number *(if know)* _____

CBE GROUP   Line **4.7** of *(Check one):*   ☐ Part 1: Creditors with Priority Unsecured Claims
17 Technical Park Drive   ■ Part 2: Creditors with Nonpriority Unsecured Claims
Sacramento, CA 95823
Last 4 digits of account number _____

| Part 4: | Add the Amounts for Each Type of Unsecured Claim |

6. Total the amounts of certain types of unsecured claims. This information is for statistical reporting purposes only. 28 U.S.C. §159. Add the amounts for each type of unsecured claim.

			Total Claim
Total claims from Part 1	6a. **Domestic support obligations**	6a.	$ 4,500.00
	6b. **Taxes and certain other debts you owe the government**	6b.	$ 3,000.00
	6c. **Claims for death or personal injury while you were intoxicated**	6c.	$ 0.00
	6d. **Other.** Add all other priority unsecured claims. Write that amount here.	6d.	$ 0.00
	6e. **Total Priority.** Add lines 6a through 6d.	6e.	$ 7,500.00

			Total Claim
Total claims from Part 2	6f. **Student loans**	6f.	$ 10,000.00
	6g. **Obligations arising out of a separation agreement or divorce that you did not report as priority claims**	6g.	$ 0.00
	6h. **Debts to pension or profit-sharing plans, and other similar debts**	6h.	$ 0.00
	6i. **Other.** Add all other nonpriority unsecured claims. Write that amount here.	6i.	$ 70,815.00
	6j. **Total Nonpriority.** Add lines 6f through 6i.	6j.	$ 80,815.00

DRAFT

Fill in this information to identify your case:

Debtor 1	**Carrie Anne Edwards**		
	First Name	Middle Name	Last Name
Debtor 2			
(Spouse if, filing)	First Name	Middle Name	Last Name

United States Bankruptcy Court for the: EASTERN DISTRICT OF CALIFORNIA

Case number
(if known) _____

☐ Check if this is an amended filing

Official Form 106G
Schedule G: Executory Contracts and Unexpired Leases   12/15

Be as complete and accurate as possible. If two married people are filing together, both are equally responsible for supplying correct information. If more space is needed, copy the additional page, fill it out, number the entries, and attach it to this page. On the top of any additional pages, write your name and case number (if known).

1. Do you have any executory contracts or unexpired leases?
   ☐ No. Check this box and file this form with the court with your other schedules. You have nothing else to report on this form.
   ■ Yes. Fill in all of the information below even if the contacts of leases are listed on *Schedule A/B:Property* (Official Form 106 A/B).

2. List separately each person or company with whom you have the contract or lease. Then state what each contract or lease is for (for example, rent, vehicle lease, cell phone). See the instructions for this form in the instruction booklet for more examples of executory contracts and unexpired leases.

Person or company with whom you have the contract or lease Name, Number, Street, City, State and ZIP Code	State what the contract or lease is for
2.1 **Beauty Products Leasing Co.** 44332 Eighth St. Geismar, LA 70734	Laser skin treatment machine. Lease for 5-year period that expires on May 2020
2.2 **Jess Allen Pest Control** 1770 N. Loop Avenue Sacramento, CA 95814	Pest control contract for debtor's home entered into between debtor and Jess Allen on 2/1/2017

Fill in this information to identify your case:

Debtor 1	**Carrie Anne Edwards**		
	First Name	Middle Name	Last Name
Debtor 2			
(Spouse if, filing)	First Name	Middle Name	Last Name
United States Bankruptcy Court for the:	EASTERN DISTRICT OF CALIFORNIA		
Case number			
(if known)			

☐ Check if this is an amended filing

Official Form 106H
Schedule H: Your Codebtors

12/15

Codebtors are people or entities who are also liable for any debts you may have. Be as complete and accurate as possible. If two married people are filing together, both are equally responsible for supplying correct information. If more space is needed, copy the Additional Page, fill it out, and number the entries in the boxes on the left. Attach the Additional Page to this page. On the top of any Additional Pages, write your name and case number (if known). Answer every question.

1. Do you have any codebtors? (If you are filing a joint case, do not list either spouse as a codebtor.)

☐ No
■ Yes

2. Within the last 8 years, have you lived in a community property state or territory? (*Community property states and territories* include Arizona, California, Idaho, Louisiana, Nevada, New Mexico, Puerto Rico, Texas, Washington, and Wisconsin.)

☐ No. Go to line 3.
■ Yes. Did your spouse, former spouse, or legal equivalent live with you at the time?

   ■ No
   ☐ Yes.

   In which community state or territory did you live?   -NONE-   . Fill in the name and current address of that person.

   _____
   Name of your spouse, former spouse, or legal equivalent
   Number, Street, City, State & Zip Code

3. In Column 1, list all of your codebtors. Do not include your spouse as a codebtor if your spouse is filing with you. List the person shown in line 2 again as a codebtor only if that person is a guarantor or cosigner. Make sure you have listed the creditor on Schedule D (Official Form 106D), Schedule E/F (Official Form 106E/F), or Schedule G (Official Form 106G). Use Schedule D, Schedule E/F, or Schedule G to fill out Column 2.

Column 1: Your codebtor Name, Number, Street, City, State and ZIP Code	*Column 2:* The creditor to whom you owe the debt Check all schedules that apply:
3.1 **Bonnie Johnson** **3335 Irving St.** **Clearlake, CA 95422**	■ Schedule D, line __2.1__ ☐ Schedule E/F, line _____ ☐ Schedule G _____ **Fannie's Furniture**

Fill in this information to identify your case:

Debtor 1   **Carrie Anne Edwards**

Debtor 2
(Spouse, if filing)

United States Bankruptcy Court for the: EASTERN DISTRICT OF CALIFORNIA

Case number
(If known)

Check if this is:

☐ An amended filing

☐ A supplement showing postpetition chapter 13 income as of the following date:

_____
MM / DD/ YYYY

Official Form 106I
Schedule I: Your Income

12/15

Be as complete and accurate as possible. If two married people are filing together (Debtor 1 and Debtor 2), both are equally responsible for supplying correct information. If you are married and not filing jointly, and your spouse is living with you, include information about your spouse. If you are separated and your spouse is not filing with you, do not include information about your spouse. If more space is needed, attach a separate sheet to this form. On the top of any additional pages, write your name and case number (if known). Answer every question.

Part 1:   Describe Employment

1. **Fill in your employment information.**

   If you have more than one job, attach a separate page with information about additional employers.

   Include part-time, seasonal, or self-employed work.

   Occupation may include student or homemaker, if it applies.

	Debtor 1	Debtor 2 or non-filing spouse
Employment status	■ Employed ☐ Not employed	☐ Employed ☐ Not employed
Occupation	Retail	
Employer's name	Macy's	
Employer's address	2356 Cleveland Ave. Sacramento, CA 95827	
How long employed there?	2 years	

Part 2:   Give Details About Monthly Income

Estimate monthly income as of the date you file this form. If you have nothing to report for any line, write $0 in the space. Include your non-filing spouse unless you are separated.

If you or your non-filing spouse have more than one employer, combine the information for all employers for that person on the lines below. If you need more space, attach a separate sheet to this form.

		For Debtor 1	For Debtor 2 or non-filing spouse
2.	List monthly gross wages, salary, and commissions (before all payroll deductions). If not paid monthly, calculate what the monthly wage would be.	2. $ 5,276.00	$ N/A
3.	Estimate and list monthly overtime pay.	3. +$ 0.00	+$ N/A
4.	Calculate gross income. Add line 2 + line 3.	4. $ 5,276.00	$ N/A

Debtor 1 **Carrie Anne Edwards**   Case number (*if known*) _____

		For Debtor 1	For Debtor 2 or non-filing spouse
	Copy line 4 here	4. $ **5,276.00**	$ **N/A**

5. **List all payroll deductions:**

			For Debtor 1	For Debtor 2 or non-filing spouse
5a.	Tax, Medicare, and Social Security deductions	5a.	$ **632.00**	$ **N/A**
5b.	Mandatory contributions for retirement plans	5b.	$ **0.00**	$ **N/A**
5c.	Voluntary contributions for retirement plans	5c.	$ **136.00**	$ **N/A**
5d.	Required repayments of retirement fund loans	5d.	$ **0.00**	$ **N/A**
5e.	Insurance	5e.	$ **187.00**	$ **N/A**
5f.	Domestic support obligations	5f.	$ **0.00**	$ **N/A**
5g.	Union dues	5g.	$ **0.00**	$ **N/A**
5h.	Other deductions. Specify: ____	5h.+	$ **0.00** +	$ **N/A**

6. **Add the payroll deductions.** Add lines 5a+5b+5c+5d+5e+5f+5g+5h. 6. $ **955.00** $ **N/A**

7. **Calculate total monthly take-home pay.** Subtract line 6 from line 4. 7. $ **4,321.00** $ **N/A**

8. **List all other income regularly received:**

8a. **Net income from rental property and from operating a business, profession, or farm**
Attach a statement for each property and business showing gross receipts, ordinary and necessary business expenses, and the total monthly net income. 8a. $ **0.00** $ **N/A**

8b. **Interest and dividends** 8b. $ **0.00** $ **N/A**

8c. **Family support payments that you, a non-filing spouse, or a dependent regularly receive**
Include alimony, spousal support, child support, maintenance, divorce settlement, and property settlement. 8c. $ **400.00** $ **N/A**

8d. **Unemployment compensation** 8d. $ **0.00** $ **N/A**

8e. **Social Security** 8e. $ **0.00** $ **N/A**

8f. **Other government assistance that you regularly receive**
Include cash assistance and the value (if known) of any non-cash assistance that you receive, such as food stamps (benefits under the Supplemental Nutrition Assistance Program) or housing subsidies.
Specify: ____ 8f. $ **0.00** $ **N/A**

8g. **Pension or retirement income** 8g. $ **0.00** $ **N/A**

8h. **Other monthly income. Specify:** ____ 8h.+ $ **0.00** + $ **N/A**

9. **Add all other income.** Add lines 8a+8b+8c+8d+8e+8f+8g+8h. 9. $ **400.00** $ **N/A**

10. **Calculate monthly income.** Add line 7 + line 9. 10. $ **4,721.00** + $ **N/A** = $ **4,721.00**
Add the entries in line 10 for Debtor 1 and Debtor 2 or non-filing spouse.

11. **State all other regular contributions to the expenses that you list in *Schedule J*.**
Include contributions from an unmarried partner, members of your household, your dependents, your roommates, and other friends or relatives.
Do not include any amounts already included in lines 2-10 or amounts that are not available to pay expenses listed in *Schedule J*.
Specify: ____ 11. +$ **0.00**

12. **Add the amount in the last column of line 10 to the amount in line 11.** The result is the combined monthly income. Write that amount on the *Summary of Schedules* and *Statistical Summary of Certain Liabilities* and Related *Data*, if it applies 12. $ **4,721.00**
Combined monthly income

13. **Do you expect an increase or decrease within the year after you file this form?**
■ No.
☐ Yes. Explain: ____

Fill in this information to identify your case:

Debtor 1	**Carrie Anne Edwards**
Debtor 2 (Spouse, if filing)	
United States Bankruptcy Court for the:	EASTERN DISTRICT OF CALIFORNIA
Case number (If known)	

Check if this is:

☐ An amended filing

☐ A supplement showing postpetition chapter 13 expenses as of the following date:

_____
MM / DD / YYYY

Official Form 106J
Schedule J: Your Expenses

12/15

Be as complete and accurate as possible. If two married people are filing together, both are equally responsible for supplying correct information. If more space is needed, attach another sheet to this form. On the top of any additional pages, write your name and case number (if known). Answer every question.

Part 1:   Describe Your Household

1. **Is this a joint case?**

   ■ No. Go to line 2.

   ☐ Yes. **Does Debtor 2 live in a separate household?**

       ☐ No

       ☐ Yes. Debtor 2 must file Official Form 106J-2, *Expenses for Separate Household* of Debtor 2.

2. **Do you have dependents?** ☐ No

   Do not list Debtor 1 and Debtor 2.

   ■ Yes. Fill out this information for each dependent..........

   Do not state the dependents names.

	Dependent's relationship to Debtor 1 or Debtor 2	Dependent's age	Does dependent live with you?
	Daughter	14	☐ No ■ Yes
	Son	16	☐ No ■ Yes
			☐ No ☐ Yes
			☐ No ☐ Yes

3. **Do you your expenses include expenses of people other than yourself and your dependents?** ■ No ☐ Yes

Part 2:   Estimate Your Ongoing Monthly Expenses

Estimate your expenses as of your bankruptcy filing date unless you are using this form as a supplement in a Chapter 13 case to report expenses as of a date after the bankruptcy is filed. If this is a supplemental *Schedule J*, check the box at the top of the form and fill in the applicable date.

Include expenses paid for with non-cash government assistance if you know the value of such assistance and have included it on *Schedule I: Your Income* (Official Form 106I.)

Your expenses

4.	The rental or home ownership expenses for your residence. Include first mortgage payments and any rent for the ground or lot.	4. $	1,175.00
	If not included in line 4:		
4a.	Real estate taxes	4a. $	0.00
4b.	Property, homeowner's, or renter's insurance	4b. $	0.00
4c.	Home maintenance, repair, and upkeep expenses	4c. $	100.00
4d.	Homeowner's association or condominium dues	4d. $	0.00
5.	Additional mortgage payments for your residence, such as home equity loans	5. $	0.00

Debtor 1   **Carrie Anne Edwards**   Case number (if known) _____

6. **Utilities:**
    6a.   Electricity, heat, natural gas   6a. $ 250.00
    6b.   Water, sewer, garbage collection   6b. $ 150.00
    6c.   Telephone, cell phone, Internet, satellite, and cable services   6c. $ 350.00
    6d.   Other. Specify: _____   6d. $ 0.00
7. **Food and housekeeping supplies**   7. $ 750.00
8. **Childcare and children's education costs**   8. $ 0.00
9. **Clothing, laundry, and dry cleaning**   9. $ 100.00
10. **Personal care products and services**   10. $ 75.00
11. **Medical and dental expenses**   11. $ 150.00
12. **Transportation.** Include gas, maintenance, bus or train fare.
    Do not include car payments.   12. $ 400.00
13. **Entertainment, clubs, recreation, newspapers, magazines, and books** 13. $ 150.00
14. **Charitable contributions and religious donations**   14. $ 250.00
15. **Insurance.**
    Do not include insurance deducted from your pay or included in lines 4 or 20.
    15a. Life insurance   15a. $ 64.00
    15b. Health insurance   15b. $ 0.00
    15c. Vehicle insurance   15c. $ 200.00
    15d. Other insurance. Specify: _____   15d. $ 0.00
16. **Taxes.** Do not include taxes deducted from your pay or included in lines 4 or 20.
    Specify: _____   16. $ 0.00
17. **Installment or lease payments:**
    17a. Car payments for Vehicle 1   17a. $ 375.00
    17b. Car payments for Vehicle 2   17b. $ 0.00
    17c. Other. Specify: _____   17c. $ 0.00
    17d. Other. Specify: _____   17d. $ 0.00
18. **Your payments of alimony, maintenance, and support that you did not report as
    deducted from your pay on line 5,** *Schedule I, Your Income* (Official Form 106I). 18. $ 0.00
19. **Other payments you make to support others who do not live with you.** $ 0.00
    Specify: _____   19.
20. **Other real property expenses not included in lines 4 or 5** of this form or on *Schedule I: Your Income.*
    20a. Mortgages on other property   20a. $ 0.00
    20b. Real estate taxes   20b. $ 0.00
    20c. Property, homeowner's, or renter's insurance   20c. $ 0.00
    20d. Maintenance, repair, and upkeep expenses   20d. $ 0.00
    20e. Homeowner's association or condominium dues   20e. $ 75.00
21. **Other: Specify:**   **Pet care**   21. +$ 75.00

22. **Calculate your monthly expenses**
    22a. Add lines 4 through 21. $ 4,689.00
    22b. Copy line 22 (monthly expenses for Debtor 2), if any, from Official Form 106J-2 $
    22c. Add line 22a and 22b. The result is your monthly expenses. $ 4,689.00

23. **Calculate your monthly net income.**
    23a. Copy line 12 *(your combined monthly income)* from Schedule I.   23a. $ 4,721.00
    23b. Copy your monthly expenses from line 22c above.   23b. -$ 4,689.00

    23c. Subtract your monthly expenses from your monthly income.
         The result is your *monthly net income.*   23c. $ 32.00

24. **Do you expect an increase or decrease in your expenses within the year after you file this form?**
    For example, do you expect to finish paying for your car loan within the year or do you expect your mortgage payment to increase or decrease because of a modification to the terms of your mortgage?

    ■ No.
    ☐ Yes.   Explain here: _____

Fill in this information to identify your case:

Debtor 1	**Carrie Anne Edwards**
	First Name Middle Name Last Name
Debtor 2	
(Spouse if, filing)	First Name Middle Name Last Name

United States Bankruptcy Court for the: EASTERN DISTRICT OF CALIFORNIA

Case number _____
(if known)

☐ Check if this is an
amended filing

Official Form 106Dec

Declaration About an Individual Debtor's Schedules

12/15

If two married people are filing together, both are equally responsible for supplying correct information.

You must file this form whenever you file bankruptcy schedules or amended schedules. Making a false statement, concealing property, or obtaining money or property by fraud in connection with a bankruptcy case can result in fines up to $250,000, or imprisonment for up to 20 years, or both. 18 U.S.C. §§ 152, 1341, 1519, and 3571.

Sign Below

Did you pay or agree to pay someone who is NOT an attorney to help you fill out bankruptcy forms?

■ No

☐ Yes. Name of person _____   Attach *Bankruptcy Petition Preparer's Notice, Declaration, and Signature* (Official Form 119)

Under penalty of perjury, I declare that I have read the summary and schedules filed with this declaration and that they are true and correct.

X **/s/ Carrie Anne Edwards**   X _____
   Carrie Anne Edwards   Signature of Debtor 2
   Signature of Debtor 1

   Date **October 2, 2017**   Date _____

Official Form 106Dec   Declaration About an Individual Debtor's Schedules

Fill in this information to identify your case:

Debtor 1	**Carrie Anne Edwards**		
	First Name	Middle Name	Last Name
Debtor 2			
(Spouse if, filing)	First Name	Middle Name	Last Name
United States Bankruptcy Court for the:	EASTERN DISTRICT OF CALIFORNIA		
Case number (if known)			

☐ Check if this is an amended filing

Official Form 107
Statement of Financial Affairs for Individuals Filing for Bankruptcy

4/16

Be as complete and accurate as possible. If two married people are filing together, both are equally responsible for supplying correct information. If more space is needed, attach a separate sheet to this form. On the top of any additional pages, write your name and case number (if known). Answer every question.

Part 1: Give Details About Your Marital Status and Where You Lived Before

1. **What is your current marital status?**

   ☐ Married
   ■ Not married

2. **During the last 3 years, have you lived anywhere other than where you live now?**

   ☐ No
   ■ Yes. List all of the places you lived in the last 3 years. Do not include where you live now.

Debtor 1 Prior Address:	Dates Debtor 1 lived there	Debtor 2 Prior Address:	Dates Debtor 2 lived there
21 Scarborough Rd. Cleveland, OH 44118	From-To: 1/1/2014 9/1/201	☐ Same as Debtor 1	☐ Same as Debtor 1 From-To:

3. **Within the last 8 years, did you ever live with a spouse or legal equivalent in a community property state or territory?** (*Community property states and territories* include Arizona, California, Idaho, Louisiana, Nevada, New Mexico, Puerto Rico, Texas, Washington and Wisconsin.)

   ■ No
   ☐ Yes. Make sure you fill out *Schedule H: Your Codebtors* (Official Form 106H).

Part 2 Explain the Sources of Your Income

4. **Did you have any income from employment or from operating a business during this year or the two previous calendar years?**
   Fill in the total amount of income you received from all jobs and all businesses, including part-time activities.
   If you are filing a joint case and you have income that you receive together, list it only once under Debtor 1.

   ☐ No
   ■ Yes. Fill in the details.

	Debtor 1		Debtor 2	
	Sources of income Check all that apply.	Gross income (before deductions and exclusions)	Sources of income Check all that apply.	Gross income (before deductions and exclusions)
From January 1 of current year until the date you filed for bankruptcy:	■ Wages, commissions, bonuses, tips	$36,765.00	☐ Wages, commissions, bonuses, tips	
	☐ Operating a business		☐ Operating a business	

Debtor 1   **Carrie Anne Edwards**   Case number (*if known*) _____

	Debtor 1		Debtor 2	
	Sources of income Check all that apply.	**Gross income** (before deductions and exclusions)	**Sources of income** Check all that apply.	**Gross income** (before deductions and exclusions)
For last calendar year: (January 1 to December 31, 2016)	■ Wages, commissions, bonuses, tips ☐ Operating a business	**$54,100.00**	☐ Wages, commissions, bonuses, tips ☐ Operating a business	
For the calendar year before that: (January 1 to December 31, 2015)	■ Wages, commissions, bonuses, tips ☐ Operating a business	**$60,100.00**	☐ Wages, commissions, bonuses, tips ☐ Operating a business	

5. **Did you receive any other income during this year or the two previous calendar years?**
Include income regardless of whether that income is taxable. Examples of *other income* are alimony; child support; Social Security, unemployment, and other public benefit payments; pensions; rental income; interest; dividends; money collected from lawsuits; royalties; and gambling and lottery winnings. If you are filing a joint case and you have income that you received together, list it only once under Debtor 1.

List each source and the gross income from each source separately. Do not include income that you listed in line 4.

■ No
☐ Yes. Fill in the details.

	Debtor 1		Debtor 2	
	Sources of income Describe below.	**Gross income from each source** (before deductions and exclusions)	**Sources of income** Describe below.	**Gross income** (before deductions and exclusions)

Part 3:   List Certain Payments You Made Before You Filed for Bankruptcy

6. **Are either Debtor 1's or Debtor 2's debts primarily consumer debts?**

☐ No.   **Neither Debtor 1 nor Debtor 2 has primarily consumer debts.** *Consumer debts* are defined in 11 U.S.C. § 101(8) as "incurred by an individual primarily for a personal, family, or household purpose."

     During the 90 days before you filed for bankruptcy, did you pay any creditor a total of $6,425* or more?

     ☐ No.   Go to line 7.

     ☐ Yes   List below each creditor to whom you paid a total of $6,425* or more in one or more payments and the total amount you paid that creditor. Do not include payments for domestic support obligations, such as child support and alimony. Also, do not include payments to an attorney for this bankruptcy case.
     * Subject to adjustment on 4/01/19 and every 3 years after that for cases filed on or after the date of adjustment.

■ Yes.   **Debtor 1 or Debtor 2 or both have primarily consumer debts.**
     During the 90 days before you filed for bankruptcy, did you pay any creditor a total of $600 or more?

     ☐ No.   Go to line 7.

     ■ Yes   List below each creditor to whom you paid a total of $600 or more and the total amount you paid that creditor. Do not include payments for domestic support obligations, such as child support and alimony. Also, do not include payments to an attorney for this bankruptcy case.

Creditor's Name and Address	Dates of payment	Total amount paid	Amount you still owe	Was this payment for ...
Lonetree **PO Box 305** **Lucerne, CA 95458**	6/1/2017	$900.00	$18,000.00	■ Mortgage ☐ Car ☐ Credit Card ☐ Loan Repayment ☐ Suppliers or vendors ☐ Other__

Debtor 1   **Carrie Anne Edwards**   Case number *(if known)* _____

7. **Within 1 year before you filed for bankruptcy, did you make a payment on a debt you owed anyone who was an insider?**
Insiders include your relatives; any general partners; relatives of any general partners; partnerships of which you are a general partner; corporations of which you are an officer, director, person in control, or owner of 20% or more of their voting securities; and any managing agent, including one for a business you operate as a sole proprietor. 11 U.S.C. § 101. Include payments for domestic support obligations, such as child support and alimony.

  ■ No
  ☐ Yes. List all payments to an insider.

Insider's Name and Address	Dates of payment	Total amount paid	Amount you still owe	Reason for this payment

8. **Within 1 year before you filed for bankruptcy, did you make any payments or transfer any property on account of a debt that benefited an insider?**
Include payments on debts guaranteed or cosigned by an insider.

  ■ No
  ☐ Yes. List all payments to an insider

Insider's Name and Address	Dates of payment	Total amount paid	Amount you still owe	Reason for this payment Include creditor's name

Part 4: Identify Legal Actions, Repossessions, and Foreclosures

9. **Within 1 year before you filed for bankruptcy, were you a party in any lawsuit, court action, or administrative proceeding?**
List all such matters, including personal injury cases, small claims actions, divorces, collection suits, paternity actions, support or custody modifications, and contract disputes.

  ☐ No
  ■ Yes. Fill in the details.

Case title Case number	Nature of the case	Court or agency	Status of the case
Bob Jones III v. Carrie Anne Edwards Case No.: MCV-34457	Civil	**Placer County Superior Court 10820 Justice Center Drive Roseville, CA 95678**	■ Pending ☐ On appeal ☐ Concluded **Negligence action for auto accident**

10. **Within 1 year before you filed for bankruptcy, was any of your property repossessed, foreclosed, garnished, attached, seized, or levied?**
Check all that apply and fill in the details below.

  ☐ No. Go to line 11.
  ■ Yes. Fill in the information below.

Creditor Name and Address	Describe the Property Explain what happened	Date	Value of the property
JNR Adjustment Co. PO Box 27070 Minneapolis, MN 55427	**Wage garnishment for two months totaling $510 for judgment on debt owed to DVD club.** ☐ Property was repossessed. ☐ Property was foreclosed. ■ Property was garnished. ☐ Property was attached, seized or levied.	4/7/2017	$510.00

Debtor 1   **Carrie Anne Edwards**   Case number (if known) _____

Creditor Name and Address	Describe the Property Explain what happened	Date	Value of the property
Eskanos & Adler **2325 Clayton Rd.** **Concord, CA 94520**	**Repossessed furniture worth $800** ■ Property was repossessed. ☐ Property was foreclosed. ☐ Property was garnished. ☐ Property was attached, seized or levied.	**4/30/2017**	**$800.00**
Grand Junction Mortgage **3456 Eighth St.** **Clearlake, CA 95422**	**Home described in Schedule A/B. Sale is scheduled but hasn't happened yet.** ☐ Property was repossessed. ☐ Property was foreclosed. ☐ Property was garnished. ☐ Property was attached, seized or levied.	**Notice of Default Sent 10/1/2016**	**Unknown**

11. **Within 90 days before you filed for bankruptcy, did any creditor, including a bank or financial institution, set off any amounts from your accounts or refuse to make a payment because you owed a debt?**

  ■ No
  ☐ Yes. Fill in the details.

Creditor Name and Address	Describe the action the creditor took	Date action was taken	Amount

12. **Within 1 year before you filed for bankruptcy, was any of your property in the possession of an assignee for the benefit of creditors, a court-appointed receiver, a custodian, or another official?**

  ■ No
  ☐ Yes

Part 5:	List Certain Gifts and Contributions

13. **Within 2 years before you filed for bankruptcy, did you give any gifts with a total value of more than $600 per person?**

  ■ No
  ☐ Yes. Fill in the details for each gift.

Gifts with a total value of more than $600 per person Person to Whom You Gave the Gift and Address:	Describe the gifts	Dates you gave the gifts	Value

14. **Within 2 years before you filed for bankruptcy, did you give any gifts or contributions with a total value of more than $600 to any charity?**

  ☐ No
  ■ Yes. Fill in the details for each gift or contribution.

Gifts or contributions to charities that total more than $600 Charity's Name Address (Number, Street, City, State and ZIP Code)	Describe what you contributed	Dates you contributed	Value
Universal Life Church **43322 First Street** **Citrus Heights, CA 95621**	**Charitable contributions (tithing) of $250 per month**	**2015 - 2017**	**$6,000.00**

Debtor 1   **Carrie Anne Edwards**   Case number *(if known)* _____

Part 6:   List Certain Losses

15. Within 1 year before you filed for bankruptcy or since you filed for bankruptcy, did you lose anything because of theft, fire, other disaster, or gambling?

    ■   No
    ☐   Yes. Fill in the details.

Describe the property you lost and how the loss occurred	Describe any insurance coverage for the loss Include the amount that insurance has paid. List pending insurance claims on line 33 of *Schedule A/B: Property.*	Date of your loss	Value of property lost

Part 7:   List Certain Payments or Transfers

16. Within 1 year before you filed for bankruptcy, did you or anyone else acting on your behalf pay or transfer any property to anyone you consulted about seeking bankruptcy or preparing a bankruptcy petition?
Include any attorneys, bankruptcy petition preparers, or credit counseling agencies for services required in your bankruptcy.

    ☐   No
    ■   Yes. Fill in the details.

Person Who Was Paid Address Email or website address Person Who Made the Payment, if Not You	Description and value of any property transferred	Date payment or transfer was made	Amount of payment
Jim McDonald, Esq. 444 State St. Ukiah, CA 95482 mcdonaldlaw@email.com	$100 for bankruptcy advice	7/21/2017	$100.00
ABC Bankruptcy Counseling 1731 Second St. Bloomfield, NJ 07003 bkcounseling@abc.com	$30 for pre-filing bankruptcy counseling course	6/1/2017	$30.00

17. Within 1 year before you filed for bankruptcy, did you or anyone else acting on your behalf pay or transfer any property to anyone who promised to help you deal with your creditors or to make payments to your creditors?
Do not include any payment or transfer that you listed on line 16.

    ■   No
    ☐   Yes. Fill in the details.

Person Who Was Paid Address	Description and value of any property transferred	Date payment or transfer was made	Amount of payment

18. Within 2 years before you filed for bankruptcy, did you sell, trade, or otherwise transfer any property to anyone, other than property transferred in the ordinary course of your business or financial affairs?
Include both outright transfers and transfers made as security (such as the granting of a security interest or mortgage on your property). Do not include gifts and transfers that you have already listed on this statement.

    ☐   No
    ■   Yes. Fill in the details.

Person Who Received Transfer Address Person's relationship to you	Description and value of property transferred	Describe any property or payments received or debts paid in exchange	Date transfer was made
Robert James 5554 15th St. Orangevale, CA 95662 None - Arm's length transaction	2009 Infinity sold for $8,000, fair market value according to www.kbb.com, money spent on house payment, car payment, and bills.	None.	3/23/2017

19. Within 10 years before you filed for bankruptcy, did you transfer any property to a self-settled trust or similar device of which you are a

Debtor 1   Carrie Anne Edwards   Case number *(if known)* _____

beneficiary? (These are often called *asset-protection devices*.)
- ■ No
- ☐ Yes. Fill in the details.

Name of trust	Description and value of the property transferred	Date Transfer was made

Part 8:   List of Certain Financial Accounts, Instruments, Safe Deposit Boxes, and Storage Units

20. Within 1 year before you filed for bankruptcy, were any financial accounts or instruments held in your name, or for your benefit, closed, sold, moved, or transferred?
Include checking, savings, money market, or other financial accounts; certificates of deposit; shares in banks, credit unions, brokerage houses, pension funds, cooperatives, associations, and other financial institutions.
- ☐ No
- ■ Yes. Fill in the details.

Name of Financial Institution and Address (Number, Street, City, State and ZIP Code)	Last 4 digits of account number	Type of account or instrument	Date account was closed, sold, moved, or transferred	Last balance before closing or transfer
WestAmerica Bank 444 North Main St. Rocklin, CA 95677	XXXX-5252	■ Checking ☐ Savings ☐ Money Market ☐ Brokerage ☐ Other	Final balance ($150) 7/1/2017	$150.00

21. Do you now have, or did you have within 1 year before you filed for bankruptcy, any safe deposit box or other depository for securities, cash, or other valuables?

- ■ No
- ☐ Yes. Fill in the details.

Name of Financial Institution Address (Number, Street, City, State and ZIP Code)	Who else had access to it? Address (Number, Street, City, State and ZIP Code)	Describe the contents	Do you still have it?

22. Have you stored property in a storage unit or place other than your home within 1 year before you filed for bankruptcy?

- ■ No
- ☐ Yes. Fill in the details.

Name of Storage Facility Address (Number, Street, City, State and ZIP Code)	Who else has or had access to it? Address (Number, Street, City, State and ZIP Code)	Describe the contents	Do you still have it?

Part 9:   Identify Property You Hold or Control for Someone Else

23. Do you hold or control any property that someone else owns? Include any property you borrowed from, are storing for, or hold in trust for someone.

- ☐ No
- ■ Yes. Fill in the details.

Owner's Name Address (Number, Street, City, State and ZIP Code)	Where is the property? (Number, Street, City, State and ZIP Code)	Describe the property	Value
Bonnie Johnson 3335 Irving St. Clearlake, CA 95422	Edwards residence	Poodle (Binkie) $300	$300.00

Part 10:   Give Details About Environmental Information

For the purpose of Part 10, the following definitions apply:

- ■ *Environmental law* means any federal, state, or local statute or regulation concerning pollution, contamination, releases of hazardous or

Debtor 1   **Carrie Anne Edwards**   Case number *(if known)*

toxic substances, wastes, or material into the air, land, soil, surface water, groundwater, or other medium, including statutes or regulations controlling the cleanup of these substances, wastes, or material.

- *Site* means any location, facility, or property as defined under any environmental law, whether you now own, operate, or utilize it or used to own, operate, or utilize it, including disposal sites.
- *Hazardous material* means anything an environmental law defines as a hazardous waste, hazardous substance, toxic substance, hazardous material, pollutant, contaminant, or similar term.

Report all notices, releases, and proceedings that you know about, regardless of when they occurred.

24. Has any governmental unit notified you that you may be liable or potentially liable under or in violation of an environmental law?

■ No
□ Yes. Fill in the details.

Name of site Address (Number, Street, City, State and ZIP Code)	Governmental unit Address (Number, Street, City, State and ZIP Code)	Environmental law, if you know it	Date of notice

25. Have you notified any governmental unit of any release of hazardous material?

■ No
□ Yes. Fill in the details.

Name of site Address (Number, Street, City, State and ZIP Code)	Governmental unit Address (Number, Street, City, State and ZIP Code)	Environmental law, if you know it	Date of notice

26. Have you been a party in any judicial or administrative proceeding under any environmental law? Include settlements and orders.

■ No
□ Yes. Fill in the details.

Case Title Case Number	Court or agency Name Address (Number, Street, City, State and ZIP Code)	Nature of the case	Status of the case

Part 11:   Give Details About Your Business or Connections to Any Business

27. Within 4 years before you filed for bankruptcy, did you own a business or have any of the following connections to any business?

□ A sole proprietor or self-employed in a trade, profession, or other activity, either full-time or part-time

□ A member of a limited liability company (LLC) or limited liability partnership (LLP)

□ A partner in a partnership

□ An officer, director, or managing executive of a corporation

□ An owner of at least 5% of the voting or equity securities of a corporation

■ No. None of the above applies. Go to Part 12.
□ Yes. Check all that apply above and fill in the details below for each business.

Business Name Address (Number, Street, City, State and ZIP Code)	Describe the nature of the business Name of accountant or bookkeeper	Employer Identification number Do not include Social Security number or ITIN. Dates business existed

28. Within 2 years before you filed for bankruptcy, did you give a financial statement to anyone about your business? Include all financial institutions, creditors, or other parties.

■ No
□ Yes. Fill in the details below.

Name Address (Number, Street, City, State and ZIP Code)	Date Issued

Part 12:   Sign Below

I have read the answers on this *Statement of Financial Affairs* and any attachments, and I declare under penalty of perjury that the answers

Debtor 1   **Carrie Anne Edwards**   Case number *(if known)* _____

are true and correct. I understand that making a false statement, concealing property, or obtaining money or property by fraud in connection with a bankruptcy case can result in fines up to $250,000, or imprisonment for up to 20 years, or both. 18 U.S.C. §§ 152, 1341, 1519, and 3571.

/s/ Carrie Anne Edwards
_____   _____
Carrie Anne Edwards   **Signature of Debtor 2**
Signature of Debtor 1

Date   **October 2, 2017**   Date   _____

Did you attach additional pages to *Your Statement of Financial Affairs for Individuals Filing for Bankruptcy* **(Official Form 107)?**
■ No
☐ Yes

Did you pay or agree to pay someone who is not an attorney to help you fill out bankruptcy forms?
■ No
☐ Yes. Name of Person _____. Attach the *Bankruptcy Petition Preparer's Notice, Declaration, and Signature* (Official Form 119).

Fill in this information to identify your case:

Debtor 1	**Carrie Anne Edwards**
	First Name Middle Name Last Name
Debtor 2	
(Spouse if, filing)	First Name Middle Name Last Name
United States Bankruptcy Court for the:	EASTERN DISTRICT OF CALIFORNIA
Case number	
(if known)	

☐ Check if this is an
amended filing

Official Form 108

Statement of Intention for Individuals Filing Under Chapter 7

12/15

If you are an individual filing under chapter 7, you must fill out this form if:

■ creditors have claims secured by your property, or

■ you have leased personal property and the lease has not expired.

You must file this form with the court within 30 days after you file your bankruptcy petition or by the date set for the meeting of creditors, whichever is earlier, unless the court extends the time for cause. You must also send copies to the creditors and lessors you list on the form

If two married people are filing together in a joint case, both are equally responsible for supplying correct information. Both debtors must sign and date the form.

Be as complete and accurate as possible. If more space is needed, attach a separate sheet to this form. On the top of any additional pages, write your name and case number (if known).

Part 1:	List Your Creditors Who Have Secured Claims

1. For any creditors that you listed in Part 1 of Schedule D: Creditors Who Have Claims Secured by Property (Official Form 106D), fill in the information below.

Identify the creditor and the property that is collateral	What do you intend to do with the property that secures a debt?	Did you claim the property as exempt on Schedule C?
Creditor's name: **Fannie's Furniture** Description of property securing debt: **Used bedroom set**	☐ Surrender the property. ■ Retain the property and redeem it. ☐ Retain the property and enter into a *Reaffirmation Agreement*. ☐ Retain the property and [explain]:	☐ No ■ Yes
Creditor's name: **GMAC** Description of property securing debt: **2014 Toyota Camry 45,000 miles good condition (fair market value - nada.com) Location: 3045 Berwick St., Rocklin, CA**	☐ Surrender the property. ☐ Retain the property and redeem it. ■ Retain the property and enter into a *Reaffirmation Agreement*. ☐ Retain the property and [explain]:	■ No ☐ Yes
Creditor's name: **Grand Junction Mortgage** Description of **3045 Berwick St. Rocklin, CA**	☐ Surrender the property. ☐ Retain the property and redeem it. ☐ Retain the property and enter into a *Reaffirmation Agreement*.	■ No ☐ Yes

Official Form 108   Statement of Intention for Individuals Filing Under Chapter 7   page 1

Debtor 1   **Carrie Anne Edwards**   Case number *(if known)* _____

property   **95765**
securing debt:

☑ Retain the property and [explain]:
Debtor will retain collateral and continue to make regular payments.

Creditor's name: **Lending Tree**

Description of property securing debt: **3045 Berwick St. Rocklin, CA 95765**

☐ Surrender the property.
☐ Retain the property and redeem it.
☐ Retain the property and enter into a *Reaffirmation Agreement.*
☑ Retain the property and [explain]:
Debtor will retain collateral and continue to make regular payments.

☑ No
☐ Yes

Part 2:   **List Your Unexpired Personal Property Leases**

For any unexpired personal property lease that you listed in Schedule G: Executory Contracts and Unexpired Leases (Official Form 106G), fill in the information below. Do not list real estate leases. Unexpired leases are leases that are still in effect; the lease period has not yet ended. You may assume an unexpired personal property lease if the trustee does not assume it. 11 U.S.C. § 365(p)(2).

Describe your unexpired personal property leases   **Will the lease be assumed?**

Lessor's name: **Beauty Products Leasing Co.**

☐ No

☑ Yes

Description of leased Property: **Laser skin treatment machine. Leas** for 5-year **period that expires on May 2020**

Part 3:   **Sign Below**

Under penalty of perjury, I declare that I have indicated my intention about any property of my estate that secures a debt and any personal property that is subject to an unexpired lease.

X   **/s/ Carrie Anne Edwards**   X _____
      Carrie Anne Edwards   Signature of Debtor 2
      Signature of Debtor 1

Date   **October 2, 2017**   Date _____

Notice Required by 11 U.S.C. § 342(b) for Individuals Filing for Bankruptcy (Form 2010)

This notice is for you if:

You are an individual filing for bankruptcy, and

Your debts are primarily consumer debts. *Consumer debts* are defined in 11 U.S.C. § 101(8) as "incurred by an individual primarily for a personal, family, or household purpose."

The types of bankruptcy that are available to individuals

Individuals who meet the qualifications may file under one of four different chapters of Bankruptcy Code:

    Chapter 7 - Liquidation

    Chapter 11 - Reorganization

    Chapter 12 - Voluntary repayment plan for family farmers or fishermen

    Chapter 13 - Voluntary repayment plan for individuals with regular income

You should have an attorney review your decision to file for bankruptcy and the choice of chapter.

Chapter 7:	Liquidation
$245	filing fee
$75	administrative fee
+ $15	trustee surcharge
$335	total fee

Chapter 7 is for individuals who have financial difficulty preventing them from paying their debts and who are willing to allow their nonexempt property to be used to pay their creditors. The primary purpose of filing under chapter 7 is to have your debts discharged. The bankruptcy discharge relieves you after bankruptcy from having to pay many of your pre-bankruptcy debts. Exceptions exist for particular debts, and liens on property may still be enforced after discharge. For example, a creditor may have the right to foreclose a home mortgage or repossess an automobile.

However, if the court finds that you have committed certain kinds of improper conduct described in the Bankruptcy Code, the court may deny your discharge.

You should know that even if you file chapter 7 and you receive a discharge, some debts are not discharged under the law. Therefore, you may still be responsible to pay:

    most taxes;

    most student loans;

    domestic support and property settlement obligations;

most fines, penalties, forfeitures, and criminal restitution obligations; and

certain debts that are not listed in your bankruptcy papers.

You may also be required to pay debts arising from:

fraud or theft;

fraud or defalcation while acting in breach of fiduciary capacity;

intentional injuries that you inflicted; and

death or personal injury caused by operating a motor vehicle, vessel, or aircraft while intoxicated from alcohol or drugs.

If your debts are primarily consumer debts, the court can dismiss your chapter 7 case if it finds that you have enough income to repay creditors a certain amount. You must file *Chapter 7 Statement of Your Current Monthly Income* (Official Form 122A–1) if you are an individual filing for bankruptcy under chapter 7. This form will determine your current monthly income and compare whether your income is more than the median income that applies in your state.

If your income is not above the median for your state, you will not have to complete the other chapter 7 form, the *Chapter 7 Means Test Calculation* (Official Form 122A–2).

If your income is above the median for your state, you must file a second form —the *Chapter 7 Means Test Calculation* (Official Form 122A–2). The calculations on the form— sometimes called the *Means Test*—deduct from your income living expenses and payments on certain debts to determine any amount available to pay unsecured creditors. If

your income is more than the median income for your state of residence and family size, depending on the results of the *Means Test*, the U.S. trustee, bankruptcy administrator, or creditors can file a motion to dismiss your case under § 707(b) of the Bankruptcy Code. If a motion is filed, the court will decide if your case should be dismissed. To avoid dismissal, you may choose to proceed under another chapter of the Bankruptcy Code.

If you are an individual filing for chapter 7 bankruptcy, the trustee may sell your property to pay your debts, subject to your right to exempt the property or a portion of the proceeds from the sale of the property. The property, and the proceeds from property that your bankruptcy trustee sells or liquidates that you are entitled to, is called *exempt property*. Exemptions may enable you to keep your home, a car, clothing, and household items or to receive some of the proceeds if the property is sold.

Exemptions are not automatic. To exempt property, you must list it on *Schedule C: The Property You Claim as Exempt* (Official Form 106C). If you do not list the property, the trustee may sell it and pay all of the proceeds to your creditors.

Chapter 11: Reorganization

	$1,167	filing fee
+	$550	administrative fee
	$1,717	total fee

Chapter 11 is often used for reorganizing a business, but is also available to individuals. The provisions of chapter 11 are too complicated to summarize briefly.

Read These Important Warnings

Because bankruptcy can have serious long-term financial and legal consequences, including loss of your property, you should hire an attorney and carefully consider all of your options before you file. Only an attorney can give you legal advice about what can happen as a result of filing for bankruptcy and what your options are. If you do file for bankruptcy, an attorney can help you fill out the forms properly and protect you, your family, your home, and your possessions.

Although the law allows you to represent yourself in bankruptcy court, you should understand that many people find it difficult to represent themselves successfully. The rules are technical, and a mistake or inaction may harm you. If you file without an attorney, you are still responsible for knowing and following all of the legal requirements.

You should not file for bankruptcy if you are not eligible to file or if you do not intend to file the necessary documents.

Bankruptcy fraud is a serious crime; you could be fined and imprisoned if you commit fraud in your bankruptcy case. Making a false statement, concealing property, or obtaining money or property by fraud in connection with a bankruptcy case can result in fines up to $250,000, or imprisonment for up to 20 years, or both. 18 U.S.C. §§ 152, 1341, 1519, and 3571.

Chapter 12: Repayment plan for family farmers or fishermen

	$200	filing fee
+	$75	administrative fee
	$275	total fee

Similar to chapter 13, chapter 12 permits family farmers and fishermen to repay their debts over a period of time using future earnings and to discharge some debts that are not paid.

Chapter 13: Repayment plan for individuals with regular income

	$235	filing fee
+	$75	administrative fee
	$310	total fee

Chapter 13 is for individuals who have regular income and would like to pay all or part of their debts in installments over a period of time and to discharge some debts that are not paid. You are eligible for chapter 13 only if your debts are not more than certain dollar amounts set forth in 11 U.S.C. § 109.

Under chapter 13, you must file with the court a plan to repay your creditors all or part of the money that you owe them, usually using your future earnings. If the court approves your plan, the court will allow you to repay your debts, as adjusted by the plan, within 3 years or 5 years, depending on your income and other factors.

After you make all the payments under your plan, many of your debts are discharged. The debts that are not discharged and that you may still be responsible to pay include:

domestic support obligations,

most student loans,

certain taxes,

debts for fraud or theft,

debts for fraud or defalcation while acting in a fiduciary capacity,

most criminal fines and restitution obligations,

certain debts that are not listed in your bankruptcy papers,

certain debts for acts that caused death or personal injury, and

certain long-term secured debts.

Warning: File Your Forms on Time

Section 521(a)(1) of the Bankruptcy Code requires that you promptly file detailed information about your creditors, assets, liabilities, income, expenses and general financial condition. The court may dismiss your bankruptcy case if you do not file this information within the deadlines set by the Bankruptcy Code, the Bankruptcy Rules, and the local rules of the court.

For more information about the documents and their deadlines, go to:
http://www.uscourts.gov/bkforms/bankruptcy_forms.html#procedure.

Bankruptcy crimes have serious consequences

If you knowingly and fraudulently conceal assets or make a false oath or statement under penalty of perjury—either orally or in writing—in connection with a bankruptcy case, you may be fined, imprisoned, or both.

All information you supply in connection with a bankruptcy case is subject to examination by the Attorney General acting through the Office of the U.S. Trustee, the Office of the U.S. Attorney, and other offices and employees of the U.S. Department of Justice.

Make sure the court has your mailing address

The bankruptcy court sends notices to the mailing address you list on *Voluntary Petition for Individuals Filing for Bankruptcy* (Official Form 101). To ensure that you receive information about your case, Bankruptcy Rule 4002 requires that you notify the court of any changes in your address.

A married couple may file a bankruptcy case together—called a *joint case*. If you file a joint case and each spouse lists the same mailing address on the bankruptcy petition, the bankruptcy court generally will mail you and your spouse one copy of each notice, unless you file a statement with the court asking that each spouse receive separate copies.

Understand which services you could receive from credit counseling agencies

The law generally requires that you receive a credit counseling briefing from an approved credit counseling agency. 11 U.S.C. § 109(h). If you are filing a joint case, both spouses must receive the briefing. With limited exceptions, you must receive it within the 180 days *before* you file your bankruptcy petition. This briefing is usually conducted by telephone or on the Internet.

In addition, after filing a bankruptcy case, you generally must complete a financial management instructional course before you can receive a discharge. If you are filing a joint case, both spouses must complete the course.

You can obtain the list of agencies approved to provide both the briefing and the instructional course from: http://justice.gov/ust/eo/hapcpa/ccde/cc_approved.html.

In Alabama and North Carolina, go to: http://www.uscourts.gov/FederalCourts/Bankruptcy/BankruptcyResources/ApprovedCredit AndDebtCounselors.aspx.

If you do not have access to a computer, the clerk of the bankruptcy court may be able to help you obtain the list.

United States Bankruptcy Court
Northern District of California

IN RE: Case No. _____

Edwards, Carrie Anne _____ Chapter **7**_____
                            Debtor(s)

CREDITOR MATRIX COVER SHEET

I declare that the attached Creditor Mailing Matrix, consisting of _____**3** sheets, contains the correct, complete and current names and addresses of all priority, secured and unsecured creditors listed in debtor's filing and that this matrix conforms with the Clerk's promulgated requirements.

DATED:

_____
Signature of Debtor's Attorney or Pro Per Debtor

Creditor Mailing Matrix

In re ___Carrie Ann Edwards___   Case No. _____
             Debtor(s)   Chapter ____7_____

Alan Accountant
5 Green St
Cleveland, OH 44118

American Allowance
PO Box 1
New York, NY 10001

Angel Of Mercy Hospital
4444 Elevisior St
Belmont, CA 94003

Beauty Products Leasing Co
44332 Eighth St
Geismar, LA 70734

Bob Jones III
4566 Fifth Ave
New York, NY 10020

Bonnie Johnson
3335 Irving St
Clearlake, CA 95422

Cal State Central Credit Union
1205 N Dutton Av
Santa Rosa, CA 95401

Citibank
200 East North St
Columbus, OH 43266

Dr Dennis Dentist
45 Superior Way
Cleveland, OH 44118

Dr Helen Jones
443 First St
Soledad, CA 94750

Fannie's Furniture
55544 Grove St
Berkeley, CA 94710

GMAC
PO Box 23567
Duchesne, UT 84021

Grand Junction Mortage
3456 Eight St
Clearlake, CA 95422

Herman Jones
45543 Woodleigh Court
Smith River, CA 95567

Illuminating Co
20245 Old Hwy 53
Clearlake, CA 95422

IRS
Columbus, OH 43266

John White Esq
PO Box 401
Finley, CA 95435

Jon Edwards
900 Grand View
Jackson, WY 83001

Lending Tree
PO Box 3333
Palo Alto, CA 94310

PG & E
315 North Forbes St
Lakeport, CA 95453

Sears
PO Box 11
Chicago, IL 60619

DRAFT

Fill in this information to identify the case:

Debtor 1 _____
First Name   Middle Name   Last Name

Debtor 2 _____
(Spouse, if filing) First Name   Middle Name   Last Name

United States Bankruptcy Court for the: _____ District of _____

Case number _____ Chapter _____
(If known)

Official Form 119

Bankruptcy Petition Preparer's Notice, Declaration, and Signature   12/15

Bankruptcy petition preparers as defined in 11 U.S.C. § 110 must fill out this form every time they help prepare documents that are filed in the case. If more than one bankruptcy petition preparer helps with the documents, each must sign in Part 2. A bankruptcy petition preparer who does not comply with the provisions of title 11 of the United States Code and the Federal Rules of Bankruptcy Procedure may be fined, imprisoned, or both. 11 U.S.C. § 110; 18 U.S.C. § 156.

Part 1:	Notice to Debtor

Bankruptcy petition preparers must give the debtor a copy of this form and have the debtor sign it before they prepare any documents for filing or accept any compensation. A signed copy of this form must be filed with any document prepared.

Bankruptcy petition preparers are not attorneys and may not practice law or give you legal advice, including the following:

- whether to file a petition under the Bankruptcy Code (11 U.S.C. § 101 et seq.);

- whether filing a case under chapter 7, 11, 12, or 13 is appropriate;

- whether your debts will be eliminated or discharged in a case under the Bankruptcy Code;

- whether you will be able to keep your home, car, or other property after filing a case under the Bankruptcy Code;

- what tax consequences may arise because a case is filed under the Bankruptcy Code;

- whether any tax claims may be discharged;

- whether you may or should promise to repay debts to a creditor or enter into a reaffirmation agreement;

- how to characterize the nature of your interests in property or your debts; or

- what procedures and rights apply in a bankruptcy case.

The bankruptcy petition preparer _____ has notified me of
Name

any maximum allowable fee before preparing any document for filing or accepting any fee.

_____   Date _____
Signature of Debtor 1 acknowledging receipt of this notice   MM / DD / YYYY

_____   Date _____
Signature of Debtor 2 acknowledging receipt of this notice   MM / DD / YYYY

Debtor 1 _____   Case number *(if known)*_____
　　　　　First Name　　　Middle Name　　　Last Name

Part 2:　Declaration and Signature of the Bankruptcy Petition Preparer

Under penalty of perjury, I declare that:

■ I am a bankruptcy petition preparer or the officer, principal, responsible person, or partner of a bankruptcy petition preparer;

■ I or my firm prepared the documents listed below and gave the debtor a copy of them and the *Notice to Debtor by Bankruptcy Petition Preparer* as required by 11 U.S.C. §§ 110(b), 110(h), and 342(b); and

■ if rules or guidelines are established according to 11 U.S.C. § 110(h) setting a maximum fee for services that bankruptcy petition preparers may charge, I or my firm notified the debtor of the maximum amount before preparing any document for filing or before accepting any fee from the debtor.

_____　_____　_____
Printed name　　　　　　　　　　Title, if any　　　　　　　Firm name, if it applies

_____　_____
Number　　　　Street

_____　_____　_____　_____
City　　　　　　　　　　　　　　State　　　ZIP Code　　　Contact phone

I or my firm prepared the documents checked below and the completed declaration is made a part of each document that I check:
(Check all that apply.)

❑ Voluntary Petition (Form 101)

❑ Statement About Your Social Security Numbers (Form 121)

❑ Summary of Your Assets and Liabilities and Certain Statistical Information (Form 106Sum)

❑ Schedule A/B (Form 106A/B)

❑ Schedule C (Form 106C)

❑ Schedule D (Form 106D)

❑ Schedule E/F (Form 106E/F)

❑ Schedule G (Form 106G)

❑ Schedule H (Form 106H)

❑ Schedule I (Form 106I)

❑ Schedule J (Form 106J)

❑ Declaration About an Individual Debtor's Schedules (Form 106Dec)

❑ Statement of Financial Affairs (Form 107)

❑ Statement of Intention for Individuals Filing Under Chapter 7 (Form 108)

❑ Chapter 7 Statement of Your Current Monthly Income (Form 122A-1)

❑ Statement of Exemption from Presumption of Abuse Under § 707(b)(2) (Form 122A-1Supp)

❑ Chapter 7 Means Test Calculation (Form 122A-2)

❑ Chapter 11 Statement of Your Current Monthly Income (Form 122B)

❑ Chapter 13 Statement of Your Current Monthly Income and Calculation of Commitment Period (Form 122C-1)

❑ Chapter 13 Calculation of Your Disposable Income (Form 122C-2)

❑ Application to Pay Filing Fee in Installments (Form 103A)

❑ Application to Have Chapter 7 Filing Fee Waived (Form 103B)

❑ A list of names and addresses of all creditors (*creditor or mailing matrix*)

❑ Other _____

Bankruptcy petition preparers must sign and give their Social Security numbers. If more than one bankruptcy petition preparer prepared the documents to which this declaration applies, the signature and Social Security number of each preparer must be provided. 11 U.S.C. § 110.

_____　__ __ __ — __ __ — __ __ __ __　Date _____
Signature of bankruptcy petition preparer or officer, principal, responsible　　Social Security number of person who signed　　MM / DD / YYYY
person, or partner

_____
Printed name

_____　__ __ __ — __ __ — __ __ __ __　Date _____
Signature of bankruptcy petition preparer or officer, principal, responsible　　Social Security number of person who signed　　MM / DD / YYYY
person, or partner

_____
Printed name

United States Bankruptcy Court for the:

EASTERN DISTRICT OF CALIFORNIA

Case number *(if known)*: _____

Official Form 121
Statement About Your Social Security Numbers

12/15

Use this form to tell the court about any Social Security or federal Individual Taxpayer Identification numbers you have used. Do not file this form as part of the public case file. This form must be submitted separately and must not be included in the court's public electronic records. Please consult local court procedures for submission requirements.

To protect your privacy, the court will not make this form available to the public. You should not include a full Social Security Number or Individual Taxpayer Number on any other document filed with the court. The court will make only the last four digits of your numbers known to the public. However, the full numbers will be available to your creditors, the U.S. Trustee or bankruptcy administrator, and the trustee assigned to your case.

Making a false statement, concealing property, or obtaining money or property by fraud in connection with a bankruptcy case can result in fines up to $250,000, or imprisonment for up to 20 years, or both. 18 U.S.C. §§ 152, 1341, 1519, and 3571.

Part 1: Tell the Court About Yourself and Your spouse if Your Spouse is Filing With You

	For Debtor 1:	For Debtor 2 (Only if Spouse is Filing:)
1. Your name	**Carrie** First name	First name
	Anne Middle name	Middle name
	Edwards Last name	Last name

Part 2: Tell the Court About all of Your Social Security or Federal Individual Taxpayer Identification Numbers

2. All Social Security Numbers you have used	000-00-628▮ ☐ You do not have a Social Security Number	☐ You do not have a Social Security Number
3. All federal Individual Taxpayer Identification Numbers (ITIN) you have used	■ You do not have an ITIN.	☐ You do not have an ITIN.

Part 3: Sign Below

Under penalty of perjury, I declare that the information I have provided in this form is true and correct.	Under penalty of perjury, I declare that the information I have provided in this form is true and correct.
X **/s/ Carrie Anne Edwards** **Carrie Anne Edwards** Signature of Debtor 1	X _____ Signature of Debtor 2
Date **October 2, 2017**	Date _____

Fill in this information to identify your case:

Debtor 1   **Carrie Anne Edwards**

Debtor 2
(Spouse, if filing)

United States Bankruptcy Court for the: Eastern District of California

Case number
(if known)

Check one box only as directed in this form and in Form 122A-1Supp:

■ 1. There is no presumption of abuse

☐ 2. The calculation to determine if a presumption of abuse applies will be made under *Chapter 7 Means Test Calculation* (Official Form 122A-2).

☐ 3. The Means Test does not apply now because of qualified military service but it could apply later.

☐ Check if this is an amended filing

Official Form 122A - 1
Chapter 7 Statement of Your Current Monthly Income

12/15

Be as complete and accurate as possible. If two married people are filing together, both are equally responsible for being accurate. If more space is needed, attach a separate sheet to this form. Include the line number to which the additional information applies. On the top of any additional pages, write your name and case number (if known). If you believe that you are exempted from a presumption of abuse because you do not have primarily consumer debts or because of qualifying military service, complete and file *Statement of Exemption from Presumption of Abuse Under § 707(b)(2)* (Official Form 122A-1Supp) with this form.

Part 1:	Calculate Your Current Monthly Income

1. **What is your marital and filing status?** Check one only.

  ■ **Not married.** Fill out Column A, lines 2-11.

  ☐ **Married and your spouse is filing with you.** Fill out both Columns A and B, lines 2-11.

  ☐ **Married and your spouse is NOT filing with you.** You and your spouse are:

    ☐ **Living in the same household and are not legally separate.** Fill out both Columns A and B, lines 2-11.

    ☐ **Living separately or are legally separated.** Fill out Column A, lines 2-11; do not fill out Column B. By checking this box, you declare under penalty of perjury that you and your spouse are legally separated under nonbankruptcy law that applies or that you and your spouse are living apart for reasons that do not include evading the Means Test requirements. 11 U.S.C § 707(b)(7)(B).

Fill in the average monthly income that you received from all sources, derived during the 6 full months before you file this bankruptcy case. 11 U.S.C. § 101(10A). For example, if you are filing on September 15, the 6-month period would be March 1 through August 31. If the amount of your monthly income varied during the 6 months, add the income for all 6 months and divide the total by 6. Fill in the result. Do not include any income amount more than once. For example, if both spouses own the same rental property, put the income from that property in one column only. If you have nothing to report for any line, write $0 in the space.

		Column A Debtor 1	Column B Debtor 2 or non-filing spouse
2.	**Your gross wages, salary, tips, bonuses, overtime, and commissions** (before all payroll deductions).	$ 5,276.00	$
3.	**Alimony and maintenance payments.** Do not include payments from a spouse if Column B is filled in.	$ 0.00	$
4.	**All amounts from any source which are regularly paid for household expenses of you or your dependents, including child support.** Include regular contributions from an unmarried partner, members of your household, your dependents, parents, and roommates. Include regular contributions from a spouse only if Column B is not filled in. Do not include payments you listed on line 3.	$ 400.00	$

5. **Net income from operating a business, profession, or farm**

	Debtor 1		
Gross receipts (before all deductions)	$	0.00	
Ordinary and necessary operating expenses	-$	0.00	
Net monthly income from a business, profession, or farm	$	0.00	Copy here -> $ 0.00 $

6. **Net income from rental and other real property**

	Debtor 1		
Gross receipts (before all deductions)	$	0.00	
Ordinary and necessary operating expenses	-$	0.00	
Net monthly income from rental or other real property	$	0.00	Copy here -> $ 0.00 $

7. **Interest, dividends, and royalties** $ 0.00 $

Debtor 1 **Carrie Anne Edwards**   Case number (if known) _____

		Column A Debtor 1	Column B Debtor 2 or non-filing spouse
8.	**Unemployment compensation**	$ 0.00	$
	Do not enter the amount if you contend that the amount received was a benefit under the Social Security Act. Instead, list it here:		
	For you $	0.00	
	For your spouse $		
9.	**Pension or retirement income.** Do not include any amount received that was a benefit under the Social Security Act.	$ 0.00	$
10.	**Income from all other sources not listed above.** Specify the source and amount. Do not include any benefits received under the Social Security Act or payments received as a victim of a war crime, a crime against humanity, or international or domestic terrorism. If necessary, list other sources on a separate page and put the total below.		
	_____	$ 0.00	$
	_____	$ 0.00	$
	Total amounts from separate pages, if any.	+ $ 0.00	$

11. **Calculate your total current monthly income.** Add lines 2 through 10 for each column. Then add the total for Column A to the total for Column B.

$ **5,676.00** + $ _____ = $ **5,676.00**

Total current monthly income

Part 2: Determine Whether the Means Test Applies to You

12. **Calculate your current monthly income for the year.** Follow these steps:

12a. Copy your total current monthly income from line 11. _____ Copy line 11 here=> $ **5,676.00**

Multiply by 12 (the number of months in a year)   x 12

12b. The result is your annual income for this part of the form   12b. $ **68,112.00**

13. **Calculate the median family income that applies to you.** Follow these steps:

Fill in the state in which you live.   **CA**

Fill in the number of people in your household.   **3**

Fill in the median family income for your state and size of household. _____   13. $ **75,160.00**

To find a list of applicable median income amounts, go online using the link specified in the separate instructions for this form. This list may also be available at the bankruptcy clerk's office.

14. **How do the lines compare?**

14a. ■ Line 12b is less than or equal to line 13. On the top of page 1, check box 1, *There is no presumption of abuse.* Go to Part 3.

14b. ☐ Line 12b is more than line 13. On the top of page 1, check box 2, *The presumption of abuse is determined by Form 122A-2.* Go to Part 3 and fill out Form 122A-2.

Part 3: Sign Below

By signing here, I declare under penalty of perjury that the information on this statement and in any attachments is true and correct.

X **/s/ Carrie Anne Edwards**
    Carrie Anne Edwards
    Signature of Debtor 1

Date **October 2, 2017**
    MM / DD / YYYY

If you checked line 14a, do NOT fill out or file Form 122A-2.

If you checked line 14b, fill out Form 122A-2 and file it with this form.

Fill in this information to identify your case:

Debtor 1 _____
        First Name   Middle Name   Last Name

Debtor 2 _____
(Spouse, if filing) First Name   Middle Name   Last Name

United States Bankruptcy Court for the: _____ District of _____

Case number _____
(If known)

☐ Check if this is an amended filing

Official Form 122A—1Supp

Statement of Exemption from Presumption of Abuse Under § 707(b)(2) 12/15

File this supplement together with *Chapter 7 Statement of Your Current Monthly Income* **(Official Form 122A-1), if you believe that you are exempted from a presumption of abuse. Be as complete and accurate as possible. If two married people are filing together, and any of the exclusions in this statement applies to only one of you, the other person should complete a separate Form 122A-1 if you believe that this is required by 11 U.S.C. § 707(b)(2)(C).**

Part 1: Identify the Kind of Debts You Have

1. **Are your debts primarily consumer debts?** *Consumer debts* are defined in 11 U.S.C. § 101(8) as "incurred by an individual primarily for a personal, family, or household purpose." Make sure that your answer is consistent with the answer you gave at line 16 of the *Voluntary Petition for Individuals Filing for Bankruptcy* (Official Form 101).

   ☐ No. Go to Form 122A-1; on the top of page 1 of that form, check box 1, *There is no presumption of abuse,* and sign Part 3. Then submit this supplement with the signed Form 122A-1.

   ☐ Yes. Go to Part 2.

Part 2: Determine Whether Military Service Provisions Apply to You

2. **Are you a disabled veteran** (as defined in 38 U.S.C. § 3741(1))?

   ☐ No. Go to line 3.

   ☐ Yes. Did you incur debts mostly while you were on active duty or while you were performing a homeland defense activity? 10 U.S.C. § 101(d)(1); 32 U.S.C. § 901(1).

      ☐ No. Go to line 3.

      ☐ Yes. Go to Form 122A-1; on the top of page 1 of that form, check box 1, *There is no presumption of abuse,* and sign Part 3. Then submit this supplement with the signed Form 122A-1.

3. **Are you or have you been a Reservist or member of the National Guard?**

   ☐ No. Complete Form 122A-1. Do not submit this supplement.

   ☐ Yes. Were you called to active duty or did you perform a homeland defense activity? 10 U.S.C. § 101(d)(1); 32 U.S.C. § 901(1).

     ☐ No. Complete Form 122A-1. Do not submit this supplement.

     ☐ Yes. Check any one of the following categories that applies:

       ☐ **I was called to active duty after September 11, 2001,** for at least 90 days and remain on active duty.

       ☐ **I was called to active duty after September 11, 2001,** for at least 90 days and was released from active duty on _____, which is fewer than 540 days before I file this bankruptcy case.

       ☐ **I am performing a homeland defense activity for at least 90 days.**

       ☐ **I performed a homeland defense activity for at least 90 days,** ending on _____, which is fewer than 540 days before I file this bankruptcy case.

If you checked one of the categories to the left, go to Form 122A-1. On the top of page 1 of Form 122A-1, check box 3, *The Means Test does not apply now,* and sign Part 3. Then submit this supplement with the signed Form 122A-1. You are not required to fill out the rest of Official Form 122A-1 during the exclusion period. The *exclusion period* means the time you are on active duty or are performing a homeland defense activity, and for 540 days afterward. 11 U.S.C. § 707(b)(2)(D)(ii).

If your exclusion period ends before your case is closed, you may have to file an amended form later.

Official Form 122A-1Supp   Statement of Exemption from Presumption of Abuse Under § 707(b)(2)

Fill in this information to identify your case:

Debtor 1 _____
First Name   Middle Name   Last Name

Debtor 2 _____
(Spouse, if filing) First Name   Middle Name   Last Name

United States Bankruptcy Court for the: _____ District of _____

Case number _____
(If known)

Check the appropriate box as directed in lines 40 or 42:

According to the calculations required by this Statement:

❑ 1. There is no presumption of abuse.

❑ 2. There is a presumption of abuse.

❑ Check if this is an amended filing

Official Form 122A–2
Chapter 7 Means Test Calculation
04/16

To fill out this form, you will need your completed copy of *Chapter 7 Statement of Your Current Monthly Income* (Official Form 122A-1).

Be as complete and accurate as possible. If two married people are filing together, both are equally responsible for being accurate. If more space is needed, attach a separate sheet to this form. Include the line number to which the additional information applies. On the top of any additional pages, write your name and case number (if known).

Part 1:   Determine Your Adjusted Income

1. Copy your total current monthly income... Copy line 11 from Official Form 122A-1 here➔ .... $_____

2. Did you fill out Column B in Part 1 of Form 122A-1?
   ❑ No. Fill in $0 for the total on line 3.
   ❑ Yes. Is your spouse filing with you?
      ❑ No. Go to line 3.
      ❑ Yes. Fill in $0 for the total on line 3.

3. Adjust your current monthly income by subtracting any part of your spouse's income not used to pay for the household expenses of you or your dependents. Follow these steps:

   On line 11, Column B of Form 122A–1, was any amount of the income you reported for your spouse NOT regularly used for the household expenses of you or your dependents?

   ❑ No. Fill in 0 for the total on line 3.
   ❑ Yes. Fill in the information below:

State each purpose for which the income was used For example, the income is used to pay your spouse's tax debt or to support people other than you or your dependents	Fill in the amount you are subtracting from your spouse's income
_____	$_____
_____	$_____
_____	+ $_____
Total.	$_____ Copy total here ....➔ − $_____

4. Adjust your current monthly income. Subtract the total on line 3 from line 1. $_____

Debtor 1 _____   Case number (if known)_____
         First Name   Middle Name   Last Name

Part 2:	Calculate Your Deductions from Your Income

The Internal Revenue Service (IRS) issues National and Local Standards for certain expense amounts. Use these amounts to answer the questions in lines 6-15. To find the IRS standards, go online using the link specified in the separate instructions for this form. This information may also be available at the bankruptcy clerk's office.

Deduct the expense amounts set out in lines 6-15 regardless of your actual expense. In later parts of the form, you will use some of your actual expenses if they are higher than the standards. Do not deduct any amounts that you subtracted from your spouse's income in line 3 and do not deduct any operating expenses that you subtracted from income in lines 5 and 6 of Form 122A–1.

If your expenses differ from month to month, enter the average expense.

Whenever this part of the form refers to *you*, it means both you and your spouse if Column B of Form 122A–1 is filled in.

5. **The number of people used in determining your deductions from income**

   Fill in the number of people who could be claimed as exemptions on your federal income tax return, plus the number of any additional dependents whom you support. This number may be different from the number of people in your household.

National Standards   You must use the IRS National Standards to answer the questions in lines 6-7.

6. **Food, clothing, and other items:** Using the number of people you entered in line 5 and the IRS National Standards, fill in the dollar amount for food, clothing, and other items. $_____

7. **Out-of-pocket health care allowance:** Using the number of people you entered in line 5 and the IRS National Standards, fill in the dollar amount for out-of-pocket health care. The number of people is split into two categories—people who are under 65 and people who are 65 or older—because older people have a higher IRS allowance for health care costs. If your actual expenses are higher than this IRS amount, you may deduct the additional amount on line 22.

   People who are under 65 years of age

   7a.   Out-of-pocket health care allowance per person $_____

   7b.   Number of people who are under 65   X _____

   7c.   **Subtotal.** Multiply line 7a by line 7b. $_____   Copy here➔ $_____

   People who are 65 years of age or older

   7d.   Out-of-pocket health care allowance per person $_____

   7e.   Number of people who are 65 or older   X _____

   7f.   **Subtotal.** Multiply line 7d by line 7e. $_____   Copy here➔   + $_____

   7g.   **Total.** Add lines 7c and 7f.. $_____   Copy total here➔ $_____

Debtor 1 _____   Case number (*if known*)_____
       First Name   Middle Name   Last Name

Local Standards   You must use the IRS Local Standards to answer the questions in lines 8-15.

Based on information from the IRS, the U.S. Trustee Program has divided the IRS Local Standard for housing for bankruptcy purposes into two parts:

- **Housing and utilities – Insurance and operating expenses**
- **Housing and utilities – Mortgage or rent expenses**

To answer the questions in lines 8-9, use the U.S. Trustee Program chart.

To find the chart, go online using the link specified in the separate instructions for this form. This chart may also be available at the bankruptcy clerk's office.

8. **Housing and utilities – Insurance and operating expenses:** Using the number of people you entered in line 5, fill in the dollar amount listed for your county for insurance and operating expenses. .... $_____

9. **Housing and utilities – Mortgage or rent expenses:**

    9a. Using the number of people you entered in line 5, fill in the dollar amount listed for your county for mortgage or rent expenses.. $_____

    9b. Total average monthly payment for all mortgages and other debts secured by your home.

       To calculate the total average monthly payment, add all amounts that are contractually due to each secured creditor in the 60 months after you file for bankruptcy. Then divide by 60.

Name of the creditor	Average monthly payment
_____	$_____
_____	$_____
_____	+ $_____

       Total average monthly payment $_____   Copy here➡   – $_____   Repeat this amount on line 33a.

    9c. Net mortgage or rent expense.

       Subtract line 9b (*total average monthly payment*) from line 9a (*mortgage or rent expense*). If this amount is less than $0, enter $0. .... $_____   Copy here➡ $_____

10. **If you claim that the U.S. Trustee Program's division of the IRS Local Standard for housing is incorrect and affects the calculation of your monthly expenses, fill in any additional amount you claim.** $_____

    Explain why: _____
            _____

11. **Local transportation expenses:** Check the number of vehicles for which you claim an ownership or operating expense.

    ❑ 0. Go to line 14.
    ❑ 1. Go to line 12.
    ❑ 2 or more. Go to line 12.

12. **Vehicle operation expense:** Using the IRS Local Standards and the number of vehicles for which you claim the operating expenses, fill in the *Operating Costs* that apply for your Census region or metropolitan statistical area. $_____

Official Form 122A–2   **Chapter 7 Means Test Calculation**   page **3**

Debtor 1 _____   Case number (if known)_____
First Name   Middle Name   Last Name

13. **Vehicle ownership or lease expense:** Using the IRS Local Standards, calculate the net ownership or lease expense for each vehicle below. You may not claim the expense if you do not make any loan or lease payments on the vehicle. In addition, you may not claim the expense for more than two vehicles.

Vehicle 1 **Describe Vehicle 1:** _____
_____

13a. Ownership or leasing costs using IRS Local Standard. .... $_____

13b. Average monthly payment for all debts secured by Vehicle 1.
Do not include costs for leased vehicles.

To calculate the average monthly payment here and on line 13e, add all amounts that are contractually due to each secured creditor in the 60 months after you filed for bankruptcy. Then divide by 60.

Name of each creditor for Vehicle 1	Average monthly payment
_____	$_____
_____	+ $_____
Total average monthly payment	$_____

Copy here ➡   − $_____   Repeat this amount on line 33b.

13c. Net Vehicle 1 ownership or lease expense
Subtract line 13b from line 13a. If this amount is less than $0, enter $0. .... $_____

Copy net Vehicle 1 expense here ..... ➡ $_____

Vehicle 2 **Describe Vehicle 2:** _____
_____

13d. Ownership or leasing costs using IRS Local Standard. .... $_____

13e. Average monthly payment for all debts secured by Vehicle 2.
Do not include costs for leased vehicles.

Name of each creditor for Vehicle 2	Average monthly payment
_____	$_____
_____	+ $_____
Total average monthly payment	$_____

Copy here ➡   − $_____   Repeat this amount on line 33c.

13f. Net Vehicle 2 ownership or lease expense
Subtract line 13e from 13d. If this amount is less than $0, enter $0. .... $_____

Copy net Vehicle 2 expense here ... ➡ $_____

14. **Public transportation expense:** If you claimed 0 vehicles in line 11, using the IRS Local Standards, fill in the *Public Transportation* expense allowance regardless of whether you use public transportation. $_____

15. **Additional public transportation expense:** If you claimed 1 or more vehicles in line 11 and if you claim that you may also deduct a public transportation expense, you may fill in what you believe is the appropriate expense, but you may not claim more than the IRS Local Standard for *Public Transportation*. $_____

Debtor 1 _____   Case number (*if known*)_____

      First Name   Middle Name   Last Name

Other Necessary Expenses   In addition to the expense deductions listed above, you are allowed your monthly expenses for the following IRS categories.

16. **Taxes:** The total monthly amount that you will actually owe for federal, state and local taxes, such as income taxes, self-employment taxes, Social Security taxes, and Medicare taxes. You may include the monthly amount withheld from your pay for these taxes. However, if you expect to receive a tax refund, you must divide the expected refund by 12 and subtract that number from the total monthly amount that is withheld to pay for taxes. $_____

    Do not include real estate, sales, or use taxes.

17. **Involuntary deductions:** The total monthly payroll deductions that your job requires, such as retirement contributions, union dues, and uniform costs.

    Do not include amounts that are not required by your job, such as voluntary 401(k) contributions or payroll savings. $_____

18. **Life insurance:** The total monthly premiums that you pay for your own term life insurance. If two married people are filing together, include payments that you make for your spouse's term life insurance. Do not include premiums for life insurance on your dependents, for a non-filing spouse's life insurance, or for any form of life insurance other than term. $_____

19. **Court-ordered payments:** The total monthly amount that you pay as required by the order of a court or administrative agency, such as spousal or child support payments.

    Do not include payments on past due obligations for spousal or child support. You will list these obligations in line 35. $_____

20. **Education:** The total monthly amount that you pay for education that is either required:
    ■ as a condition for your job, or
    ■ for your physically or mentally challenged dependent child if no public education is available for similar services. $_____

21. **Childcare:** The total monthly amount that you pay for childcare, such as babysitting, daycare, nursery, and preschool.

    Do not include payments for any elementary or secondary school education. $_____

22. **Additional health care expenses, excluding insurance costs:** The monthly amount that you pay for health care that is required for the health and welfare of you or your dependents and that is not reimbursed by insurance or paid by a health savings account. Include only the amount that is more than the total entered in line 7. Payments for health insurance or health savings accounts should be listed only in line 25. $_____

23. **Optional telephones and telephone services:** The total monthly amount that you pay for telecommunication services for you and your dependents, such as pagers, call waiting, caller identification, special long distance, or business cell phone service, to the extent necessary for your health and welfare or that of your dependents or for the production of income, if it is not reimbursed by your employer.   + $_____

    Do not include payments for basic home telephone, internet and cell phone service. Do not include self-employment expenses, such as those reported on line 5 of Official Form 122A-1, or any amount you previously deducted.

24. **Add all of the expenses allowed under the IRS expense allowances.**

    Add lines 6 through 23. $_____

Debtor 1 _____   Case number *(if known)* _____
  First Name   Middle Name   Last Name

Additional Expense Deductions	These are additional deductions allowed by the Means Test.
	Note: Do not include any expense allowances listed in lines 6-24.

25. **Health insurance, disability insurance, and health savings account expenses.** The monthly expenses for health insurance, disability insurance, and health savings accounts that are reasonably necessary for yourself, your spouse, or your dependents.

Health insurance $_____

Disability insurance $_____

Health savings account   **+** $_____

Total $_____   Copy total here➔ .... $_____

Do you actually spend this total amount?

☐ No. How much do you actually spend? $_____
☐ Yes

26. **Continuing contributions to the care of household or family members.** The actual monthly expenses that you will continue to pay for the reasonable and necessary care and support of an elderly, chronically ill, or disabled member of your household or member of your immediate family who is unable to pay for such expenses. These expenses may include contributions to an account of a qualified ABLE program. 26 U.S.C. § 529A(b). $_____

27. **Protection against family violence.** The reasonably necessary monthly expenses that you incur to maintain the safety of you and your family under the Family Violence Prevention and Services Act or other federal laws that apply. $_____

By law, the court must keep the nature of these expenses confidential.

28. **Additional home energy costs.** Your home energy costs are included in your insurance and operating expenses on line 8.

If you believe that you have home energy costs that are more than the home energy costs included in expenses on line 8, then fill in the excess amount of home energy costs. $_____

You must give your case trustee documentation of your actual expenses, and you must show that the additional amount claimed is reasonable and necessary.

29. **Education expenses for dependent children who are younger than 18.** The monthly expenses (not more than $160.42* per child) that you pay for your dependent children who are younger than 18 years old to attend a private or public elementary or secondary school. $_____

You must give your case trustee documentation of your actual expenses, and you must explain why the amount claimed is reasonable and necessary and not already accounted for in lines 6-23.

* Subject to adjustment on 4/01/19, and every 3 years after that for cases begun on or after the date of adjustment.

30. **Additional food and clothing expense.** The monthly amount by which your actual food and clothing expenses are higher than the combined food and clothing allowances in the IRS National Standards. That amount cannot be more than 5% of the food and clothing allowances in the IRS National Standards. $_____

To find a chart showing the maximum additional allowance, go online using the link specified in the separate instructions for this form. This chart may also be available at the bankruptcy clerk's office.

You must show that the additional amount claimed is reasonable and necessary.

31. **Continuing charitable contributions.** The amount that you will continue to contribute in the form of cash or financial instruments to a religious or charitable organization. 26 U.S.C. § 170(c)(1)-(2).   **+** $_____

32. **Add all of the additional expense deductions.** $_____
Add lines 25 through 31.

Debtor 1 _____   Case number (if known) _____
First Name   Middle Name   Last Name

Deductions for Debt Payment

33. **For debts that are secured by an interest in property that you own, including home mortgages, vehicle loans, and other secured debt, fill in lines 33a through 33e.**

To calculate the total average monthly payment, add all amounts that are contractually due to each secured creditor in the 60 months after you file for bankruptcy. Then divide by 60.

		Average monthly payment
Mortgages on your home:		
33a. Copy line 9b here .... ➔	$_____	
Loans on your first two vehicles:		
33b. Copy line 13b here. .... ➔	$_____	
33c. Copy line 13e here. .... ➔	$_____	

33d. List other secured debts:

Name of each creditor for other secured debt	Identify property that secures the debt	Does payment include taxes or insurance?	
_____	_____	☐ No / ☐ Yes	$_____
_____	_____	☐ No / ☐ Yes	$_____
_____	_____	☐ No / ☐ Yes	+ $_____

33e. Total average monthly payment. Add lines 33a through 33d.................... | $_____ | Copy total here ➔ | $_____

34. **Are any debts that you listed in line 33 secured by your primary residence, a vehicle, or other property necessary for your support or the support of your dependents?**

☐ No. Go to line 35.

☐ Yes. State any amount that you must pay to a creditor, in addition to the payments listed in line 33, to keep possession of your property (called the *cure amount*). Next, divide by 60 and fill in the information below.

Name of the creditor	Identify property that secures the debt	Total cure amount		Monthly cure amount
_____	_____	$_____	÷ 60 =	$_____
_____	_____	$_____	÷ 60 =	$_____
_____	_____	$_____	÷ 60 =	+ $_____
		Total	$_____	Copy total here ➔	$_____

35. **Do you owe any priority claims such as a priority tax, child support, or alimony — that are past due as of the filing date of your bankruptcy case?** 11 U.S.C. § 507.

☐ No. Go to line 36.

☐ Yes. Fill in the total amount of all of these priority claims. Do not include current or ongoing priority claims, such as those you listed in line 19.

Total amount of all past-due priority claims .... | $_____ | ÷ 60 = | $_____

Debtor 1 _____ Case number *(if known)*_____
First Name   Middle Name   Last Name

36. **Are you eligible to file a case under Chapter 13?** 11 U.S.C. § 109(e).
For more information, go online using the link for *Bankruptcy Basics* specified in the separate
instructions for this form. *Bankruptcy Basics* may also be available at the bankruptcy clerk's office.

☐ No. Go to line 37.

☐ Yes. Fill in the following information.

Projected monthly plan payment if you were filing under Chapter 13 $_____

Current multiplier for your district as stated on the list issued by the
Administrative Office of the United States Courts (for districts in Alabama and
North Carolina) or by the Executive Office for United States Trustees (for all
other districts).   X _____

To find a list of district multipliers that includes your district, go online using the
link specified in the separate instructions for this form. This list may also be
available at the bankruptcy clerk's office.

Average monthly administrative expense if you were filing under Chapter 13 $_____   Copy total here ➜ $_____

37. **Add all of the deductions for debt payment.**
Add lines 33e through 36. .... $_____

Total Deductions from Income

38. **Add all of the allowed deductions.**

Copy line 24, *All of the expenses allowed under IRS expense allowances* .... $_____

Copy line 32, *All of the additional expense deductions*.... $_____

Copy line 37, *All of the deductions for debt payment*....... $_____

Total deductions $_____   Copy total here .... ➜ $_____

Part 3:   Determine Whether There Is a Presumption of Abuse

39. **Calculate monthly disposable income for 60 months**

39a. Copy line 4, *adjusted current monthly income* ..... $_____

39b. Copy line 38, *Total deductions*.......... − $_____

39c. Monthly disposable income. 11 U.S.C. § 707(b)(2).
Subtract line 39b from line 39a. $_____   Copy here ➜ $_____

For the next 60 months (5 years)...   x 60

39d. **Total.** Multiply line 39c by 60. .... $_____   Copy here ➜ $_____

40. **Find out whether there is a presumption of abuse.** Check the box that applies:

☐ **The line 39d is less than $7,700*.** On the top of page 1 of this form, check box 1, *There is no presumption of abuse.* Go to Part 5.

☐ **The line 39d is more than $12,850*.** On the top of page 1 of this form, check box 2, *There is a presumption of abuse.* You may fill out Part 4 if you claim special circumstances. Then go to Part 5.

☐ **The line 39d is at least $7,700*, but not more than $12,850*.** Go to line 41.

* Subject to adjustment on 4/01/19, and every 3 years after that for cases filed on or after the date of adjustment.

Official Form 122A–2   **Chapter 7 Means Test Calculation**   page **8**

Debtor 1 _____   Case number (*if known*)_____
First Name   Middle Name   Last Name

41. 41a. **Fill in the amount of your total nonpriority unsecured debt.** If you filled out *A Summary of Your Assets and Liabilities and Certain Statistical Information Schedules* (Official Form 106Sum), you may refer to line 3b on that form... $_____

x .25

41b. **25% of your total nonpriority unsecured debt.** 11 U.S.C. § 707(b)(2)(A)(i)(I).
Multiply line 41a by 0.25. .... $_____   Copy here ➡ $_____

42. **Determine whether the income you have left over after subtracting all allowed deductions is enough to pay 25% of your unsecured, nonpriority debt.**
Check the box that applies:

❑ **Line 39d is less than line 41b.** On the top of page 1 of this form, check box 1, *There is no presumption of abuse.* Go to Part 5.

❑ **Line 39d is equal to or more than line 41b.** On the top of page 1 of this form, check box 2, *There is a presumption of abuse.* You may fill out Part 4 if you claim special circumstances. Then go to Part 5.

Part 4:	Give Details About Special Circumstances

43. **Do you have any special circumstances that justify additional expenses or adjustments of current monthly income for which there is no reasonable alternative?** 11 U.S.C. § 707(b)(2)(B).

❑ No. Go to Part 5.

❑ Yes. Fill in the following information. All figures should reflect your average monthly expense or income adjustment for each item. You may include expenses you listed in line 25.

You must give a detailed explanation of the special circumstances that make the expenses or income adjustments necessary and reasonable. You must also give your case trustee documentation of your actual expenses or income adjustments.

Give a detailed explanation of the special circumstances	Average monthly expense or income adjustment
_____	$_____
_____	$_____
_____	$_____
_____	$_____

Part 5:	Sign Below

By signing here, I declare under penalty of perjury that the information on this statement and in any attachments is true and correct.

✖ _____   ✖ _____
Signature of Debtor 1   Signature of Debtor 2

Date _____   Date _____
MM / DD / YYYY   MM / DD / YYYY

Fill in this information to identify the case:

Debtor 1 _____
         First Name   Middle Name   Last Name

Debtor 2 _____
(Spouse, if filing) First Name   Middle Name   Last Name

United States Bankruptcy Court for the: _____ District of _____

Case number _____
(If known)

Official Form 423

Certification About a Financial Management Course

12/15

If you are an individual, you must take an approved course about personal financial management if:

- **you filed for bankruptcy under chapter 7 or 13, or**
- **you filed for bankruptcy under chapter 11 and § 1141 (d)(3) applies.**

In a joint case, each debtor must take the course. 11 U.S.C. §§ 727(a)(11) and 1328(g).

After you finish the course, the provider will give you a certificate. The provider may notify the court that you have completed the course. If the provider does notify the court, you need not file this form. If the provider does not notify the court, then Debtor 1 and Debtor 2 must each file this form with the certificate number before your debts will be discharged.

- If you filed under chapter 7 and you need to file this form, file it within 60 days after the first date set for the meeting of creditors under § 341 of the Bankruptcy Code.

- If you filed under chapter 11 or 13 and you need to file this form, file it before you make the last payment that your plan requires or before you file a motion for a discharge under § 1141(d)(5)(B) or § 1328(b) of the Bankruptcy Code. Fed. R. Bankr. P. 1007(c).

In some cases, the court can waive the requirement to take the financial management course. To have the requirement waived, you must file a motion with the court and obtain a court order.

Part 1:   **Tell the Court About the Required Course**

You must check one:

- ☐ **I completed an approved course in personal financial management:**

   Date I took the course   _____
                          MM / DD / YYYY

   Name of approved provider   _____

   Certificate number   _____

- ☐ **I am not required to complete a course in personal financial management because the court has granted my motion for a waiver of the requirement based on** *(check one)*:

   - ☐ **Incapacity.** I have a mental illness or a mental deficiency that makes me incapable of realizing or making rational decisions about finances.

   - ☐ **Disability.** My physical disability causes me to be unable to complete a course in personal financial management in person, by phone, or through the internet, even after I reasonably tried to do so.

   - ☐ **Active duty.** I am currently on active military duty in a military combat zone.

   - ☐ **Residence.** I live in a district in which the United States trustee (or bankruptcy administrator) has determined that the approved instructional courses cannot adequately meet my needs.

Part 2:   **Sign Here**

I certify that the information I have provided is true and correct.

_____   _____   Date _____
Signature of debtor named on certificate   Printed name of debtor   MM / DD / YYYY

Official Form 423   **Certification About a Financial Management Course**

B2030 (Form 2030) (12/15)

United States Bankruptcy Court

_____ District Of _____

In re

Case No. _____

Debtor

Chapter _____

DISCLOSURE OF COMPENSATION OF ATTORNEY FOR DEBTOR

1. Pursuant to 11 U .S.C. § 329(a) and Fed. Bankr. P. 2016(b), I certify that I am the attorney for the above named debtor(s) and that compensation paid to me within one year before the filing of the petition in bankruptcy, or agreed to be paid to me, for services rendered or to be rendered on behalf of the debtor(s) in contemplation of or in connection with the bankruptcy case is as follows:

    For legal services, I have agreed to accept . . . . $_____

    Prior to the filing of this statement I have received . . . . $_____

    Balance Due . . . . $_____

2. The source of the compensation paid to me was:

    ☐ Debtor   ☐ Other (specify)

3. The source of compensation to be paid to me is:

    ☐ Debtor   ☐ Other (specify)

4. ☐ I have not agreed to share the above-disclosed compensation with any other person unless they are members and associates of my law firm.

    ☐ I have agreed to share the above-disclosed compensation with a other person or persons who are not members or associates of my law firm. A copy of the agreement, together with a list of the names of the people sharing in the compensation, is attached.

5. In return for the above-disclosed fee, I have agreed to render legal service for all aspects of the bankruptcy case, including:

    a. Analysis of the debtor' s financial situation, and rendering advice to the debtor in determining whether to file a petition in bankruptcy;

    b. Preparation and filing of any petition, schedules, statements of affairs and plan which may be required;

    c. Representation of the debtor at the meeting of creditors and confirmation hearing, and any adjourned hearings thereof;

B2030 (Form 2030) (12/15)

    d.   Representation of the debtor in adversary proceedings and other contested bankruptcy matters;

    e.   [Other provisions as needed]

6.   By agreement with the debtor(s), the above-disclosed fee does not include the following services:

CERTIFICATION

    I certify that the foregoing is a complete statement of any agreement or arrangement for payment to me for representation of the debtor(s) in this bankruptcy proceeding.

_____

Date

_____

Signature of Attorney

_____

Name of law firm

Fill in this information to identify your case:

Debtor 1	Carrie	Anne	Edwards
	First Name	Middle Name	Last Name
Debtor 2			
(Spouse, if filing)	First Name	Middle Name	Last Name

United States Bankruptcy Court for the: Eastern District of California

Case number: XXXX-XXXXX
(If known)

Official Form 427

Cover Sheet for Reaffirmation Agreement

12/15

Anyone who is a party to a reaffirmation agreement may fill out and file this form. Fill it out completely, attach it to the reaffirmation agreement, and file the documents within the time set under Bankruptcy Rule 4008.

Part 1: Explain the Repayment Terms of the Reaffirmation Agreement

1. Who is the creditor?

GMAC
Name of the creditor

2. How much is the debt?

On the date that the bankruptcy case is filed $ 15,000.00

To be paid under the reaffirmation agreement $ 15,000.00

$ 375.00 per month for 40 months (if fixed interest rate)

3. What is the Annual Percentage Rate (APR) of interest? (See Bankruptcy Code § 524(k)(3)(E).)

Before the bankruptcy case was filed 8.00 %

Under the reaffirmation agreement 8.00 % ☐ Fixed rate
☐ Adjustable rate

4. Does collateral secure the debt?

☐ No
☑ Yes. Describe the collateral. 2014 Toyota Camry

Current market value $ 14,750.00

5. Does the creditor assert that the debt is nondischargeable?

☑ No
☐ Yes. Attach an explanation of the nature of the debt and the basis for contending that the debt is nondischargeable.

6. Using information from Schedule I: Your Income (Official Form 106I) and Schedule J: Your Expenses (Official Form 106J), fill in the amounts.

Income and expenses reported on Schedules I and J		Income and expenses stated on the reaffirmation agreement	
6a. Combined monthly income from line 12 of Schedule I	$ 4,721.00	6e. Monthly income from all sources after payroll deductions	$ 4,721.00
6b. Monthly expenses from line 22c of Schedule J	$ 4,314.00	6f. Monthly expenses	− $ 4,314.00
6c. Monthly payments on all reaffirmed debts not listed on Schedule J	− $ 375.00	6g. Monthly payments on all reaffirmed debts not included in monthly expenses	− $ 375.00
6d. Scheduled net monthly income Subtract lines 6b and 6c from 6a. If the total is less than 0, put the number in brackets.	$ 32.00	6h. Present net monthly income Subtract lines 6f and 6g from 6e. If the total is less than 0, put the number in brackets.	$ 32.00

Debtor 1 _____   Case number (*if known*)_____
      First Name   Middle Name   Last Name

7.	Are the income amounts on lines 6a and 6e different?	☐ No ☐ Yes. Explain why they are different and complete line 10._____ _____
8.	Are the expense amounts on lines 6b and 6f different?	☐ No ☐ Yes. Explain why they are different and complete line 10._____ _____
9.	Is the net monthly income in line 6h less than 0?	☐ No ☐ Yes. A presumption of hardship arises (unless the creditor is a credit union). Explain how the debtor will make monthly payments on the reaffirmed debt and pay other living expenses. Complete line 10. _____ _____
10.	Debtor's certification about lines 7-9 If any answer on lines 7-9 is *Yes*, the debtor must sign here. If all the answers on lines 7-9 are *No*, go to line 11.	I certify that each explanation on lines 7-9 is true and correct. ✗ _____ ✗ _____ Signature of Debtor 1 Signature of Debtor 2 (Spouse Only in a Joint Case)

11.	Did an attorney represent the debtor in negotiating the reaffirmation agreement?	☐ No
		☐ Yes. Has the attorney executed a declaration or an affidavit to support the reaffirmation agreement?
		    ☐ No
		    ☐ Yes

DRAFT

Part 2:   **Sign Here**

Whoever fills out this form must sign here.
I certify that the attached agreement is a true and correct copy of the reaffirmation agreement between the parties identified on this *Cover Sheet for Reaffirmation Agreement*.

✗ _____   Date _____
Signature   MM / DD / YYYY

_____
Printed Name

Check one:

☐   Debtor or Debtor's Attorney
☐   Creditor or Creditor's Attorney

Form 2400B (12/15)

UNITED STATES BANKRUPTCY COURT

In re Carrie Anne Edwards   ,   Case No. xxxx-xxxxx
_____
           Debtor   Chapter 7

MOTION FOR APPROVAL OF REAFFIRMATION AGREEMENT

I (we), the debtor(s), affirm the following to be true and correct:

I am not represented by an attorney in connection with this reaffirmation agreement.

I believe this reaffirmation agreement is in my best interest based on the income and expenses I have disclosed in my Statement in Support of Reaffirmation Agreement, and because *(provide any additional relevant reasons the court should consider)*:

Therefore, I ask the court for an order approving this reaffirmation agreement under the following provisions *(check all applicable boxes)*:

[✔] 11 U.S.C. § 524(c)(6) (debtor is not represented by an attorney during the course of the negotiation of the reaffirmation agreement)

[ ] 11 U.S.C. § 524(m) (presumption of undue hardship has arisen because monthly expenses exceed monthly income, as explained in Part II of Form 2400A, Reaffirmation Documents)

Signed: Carrie Anne Edwards
        (Debtor)

_____
        (Joint Debtor, if any)

Date: _____10/02/2017_____

Form 2400A (12/15)

Check one.
☐ **Presumption of Undue Hardship**
☑ **No Presumption of Undue Hardship**
See Debtor's Statement in Support of Reaffirmation,
Part II below, to determine which box to check.

UNITED STATES BANKRUPTCY COURT

Carrie Anne Edwards

In re _____,   Case No. xxxx-xxxxx _____
                    Debtor

                                                   Chapter 7 _____

REAFFIRMATION DOCUMENTS

Name of Creditor: GMAC _____

☐ Check this box if Creditor is a Credit Union

PART I. REAFFIRMATION AGREEMENT

Reaffirming a debt is a serious financial decision. Before entering into this Reaffirmation Agreement, you must review the important disclosures, instructions, and definitions found in Part V of this form.

A. Brief description of the original agreement being reaffirmed: Auto Loan _____
                                                                For example, auto loan

B. ***AMOUNT REAFFIRMED***: $_____ 15,000.00

   The Amount Reaffirmed is the entire amount that you are agreeing to pay. This may include
   unpaid principal, interest, and fees and costs (if any) arising on or before ___10/02/2017___,
   which is the date of the Disclosure Statement portion of this form (Part V).

   See the definition of "Amount Reaffirmed" in Part V, Section C below.

C. The ***ANNUAL PERCENTAGE RATE*** applicable to the Amount Reaffirmed is ___8.0000___%.

   See definition of "Annual Percentage Rate" in Part V, Section C below.

   This is a *(check one)* ☑ Fixed rate   ☐ Variable rate

If the loan has a variable rate, the future interest rate may increase or decrease from the Annual Percentage Rate disclosed here.

D. Reaffirmation Agreement Repayment Terms *(check and complete one)*:

- [✔] $ _375.00_ per month for ___40___ months starting on _11/01/2017_ .

- [ ] Describe repayment terms, including whether future payment amount(s) may be different from the initial payment amount.

E. Describe the collateral, if any, securing the debt:

        Description: 2014 Toyota Camry
        Current Market Value $_____14,750.00

F. Did the debt that is being reaffirmed arise from the purchase of the collateral described above?

- [✔] Yes. What was the purchase price for the collateral? $_____18,500.00

- [ ] No. What was the amount of the original loan? $_____

G. Specify the changes made by this Reaffirmation Agreement to the most recent credit terms on the reaffirmed debt and any related agreement:

	Terms as of the Date of Bankruptcy	Terms After Reaffirmation
Balance due *(including fees and costs)*	$_____	$_____
Annual Percentage Rate	_____%	_____%
Monthly Payment	$_____	$_____

H. [ ] Check this box if the creditor is agreeing to provide you with additional future credit in connection with this Reaffirmation Agreement. Describe the credit limit, the Annual Percentage Rate that applies to future credit and any other terms on future purchases and advances using such credit:

PART II. DEBTOR'S STATEMENT IN SUPPORT OF REAFFIRMATION AGREEMENT

A. Were you represented by an attorney during the course of negotiating this agreement?

    Check one. [ ] Yes [✔] No

B. Is the creditor a credit union?

    Check one. [ ] Yes [✔] No

Form 2400A, Reaffirmation Documents   Page 3

C. If your answer to EITHER question A. or B. above is "No," complete 1. and 2. below.

   1.   Your present monthly income and expenses are:

       a. Monthly income from all sources after payroll deductions
(take-home pay plus any other income) $ 4,721.00

       b. Monthly expenses (including all reaffirmed debts except
this one) $ 4,314.00

       c. Amount available to pay this reaffirmed debt (subtract b. from a.) $ 407.00

       d. Amount of monthly payment required for this reaffirmed debt $ 375.00

*If the monthly payment on this reaffirmed debt (line d.) is **greater than** the amount you have available to
pay this reaffirmed debt (line c.), you must check the box at the top of page one that says "Presumption
of Undue Hardship." Otherwise, you must check the box at the top of page one that says "No
Presumption of Undue Hardship."*

   2.   You believe that this reaffirmation agreement will not impose an undue hardship on you or your
dependents because:

       Check one of the two statements below, if applicable:

☑   You can afford to make the payments on the reaffirmed debt because your monthly income is
greater than your monthly expenses even after you include in your expenses the monthly
payments on all debts you are reaffirming, including this one.

☐   You can afford to make the payments on the reaffirmed debt even though your monthly income
is less than your monthly expenses after you include in your expenses the monthly payments on
all debts you are reaffirming, including this one, because:

       Use an additional page if needed for a full explanation.

D. If your answers to BOTH questions A. and B. above were "Yes," check the following
statement, if applicable:

☑   You believe this Reaffirmation Agreement is in your financial interest and you can afford to
make the payments on the reaffirmed debt.

Also, check the box at the top of page one that says "No Presumption of Undue Hardship."

Form 2400A, Reaffirmation Documents   Page 4

PART III. CERTIFICATION BY DEBTOR(S) AND SIGNATURES OF PARTIES

I hereby certify that:

(1)   I agree to reaffirm the debt described above.

(2)   Before signing this Reaffirmation Agreement, I read the terms disclosed in this Reaffirmation Agreement (Part I) and the Disclosure Statement, Instructions and Definitions included in Part V below;

(3)   The Debtor's Statement in Support of Reaffirmation Agreement (Part II above) is true and complete;

(4)   I am entering into this agreement voluntarily and am fully informed of my rights and responsibilities; and

(5)   I have received a copy of this completed and signed Reaffirmation Documents form.

SIGNATURE(S) (If this is a joint Reaffirmation Agreement, both debtors must sign.):

Date __10/02/2017__   Signature __Carrie Anne Edward_____
                                              Debtor

Date _____   Signature _____
                                              Joint Debtor, if any

Reaffirmation Agreement Terms Accepted by Creditor:

Creditor __GMAC_____   __PO Box 23567, Duchesne, UT 84021__
                Print Name   *Address*

_____   _____   _____
Print Name of Representative   *Signature*   *Date*

PART IV. CERTIFICATION BY DEBTOR'S ATTORNEY (IF ANY)

To be filed only if the attorney represented the debtor during the course of negotiating this agreement.

I hereby certify that: (1) this agreement represents a fully informed and voluntary agreement by the debtor; (2) this agreement does not impose an undue hardship on the debtor or any dependent of the debtor; and (3) I have fully advised the debtor of the legal effect and consequences of this agreement and any default under this agreement.

☐ A presumption of undue hardship has been established with respect to this agreement. In my opinion, however, the debtor is able to make the required payment.

Check box, if the presumption of undue hardship box is checked on page 1 and the creditor is not a Credit Union.

Date _____   Signature of Debtor's Attorney_____

                          Print Name of Debtor's Attorney _____

PART V. DISCLOSURE STATEMENT AND INSTRUCTIONS TO DEBTOR(S)

Before agreeing to reaffirm a debt, review the terms disclosed in the Reaffirmation Agreement (Part I above) and these additional important disclosures and instructions.

Reaffirming a debt is a serious financial decision. The law requires you to take certain steps to make sure the decision is in your best interest. If these steps, which are detailed in the Instructions provided in Part V, Section B below, are not completed, the Reaffirmation Agreement is not effective, even though you have signed it.

A.   DISCLOSURE STATEMENT

1. **What are your obligations if you reaffirm a debt?** A reaffirmed debt remains your personal legal obligation to pay. Your reaffirmed debt is not discharged in your bankruptcy case. That means that if you default on your reaffirmed debt after your bankruptcy case is over, your creditor may be able to take your property or your wages. Your obligations will be determined by the Reaffirmation Agreement, which may have changed the terms of the original agreement. If you are reaffirming an open end credit agreement, that agreement or applicable law may permit the creditor to change the terms of that agreement in the future under certain conditions.

2. **Are you required to enter into a reaffirmation agreement by any law?** No, you are not required to reaffirm a debt by any law. Only agree to reaffirm a debt if it is in your best interest. Be sure you can afford the payments that you agree to make.

3. **What if your creditor has a security interest or lien?** Your bankruptcy discharge does not eliminate any lien on your property. A "lien" is often referred to as a security interest, deed of trust, mortgage, or security deed. The property subject to a lien is often referred to as collateral. Even if you do not reaffirm and your personal liability on the debt is discharged, your creditor may still have a right under the lien to take the collateral if you do not pay or default on the debt. If the collateral is personal property that is exempt or that the trustee has abandoned, you may be able to redeem the item rather than reaffirm the debt. To redeem, you make a single payment to the creditor equal to the current value of the collateral, as the parties agree or the court determines.

4. **How soon do you need to enter into and file a reaffirmation agreement?** If you decide to enter into a reaffirmation agreement, you must do so before you receive your discharge. After you have entered into a reaffirmation agreement and all parts of this form that require a signature have been signed, either you or the creditor should file it as soon as possible. The signed agreement must be filed with the court no later than 60 days after the first date set for the meeting of creditors, so that the court will have time to schedule a hearing to approve the agreement if approval is required. However, the court may extend the time for filing, even after the 60-day period has ended.

5. **Can you cancel the agreement?** You may rescind (cancel) your Reaffirmation Agreement at any time before the bankruptcy court enters your discharge, or during the 60-day period that begins on the date your Reaffirmation Agreement is filed with the court, whichever occurs later. To rescind (cancel) your Reaffirmation Agreement, you must notify the creditor that your Reaffirmation Agreement is rescinded (or canceled). Remember that you can rescind the agreement, even if the court approves it, as long as you rescind within the time allowed.

6. **When will this Reaffirmation Agreement be effective?**

    a. **If you *were* represented by an attorney during the negotiation of your Reaffirmation Agreement and**

    i. **if the creditor is not a Credit Union**, your Reaffirmation Agreement becomes effective when it is filed with the court unless the reaffirmation is presumed to be an undue hardship. If the Reaffirmation Agreement is presumed to be an undue hardship, the court must review it and may set a hearing to determine whether you have rebutted the presumption of undue hardship.

    ii. **if the creditor is a Credit Union**, your Reaffirmation Agreement becomes effective when it is filed with the court.

    b. **If you *were not* represented by an attorney during the negotiation of your Reaffirmation Agreement**, the Reaffirmation Agreement will not be effective unless the court approves it. To have the court approve your agreement, you must file a motion. See Instruction 5, below. The court will notify you and the creditor of the hearing on your Reaffirmation Agreement. You must attend this hearing, at which time the judge will review your Reaffirmation Agreement. If the judge decides that the Reaffirmation Agreement is in your best interest, the agreement will be approved and will become effective. However, if your Reaffirmation Agreement is for a consumer debt secured by a mortgage, deed of trust, security deed, or other lien on your real property, like your home, you do not need to file a motion or get court approval of your Reaffirmation Agreement.

7. **What if you have questions about what a creditor can do?** If you have questions about reaffirming a debt or what the law requires, consult with the attorney who helped you negotiate this agreement. If you do not have an attorney helping you, you may ask the judge to explain the effect of this agreement to you at the hearing to approve the Reaffirmation Agreement. When this disclosure refers to what a creditor "may" do, it is not giving any creditor permission to do anything. The word "may" is used to tell you what might occur if the law permits the creditor to take the action.

B. INSTRUCTIONS

1. Review these Disclosures and carefully consider your decision to reaffirm. If you want to reaffirm, review and complete the information contained in the Reaffirmation Agreement (Part I above). If your case is a joint case, both spouses must sign the agreement if both are reaffirming the debt.

2. Complete the Debtor's Statement in Support of Reaffirmation Agreement (Part II above). Be sure that you can afford to make the payments that you are agreeing to make and that you have received a copy of the Disclosure Statement and a completed and signed Reaffirmation Agreement.

3. If you were represented by an attorney during the negotiation of your Reaffirmation Agreement, your attorney must sign and date the Certification By Debtor's Attorney (Part IV above).

4. You or your creditor must file with the court the original of this Reaffirmation Documents packet and a completed Reaffirmation Agreement Cover Sheet (Official Bankruptcy Form 427).

5. *If you are not represented by an attorney, you must also complete and file with the court a separate document entitled "Motion for Court Approval of Reaffirmation Agreement" unless your Reaffirmation Agreement is for a consumer debt secured by a lien on your real property, such as your home.* You can use Form 2400B to do this.

C. DEFINITIONS

1. **"Amount Reaffirmed"** means the total amount of debt that you are agreeing to pay (reaffirm) by entering into this agreement. The total amount of debt includes any unpaid fees and costs that you are agreeing to pay that arose on or before the date of disclosure, which is the date specified in the Reaffirmation Agreement (Part I, Section B above). Your credit agreement may obligate you to pay additional amounts that arise after the date of this disclosure. You should consult your credit agreement to determine whether you are obligated to pay additional amounts that may arise after the date of this disclosure.

2. **"Annual Percentage Rate"** means the interest rate on a loan expressed under the rules required by federal law. The annual percentage rate (as opposed to the "stated interest rate") tells you the full cost of your credit including many of the creditor's fees and charges. You will find the annual percentage rate for your original agreement on the disclosure statement that was given to you when the loan papers were signed or on the monthly statements sent to you for an open end credit account such as a credit card.

3. **"Credit Union"** means a financial institution as defined in 12 U.S.C. § 461(b)(1)(A)(iv). It is owned and controlled by and provides financial services to its members and typically uses words like "Credit Union" or initials like "C.U." or "F.C.U." in its name.

B2400C (Form B2400C) (12/15)

United States Bankruptcy Court

_____ Eastern _____ District of _____ California _____

In re _____ Carrie Anne Edwards _____ ,   Case No. __ XXXX-XXXXX __

Debtor   Chapter ____ 7 __

ORDER ON REAFFIRMATION AGREEMENT

The debtor(s) _____ Carrie Anne Edwards __ has (have) filed a motion for approval of the reaffirmation agreement dated _____ made between the debtor(s) and creditor _____. The court held the hearing required by 11 U.S.C. § 524(d) on notice to the debtor(s) and the creditor on _____ (date).

COURT ORDER: ☐ The court grants the debtor's motion under 11 U.S.C. § 524(c)(6)(A) and approves the reaffirmation agreement described above as not imposing an undue hardship on the debtor(s) or a dependent of the debtor(s) and as being in the best interest of the debtor(s).

☐ The court grants the debtor's motion under 11 U.S.C. § 524(k)(8) and approves the reaffirmation agreement described above.

☐ The court does not disapprove the reaffirmation agreement under 11 U.S.C. § 524(m).

☐ The court disapproves the reaffirmation agreement under 11 U.S.C. § 524(m).

☐ The court does not approve the reaffirmation agreement.

BY THE COURT

Date: __ 10/23/2017 _____   _____
                                       United States Bankruptcy Judge

Index